ARTIST'S

HANDBOOK

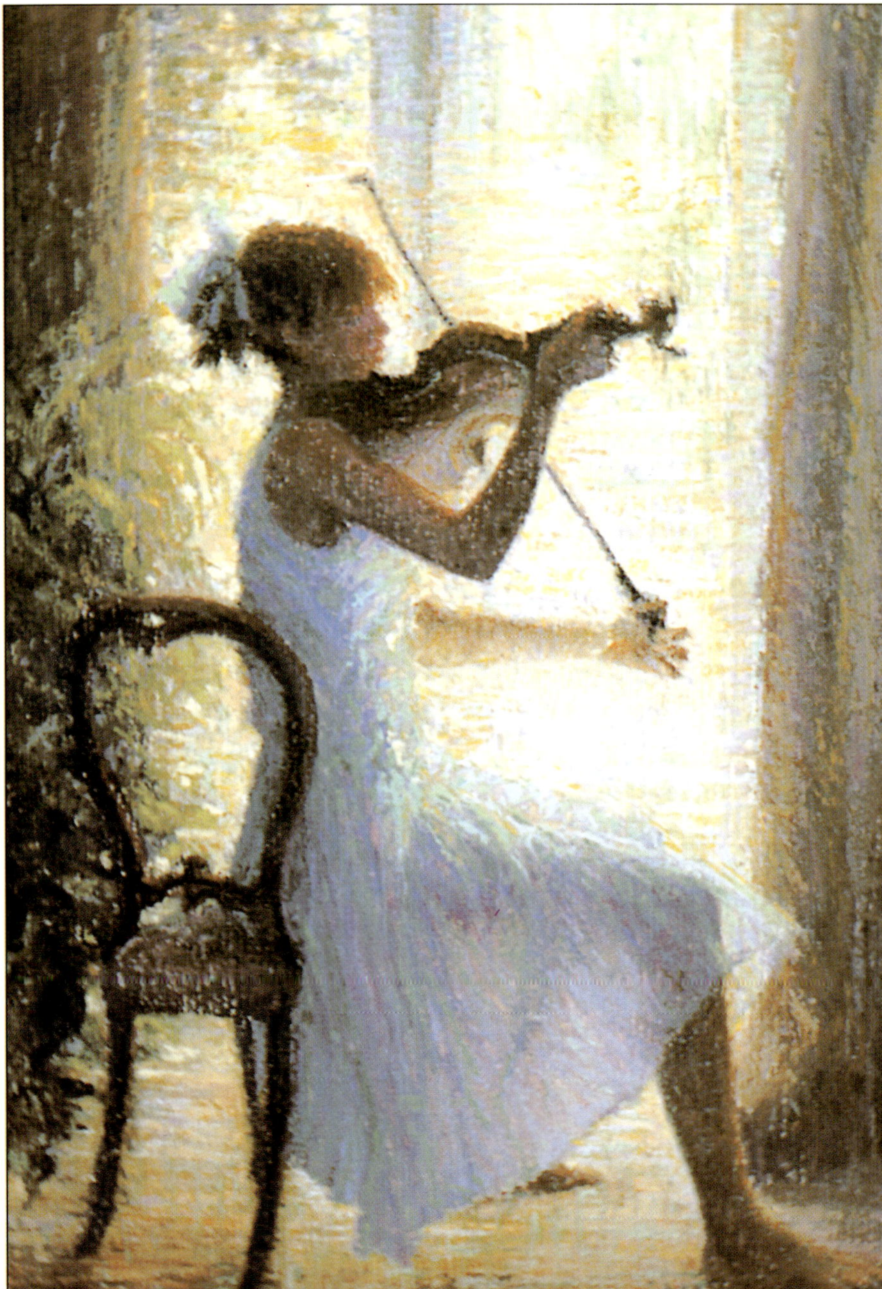

ARTIST'S
HANDBOOK

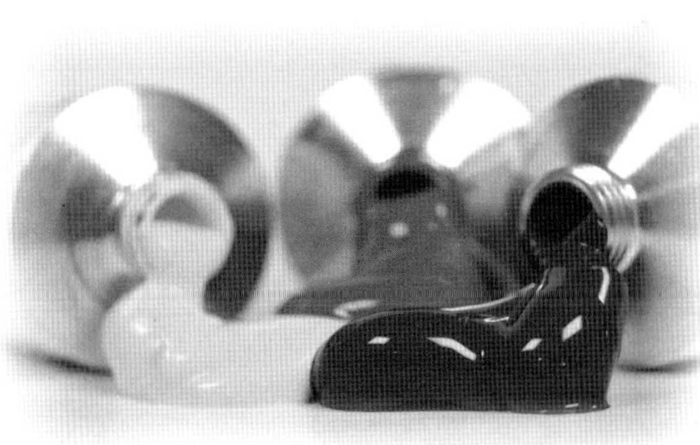

Abbeydale Press

This paperback edition printed in 2008

ISBN: 978-1-86147-247-2

1 3 5 7 9 10 8 6 4 2

Published by Abbeydale Press,
an imprint of Bookmart Limited,
Registered Number 2372865
Trading as Bookmart Limited
Blaby Road, Wigston,
Leicester, LE18 4SE, England

Originally published in 1996 by Bookmart Ltd
as *The Drawing and Painting Course*

Printed in Thailand

Contents

Introduction

Charlie Chaplin once said that nobody lives long enough to be anything but an amateur. This statement certainly applies to artists, for making any kind of art is a continuous, never-ending process of learning and discovery – which is what makes being an artist such a fascinating and rewarding occupation.

Many people lead busy lives and can only spare a few hours a week to paint and draw. If this is your case, be patient with the results and don't expect instant success. Always remember that nothing of worth is achieved without effort. If your first attempts at drawing or painting are disappointing, don't get discouraged and give up – failure is part of the learning process, and each time you paint or draw you will gain a little knowledge that you can incorporate into your next attempt. Even the great Masters experienced periods of frustration and self doubt, but what made them great was that they never gave up; they battled on regardless, and when success came it was all the sweeter for being hard-won.

Today's artist is lucky in having a vast range of painting and drawing materials to choose from. Each medium possesses its own unique characteristics, and it is worth trying out at least some of them in order to discover their expressive potential and to determine whether or not they suit your temperament and your way of working. You may, for example, enjoy the fluidity, speed and transparency of watercolour; or you may prefer the depth, richness and texture of oils, or the versatility and rich colours of pastels.

Whatever medium, or media, you choose to work with, it is important to acquire certain basic skills and practise with them before embarking on a major piece. In this book you will find an introduction to the materials, equipment and techniques associated with the most popular painting and drawing media, backed up by detailed step-by-step demonstrations and examples of work by practising painters. I hope that it will help you to achieve creditable and attractive results and inspire you to keep going, even when the going gets tough.

Angela Gair

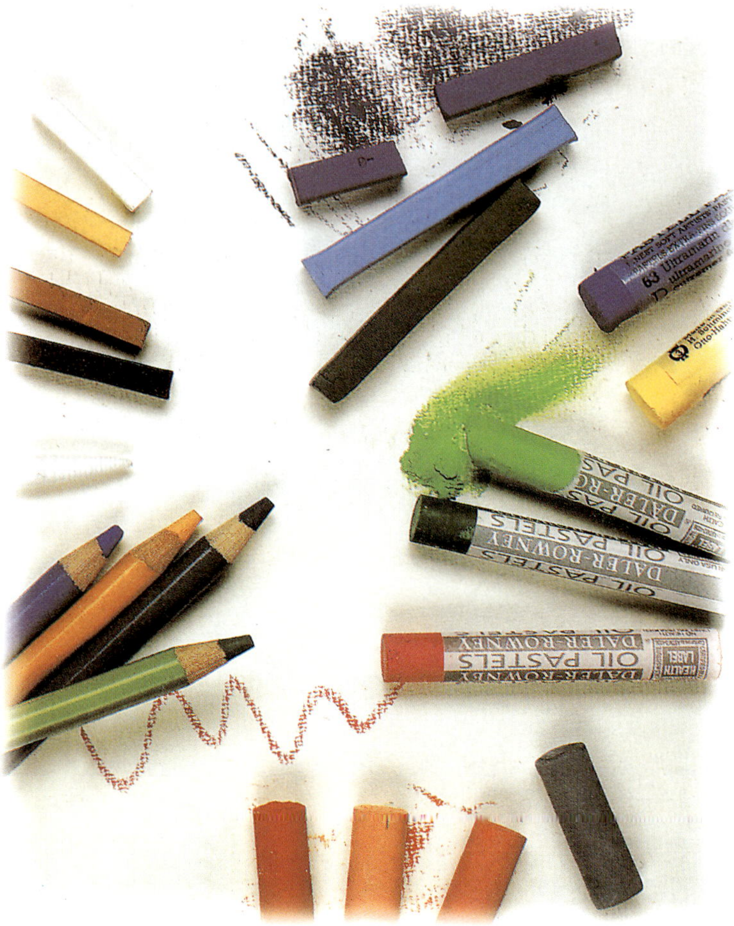

DALER-ROWNEY
OIL PASTELS

AN INTRODUCTION TO

Drawing

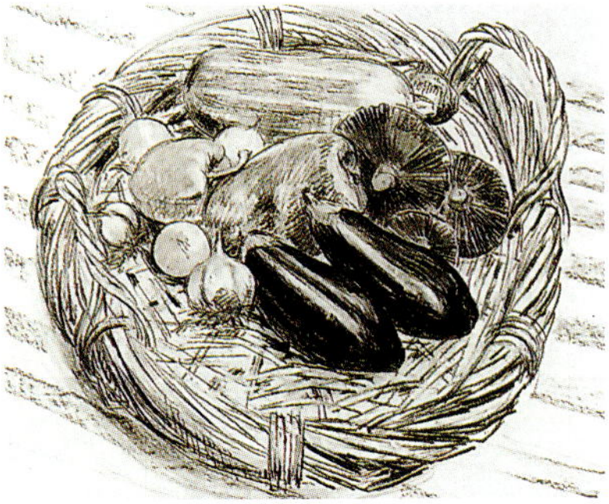

PROJECT 1

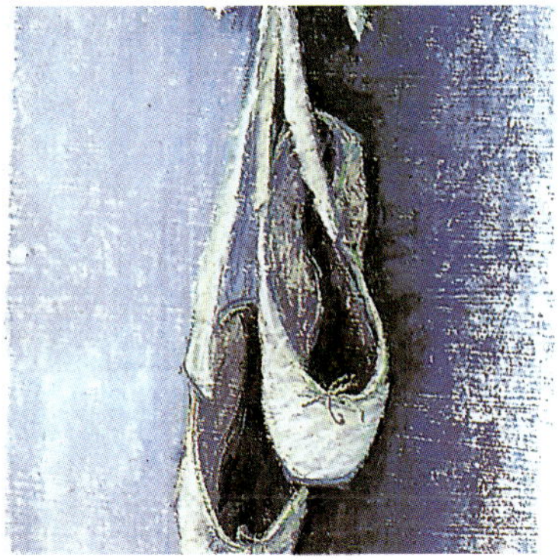

PROJECT 4

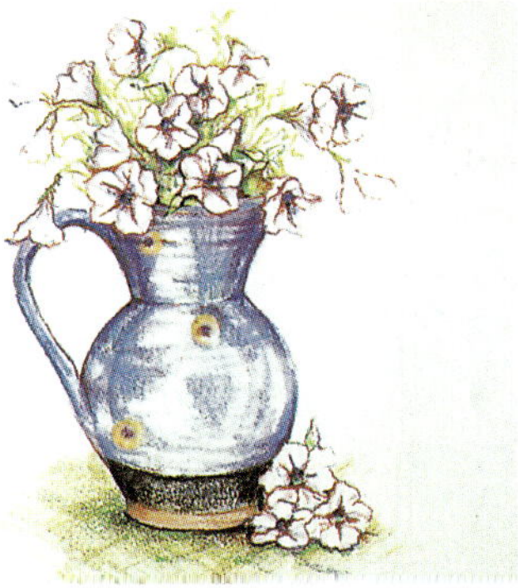

PROJECT 2

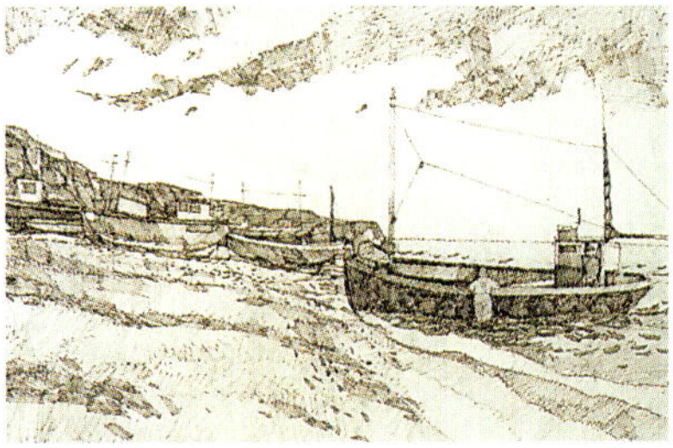

PROJECT 5

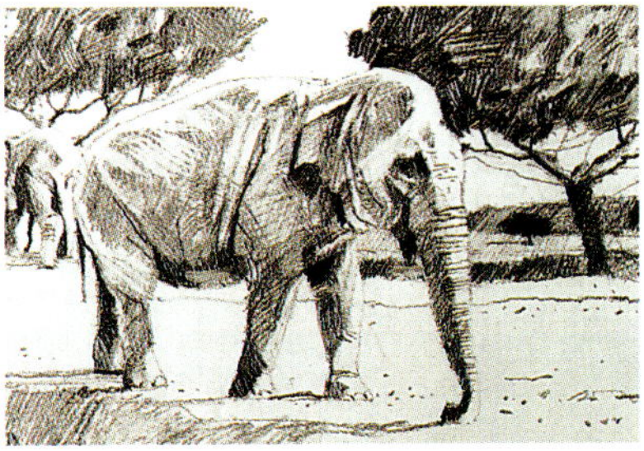

PROJECT 3

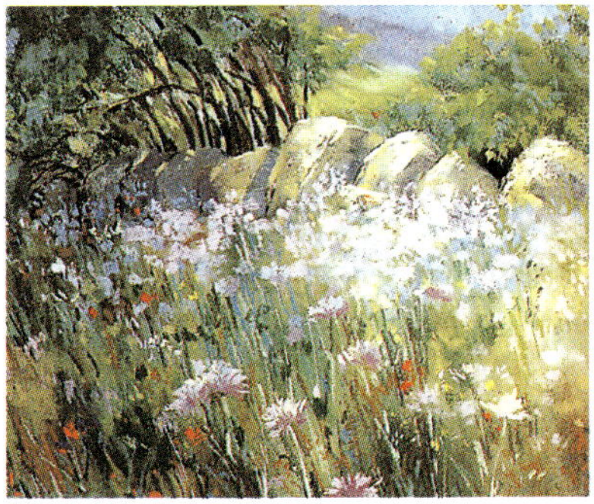

PROJECT 6

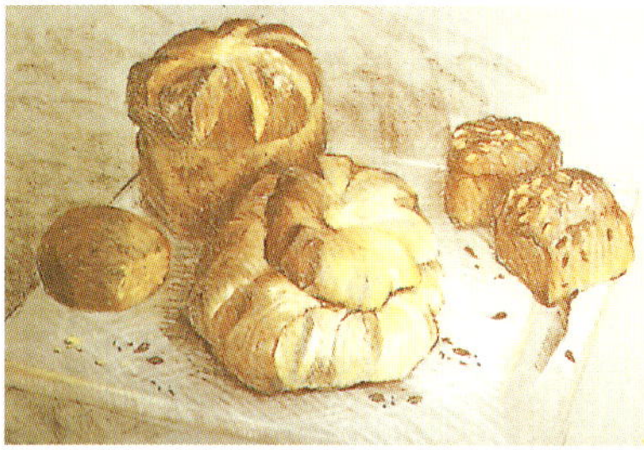

PROJECT 7

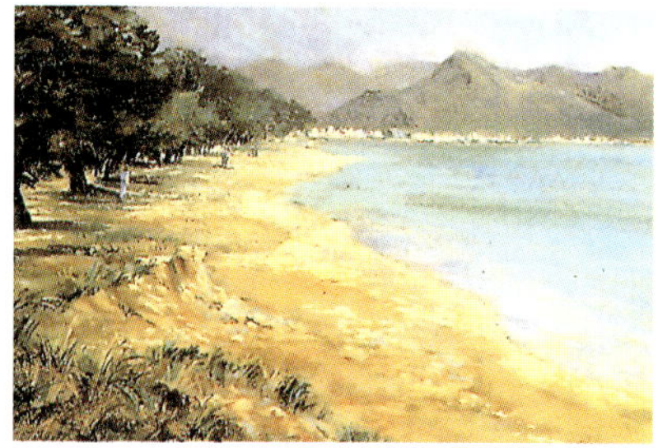

PROJECT 10

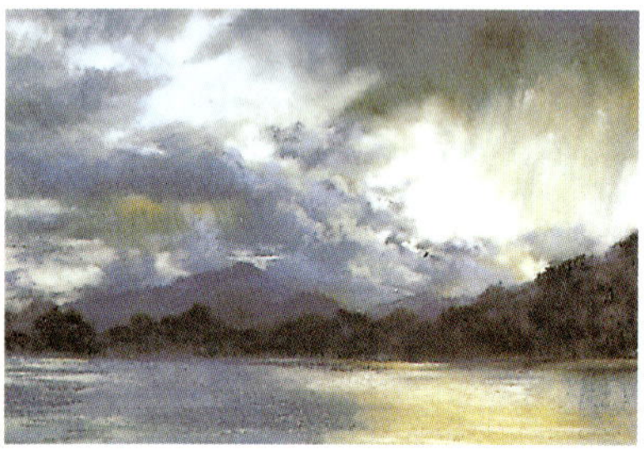

PROJECT 8

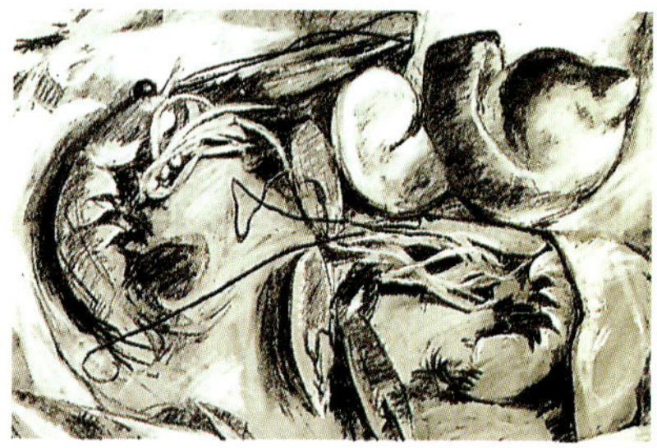

PROJECT 11

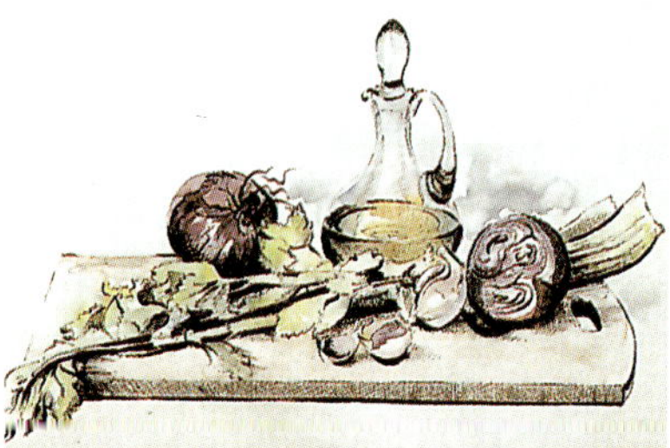

PROJECT 9

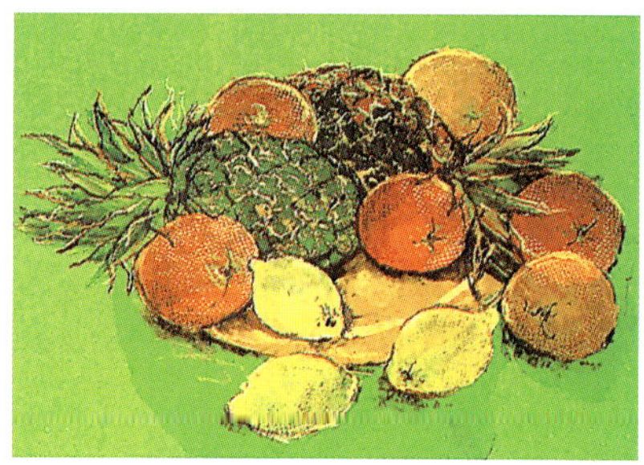

PROJECT 12

Drawing

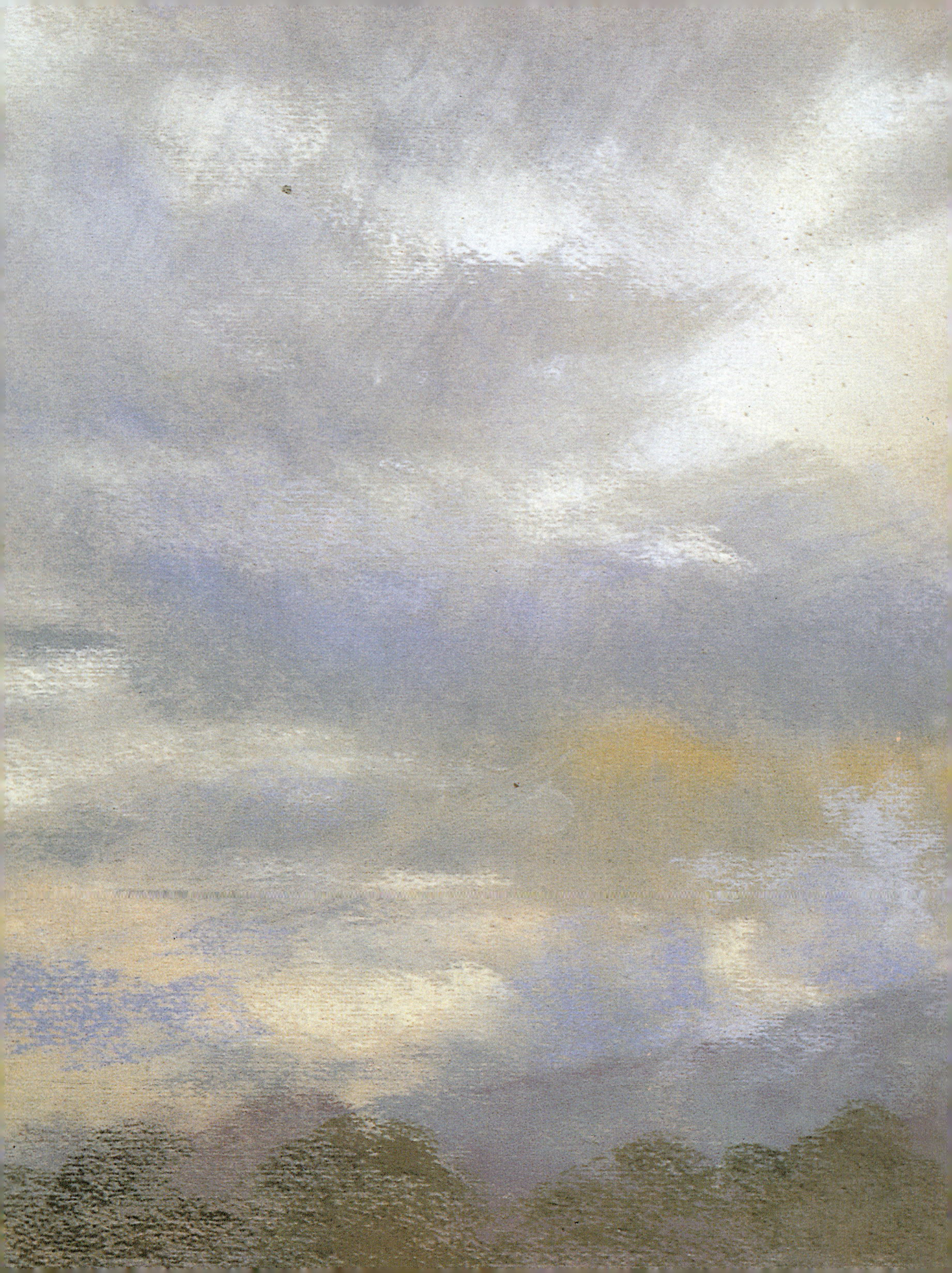

Drawing

There are many reasons for learning how to draw. To begin with, the activity of drawing is a source of much pleasure and satisfaction. Drawings and sketches are infinitely better than taking photographs as a means of recording information for a painting. But most importantly, drawing heightens our visual awareness, helping us to see the world around us with a fresh and enquiring eye.

A vast range of drawing materials, papers and equipment is now available to the artist. Each medium has its own characteristics and the opportunities for personal expression are without imit. Charcoal, for example, is perfect for bold, expressive drawings on a large scale, while coloured pencils are particularly suited to delicate, detailed work on a small scale. Your choice of medium will depend on how you work, and the reason for your drawing. Try to get into the habit of drawing a little every day, experimenting with a range of media and techniques.

Materials and Equipment

We usually associate drawing with simple lines drawn with a pencil or pen, but today the term drawing embraces a wide variety of monochrome and colour media which can be used in exciting and expressive ways.

PENCILS

The pencil is the most familiar drawing tool of all. It has a varied range, allowing for soft, velvety tones as well as delicate lines and details.

Ordinary wooden pencils comprise a thin rod of graphite encased in a hollow tube of wood. The graphite rod is known as the 'lead' – a term dating back to the sixteenth century, when graphite was first discovered and was mistakenly thought to be lead.

Pencils are graded by the H and B system, according to the relative hardness or softness of the graphite core. Typically, hard pencils range from 9H (the hardest) to H, and soft pencils

***Below** A range of materials for drawing and sketching, including hard and soft lead pencils, coloured pencils, graphite sticks, a kneaded putty eraser, and a craft knife and glasspaper block for sharpening pencils.*

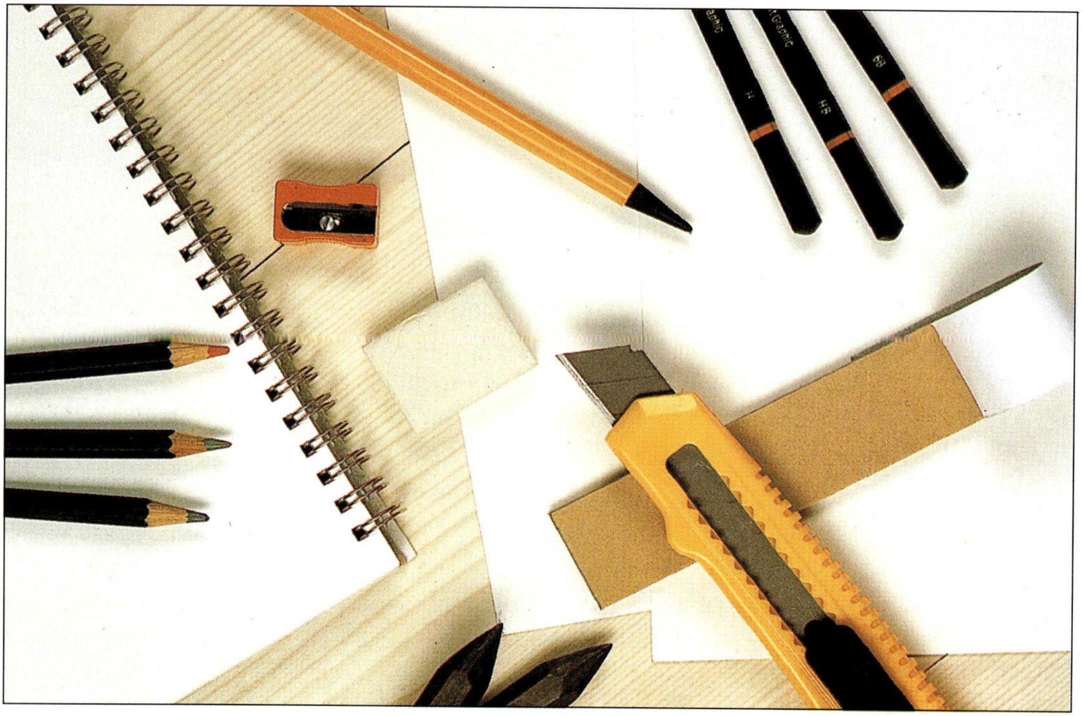

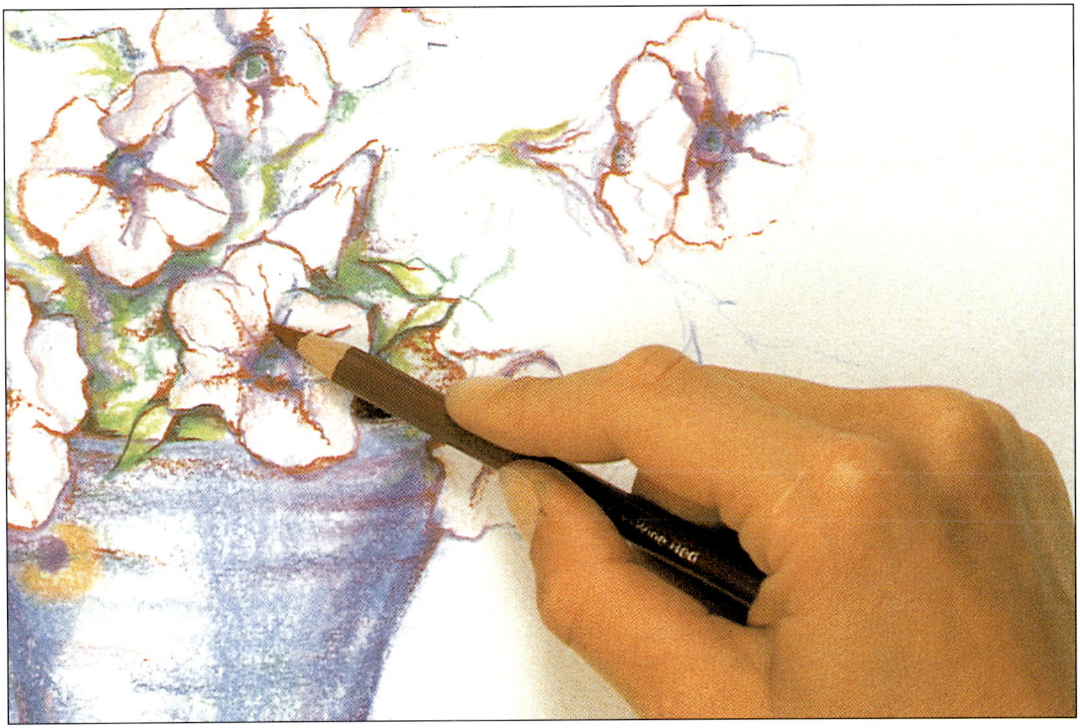

range from 8B (the softest) to B. Grades F and HB are midway between hard and soft. A very soft lead enables you to make broad, soft lines, while hard leads can be sharpened to the finest of points and are suited to fine lines and precise details. A medium grade such as 2B or 3B is probably the most popular for drawing.

Other types of pencil include propelling pencils and clutch pencils, designed to take a range of interchangeable leads. These have an advantage over wooden pencils because they don't need sharpening. Carpenters' pencils have a flat, rectangular lead that allows you to make broad, grainy marks as well as thin lines. Extremely soft pencils, known as graphite sticks, are also available. These are quite thick and produce strong, dark marks that are especially effective on rough-textured paper.

Above It is possible to produce a wide range of tones and textures with coloured pencils simply by applying different pressures to the pencil and by using both the point and the side of the lead.

Use a craft knife or scalpel blade for sharpening pencils; pencil sharpeners often break off the lead just as it is sharpened to a suitable point. A pencil that has been sharpened with a blade will retain its point far longer than one sharpened with a pencil sharpener.

Coloured pencils

An increasingly popular drawing medium, coloured pencils offer the same lively linear quality as graphite pencils, but with the added bonus of colour. The 'lead' or core of a coloured pencil consists of clay, coloured with pigment and bound with wax. Some coloured pencils are softer than others, depending on how much wax they contain. In use, coloured pencils can be overlaid to create visual blending of colours, but they cannot be mixed like paints. For this reason, they are produced in many different colours, shades and tints.

Water-soluble pencils

These are a cross between coloured pencils and watercolour paints. You can apply the colour dry, as you would with an ordinary coloured pencil, and you can also use a soft watercolour brush dipped in water to dissolve the pigment and blend colours together on the paper to create a wash-like effect.

CHARCOAL

Charcoal is the oldest drawing medium. Prehistoric man used sticks of charred wood from the fire as a tool to draw the outlines of animals on the walls of caves. Today, artists' charcoal is produced from vine and willow twigs charred in special kilns. Charcoal is simple to use and lends itself to expressive, spontaneous work. It also smudges easily, so you must draw with your hand raised off the paper and protect finished drawings with spray fixative.

Stick charcoal is available in various thicknesses. Thin sticks are suitable for sketches and delicate, detailed work. Thicker ones are better for bold work and for covering large areas quickly.

Compressed charcoal consists of powdered charcoal combined with a binder and compressed into short, thick sticks. It is stronger than stick charcoal and doesn't break so easily, and is also useful for laying in broad blocks of tone.

Charcoal pencils are made from thin sticks of compressed charcoal encased in wood. They are cleaner to handle and easier to control than stick charcoal, and have a harder texture. They make firm lines and strokes and the tip can be sharpened for detailed work.

Right *Charcoal is responsive to the slightest change in pressure, so you can produce lines and tones that vary from delicate grey to deep, positive black.*

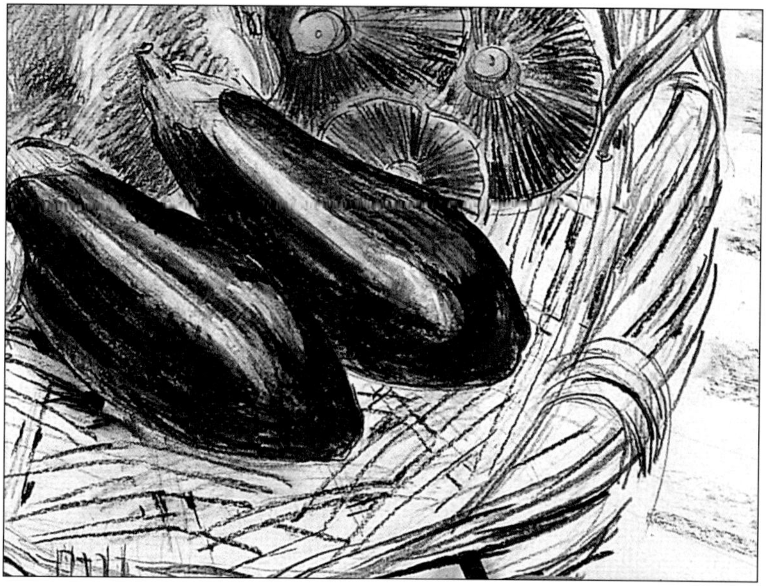

NO CONTIENE
CFC. NO
PERJUDICA
AL OZONO
Rowney
PERFIX
COLOURLESS
LOW ODOUR
FIXATIVE
For Pastel, Crayon, Charcoal drawings
FIXATIF INCOLORE
SANS ODEUR
Pour Pastels, Crayons, et Fusains
FARBLOSES GERUCHFREIES
FIXIERMITTEL
Für Pastell-, Butstift-, und
Kohlezeichnungen
FIJATIVO INCOLORO E
150 ml 210
FRANCE 728 HB

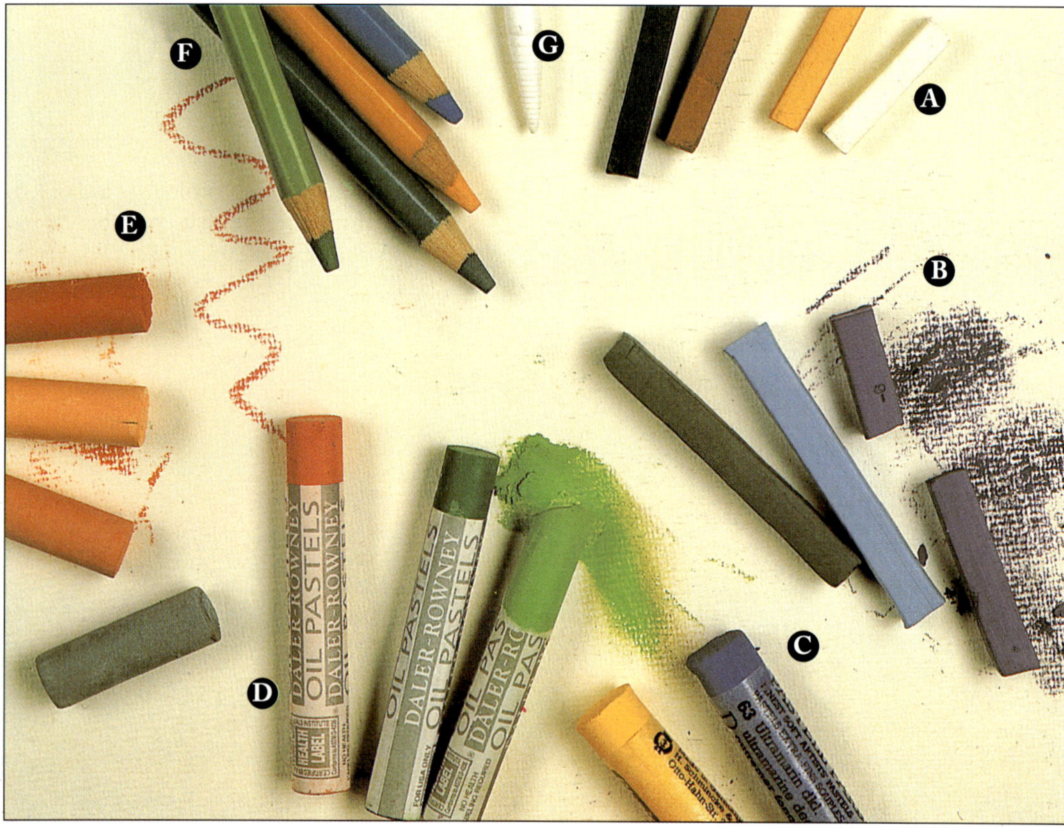

Above *Just some of the wide range of pastels and crayons available to the artist.*
A *conté crayons.* ***B*** *hard pastels.* ***C*** *soft pastels.*
D *oil pastels.* ***E*** *half-pastels.* ***F*** *pastel pencils.*
G *torchon (for blending).*

PASTELS

The main attraction of pastels is their versatility. Available in hundreds of different colours, they can be pale, soft and velvety or bold and powerful. Pastels are made from finely ground pigments bound together with gum to form a stiff paste, which is then shaped into round or square sticks and allowed to harden. Four main types are available:

Soft pastels are the most widely used of the various types because they produce the wonderful velvety bloom that is one of the main attractions of pastel art. They contain more pigment and less binder, so the colours are vibrant. The smooth, thick quality of soft pastels produces rich, painterly effects. They are easy to apply, requiring little pressure to make a mark, and can be blended and smudged with a finger, crumpled tissue or paper stump (torchon).

Hard pastels contain less pigment and more binder than the soft type. Although they have a firmer texture, the colours are less brilliant. Hard pastels can be sharpened to a point with a blade and used for crisp lines and details. Unlike soft pastels, they do not crumble and break easily, nor do they clog the tooth of the paper, so they are often used in the early stages of a drawing to outline the composition, or for adding details at the end.

Pastel pencils are thin pastel sticks encased in wood, like ordinary pencils. They are clean to use, do not break or crumble as traditional pastels do, and give greater control of handling. Pastel pencils are perfect for line sketches and detailed small-scale work, and can be used in conjunction with stick pastels.

Oil pastels are different in character from traditional pastels. The pigment and chalk are combined with an oil binder instead of gum, making the sticks stronger and harder. Oil pastels make thick, buttery strokes and their colours are clear and brilliant. Though not as controllable as soft pastels, they have a robust quality that makes them ideal for direct, spontaneous working.

Tints and shades

Pastel colours cannot be mixed before use as paints can, so each individual pastel colour comes in a wide range of tints (light tones) and shades (dark tones). The paler tints are achieved by adding progressively more white pigment to the full-strength colour, and the darker shades by adding black.

The tonal range of each colour is indicated by a system of numbering that corresponds to the various strengths of each colour. The paper label on a pastel stick bears the pastel's colour and tint number; before you throw it away, rub some colour onto a sheet of paper and write the colour name, tint and brand alongside it. This way, when you come to re-stock your colours you will know exactly which ones to buy.

CONTE CRAYONS

These are small, square sticks of very high grade compressed chalk, slightly harder and oilier than pastels. They are also available in pencil form. Traditionally used for tonal drawings, conté crayons were in the past limited to black, white, grey and three earth colours – sanguine, sepia and bistre. Recently a wide range of subtle colours has been introduced, available individually or in boxed sets.

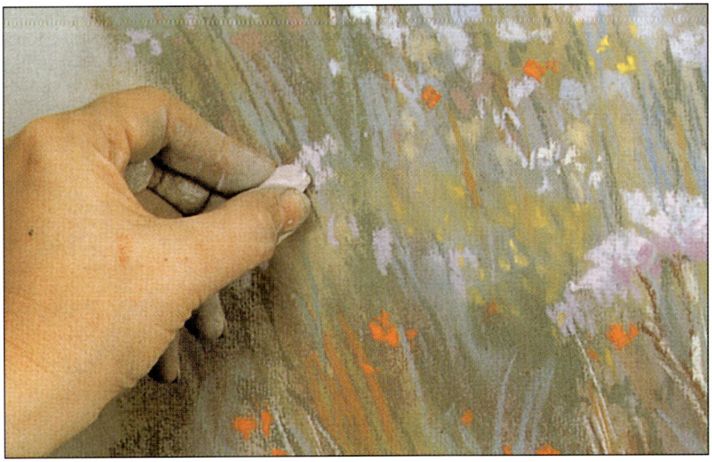

Left *Pastels and chalks have the advantage of speed and directness. There are no colours to be pre-mixed, no brushes or palettes to clean, no drying times to worry about. In short, there is nothing to get in the way of your direct response to the subject.*

PENS AND INKS

Thanks to recent manufacturing developments, there is a limitless range of pens and inks available, allowing you to produce anything from a simple monochrome sketch in black Indian ink to a detailed study in brilliant colours.

Drawing inks

There are two types of drawing ink: water-soluble and waterproof. Both types come in a wide range of colours as well as the traditional black. With water-soluble inks the drawn lines can be dissolved with water and the colours blended. With waterproof inks the lines remain intact and will not dissolve once dry, so that a wash or tint on top of the drawing may be added without spoiling the linework. Waterproof inks should never be used with reservoir pens as they contain shellac, which will clog the pen as it dries.

Coloured inks come in a range of brilliant colours. However, they are made from dyes rather than pigments and are therefore not light-fast. To minimize fading, protect finished drawings from prolonged exposure to bright daylight.

Pens

Pens made from natural materials – quills, reeds and bamboos – have been used for centuries. They are light, flexible and responsive and produce lively, animated marks.

Simple dip pens consist of a holder which can be used with a selection of nibs. They produce flowing lines that can be made to swell and thin by varying the pressure applied to the nib.

Fountain pens with their built-in supply of ink are useful for outdoor sketching because they don't need to be dipped into ink repeatedly. They are smoother to draw with than dip pens, but the nib range is more limited and most fountain pens require water-soluble ink to prevent them clogging.

Fibre-tipped pens and marker pens are available in a wide range of colours. Technical pens have tubular steel nibs that produce a controlled, even line and are suited to detailed line work.

__Right__ Drawing with pen and ink is an excellent discipline because it forces you to observe your subject carefully and make a committed mark – you can't rub out your mistakes!

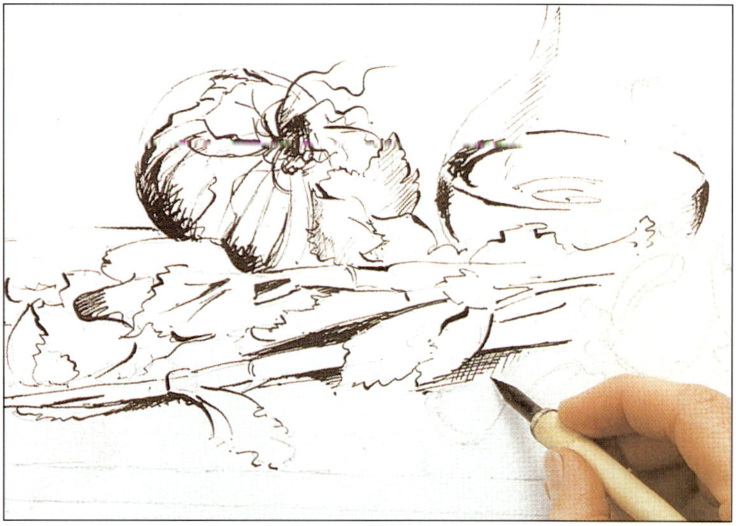

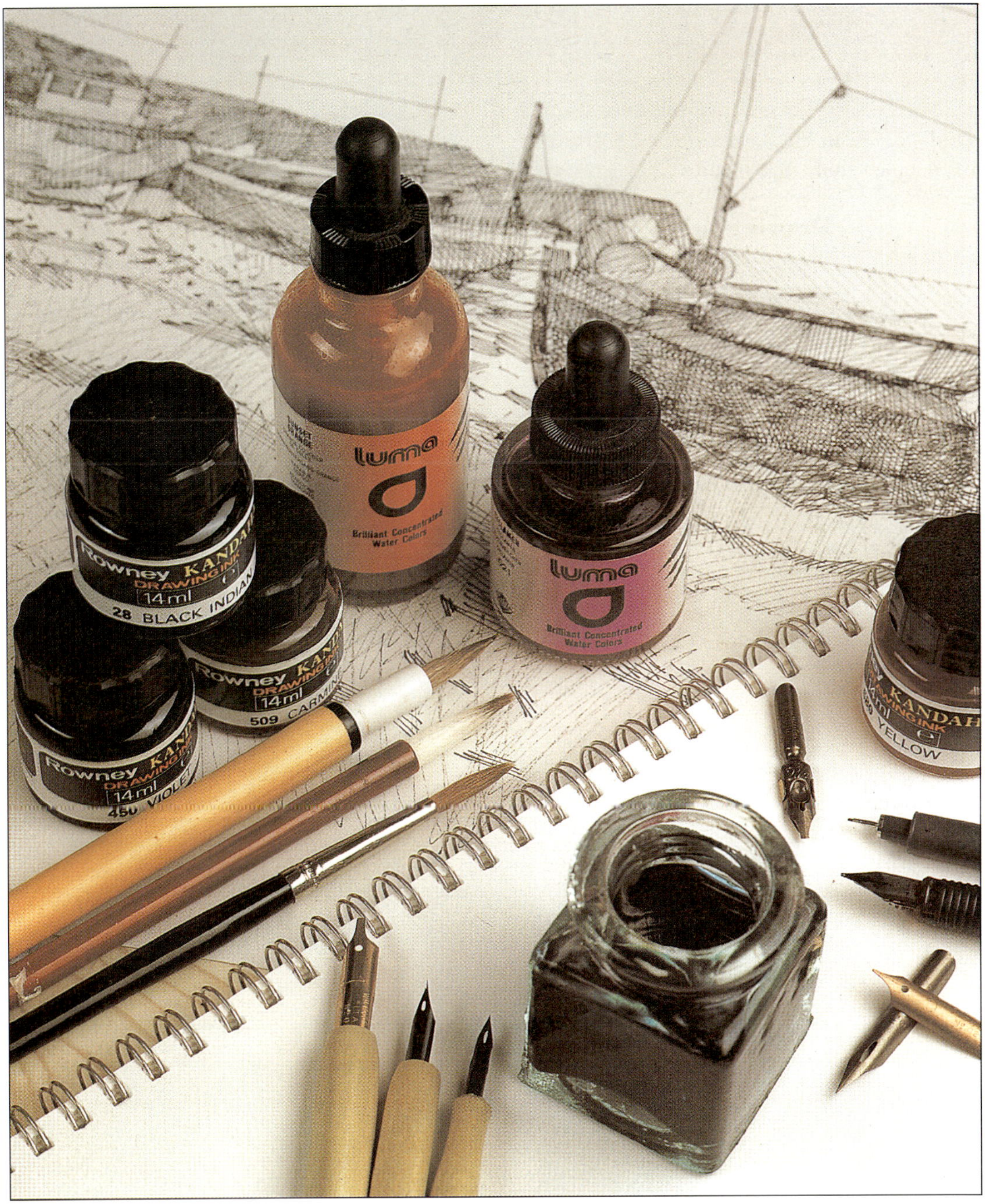
luma
Brilliant Concentrated Water Colors
luma
Brilliant Concentrated Water Colors
Rowney
DRAWING INK
14ml
28 BLACK INDIAN
Rowney
DRAWING INK
14ml
509 CARMINE
Rowney
DRAWING INK
14ml
450 VIOLET
DRAWING INK
YELLOW

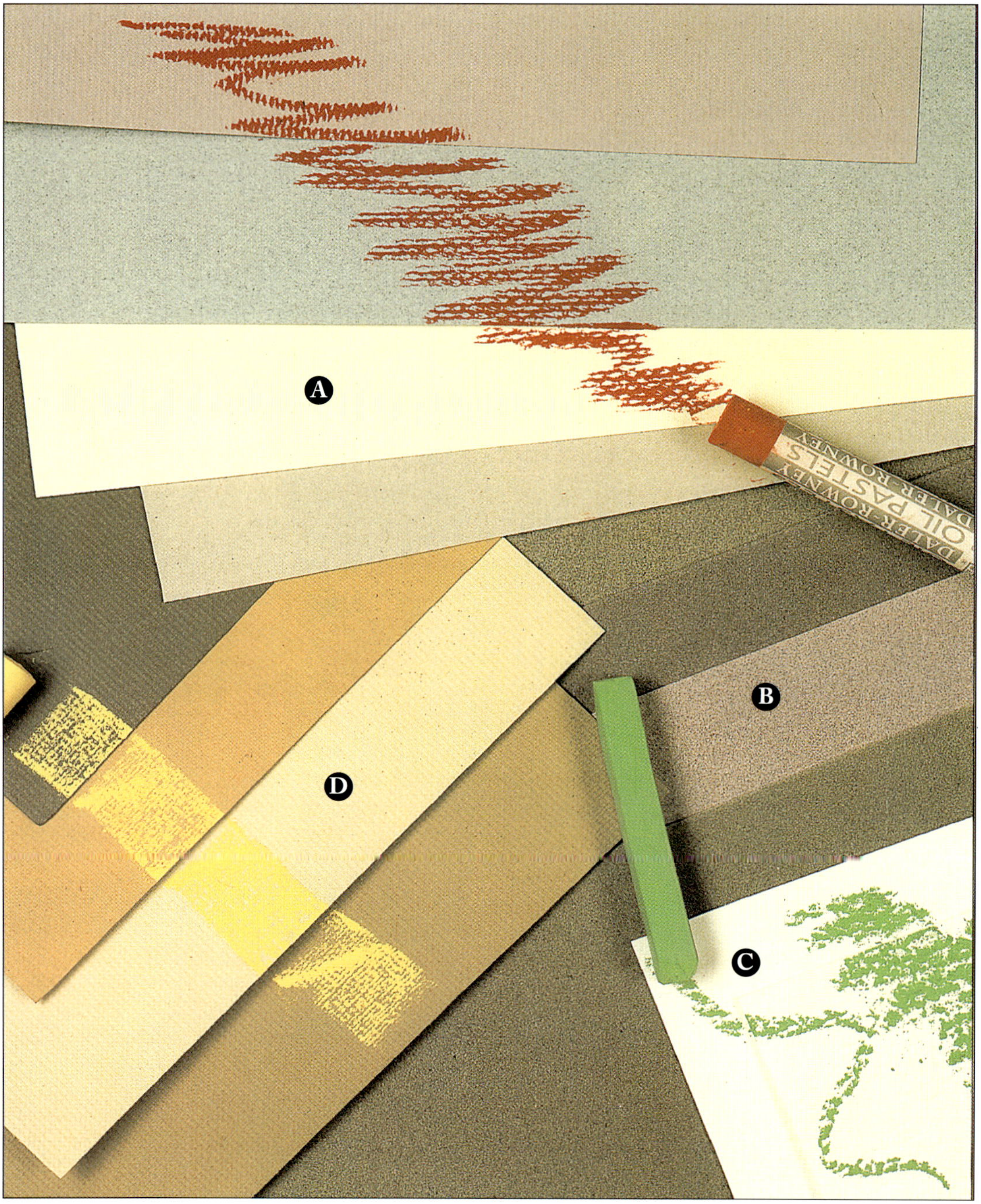
A
DALER-ROWNEY
OIL PASTELS
DALER-ROWNEY
B
D
C

PAPERS FOR DRAWING

Drawing paper is available in a wide range of weights, textures and colours, and can be purchased as single sheets, pads, sketchbooks or boards, which provide a firm support.

The character of the paper can influence a drawing quite dramatically, so it is important to choose carefully. It is worth exploring the effects of a single medium on different papers as they can vary enormously.

Textured paper

Powdery media such as pastel and charcoal need a support with enough surface texture, or 'tooth', to hold the particles of pigment. Smooth papers are unsuitable because the pastel or charcoal stick slides around and the marks are easily smudged. Papers for pastel work come in different textures, from soft velour paper that gives a rich, velvety effect, to rough sand-grain paper which is suitable for bold, vigorous work. The two best-known papers for pastel drawing are Ingres, which has a laid pattern of narrow lines and Canson, which has a fine 'wire-mesh' pattern. A wide range of colours is also available; in pastel painting, areas of the paper are often left untouched, and contribute to the picture.

Smooth paper

Hot-pressed, smooth paper is recommended for detailed work in pencil and pen and ink. Ordinary cartridge paper is fine for most purposes, but fine-nibbed pens work best on a coated paper or line board. These have a very thin, hard coating of china clay which helps to produce crisp, clean lines.

Left *Pastel papers come in a vast range of colours and textures.* ***A*** *Canson paper.* ***B*** *pastel board.* ***C*** *rough-surfaced watercolour paper.* ***D*** *Ingres paper.*

DRAWING ACCESSORIES

Erasers For erasing, plastic or kneaded putty erasers are best, as the familiar India rubber tends to smudge and can damage the paper surface. Putty erasers are malleable; small pieces can be broken off and rolled to a point to reach fine details. Use them on soft graphite, charcoal and pastel drawings, both to erase and to create highlights.

Paper stumps Also called torchons, these are used for blending or shading charcoal, pastel or soft graphite drawings. Made of tightly rolled paper, they have tapered ends for working on large areas of paper and a sharp point for small details.

Knives and sharpeners You will need a sharp craft knife or scalpel for sharpening pencils and cutting paper. A pencil sharpener is convenient, although a knife is preferable as it gives a longer point and is less liable to break the lead of the pencil. Sandpaper blocks, consisting of small, tear-off sheets of sandpaper stapled together, are useful for getting fine points on graphite sticks, pastels and charcoal sticks.

Drawing board If you usually draw on sheets of loose paper you will need a firm support to rest on. You can buy a commercial drawing board at an art supply store, but it is far cheaper to get a good piece of smooth board from a timber merchant.

Fixative If you are using pastel, chalk, charcoal or soft graphite pencil, the best way to preserve and protect your drawings is to spray them with fixative. This varnish-like fluid binds the particles of pigment to the surface of the paper so they will not smudge, smear or shake off. Fixative is available in aerosol spray form or in atomizers that you hold in your mouth and blow through to create a fine spray.

Soft Pencils

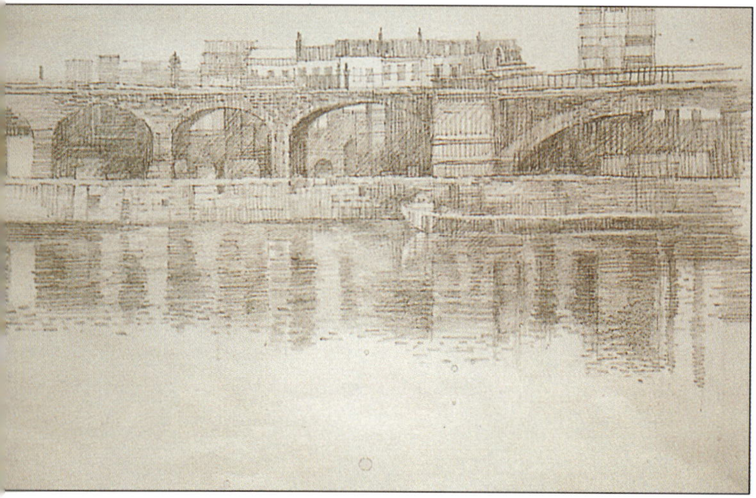

Pauline Fazakerley
LIMEHOUSE BASIN
Armed only with a soft pencil and a sketchbook, the artist was able to work on site and gather all the information she needed for a watercolour painting to be done back at the studio. The subtle nuances of tone are achieved with varying densities of hatching and crosshatching.

Artists' pencils come in various grades, ranging from the softest (8B) to the hardest (10H), with F and HB being in the middle. Hard pencils make fine, silvery lines appropriate for delicate and detailed drawing. Soft pencils are more versatile as they give more varied lines and tones. When sharpened to a fine point, they make fluid lines that can be tapered from thick to thin. When blunt, they make broad, grainy marks and you can use the side of the lead to produce solid areas of tone. You can also blend and smudge the marks laid down to produce subtle, amorphous tones and gradations, then rub back to the white paper with the corner of a kneaded putty eraser to create highlights.

Techniques

The immediacy, versatility and sensitivity of pencils make them the most popular instrument for drawing. Pencil lines can be soft and sinuous, vigorous and bold, or controlled and crisp. The character and nuance of a pencil line will be influenced by the hardness or softness of the pencil lead, the sharpness of the tip, the pressure applied and the speed with which the line is drawn.

Regular practice makes you familiar with the different marks you can produce with a pencil, and improves your drawing skills at the same time. Try to avoid making solid, continuous outlines when you draw. Grip the pencil well back from the drawing point and start by making light, exploratory marks, feeling your way into the shapes and forms you are drawing. Use fluid, fast-moving lines, and let the pencil 'dance' over the paper. Don't worry about the number of lines you make – working in pencil allows for as much elaboration and reworking as you like; in fact, some artists prefer not to rub out their mistakes and re-workings, as these give animation and life to the finished drawing.

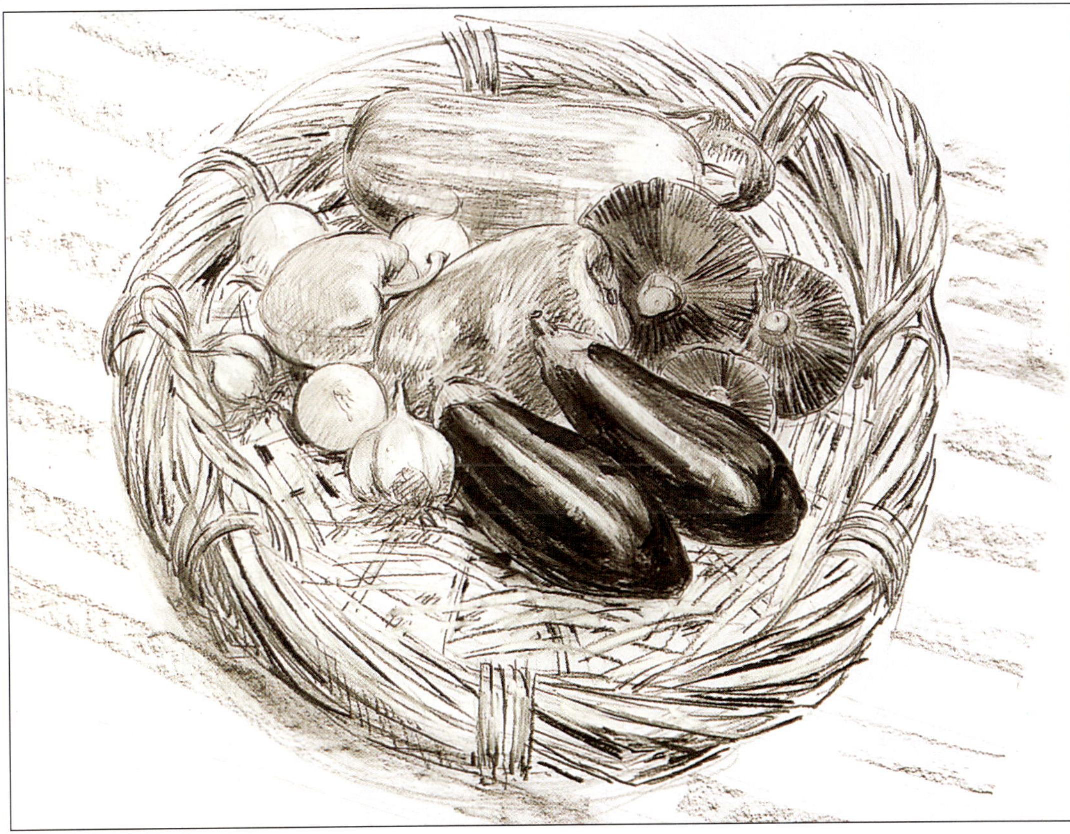

YOU WILL NEED

- *Sheet of good quality cartridge paper, 16½ x 13¼in (42 x 34cm)*
- *6B pencil*
- *White chalk*
- *Compressed charcoal*
- *Putty eraser*
- *Drawing board*
- *Drawing pins or tape*

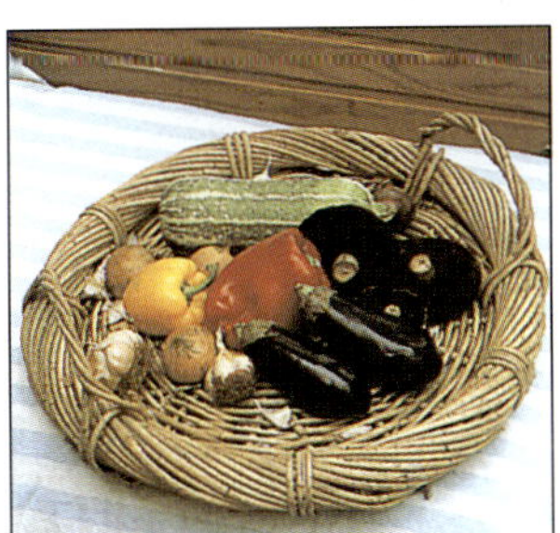

Vegetable Basket

One grade of pencil is enough to make many different kinds of mark. Soft pencils, in particular, can produce both expressive linear marks and soft, velvety tones – as in this still-life drawing, which contains lively contrasts of tone and texture.

1 Fix the paper to the drawing board with pins or tape. Grip the pencil well back from the drawing point and hold your hand off the paper surface. Working freely from your elbow, sketch in the main outlines of the still life, drawing the basket first and then the vegetables. Keep your lines loose and light, so you can rub out any errors easily. Don't concentrate on any one area for too long – keep your pencil moving over the paper and try to keep the whole thing going at once, letting the image emerge gradually.

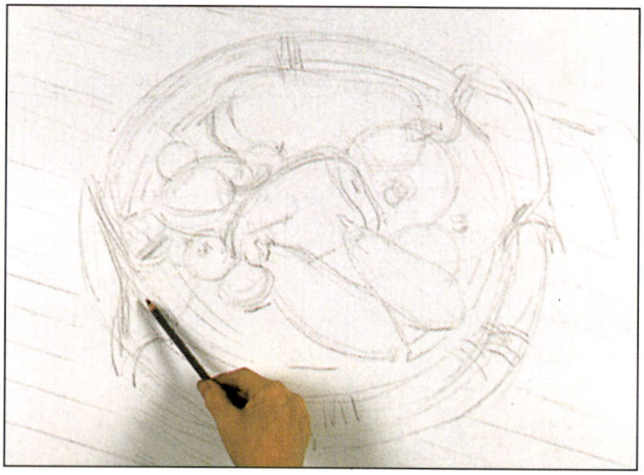

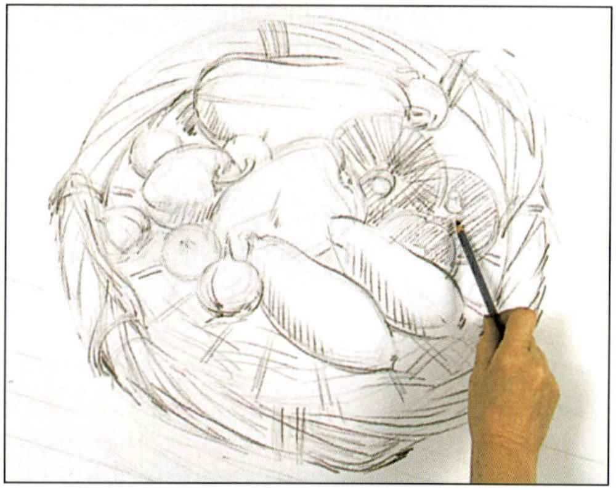

2 Pay attention to the 'negative' shapes between the vegetables, as well as their 'positive' shapes – it will help to ensure the accuracy of your drawing. When you are happy with the composition, start to define the form and volume of the vegetables, using darker lines to emphasize the bulging curves of the marrow and aubergines. Suggest the weaves and plaits of the wicker basket and start to shade in the shadows on the vegetables with loose, hatched strokes. Use the same technique to draw the dark gills of the mushrooms. Keep referring to your subject to make sure the proportions are right, correcting any mistakes as you go along.

Helpful Hint

STAND BACK FROM YOUR DRAWING FROM TIME TO TIME SO YOU CAN SEE HOW IT IS TAKING SHAPE

3 Shade in the basket and aubergines with bold pencil strokes, using the side of the lead to make soft marks. Now smudge the shading lines with your fingertips to create softly blended tones that suggest the rounded forms. This adds 'colour' to your drawing – it's like painting with a pencil.

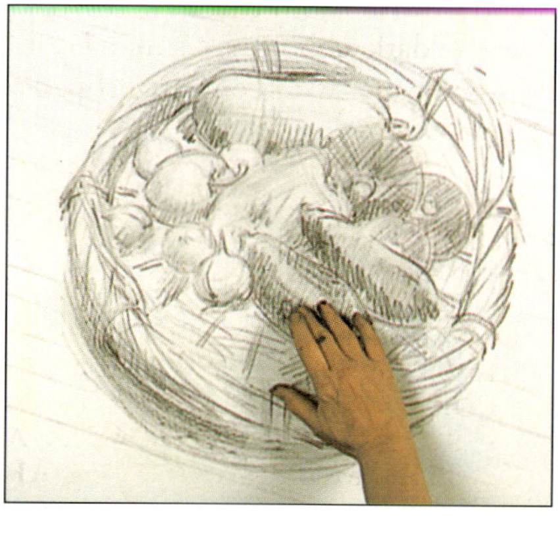

4

Continue to build up the darkest tones, using more pressure on the pencil. Vary the type of marks you make, suggesting not only form but also colour, surface pattern and texture. Again, work from one area and back again so that the drawing emerges as a unified whole. Notice here how the vegetables at the front of the group are more detailed and have stronger contrasts of light and dark tone than those at the back. This creates the illusion of depth and prevents the picture from 'tilting' forward.

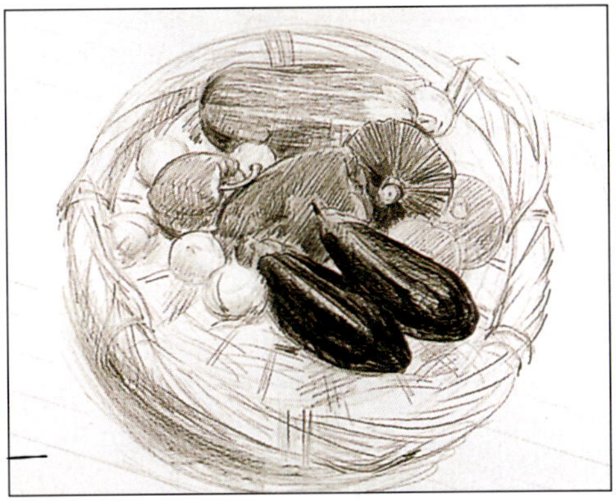

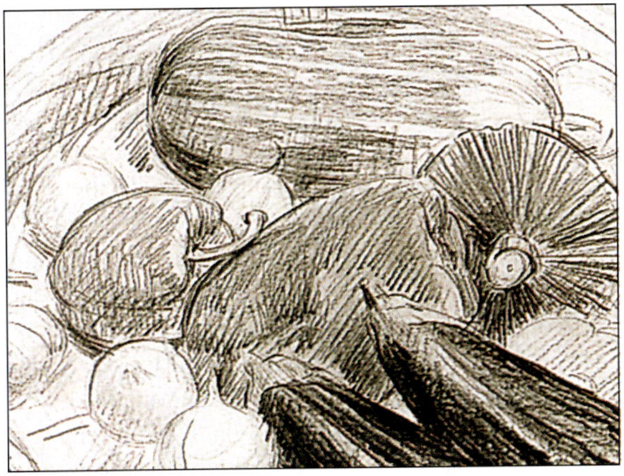

5

The shading on the marrow is done with loose, horizontal strokes that suggest the striped markings. For the peppers, use vigorous hatched strokes, pivoting from the wrist to make the lines follow their curved forms. Leave areas of white paper untouched for the lighter colours and highlights.

6

Using the side of the pencil lead, shade across the aubergines to describe their dark, shiny skin; smudge the pencil into the paper with your fingertips.

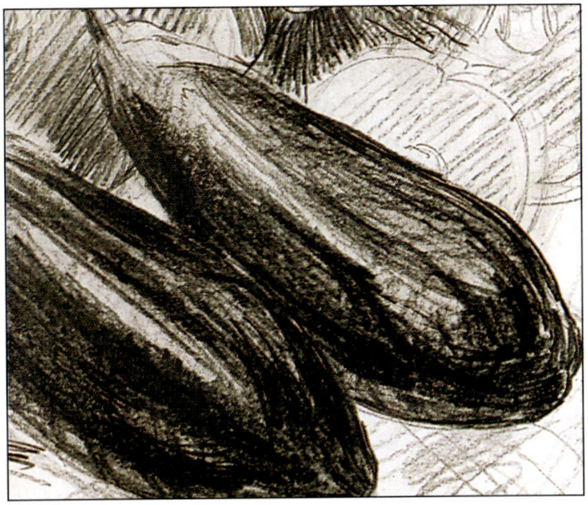

Helpful Hint

ONCE YOU HAVE ARRANGED YOUR STILL LIFE, DON'T RUSH TO START DRAWING BUT FIRST TAKE A GOOD TEN MINUTES TO OBSERVE YOUR SUBJECT CLOSELY, LOOKING AT THE VARYING SHAPES OF THE OBJECTS AND THE SHADOWS THEY MAKE.

7 Now add characteristic detail to the objects in the still life, using both the side and the point of the lead. Move across the drawing, working on all areas at the same time. Build up the shapes and textures of the onions and garlic with line and tone. Draw in the weave of the basket more firmly, varying the pressure on the pencil to suggest light and shade. Then use a sharp corner of a putty eraser to lift out soft highlights on the shiny skins of the vegetables.

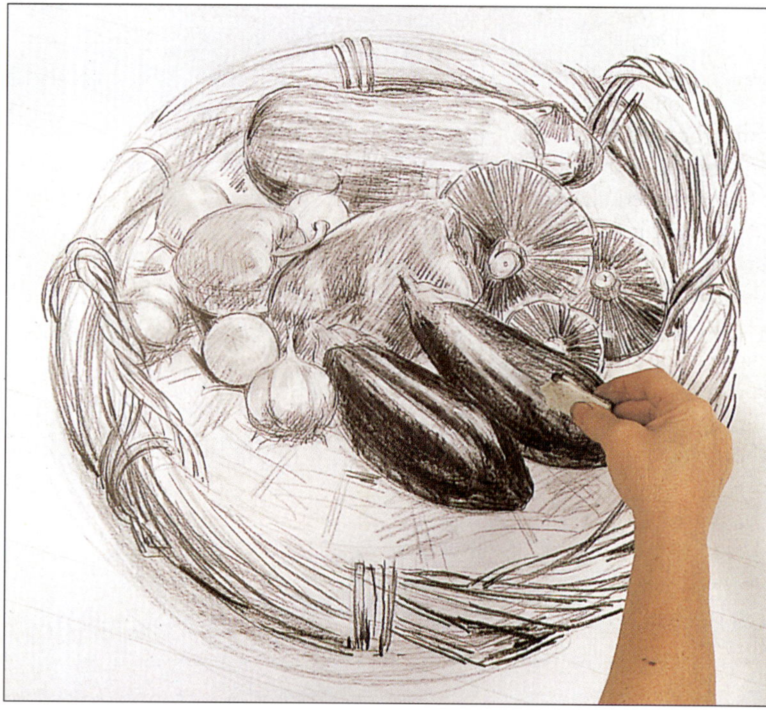

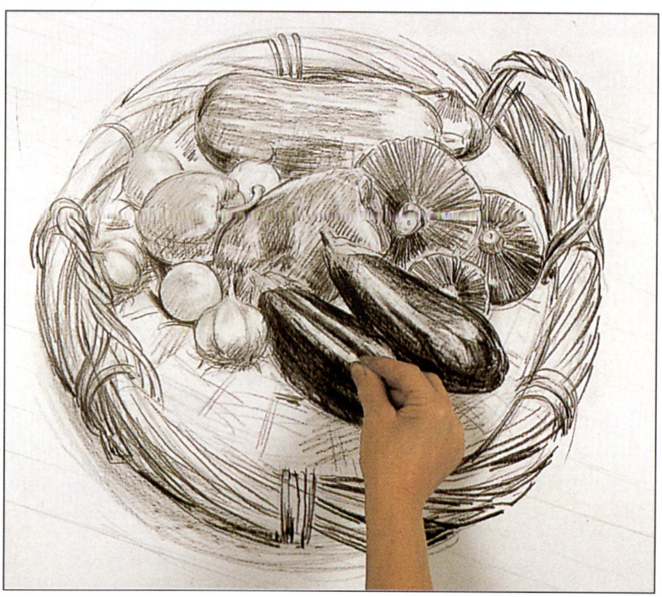

8 Work white highlights into the drawing with chalk. Concentrate especially on the dark aubergines at the front of the group, creating strong highlights to bring them forward in the picture plane.

Helpful Hint

WHEN USING SOFT PENCIL, CHARCOAL AND CHALK, IT'S A GOOD IDEA TO SPRAY YOUR FINISHED DRAWING WITH FIXATIVE, TO PREVENT ACCIDENTAL SMUDGES.

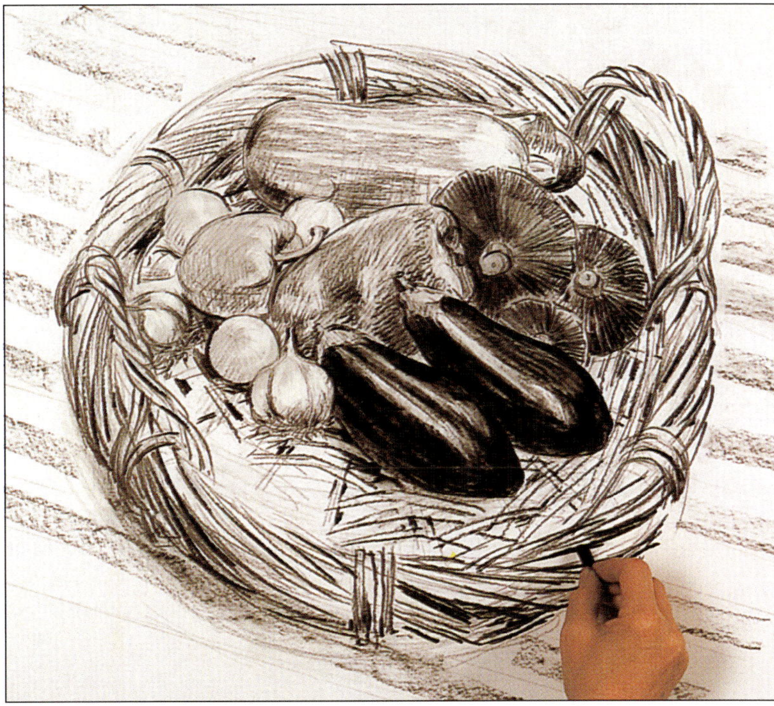

9 Deepen the darkest tones on the peppers, mushrooms and aubergines with a stick of compressed charcoal, blending it into the drawing with your fingertips. Using the side of the stick, lightly suggest the striped background fabric. Using the tip, block in the shadows between the vegetables and add further texture to the basket weave, especially at the front, to make the basket project forward.

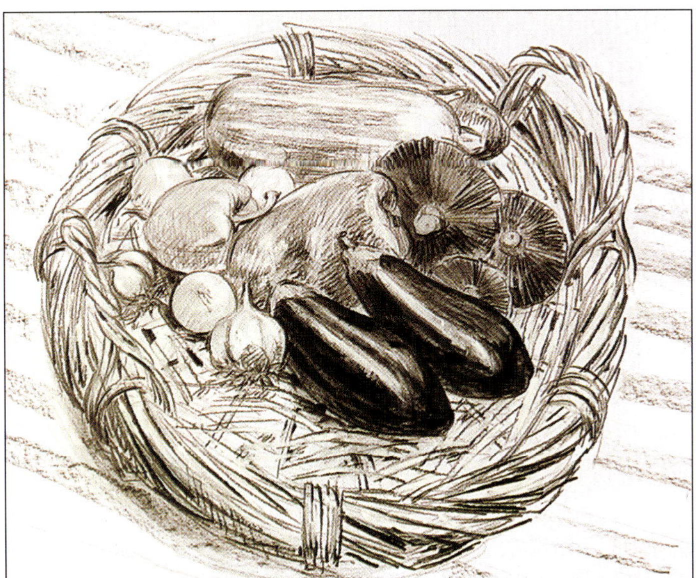

10 In the finished drawing, notice how the addition of the strong darks makes the light areas appear brighter; these tonal contrasts accentuate the wonderful textures and forms in the composition, and really bring the picture to life.

Coloured Pencils

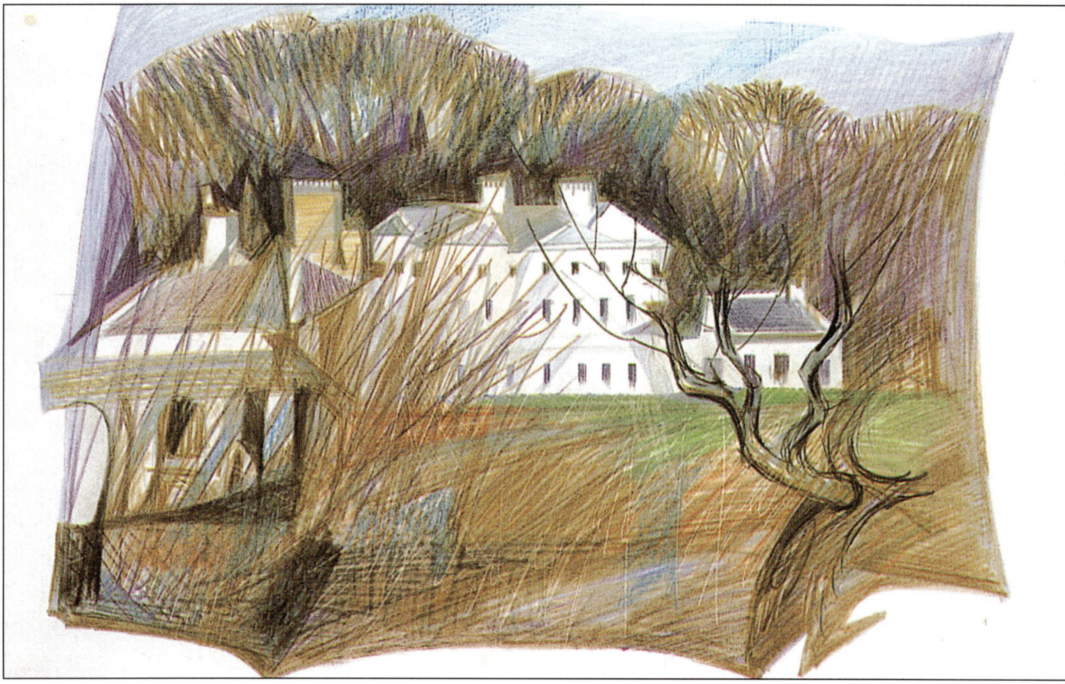

Philip Wildman
THE WHITE HOUSE
In this lively drawing the artist has applied one colour over another with loosely hatched lines to create a 'broken colour' effect. Notice how the pencil lines are worked in various directions, encouraging the eye to explore the composition.

Many of us associate coloured pencils with school and consequently underestimate their value to the artist. Being light, portable and easy to handle, coloured pencils are an excellent medium for rapid drawings and outdoor sketches. They are equally capable of creating intricate, highly detailed effects and rich blends of colour.

Because the coloured pigment is semi-transparent, light reflects off the white paper and up through the colours, lending them a soft luminosity. Most coloured-pencil drawings are characterized by a lightly textured, delicate finish that is very attractive.

The 'lead' or core of a coloured pencil is clay, coloured with pigment and bound with wax. The higher the wax content, the harder the pencil. Try out different ranges to see which you prefer – they vary in character from soft, chalky and opaque, or soft and waxy, to hard and translucent. With soft pencils, the colour comes off smoothly and evenly. A hard pencil lays down colour quite lightly and is suitable for delicate work. Many artists use both types – harder pencils for fine line work and softer ones for laying areas of solid, bold colour and for pastel-like effects.

Techniques

Hold the pencil tightly, close to the point, when laying in small intricate details. To lay in broad areas of loosely hatched colour, hold the pencil loosely, grasping it farther up the shaft and moving it in a natural sweeping motion that finds its own rhythm.

Coloured pencils are most often used on cartridge paper which has a slight tooth. With light pressure on the pencil the colour catches only on the 'peaks' of the irregular surface, producing a subtle granular finish. With heavier pressure the colour is pushed into the 'troughs' of the paper surface. It spreads more evenly and the texture of the paper is slightly flattened, resulting in a smooth, fluid layer.

A rich, 'burnished' effect is achieved by rubbing the colour into the paper surface with firm pressure using the side, rather than the tip, of the lead. The firm pressure applied fuses the colours so that they blend together in a way that is different to that achieved by overlaying colours. The brilliance of the colour can be increased further by rubbing the surface with your finger, a rag or a torchon to produce a slight sheen. When blending with solid layers of colour the surface of the paper can quickly become clogged, making further layers difficult to apply, so make sure that you choose a textured paper whose surface holds plenty of pigment.

Colour mixing

With coloured pencils you can achieve glowing and shimmering effects using methods such as hatching, crosshatching, shading and scribbling. This creates hues that are richer and more involving to look at than an area of flat colour. For example, strokes of blue laid over yellow make a green that is more subtle, lively and interesting than the flat colour you get by using a green pencil. The pure yellow and blue are still discernible, yet from the appropriate viewing distance they 'read' as green. You can also modulate the green by controlling the amount of yellow or blue.

As with pastels, the best approach is to build up the colours gradually, starting with light, open lines that let plenty of white paper show through. Hatching and crosshatching are a good way to do this because the fine, regular lines give you maximum control over the result.

Jane Strother
STUDY OF APPLES
This drawing was done as an illustration for a magazine article. The artist has skilfully combined delicate watercolour washes with finely hatched coloured pencil lines to define the three-dimensional forms of the apples. Small patches of untouched white paper help to suggest the shiny, luscious texture of the apples' skins.

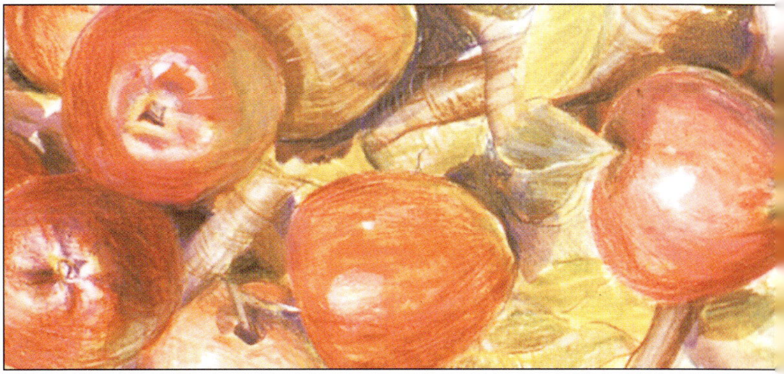

Vase of Petunias

The brilliant colours of this jug of petunias inspired the artist to tackle them using a 'burnishing' technique with coloured pencils. Layers of saturated colour were built up using the sides of the pencil leads, pushing the pigment into the surface grain of the paper to create a smooth, soft-textured finish.

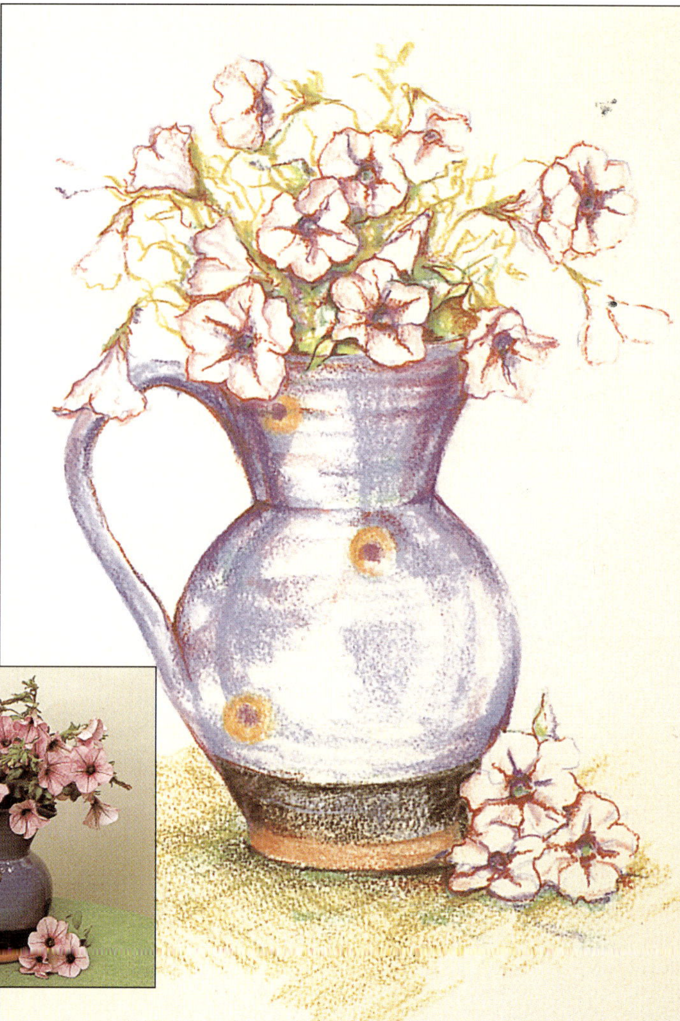

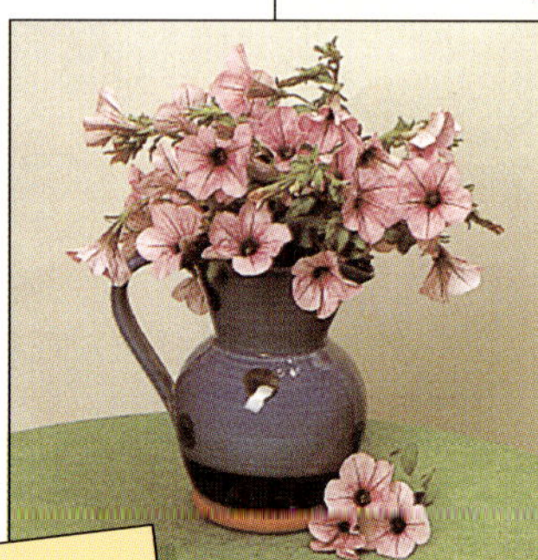

YOU WILL NEED

- ✔ *Sheet of good quality cartridge paper, 16½ x 13¼in (42 x 34cm)*

COLOURED PENCILS IN THE FOLLOWING COLOURS

- *Sky blue*
- *Dark blue*
- *Violet*
- *Deep violet*
- *Pale pink*
- *Dark green*
- *Yellow-green*
- *Sepia*
- *Cinnamon*
- *Gold ochre*
- *Wine red*

1 Start by loosely sketching the main outlines of the composition using the well-sharpened tip of a sky blue pencil. Keep your lines light and fluid – a solid, continuous outline will make your drawing appear stiff and wooden.

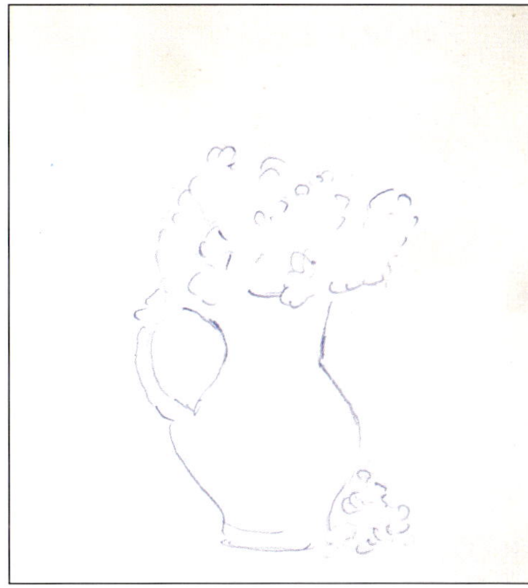

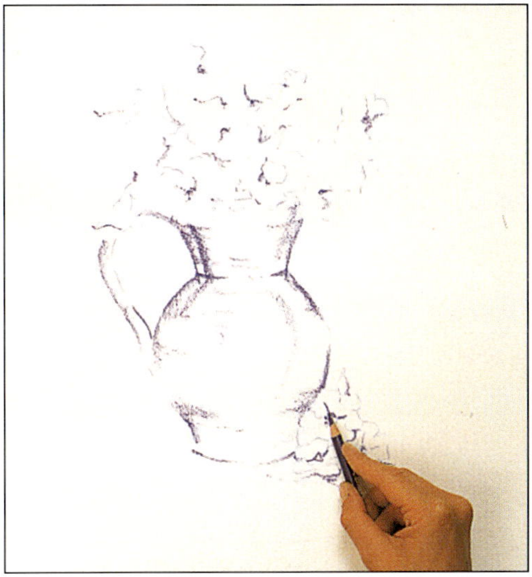

2 Switch to a dark blue pencil and pick out the dark areas in the vase, shading with the side of the pencil lead. Shade the dark centres of the petunias with the same colour. Keep your marks light – you'll build up darker colours as the drawing progresses.

Helpful Hint

FOR THIS TECHNIQUE IT'S IMPORTANT THAT YOUR PENCIL LEADS HAVE A SMOOTH EDGE, SO SHARPEN THEM WITH A PENCIL SHARPENER AND NOT A CRAFT KNIFE.

3 Continue working on the flowers using a violet pencil. Again, use the side of the pencil lead to create soft tones instead of hard lines. Start at the centres and move out, building up the colour gradually with the side of the pencil lead. Fill in the gaps between the flowers with violet to define the petals and bring the flowers forward. Work on the vase, layering smooth strokes of violet onto the blue underlayer to build up the tones.

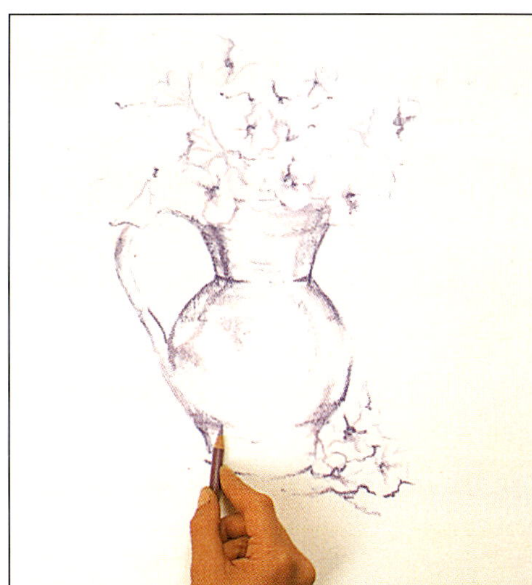

4 Shade gently with a pale pink pencil to suggest the delicate pink veining on the petals and to define their edges. Take some of this colour down into the vase.

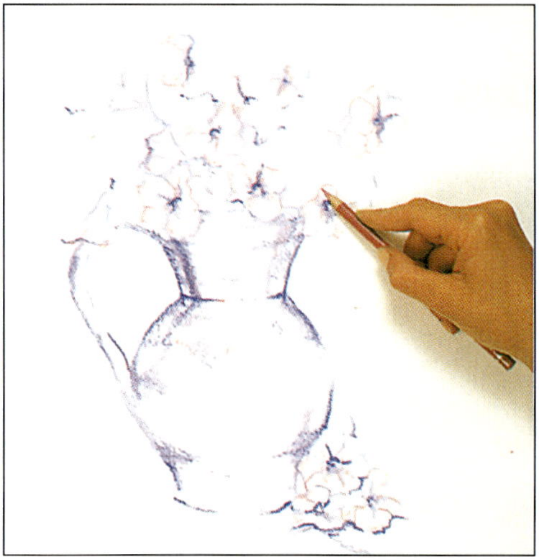

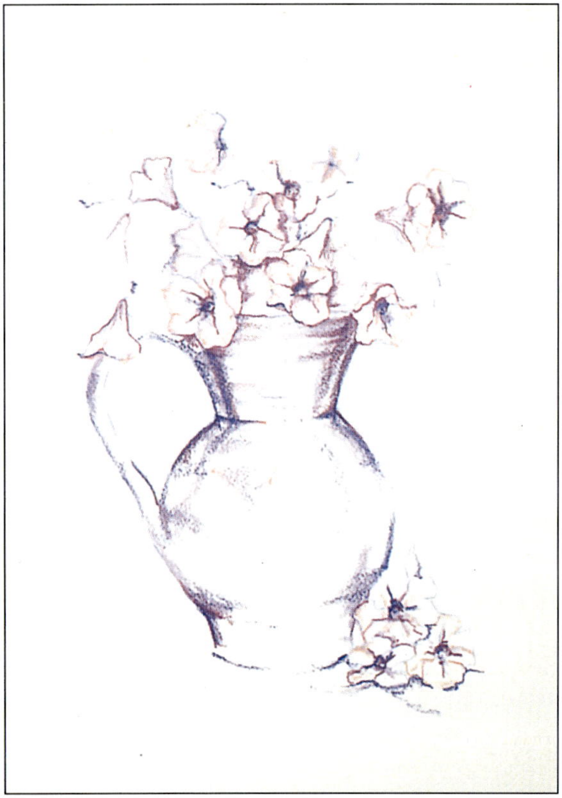

5 Work on the flowers using deep violet, shading over the existing layers of colour to build up the purplish-pink centres. Use the same colour to shade in the dark lines on the individual petals and to deepen the shadows between the blooms.

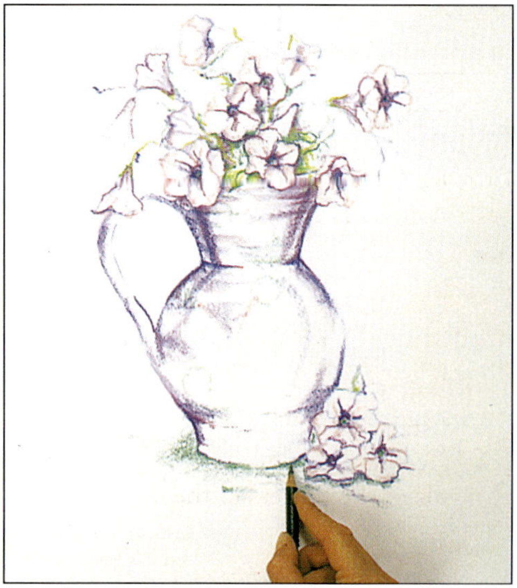

6 Define the foliage between the flowers using dark green and yellow-green. Use dark green to draw the pattern of green circles on the vase and to indicate the shadow cast by the vase and the dropped blooms on the green cloth.

7 Build up the circular pattern on the vase with strokes of pale pink overlaid with gold ochre. Fill in the centres with violet. Build up the mid tones on the vase with soft strokes of sky blue, following the rounded contours with sweeping strokes of the pencil. Leave areas of untouched white paper for the brightest highlights.

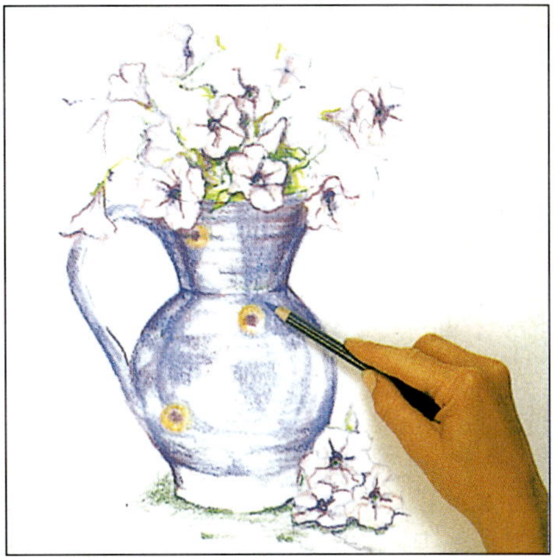

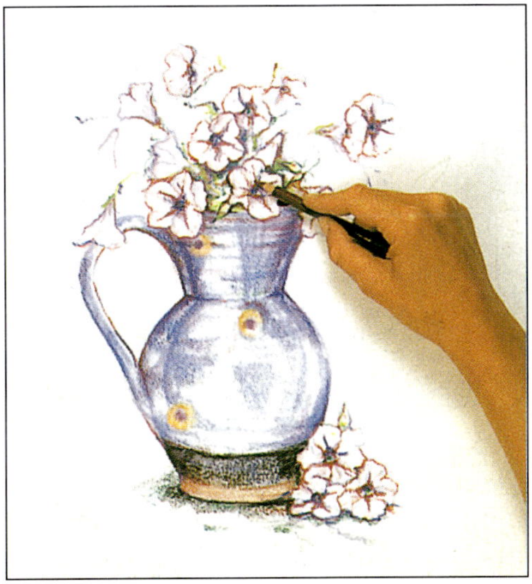

8 Fill in the dark band around the base of the vase with sepia and use cinnamon for the terracotta base. Now use wine red to introduce deeper shading on the jug, for example on the handle and on the rim. Use the same colour to go over the lines on the petals and to outline the flowers in the foreground.

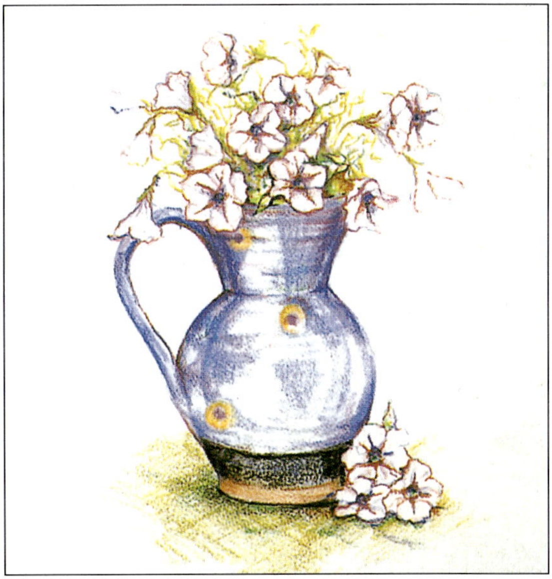

9 Finish off by shading a little more light green into the cloth with the side of the pencil. Add more leaves and stalks between the flowers with strokes of green and add touches of pink to the petals of the flowers in the background.

Drawing with Erasers

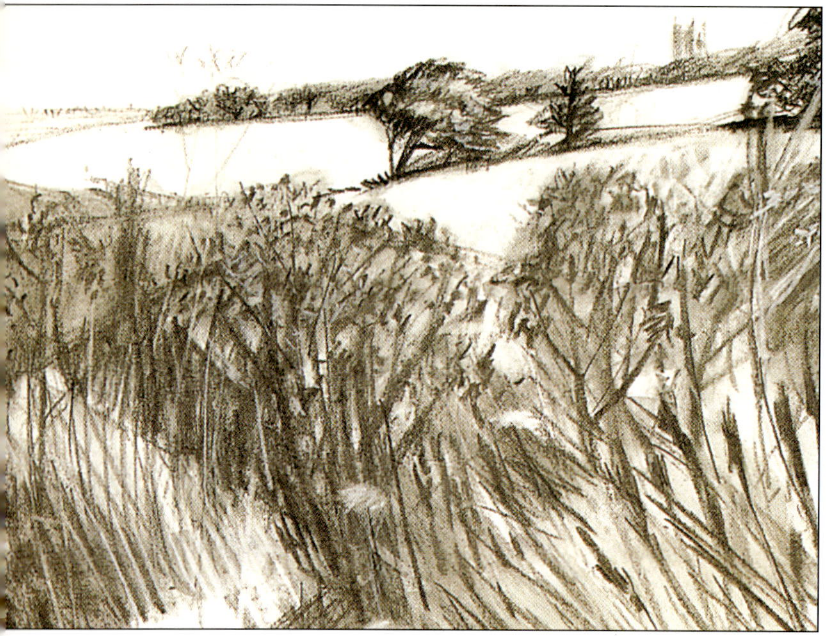

Sarah Donaldson
ACROSS THE FIELDS
This is an effective composition, with the tall grasses in the foreground forming the main focus. The artist worked into some of the charcoal marks with a putty eraser to soften the tones and emphasize the upward sweep of the grasses, which leads the eye to the landscape beyond.

Erasers aren't just used for rubbing out mistakes – they can also be used as mark-makers in their own right. For example, rather than leaving the light tones in a drawing blank or partially covered, why not try blocking in a solid area of dark tone and then use an eraser to 'draw' into it, pulling out the highlights and light areas by creating 'negative' lines and shapes.

This technique can be used with any soft drawing medium, such as graphite stick, pencil, or charcoal. It is possible to produce a different mood and surface quality depending on the type of eraser you use and the degree of pressure applied. If you want a gentle, lyrical effect, use a putty eraser and light pressure to produce soft-edged marks that impart a slightly hazy, luminous quality to the finished drawing. For a bolder, more graphic effect, use a hard eraser and apply more pressure to pull out crisp, angular shapes.

Erasers

There are several types of eraser available, each suited to different functions and different papers. Some work better on hard, glossy papers, while others are more efficient on a soft or textured surface. Putty erasers, or kneaded erasers, are soft and can be used to wipe away broad shapes. Try twisting a corner to a fine point for pulling out fine details. With heavy pressure you can get back to the white of the paper, or you can simply lighten a tone by gently caressing the surface.

Plastic erasers are firm, and their sharp corners are ideal for making crisp, hard-edged marks.

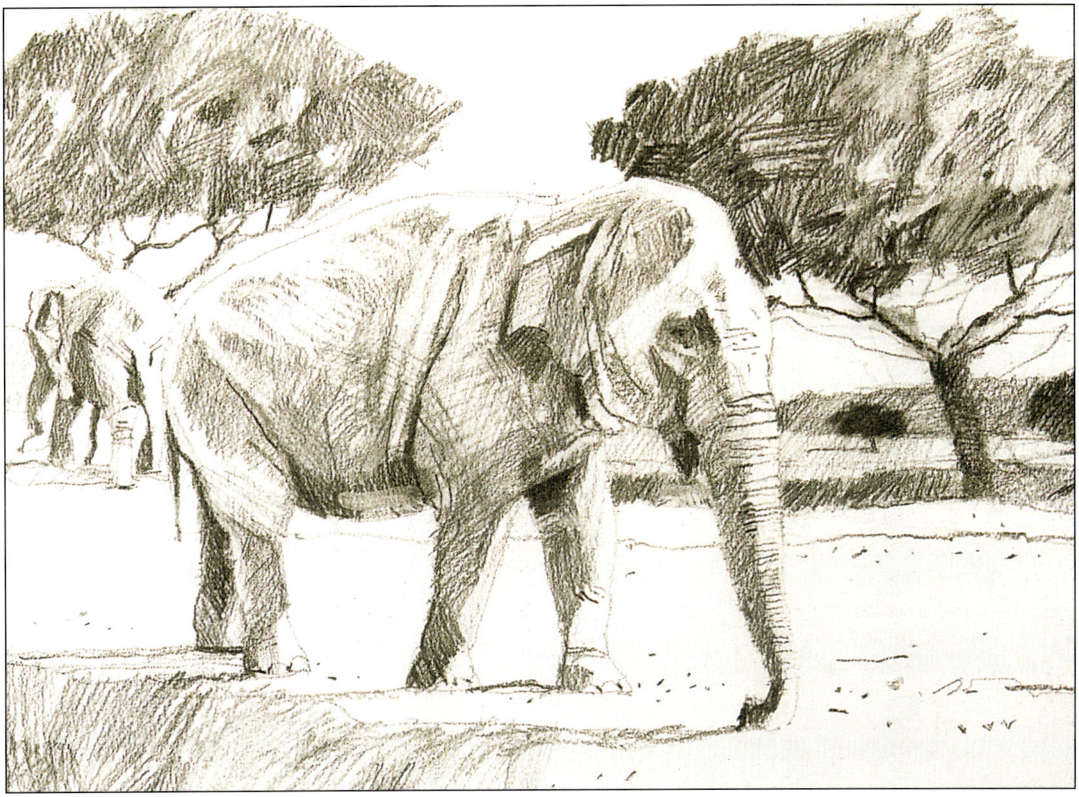

YOU WILL NEED

- *Sheet of good quality cartridge paper, 24 x 17in (61 x 43cm)*
- *Thin and thick sticks of compressed charcoal*
- *Kneadable eraser*

Elephants on Safari

This lively drawing shows how an eraser can be used, not just for correcting mistakes, but also as a drawing tool in its own right. The artist has achieved strong tonal contrasts by building up the shadows with charcoal shading, then using the corner of an eraser to pull out light tones and create a variety of interesting 'negative' shapes.

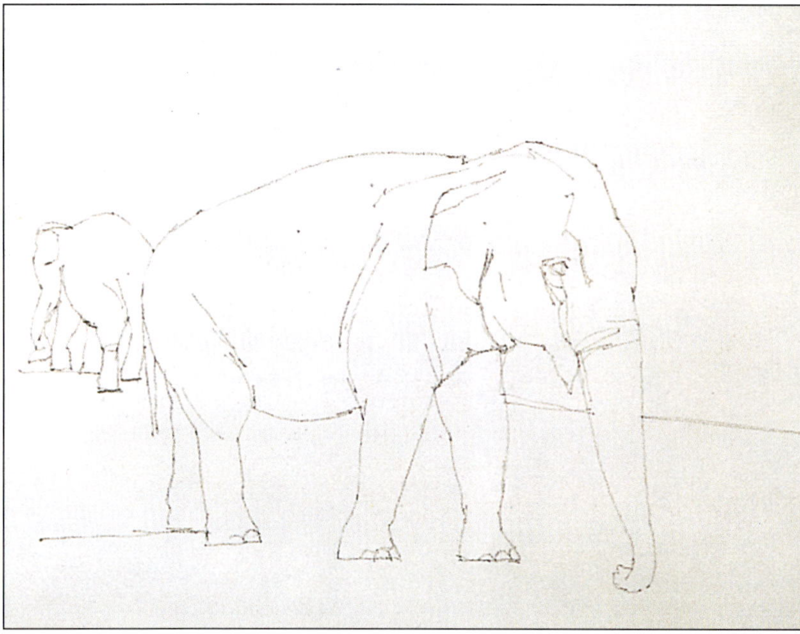

1 Using a thin stick of compressed charcoal, sketch the outlines of the elephants and indicate the horizon line.

2 Loosely draw the outlines of the trees in the background using the edge of the charcoal stick. At this stage any mistakes can be easily removed with a kneadable eraser. Sketch in the foreground elephant's features and the creases on the trunk. Don't use too much pressure with the charcoal or work for too long on any particular areas – the drawing will develop gradually as you build up areas of tone and shading across the paper.

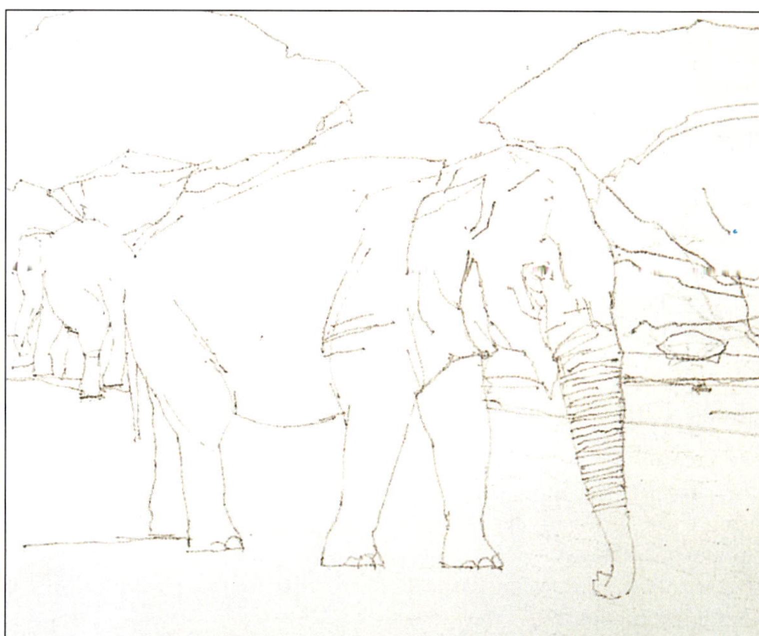

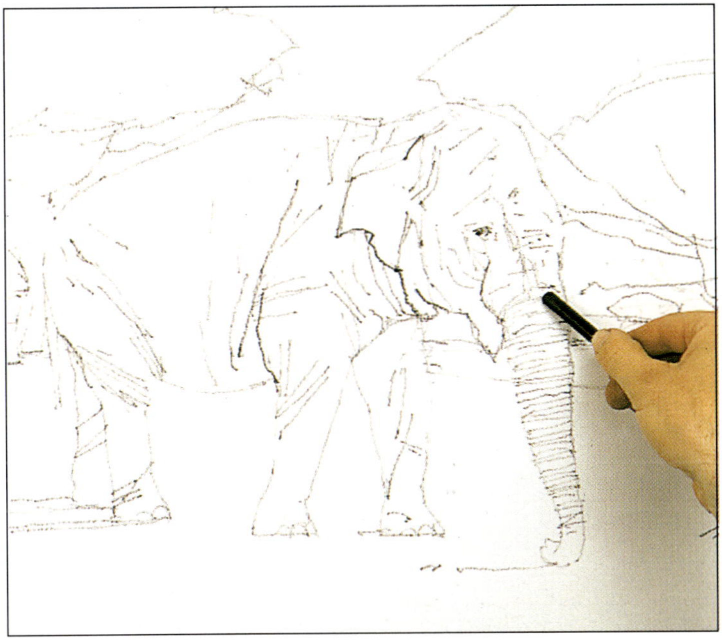

3 Continue to build up the characteristic features and details of the elephant's head, using the edge of the compressed charcoal. Work across the body, varying the pressure on the stick to create light and dark lines that indicate the play of light on the folds and creases in the skin.

4 Using a thicker stick of charcoal, build up the tones on both elephants to suggest their weight and solidity. Use loosely hatched strokes, leaving bare paper to stand for the highlights. Don't press on to the paper as you work – let the weight of the charcoal stick make the marks. Vary the direction of the strokes to follow the form of the elephants and create the texture of the skin. Shade the tree on the left using the same technique. Spray your drawing with fixative at this stage to avoid smudging the marks you've made so far.

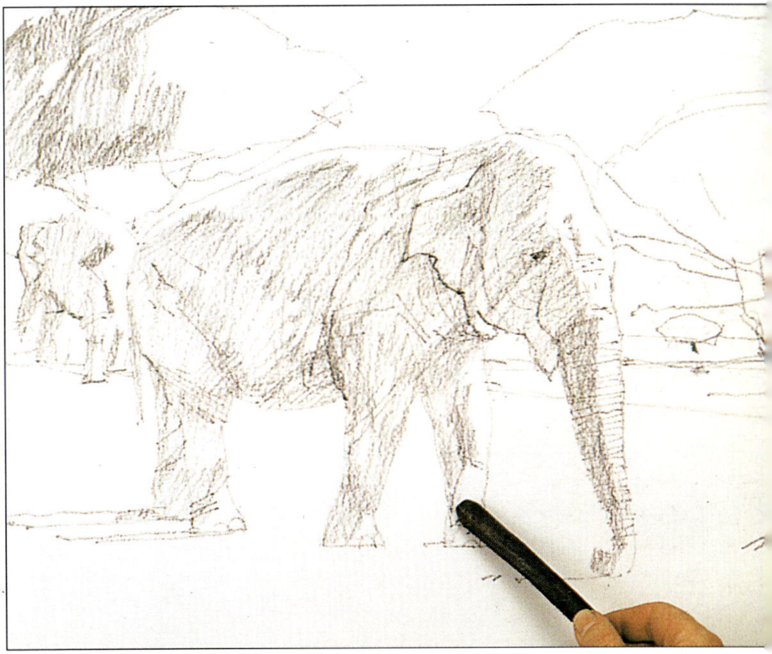

5 Rough in the shadows of the elephants, then continue working with the thicker charcoal stick to add tone and texture to the foliage and tree trunks. Vary the direction of the strokes and the density of hatching to convey the contrasting textures of the subject. Describe the hills and trees in the distance, which help to emphasize the scale of the elephants. Allow areas of the paper to show through to create highlights where sunlight is striking the subject.

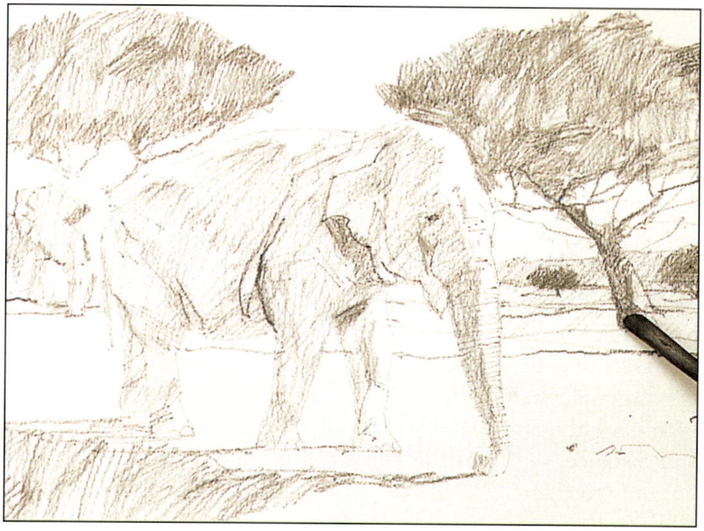

6 Add more shadows on the body of the background elephant. Switch to the thin charcoal stick and work back over the large elephant with crosshatching, using finer lines to indicate detail but keeping them spaced apart so that the tone underneath shows through. Darken the distant trees and indicate their cast shadows, and darken the tone on the left side of the tree canopy to indicate strong sunlight coming from the right. The detail (right) shows how the lightly drawn charcoal marks are broken up by the texture of the paper, which helps to describe the rugged texture of the elephant's hide. Areas of hatching and crosshatching, running in different directions, describe the weight and bulk of the animal and give the drawing a lively surface texture.

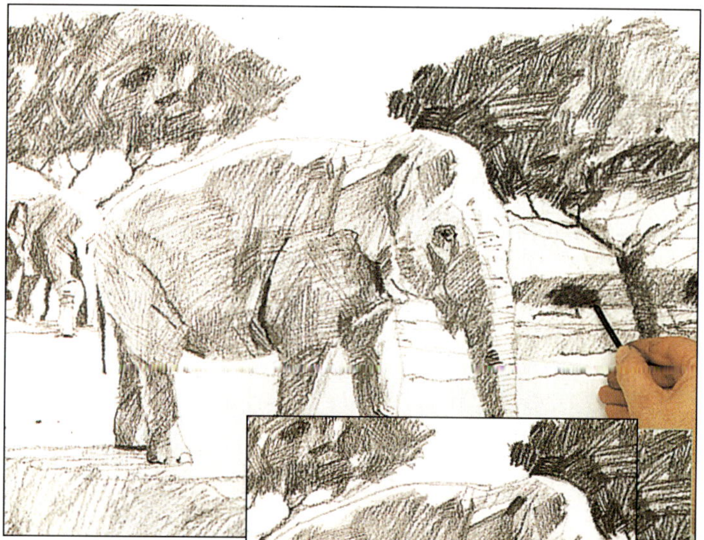

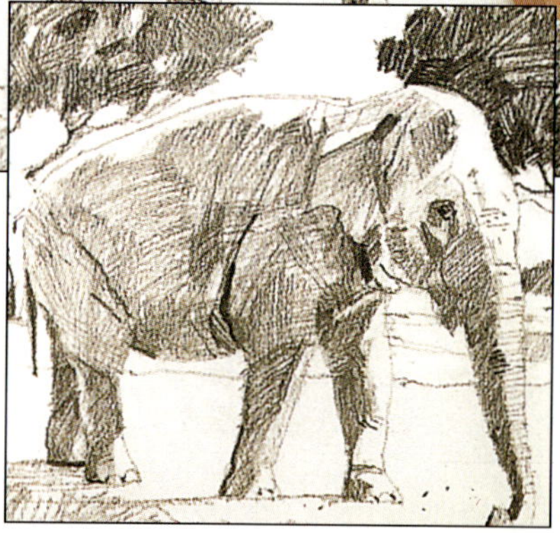

7 Now start using the kneadable eraser to remove areas of charcoal to introduce more emphatic highlights – for example, where sunlight strikes the elephant's trunk. Work back some of the dark areas with the thin charcoal stick. The strong tonal contrasts thus produced bring the larger elephant forward, increasing the sense of scale and distance. Use the eraser not only to create light and shade but also to convey texture; here, the artist is making sharp angular lines over the elephant's body, emphasizing the folds in its skin.

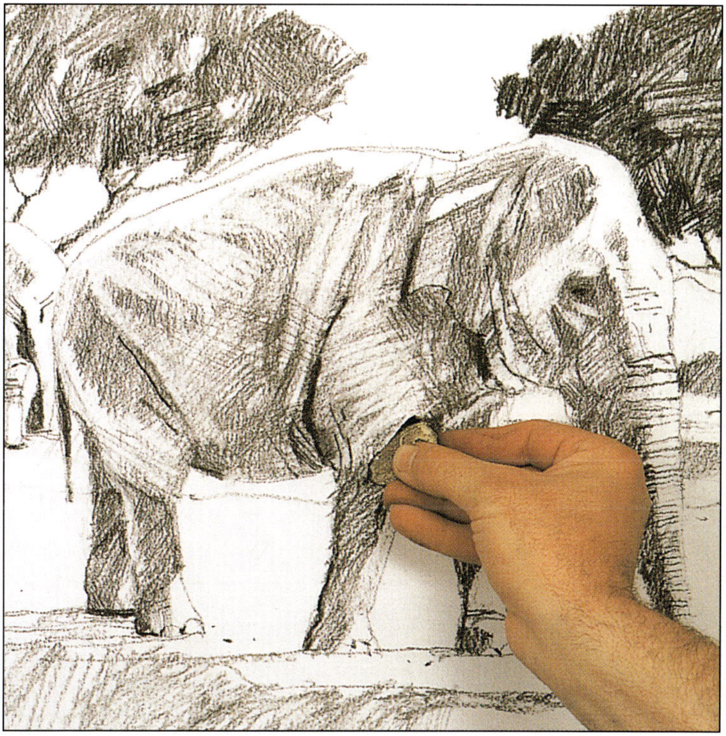

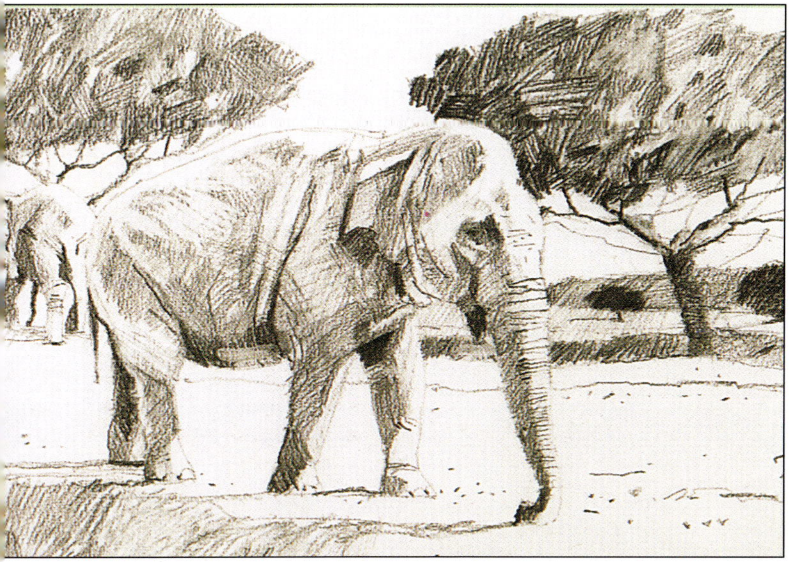

8 To complete the picture, define some of the shadow areas using denser areas of charcoal. Spray the drawing with fixative to prevent smudging. In the final drawing, the lines, shapes, forms and tones all integrate to make a bold, energetic portrait of these splendid animals.

Seeing Colour in White

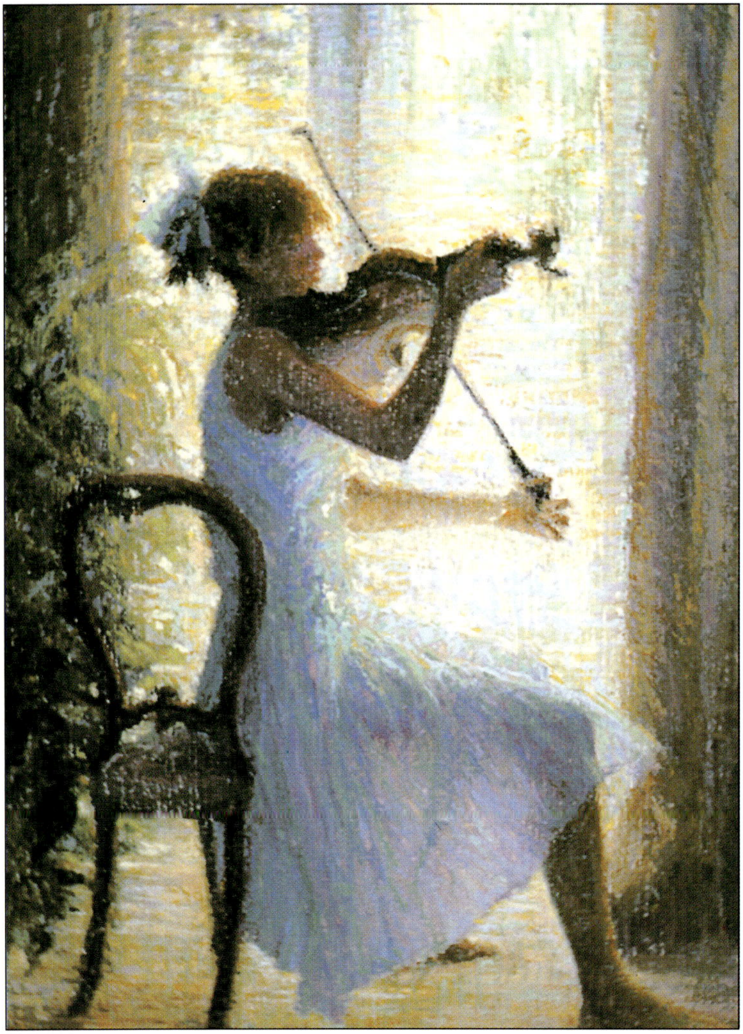

Charmian Edgerton
VIOLIN PRACTICE
Here a range of blues, pinks and greens 'read' as white in the sitter's dress.

Inexperienced painters often have problems when depicting white objects such as summer clouds, snow, ocean breakers, white buildings, or white clothing in portrait and figure paintings. On the face of it, the task is an easy one; you just use white for the highlights and grey for the shadows. But the resulting image looks flat and monotonous and somehow fails to capture the brilliance and luminosity of the subject.

This problem arises when the artist ignores what he actually sees, and paints instead what he thinks he sees. If you really look closely at a white object, particularly on a sunny day, you will soon discover that it actually contains a surprising amount of colour, ranging perhaps from warm pinks, yellows and golds in the illuminated parts to cool blues, violets and greens in the shadows. These subtle nuances of colour may not be obvious to you at first, but it is exactly such unexpected flashes of colour and reflected light that accentuate the brilliance of the whites and give a magical touch of luminosity to a snow scene or a cloudy sky, for example.

Reflected colour

White has no actual colour of its own but picks up and reflects colours from its surroundings, so that it is almost never really white but a composite of many other colours. White snow, for example, may appear yellowish on a sunny day, while the shadows that fall on it appear blue or violet because they reflect the sky. Similarly, the shadows on a white garment may appear blue or violet outdoors on a sunny day, but indoors under artificial light they may have a greenish or yellowish tinge.

As an artist, you are perfectly free to embellish or exaggerate the colours you see in nature in order to intensify the experience for those who will view your picture. Monet's paintings of snowy winter landscapes, for example, contain barely any white paint; instead he wove together cool but vibrant blues, violets and greens, offset by warm pinks and yellows. Because the colours are juxtaposed in small dabs they merge to give an impression of shimmering whiteness much more evocative than slabs of pure white.

Pastels are particularly good for drawing colourful whites. By applying strokes of different colours side by side or one over the other, it is possible to suggest tiny hints of many hues. Gradually building up the picture with small, broken colour strokes gives it a vibrant quality that suggests the play of light and shadow, and produces rich, complex layers that are far more lively than just plain white.

Jackie Simmonds

FIVE GREEK CATS, LINDOS

White buildings reflect a lot of light. In bright sunshine the light is warm and yellowish, and the shadowed areas are correspondingly cool and appear blue or violet. Here the artist has used very pale tints of yellow and ochre, rather than pure white, for the sunlit areas. Yellow-orange is the complementary of blue-violet, and when the two are juxtaposed they enhance each other and create a vibrant effect that effectively suggests bright sunlight.

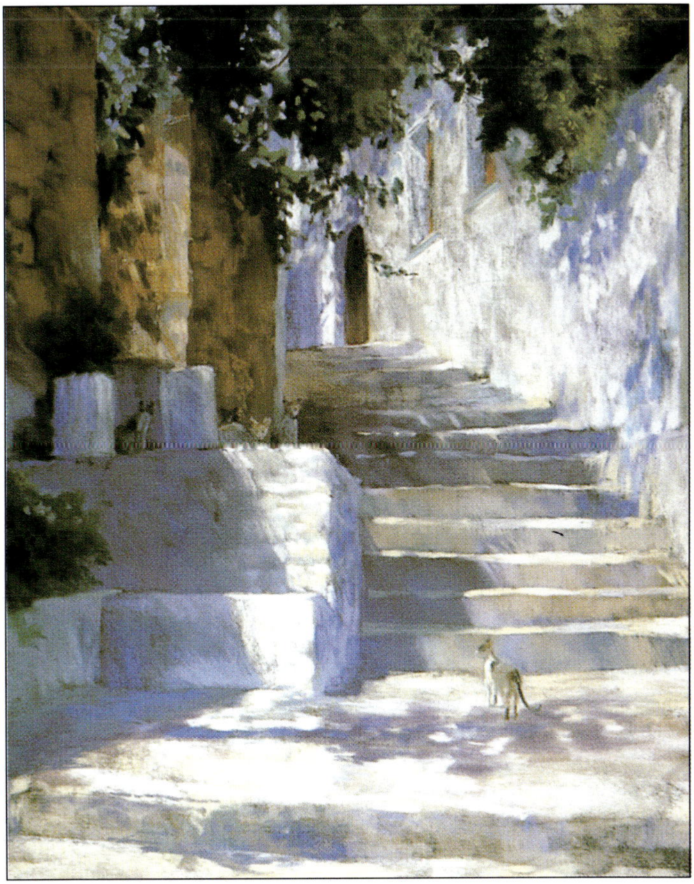

Ballet Pumps

Pastel artists most often work on a coloured ground, but a white ground can work well for delicate subjects. In this study of ballet pumps, flecks of the white paper are glimpsed through the pastel strokes, breaking up the colour and creating a lightness and vibrancy appropriate to the subject.

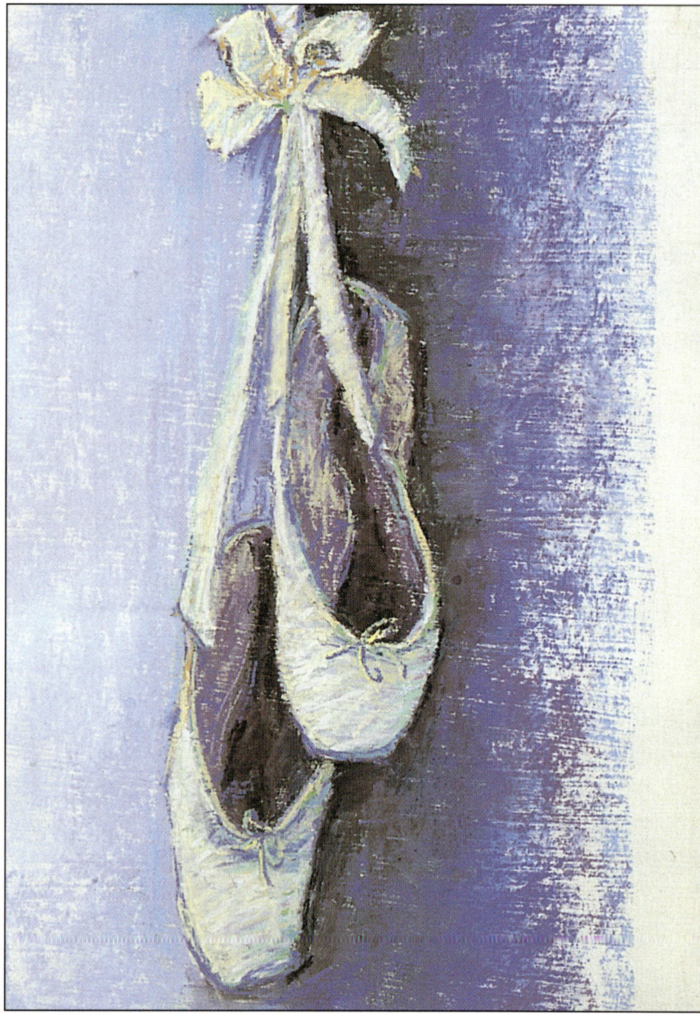

YOU WILL NEED

- ✔ *Sheet of white, rough-surfaced paper or board 17 x 13½in (43 x 34cm)*
- ✔ *Drawing board and masking tape or clips*
- ✔ *Charcoal*
- ✔ *Clean rag*

SOFT PASTELS IN THE FOLLOWING COLOURS

- *Pale tint of cerulean*
- *Pale tint of cobalt blue*
- *Mid tone ultramarine blue*
- *Dark grey-blue*
- *Pale violet*
- *Mid-tone violet*
- *Deep violet*
- *Pale tint of veridian*
- *Creamy lemon yellow*
- *Bright yellow*
- *Pale tint of orange*
- *Pale cream*

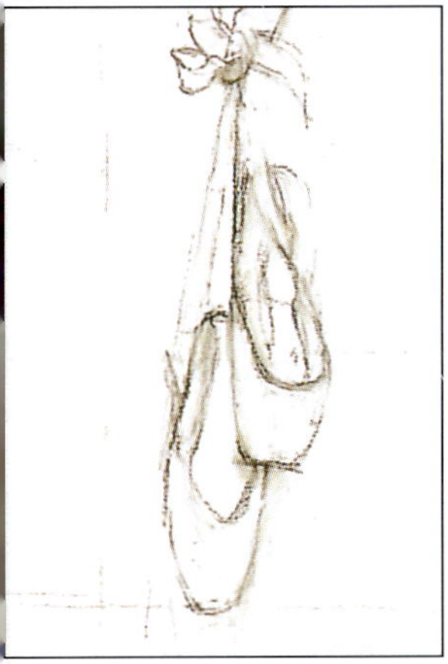

1 Sketch the ballet pumps with charcoal, using a clean rag to gently 'knock back' any excess charcoal dust so that it does not mix with the pastels and make the colours muddy.

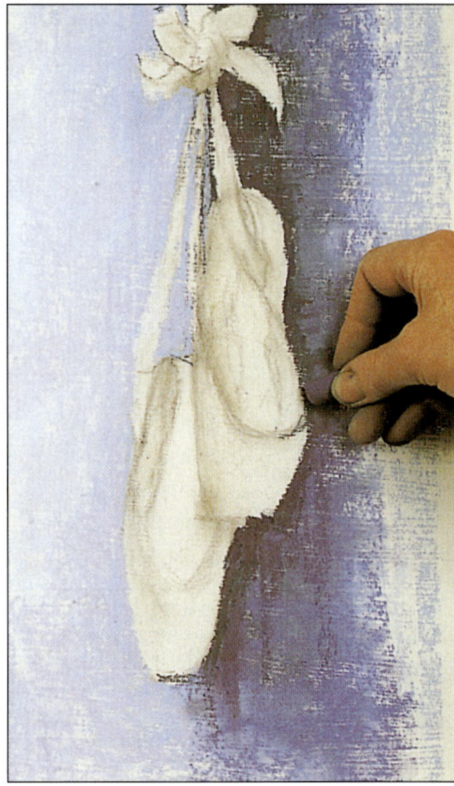

2 Block in the whole background area with pale tints of cerulean and cobalt blue; break off a short length of pastel and use the side, not the tip, to give a fairly even cover. Build up darker blues over this, to give an impression of light and shadow; use a mid-tone ultramarine blue, then overlay it with deep violet and a dark grey-blue for the darkest shadow behind the ballet pumps. Gently blend the colours together with your fingertips to smooth out any hard edges.

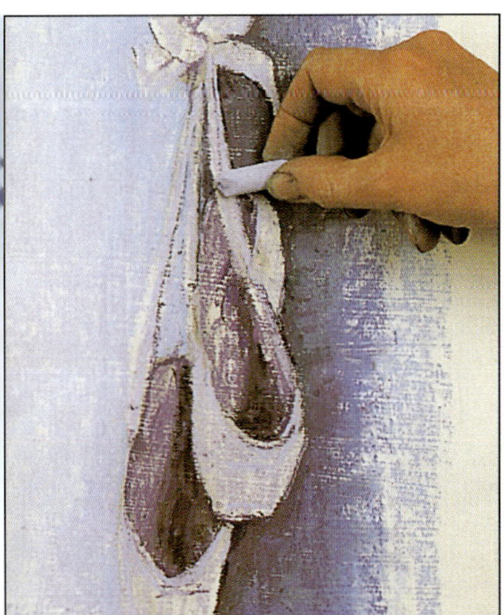

3 Define the forms of the ballet pumps using three tones of violet. Fill in the insides with a mid-tone violet, overlaid with deep violet mixed with purple-brown for the dark shadows. For the ribbons and the tops of the pumps, use a very pale violet, as shown. Apply the colours lightly, allowing some of the white paper to show through. This prevents the grain of the paper filling up too quickly, allowing you to add further layers on top.

4 Add touches of pale viridian to the outer edges of the ribbons and the rim of the pumps, where the light catches them. Add hatched strokes of creamy lemon yellow to the bow and the ribbons. Use a little pale orange for the shadows and the folds in the bow. Highlight the toes of the pumps with strokes of creamy lemon yellow and bright yellow. The base layer of pale violet pastel on the bow will show through in places as you add lively strokes of viridian, orange and yellow (see detail). This bold approach works well with pastel, giving vibrancy to the subject.

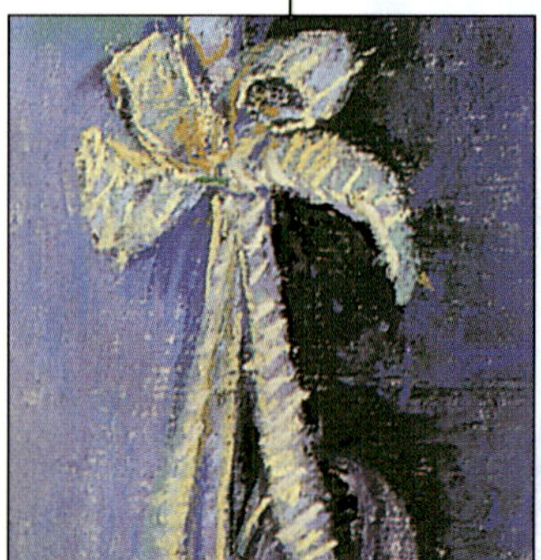

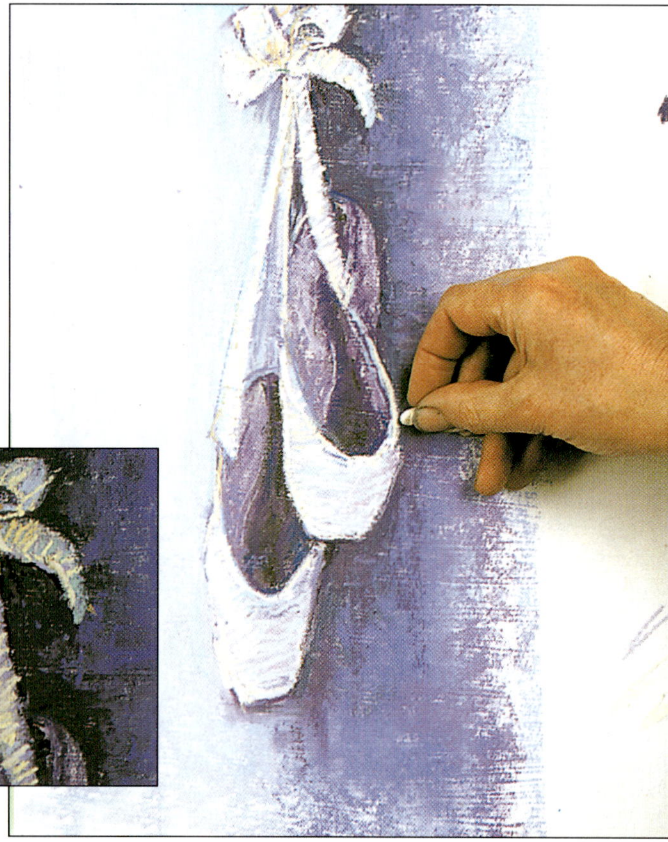

Helpful Hint

WHEN YOU'VE WORN A PASTEL DOWN TO A TINY STUMP, DON'T THROW IT AWAY – THESE SMALL PASTEL PIECES ARE IDEAL FOR DRAWING DETAILS AND INTRICATE SHAPES.

5 Using pale viridian, draw an outline around the rims of the pumps to give them more definition. To do this, break off a piece of pastel and use the sharp edge, as shown. Here you can see how the rough texture of the paper breaks up the pastel strokes and gives the colours a scintillating quality.

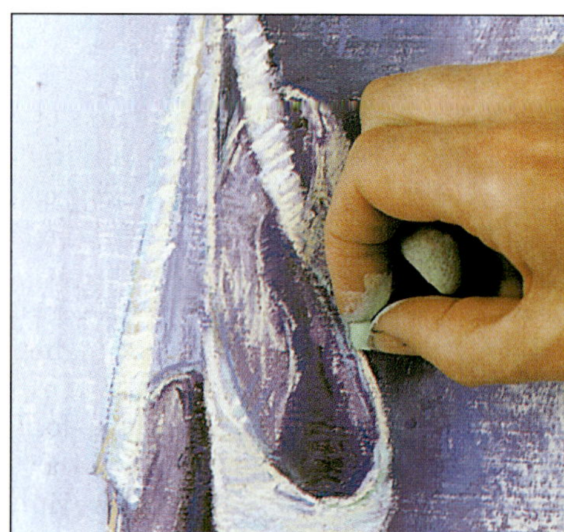

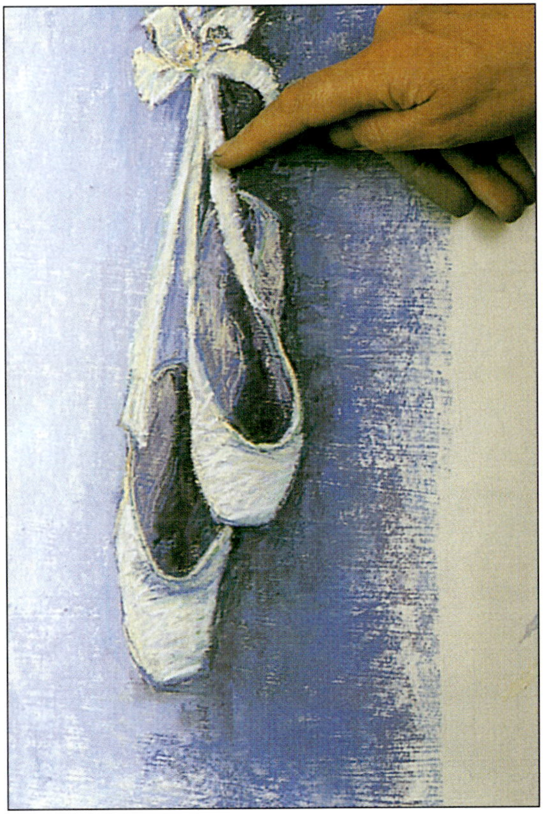

6 Add a hint of shadow to the toes of the pumps with loose strokes of pale viridian and cobalt blue. Put accents of cobalt blue around the edges of the shoes and into the shadows. Add highlights to the toes of the pumps with strokes of creamy lemon yellow and pale cream. Use your fingertip to gently smooth out the hatched lines on the ribbons; the various tones and colours will blend into each other and create the effect of shiny satin.

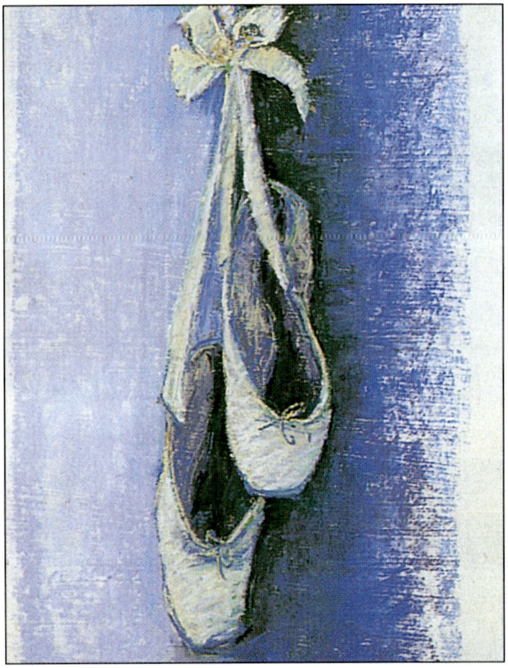

7 Now gently blend the marks on the toes of the shoes with your fingertip to create the same satiny sheen. Don't overblend, though – allow some of the marks to remain, as this gives a more lively effect than smoothly blended colour. Draw the ties at the front of the shoes, using bright yellow for the highlights and cobalt blue for the shadows (you will need tiny slithers of pastel, with a sharp edge, to draw these delicate lines). Finally, add just a touch of definition to the edges of the shoes with deep violet.

Crosshatching

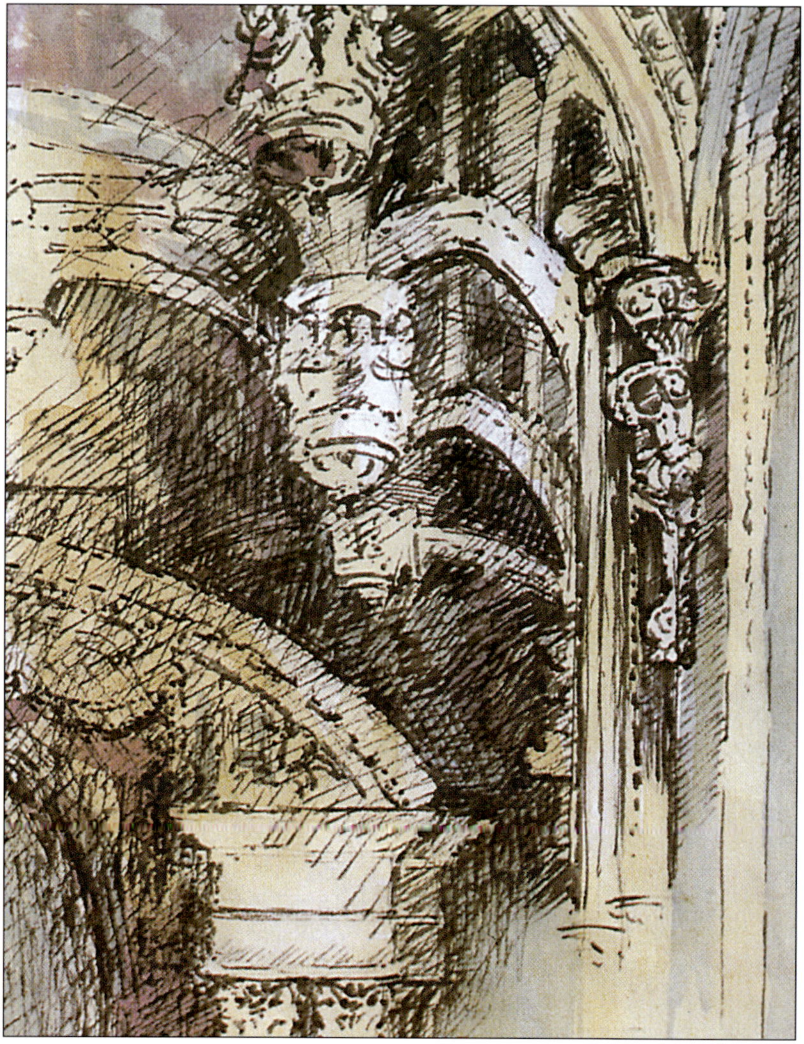

Dennis Gilbert
ARCHITECTURAL DETAIL
In this study of a church interior the artist first laid in light watercolour washes, then developed the form, light and shade with different densities of hatched and cross-hatched lines, drawn with a dip pen and black ink.

Hatching and also crosshatching have been used for centuries as a means of creating tone and texture in pen-and-ink drawings. In hatching, the lines run parallel to one another; in cross-hatching, they cross each other at an angle to create a mesh of tone. Depending on the effect you want, the lines may be carefully drawn or freely sketched.

Considerable variations from light to dark tone can be obtained by varying the pressure on the pen and the spaces between the strokes; the heavier and closer the strokes, the more solid the tone will appear. Because the white of the paper is not completely obliterated, the tone retains a luminosity that is one of the assests of this technique.

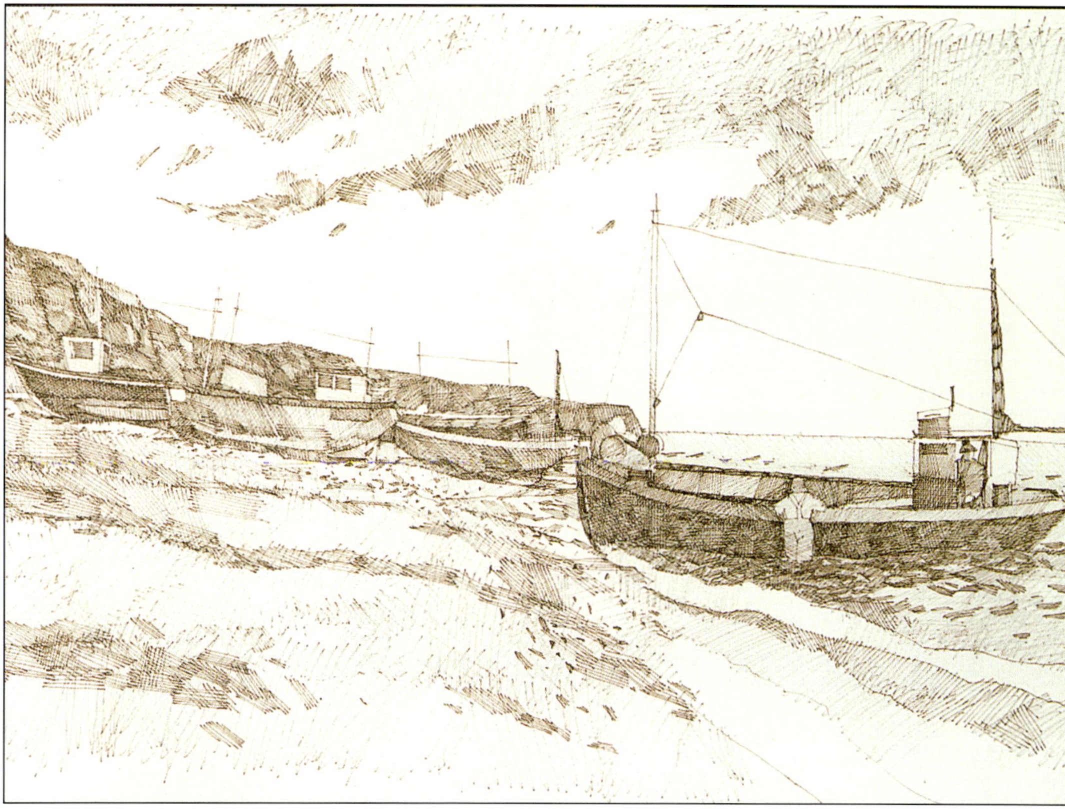

Beached Boats

YOU WILL NEED

- ✔ *Sheet of smooth, good quality cartridge paper, 24 x 17in (61 x 43cm)*
- ✔ *Black fine-liner pen, size 0.2*
- ✔ *H pencil*

An art pen with a very fine drawing tip was chosen for this black and white drawing of beached fishing boats because it produces even, regular lines. Texture and form are achieved by patiently building up small patches of hatched and crosshatched lines. By varying the density of the lines, it is possible to achieve a rich and variable range of tones, from the lightest to the darkest.

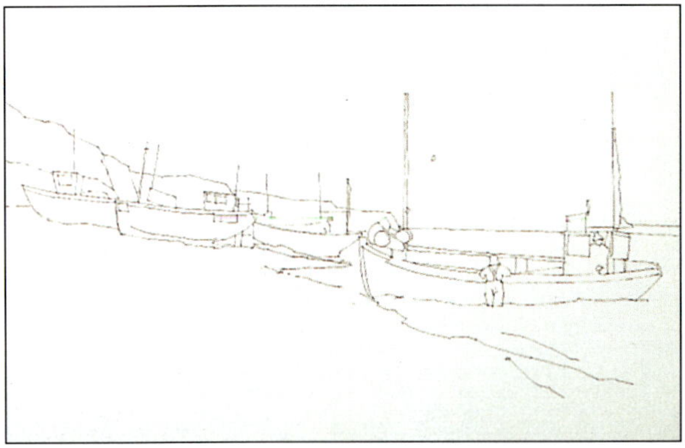

1 Lightly draw the main outlines of the scene using a sharp H pencil. When you are happy with your pencil drawing, go over the lines carefully with a size 0.2 black fine-liner drawing pen.

2 Shade the cliffs in the background by crosshatching the area in small patches, making short vertical, horizontal and diagonal lines to follow the contours of the rocks. Introduce horizontal lines to the darkest areas. The shapes of the boats gradually emerge as the background tones are built up behind them. In the detail (below) you can see how dark areas of tone are built up patch by patch in a series of rapidly drawn vertical, horizontal and diagonal lines. A fine-liner pen moves over the paper quickly and changes direction easily, so it is well suited to crosshatching.

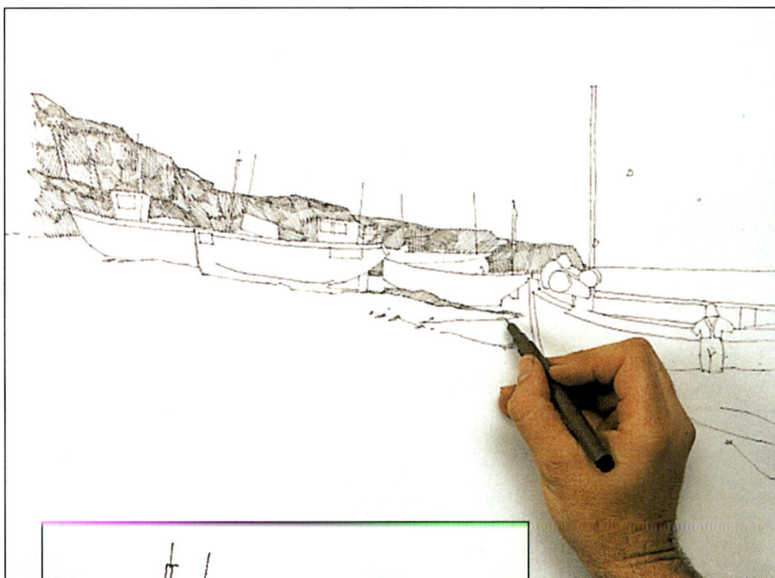

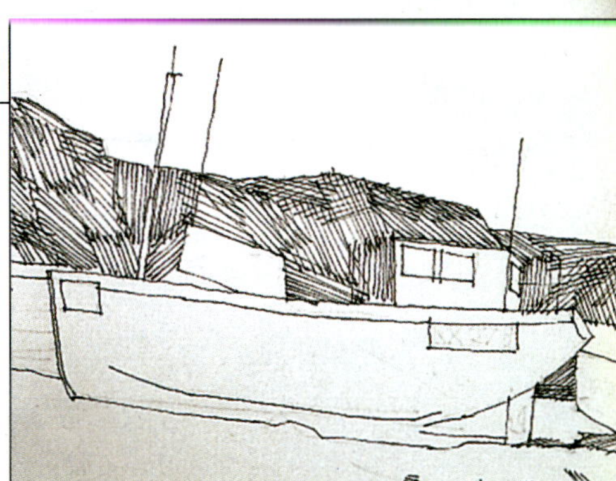

3 Begin working on the three fishing boats in the background. Use lightly hatched strokes for the lightest tones on the boat hulls, then develop areas of denser tone with cross-hatching, drawing the lines closer together. Draw the masts and put in the detailing on the cabins. Allow the white of the paper to stand for the lightest tones. A series of short, vertical lines will create the effect of a pebble beach. Use dots and dashes to indicate the pebbles. The detail (right) shows how subtle variations of light and shade can be conveyed by varying the pressure on the pen and the density of the crosshatched lines.

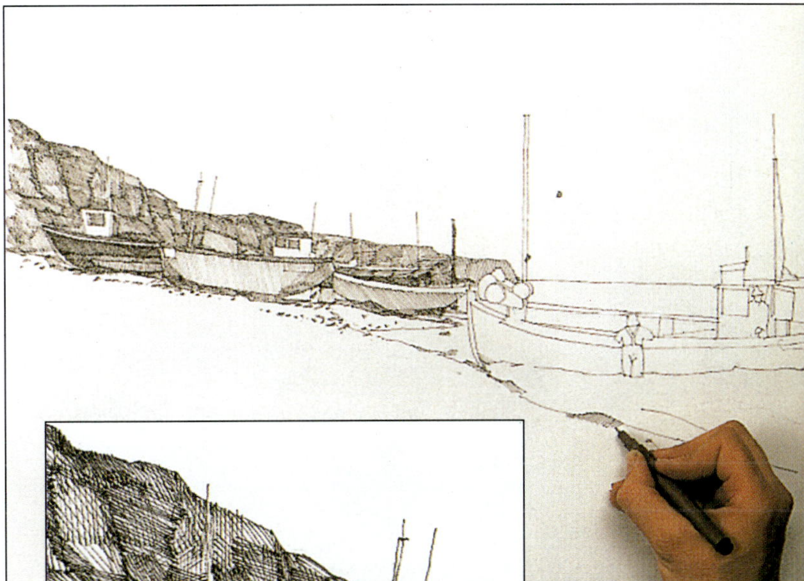

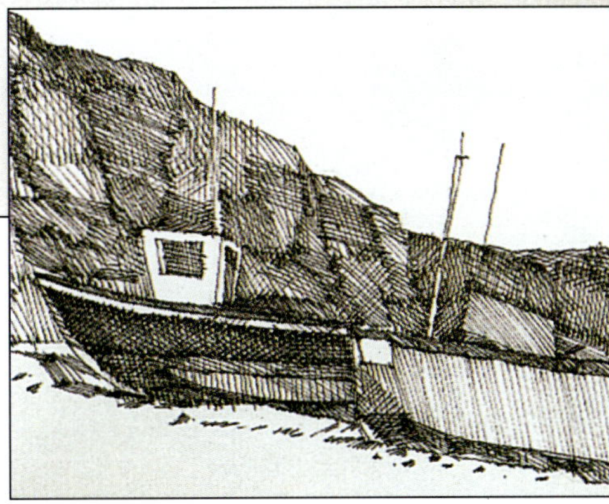

4 Now build up the detail in the drawing, working back over the boats and the cliffs. By developing all areas at once, rather than concentrating on one area at a time, your drawing will be unified, with each form relating to its neighbouring forms. Fill in the boat in the foreground using hatching and crosshatching, carefully following the contour of the boat. Draw the cabin, the sailor and the furled sail using short vertical and horizontal strokes to create a range of lights and darks. Suggest the watery reflections on the side of the hull with overlapping patches of crosshatching.

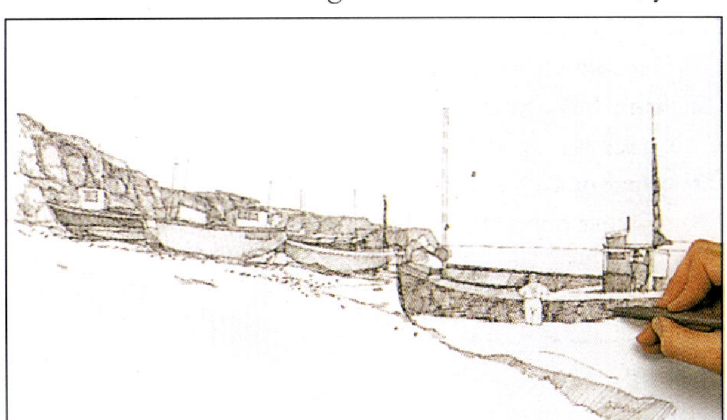

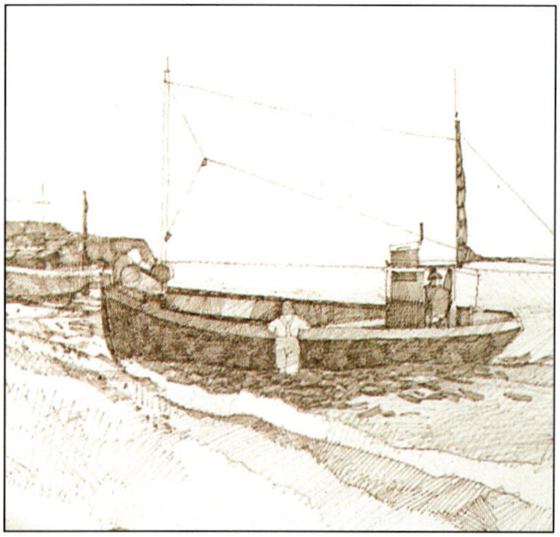

5 Intensify the tone of the foreground boat with a dense mesh of pen lines, to bring it forward in the picture plane. Carefully draw the rigging between the masts with thin, spidery lines – you'll need a steady hand for this! Shade the figure leaning over the side of the boat with a few deft strokes. Indicate the waves lapping the shore with loose crosshatching, leaving bare paper to represent the line of white surf. On top of this, use small patches of darker crosshatching to suggest the shadow cast by the boat on the choppy surface of the water.

6 Draw the rigging on the boats in the background, then suggest the contours of the beach with rapid, scribbled pen strokes worked in different directions. Don't overwork this area – keep it loose and open in contrast with the detailed work on the boat.

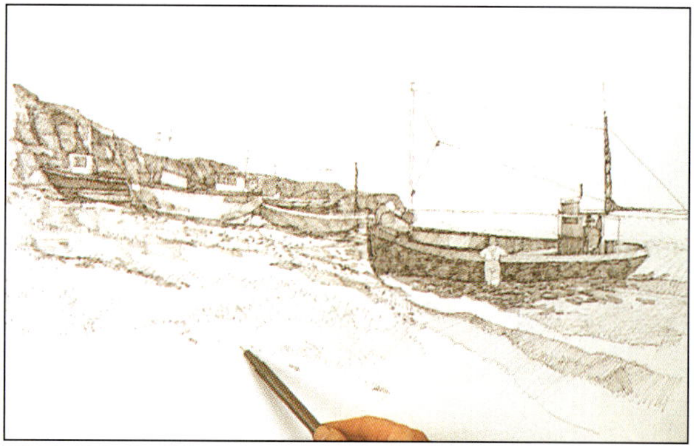

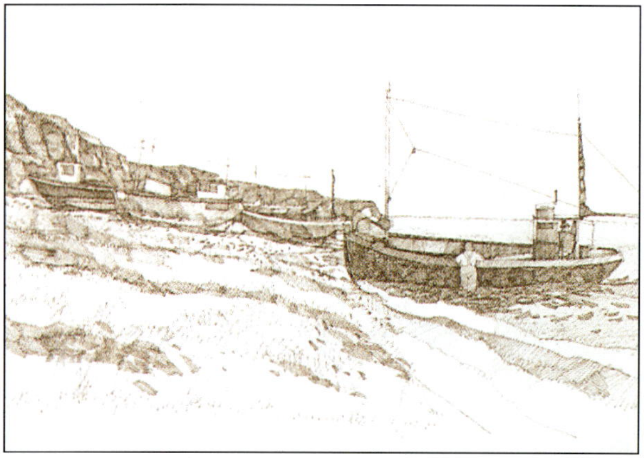

7 Continue working on the beach, building up the shadow areas by loosely hatching over the scribbled marks. Work back over the drawing, filling in the boats and the cliffs with hatching and crosshatching to convey a strong sense of texture and tonal contrast.

8 For the sky, you will need to adopt a looser approach in comparison with the more tightly worked forms of the boats and cliffs. Hold the pen further down the barrel and move it lightly across the paper to create flowing, scribbled marks. Pick out the clouds with more carefully defined areas of hatching and crosshatching. Note how the diagonal lines of cloud echo the diagonal lines of the boats, leading the eye into the picture.

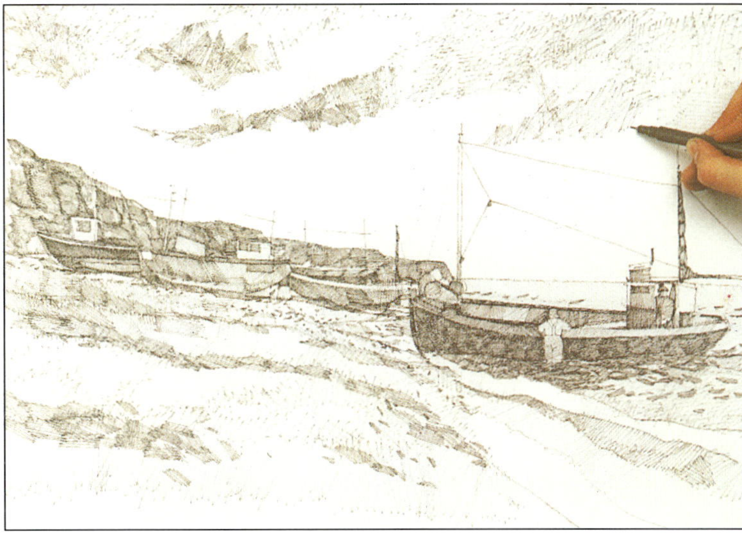

Helpful Hint

AVOID OVERWORKING THE IMAGE – THE WHITE OF THE PAPER CONTRIBUTES TO THE IMPRESSION OF LIGHT AND BREATHES AIR INTO THE DRAWING.

9 Add the final touches, clarifying tones or outlines where necessary. This technique is painstaking and requires a methodical approach, but the results are worth the effort. The final image has a graphic simplicity, and a pleasing mixture of open areas and busy, textured surfaces.

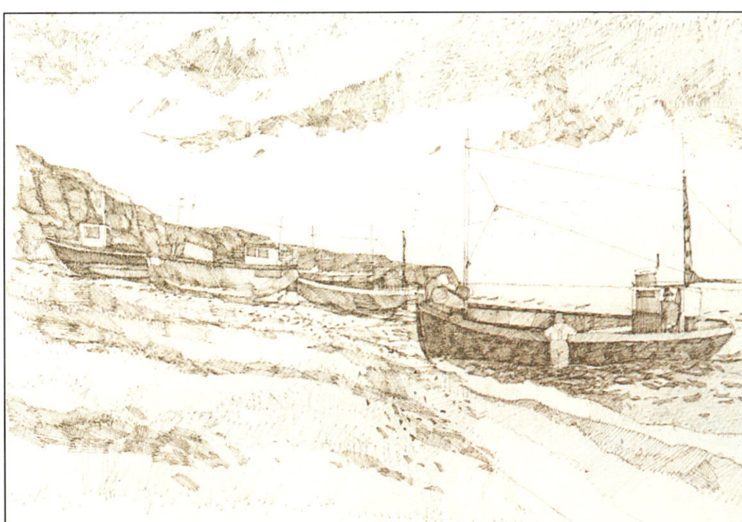

Broken Colour

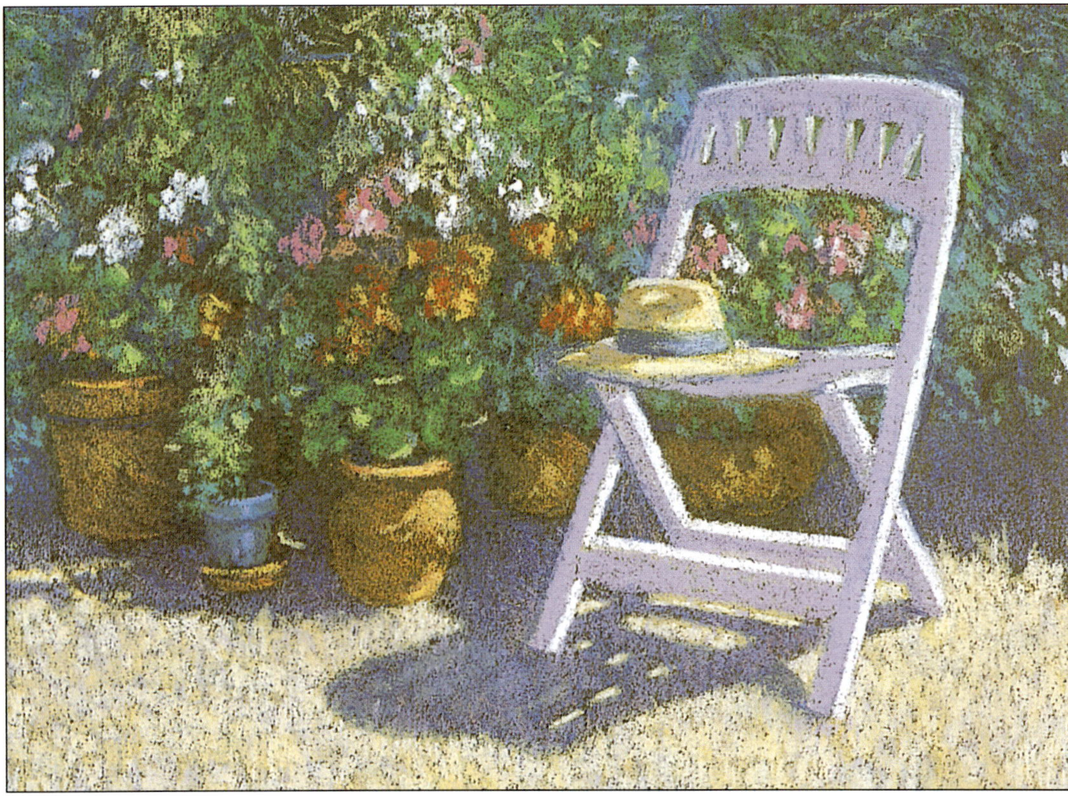

Derek Daniells
CHAIR, SUMMER
In this delightful garden scene, vibrant colour combinations suggest the atmosphere of a bright summer day. Each area of the image is formed as a mass of broken colour, consisting of interwoven and overlaid marks.

The term 'broken colour' refers to a method of building up an image with small strokes and dabs of pure colour which are not joined, but leave some of the toned paper showing through. When seen from the appropriate viewing distance, these strokes appear to merge into one mass of colour, but the effect is different from that created by a solid area of smoothly blended colour. What happens is that the small, separate flecks of colour 'vibrate' on the retina of the eye and appear to shimmer and sparkle, giving a more luminous effect than an area of flat colour.

If complementary (opposite) colours are juxtaposed, the effect is even more pronounced. For example, when dots, dabs or strokes of red and green, or yellow and violet, are intermixed, the colours are mutually enhanced by contrast and the effect is strikingly vibrant. The effect is further enhanced by working on a tinted paper, whose colour will help to unify the picture and enhance the effect of the vibrant pastel colours.

The Impressionists

This technique is used in both painting and drawing and is usually associated with the French Impressionist painters, who were the first to exploit its full potential in the late 19th century. The Impressionists were fascinated by the fleeting effects of light on the landscape and found that by building up their images with small flecks and dashes of colour they could capture visual sensations such as the glints of light on the surface of water or the dappled light beneath a tree. In addition, the many touches of colour added a shimmering quality to the picture surface, making it dance and vibrate with light.

Working methods

Pastels and coloured pencils are particularly suited to the broken colour technique owing to their pure, vibrant hues and ease of manipulation. However, it is advisable to keep to a fairly limited range of colours to achieve an overall harmony rather than a discordant hotch-potch of colours. It is also best to keep the colours fairly close in tone, otherwise the vibrant effect of light is lost.

The aim of this technique is to achieve a sense of immediacy; the colours should be applied rapidly and confidently then left with no attempt made to blend them together. Always try to vary the size, shape and density of the marks you make, otherwise the effect will be monotonous. By altering the pressure on the pencil or crayon it is possible to make a range of stippled dots and broken flecks and dabs that give life and movement to the image.

Maureen Jordan
GIRL RESTING
Here, the artist blocked in the composition freely with watercolour washes and then reworked the image in pastel. This combination of translucent, fluid watercolour washes and grainy, broken pastel marks has a depth and subtlety that effectively conveys the transient effects of light and shade.

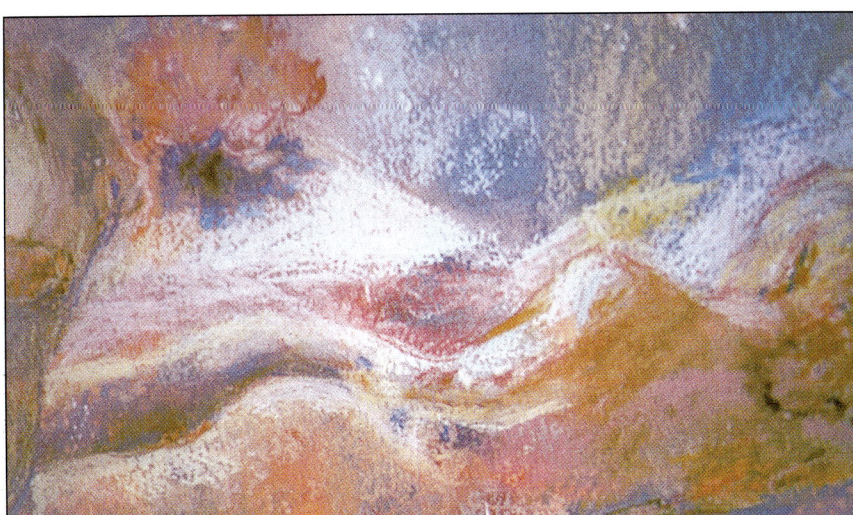

Wild Flower Field

This charming view of a field in Spain was executed on the spot. To create the variety of dense foliage, grasses and flowers, the artist freely combined softly blended areas with linear marks, building a rich impression of colour and texture.

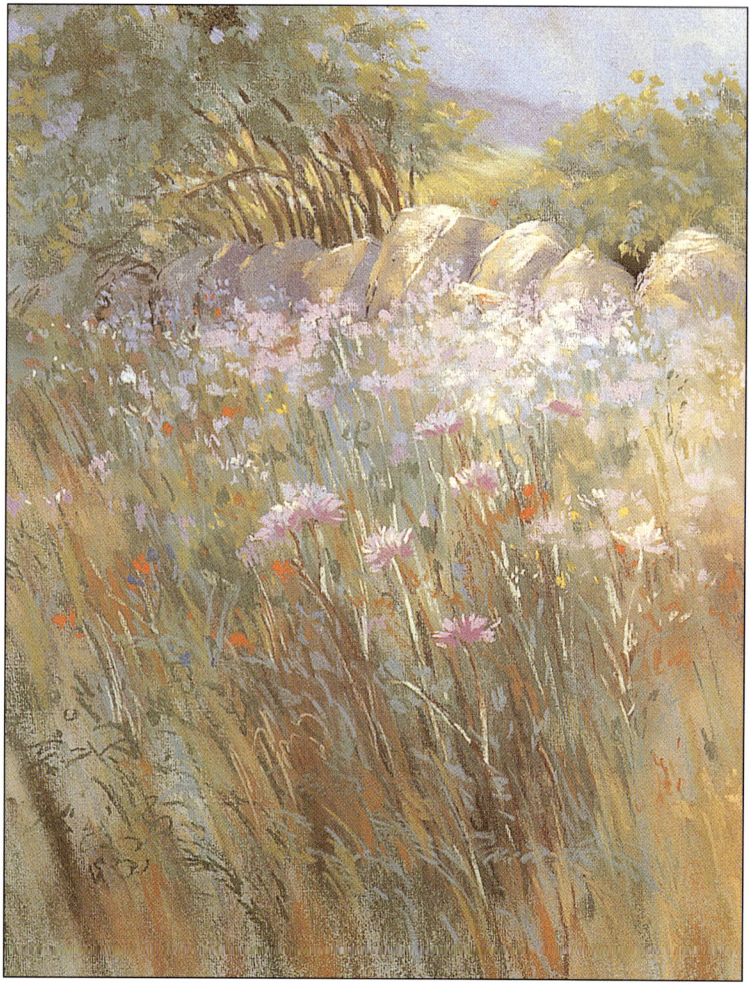

YOU WILL NEED

- ✔ *Sheet of blue-grey pastel paper, 27½ x 19¾in (70 x 50cm)*
- ✔ *Fine stick of charcoal*
- ✔ *Paper tissue*
- ✔ *Fixative spray*

SOFT PASTELS IN THE FOLLOWING COLOURS

- *Red-brown*
- *Ochre*
- *Blue-green*
- *Grey-purple*
- *Pale cobalt*
- *Blue*
- *Medium olive*
- *Green*
- *Lemon yellow*
- *Blue-grey*
- *Pale cream*
- *Golden yellow*
- *Mid brown*
- *Dark brown*
- *Purple*
- *Turquoise blue*
- *Light blue*
- *Red-grey*
- *Pale blue*
- *Orange-red*
- *Pale pink*
- *Purple-pink*
- *Pale lavender*
- *Yellow-green*

1 Working on the smooth side of the paper, start by plotting the position of the dry-stone wall and the landscape beyond using a thin stick of charcoal. The blue-grey paper provides a useful mid-tone upon which to work out the lights and darks.

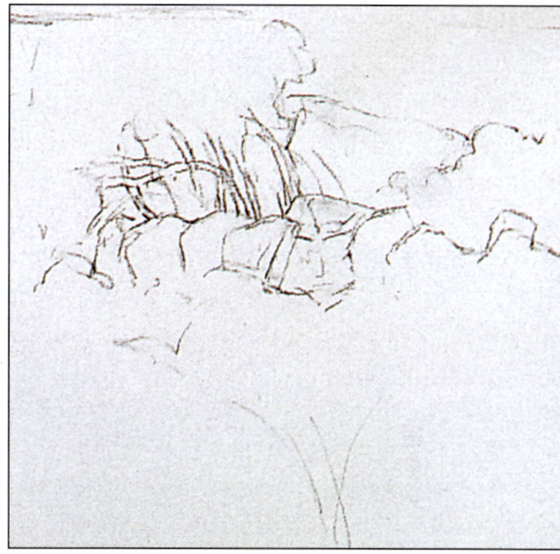

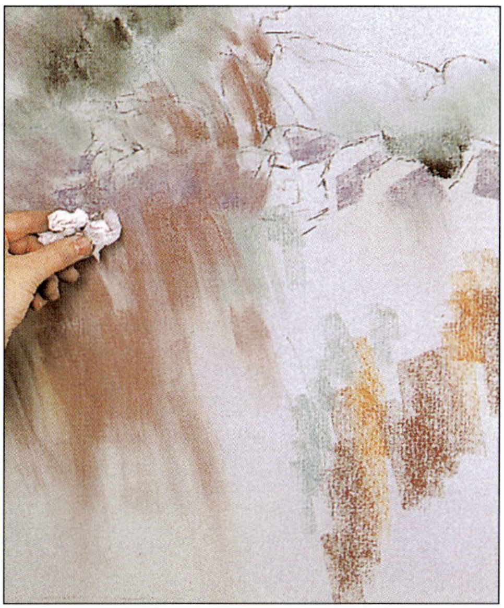

2 Rough in the main colour areas with broad side strokes. Use blue-green for the distant trees, then work across the foreground with red-browns and ochres. Add strokes of grey-purple on the wall. Blend the scribbled marks with a tissue. This creates a subtle underpainting that will underpin the marks laid over it.

3 Block in the sky with a light tint of cobalt blue, and suggest the distant hills with grey-purple. Work into the foreground field with strokes of cool blue-green and warm olive green, layering and blending the colour to build up a rich and varied surface. Use long, sweeping strokes to suggest the upward growth of the grasses. Use the same colours to define clumps of foliage in the trees.

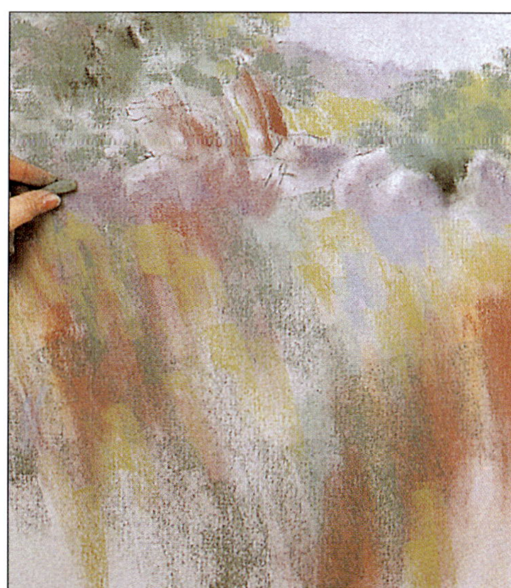

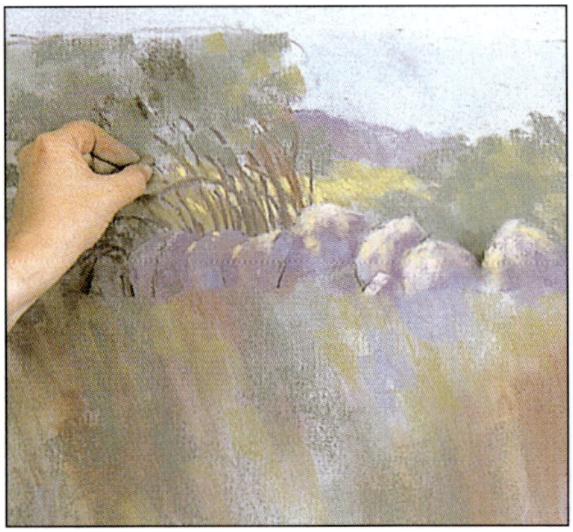

4 Lightly spray the drawing with fixative to seal the surface before the application of further colour layers. With short strokes of lemon yellow, touch in the field in the distance. Build up the shadows on the wall with short side strokes of purple, blue-grey and cobalt blue. Pick out the sunlit highlights on the wall with soft yellows, pinks and creams, then define the individual rocks with sketchy charcoal lines. Draw the tree trunks with warm and cool browns and purples, using the point of the pastel stick.

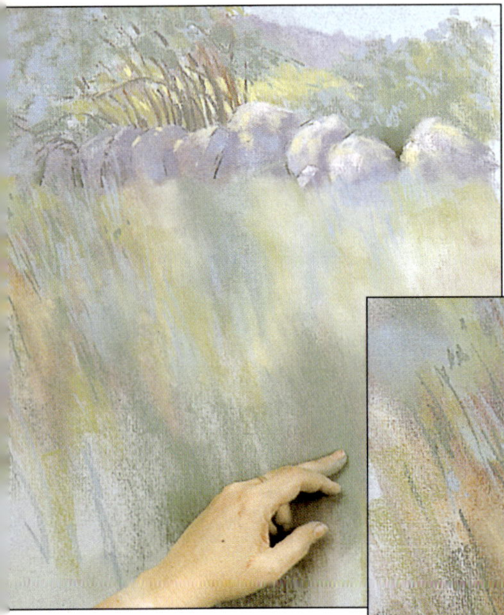

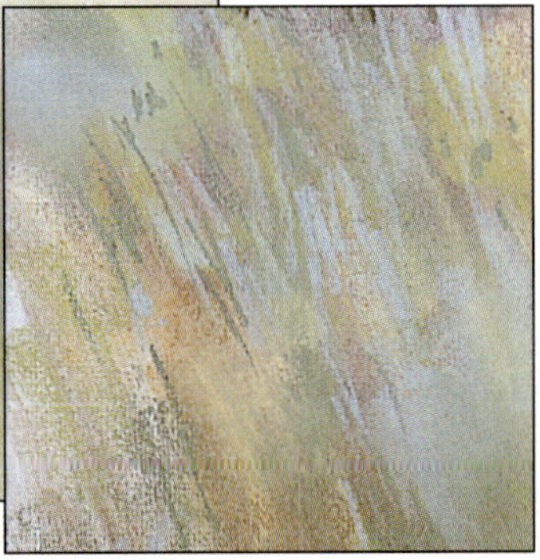

5 Suggest the cool, silvery areas of foliage with a mid-tone turquoise blue. Add strokes of this colour in the foreground field, too, creating colour echoes that help to unify the picture. Introduce lighter tones with strokes of pale cream, blending them with your finger. In the detail of the foreground field (below) we see the vibrant effect created by the combination of blended and linear marks.

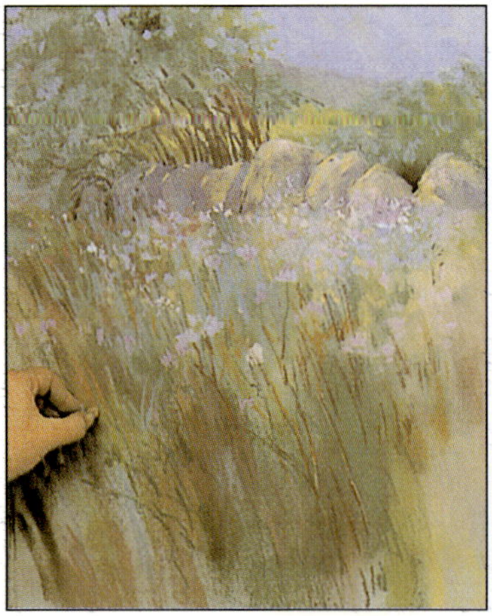

6 Work some pale cobalt blue into the foliage of the trees to open them up and suggest the sky peeping through. Stroke some golden yellow on to the rocks where the sunlight strikes them. Now start to build up linear detail over the blended marks in the foreground. Using cream, light blue, pale lavender and red-grey, and working with tip of the pastel, make lively, expressive marks for the heads of the wild flowers. Long strokes of dark green, olive green, red-brown and ochre give a lush depth to the grasses.

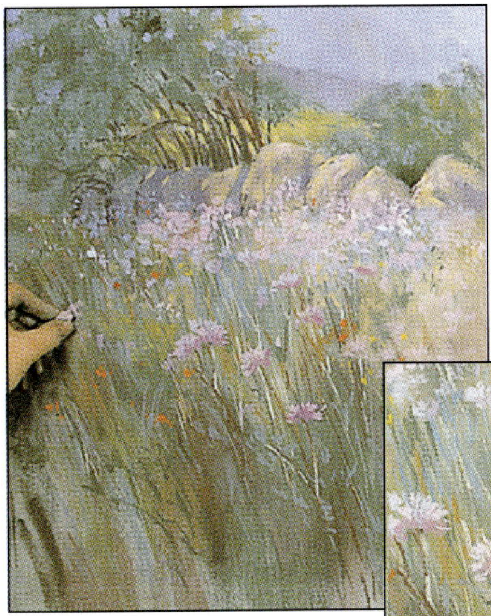

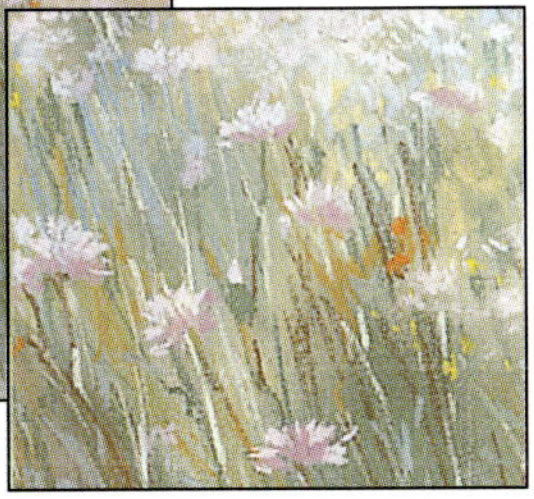

7 Use pale greens and creams to pick out the lighter grasses, and continue working on the flowers using the same colours as before. Add one or two brilliant yellow and orange-red flowers here and there – apply solid dots of pastel, then press them into the paper to create touches of vivid, saturated colour. To give the picture depth, use bigger, more emphatic marks for the nearest flowers and smaller, softer marks for those further back. Define a clump of daisies in the fore-ground with strokes of pale pink and purple-pink, to create a point of focus. In this detail you can see how the forms of the daisies are conveyed using pale pink for the inner petals and purple-pink for the undersides.

8 Knock back the hills in the background with a little pale blue to convey a sense of distance. Build up the texture of the dark grasses in the foreground with short strokes, dashes and dots of turquoise blue, blue-green and ochre to suggest movement. Suggest the tangle of leaves and grasses with random dots and little circular scribbles. To emphasize the vibrant colours of the flowers, work flecks of blue-green in between them.

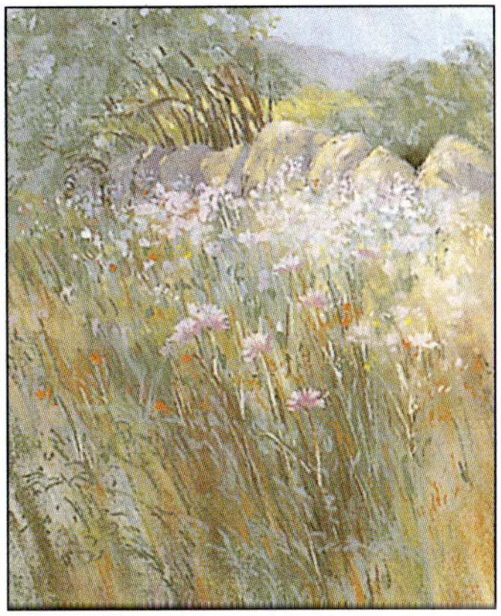

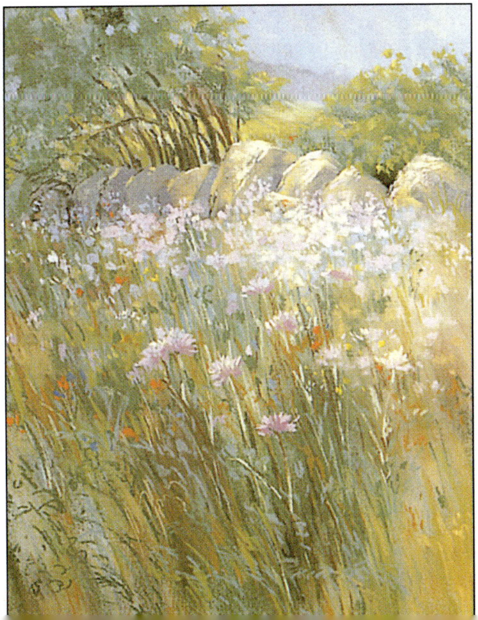

9 Add flecks of yellow-green to suggest the sunlit areas of foliage on the trees. Add touches of the same colour in the fore-ground grasses to unify the picture. Finally, add highlights to the rocks and flowers with touches of pale cream to give the picture added sparkle.

Helpful Hint

IF YOU MAKE A MISTAKE, BRUSH OFF THE POWDERY COLOUR WITH A FIRM-BRISTLED PAINTBRUSH. ALTERNATIVELY, USE A GENTLE DABBING MOTION WITH A KNEADED ERASER.

Conté Crayons

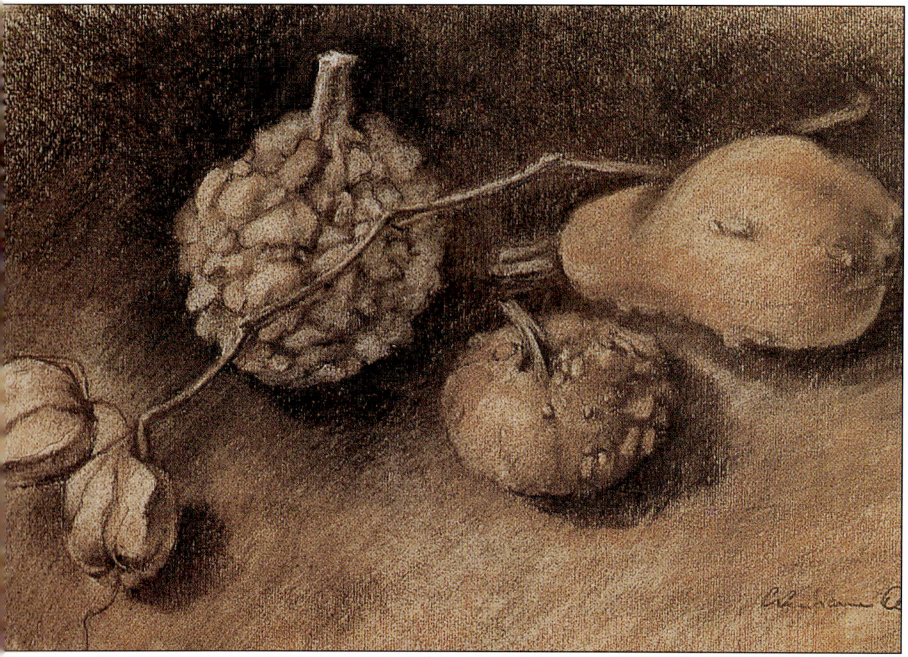

Cristiana Angelini
GOURDS
Conté crayons in traditional earth colours were used for this finely wrought still-life study. The artist has achieved subtle gradations of tone using closely hatched lines, allowing glimpses of the grey paper to serve as the highlights.

Conté comes from France and is named after its inventor, Nicolas-Jacques Conté. Conté crayons are similar to soft pastels, but slightly harder and oilier. They are made from compressed chalk and graphite bound together with gum and a little grease and formed into square-sectioned sticks. Conté is also available in pencil form.

Grades

Black and white conté crayons come in three different grades: HB (medium), B and 2B (the softest). All other colours are available in only one grade – approximately 2B. The softer the crayon, the more intense the mark it makes and the easier it is to blend.

Colours

Traditionally used for tonal drawings, conté crayons were in the past limited to black, white and three earth colours – sepia (a rich, reddish brown), sanguine (blood-red) and bistre (dark brown). Although conté is now available in a wide range of colours, many artists still favour the restrained harmony of the traditional colours, which bestows on a drawing a 'classical' look reminiscent of the beautiful chalk drawings of Leonardo da Vinci, Michelangelo and Rubens.

Papers

Conté crayons are used to best advantage on a grey, cream or buff tinted paper which provides a sympathetic background for the overlaid colours. Like pastel and charcoal, conté crayons require a paper with sufficient surface tooth for the powdery pigment to adhere to. When the textured grain of the paper is visible it becomes an integral part of the drawing, bringing out the distinctive qualities of the marks and adding an extra dimension to your work.

Techniques

As with pastels, the most practical method of using conté crayons is to snap off small pieces and use the sharp corners for linear marks and the side of the stick to block in tonal areas. Conté is also soft enough to allow colours and tones to be blended by rubbing with a finger, tissue or torchon (paper stump).

The technique known as drawing à trois crayons, (with three colours) in which sanguine, black and white conté are used together, was particularly popular in the 17th century and remains so today. Worked on grey or light brown paper, it allows tones to be translated easily and gives a rich feeling of tone and colour as well as form. The sanguine crayon is used for drawing outlines, toning and shading, with black and white used sparingly to pick out the darker tones and the highlights. You can also use hatching and crosshatching with white and sanguine together to get pink tones of various shades and intensities.

Cristiana Angelini
STILL LIFE WITH DRIED FRUIT
Here, coloured conté crayons have been used to create a high-key drawing, in contrast to the low-key one opposite. The artist has, however, used a limited range of colours in order to preserve an overall harmony.

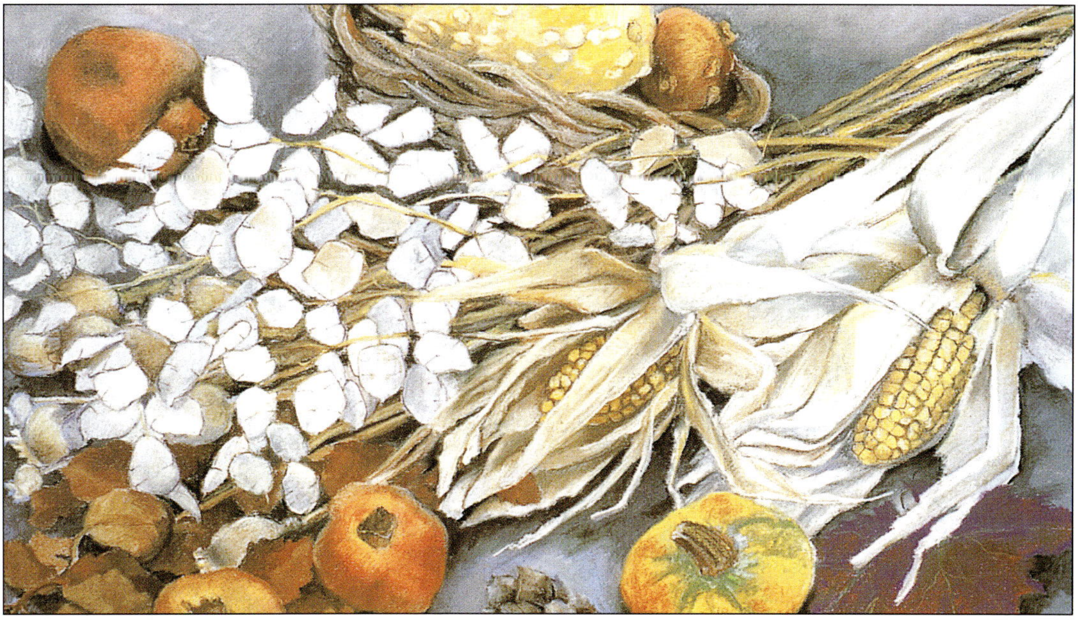

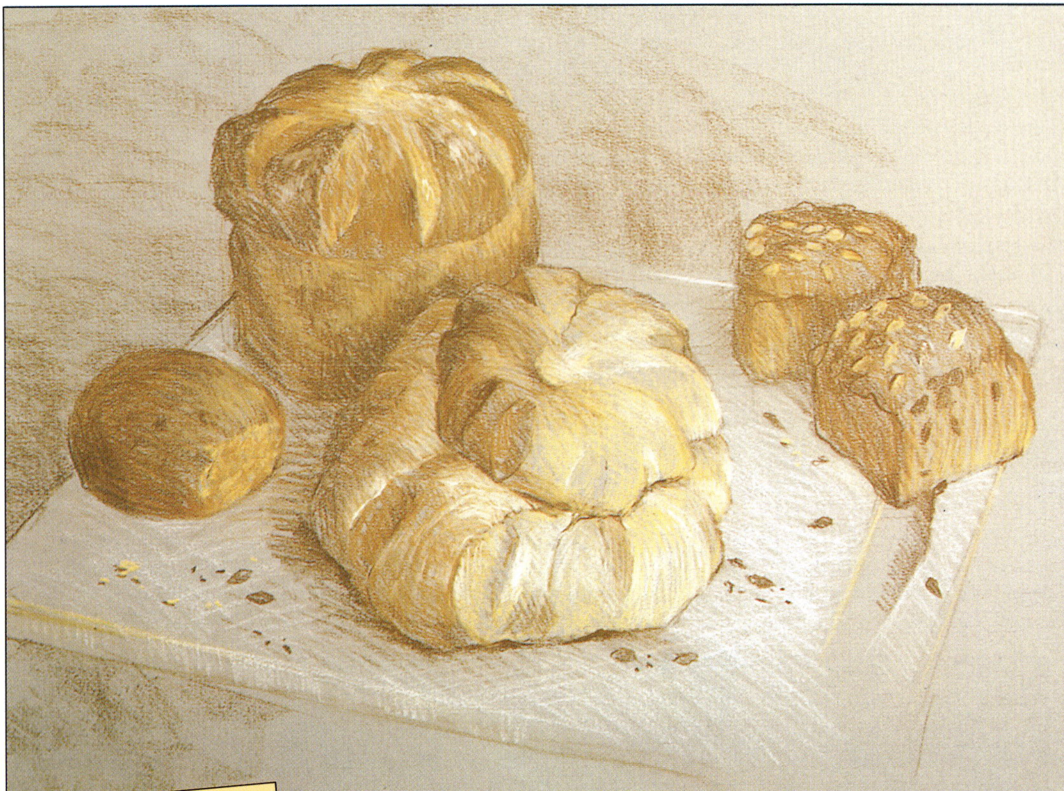

YOU WILL NEED

- *Sheet of grey pastel paper, 23¾ x 17¾in (60 x 45cm)*
- *Fixative spray*

CONTE CRAYONS IN THE FOLLOWING COLOURS

- *Bistre (dark brown)*
- *Raw Sienna*
- *Gold Ochre*
- *White*

Baker's Selection

The warm earthy tones of traditional conté crayons are perfect for capturing the golden crustiness of these freshly baked loaves. Conté crayons are shown to their best advantage on tinted paper, which gives a subtle extra dimension when incorporated into a composition. Here the grey paper provides the cool shadow tones and provides a foil for the warm earths and yellows.

1 Start by lightly sketching the composition with the bistre crayon. Use a sharp corner of the square stick to make fine lines. You may find it useful to draw light horizontal and vertical lines to help you position the objects accurately on the paper. Exaggerate some of the angles to make the composition more interesting.

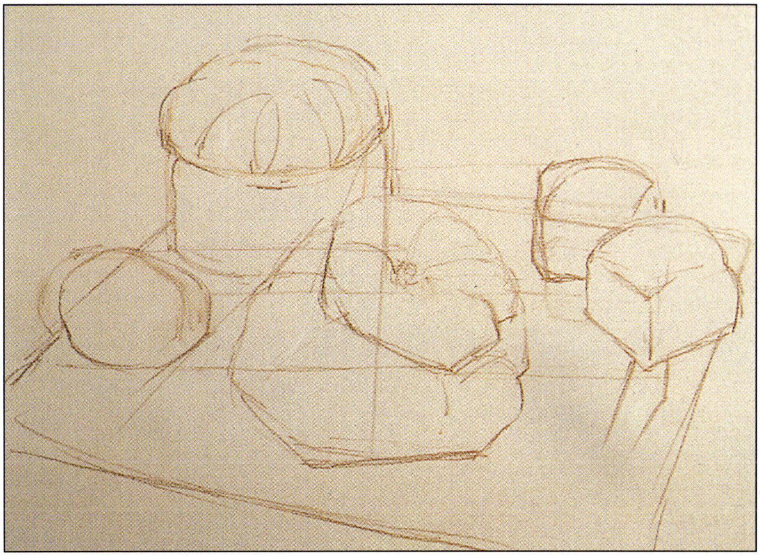

Helpful Hint

KEEP THE HATCHING LOOSE AND OPEN IN THE EARLY STAGES; IF THE WORK IS DONE TOO DENSELY AT FIRST, IT BECOMES DIFFICULT TO BUILD UP THE COLOUR AND CONTROL THE TONES.

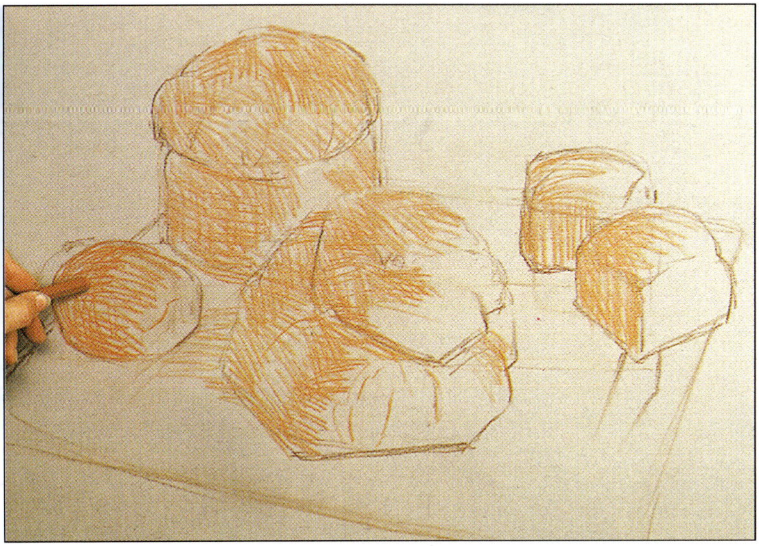

2 Switch to the raw sienna crayon and start to build up the colour of the bread and rolls with light crosshatched strokes. Change the direction of the strokes as you work, pivoting from the wrist, to emphasize the changes of plane. Leave areas of the paper untouched for the palest highlights.

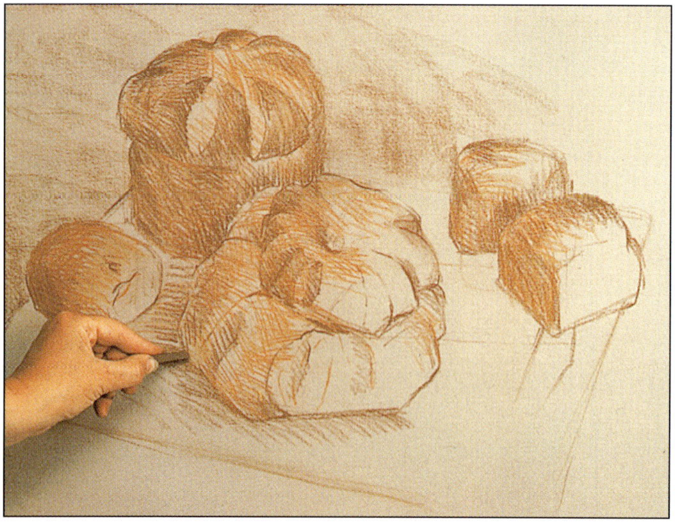

3 Work back over the drawing with the bistre crayon to define the shapes more accurately. Use hatched and crosshatched strokes to build up depth of tone and establish the forms of the loaves, but still leaving plenty of the ground showing through. Indicate the cast shadows on the cutting board with rapid hatched strokes. Lightly shade in the background, using the side of a broken piece of crayon to lay in broad, scribbled strokes.

4 The directional light picks up the sharp contours of the crusty loaves. Use the gold ochre crayon to hatch in these light-struck areas, following the contours of the loaves to create an impression of form and solidity as well as texture. Concentrate more light on the cottage loaf at the front of the group, so that it will stand out as the focal point of the finished drawing. The detail (right) reveals how, even at this midway stage, the strokes are kept loose, allowing for the brighter highlights to be added later in white conté.

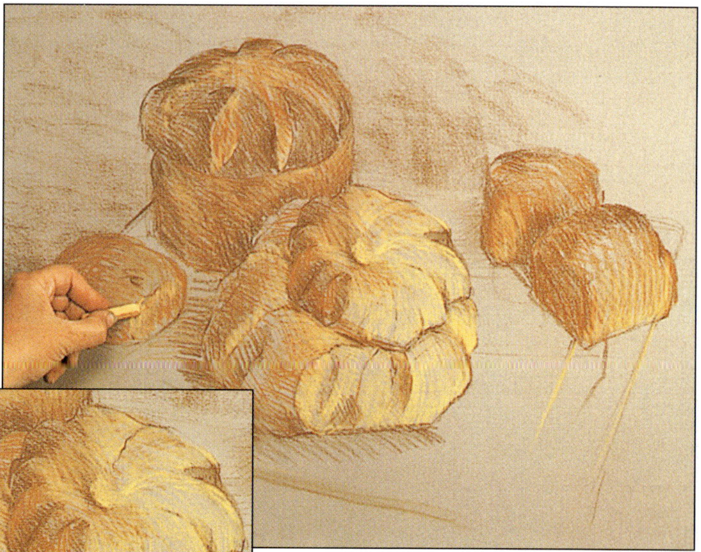

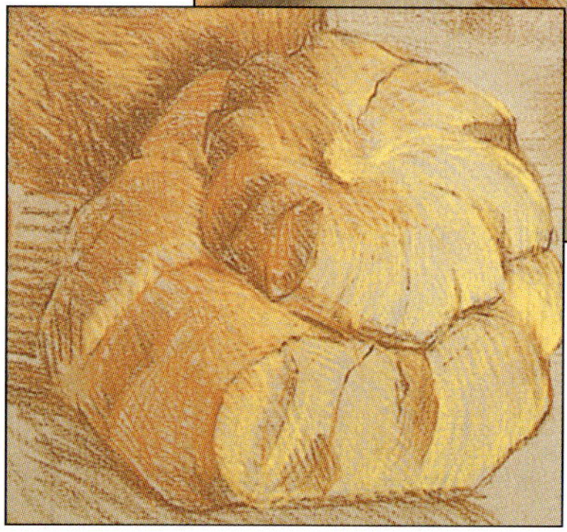

5 Accentuate the lightest highlights, applying further layers of hatched and crosshatched strokes with the white conté crayon. Then use the bistre crayon to re-define the shapes of the bread rolls. Suggest the sunflower seeds on the small rolls with a combination of bistre and gold ochre crayons.

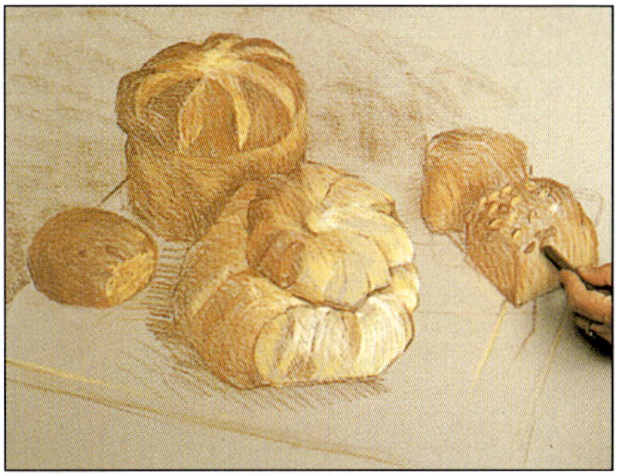

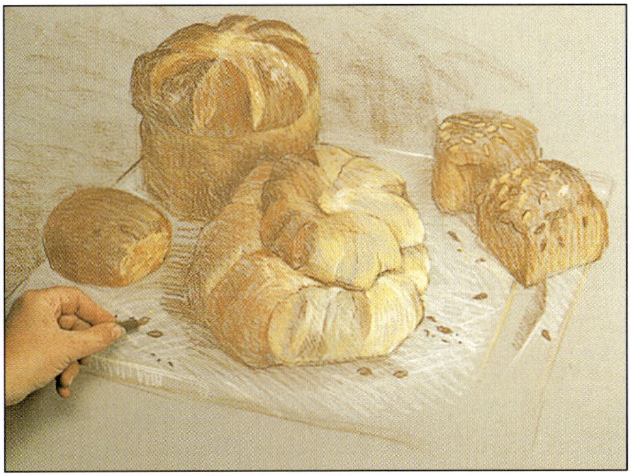

6 Work on the cutting board now, putting in the highlights with loosely hatched strokes of white conté. Draw the loose seeds on the board with the bistre crayon, adding gold ochre highlights.

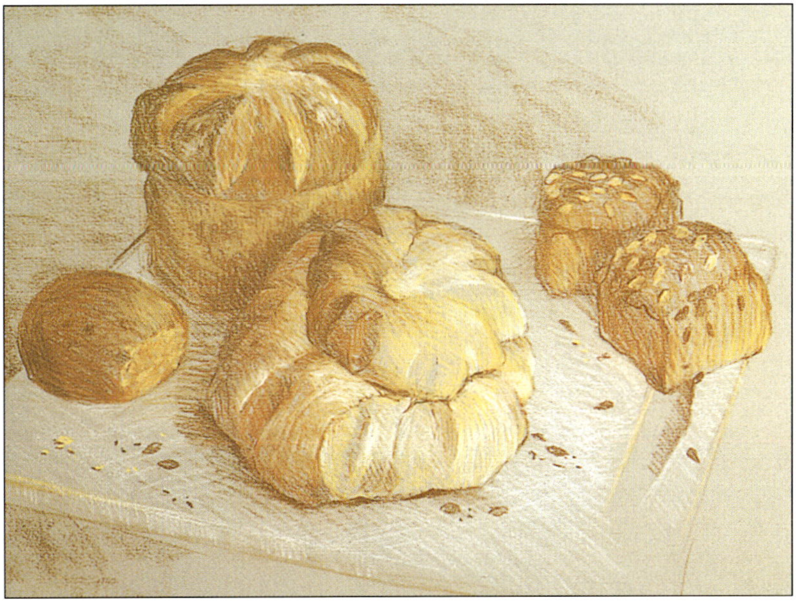

7 Using the bistre and gold ochre crayons, work back over the drawing adjusting shapes and tones and adding dark accents and final light touches. Add a few dashes of white over the tops of the loaves and bread rolls to suggest a dusting of flour. Fix your drawing with a light spray of fixative to prevent smudging.

Blending

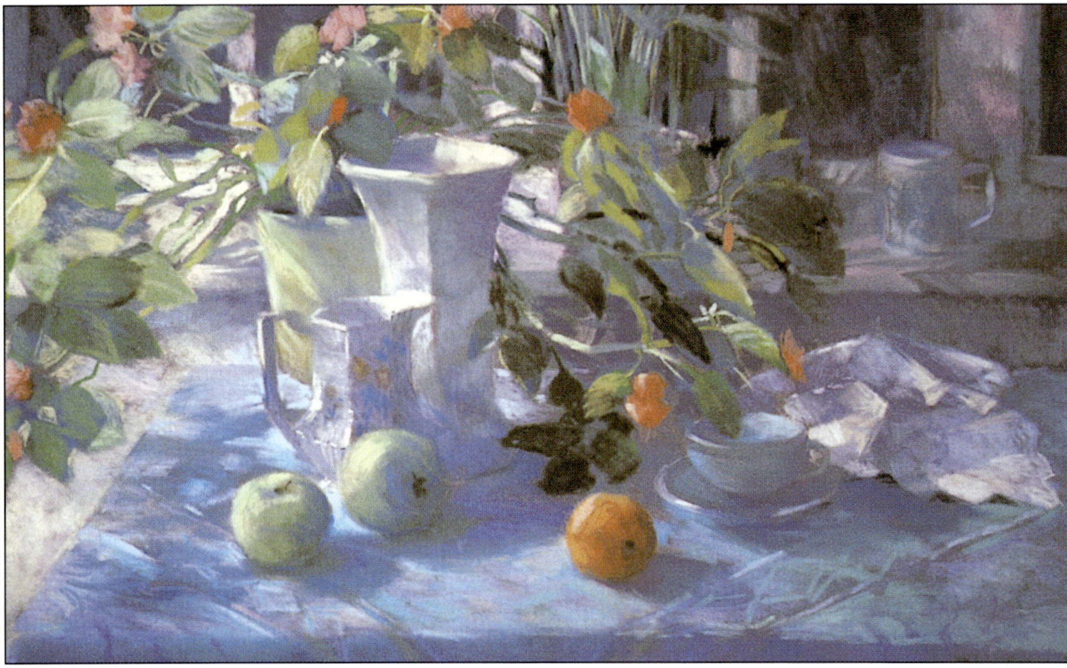

Jackie Simmonds
EVENING LIGHT
Softly blended tones give a rich, painterly quality to this still-life drawing in pastel. The artist, however, uses minimal blending with her fingers as this can muddy the colours. Instead she uses the sides of the pastel sticks to float one colour over another, letting them blend naturally on the paper.

Soft, powdery media such as pastel, conté crayon, charcoal and soft pencil can be smudged and blended very easily to create a range of subtle textures and effects. In landscape drawing, for example, blended tones can be used to suggest the soft, amorphous nature of skies, water and soft foliage, and in recreating the effects of space, distance and atmosphere.

The technique has many other uses, for example in defining the form and volume of objects using smooth gradations from light to dark, softening linear marks and details, suggesting smooth surfaces, lightening tones, and tying shapes together.

Techniques

To create an area of blended tone, either apply lightly scribbled strokes with the point of the drawing implement, or use it on its side to make a broad mark. Do not apply too much pressure – if the mark is too ingrained it will be difficult to blend it smoothly. Then lightly rub the surface with a fingertip to blend the marks and create an even tone. Repeat the process if a darker tone is required.

Similarly, two adjoining colours can be blended together where they meet to achieve a gradual colour transition, and two colours can be applied one over the other and then blended to create a solid third colour.

The finger is perhaps the most sensitive blending 'tool', but depending on the effect you want to achieve, you can use a rag, paper tissue, brush or torchon (a pencil-shaped tube of tightly rolled paper). Use your finger to blend and intensify an area of tone or colour; rags, tissues and brushes to blend large areas and to soften and lift off colour; and a torchon for precise details.

Lively colour

Blending is a very seductive technique, but when overdone it can result in a rather slick, 'boneless' drawing. With pastels in particular, over-blending can rob the colours of their freshness and bloom (this bloom is caused by light reflecting off the tiny granules of pigment clinging to the surface of the paper). You don't always have to rub or blend the colours; if you use the pastels on their sides you will find that the gradual over-laying of strokes causes them to merge where required without muddying. Always remember that a light, unblended application of one colour over another is more vibrant and exciting than a flat area of colour.

As a rule of thumb, it is best to retain the textural qualities of the drawing as much as possible and to use blending in combination with other, more linear strokes for contrast.

Tiki Regwun
FIGURE STUDY
Pastel and watercolour are a sympathetic combination. In this drawing the artist has matched the fluid, translucent quality of watercolour with the soft, powdery nature of pastel to create hazy 'pools' of colour that give depth and mystery to the image.

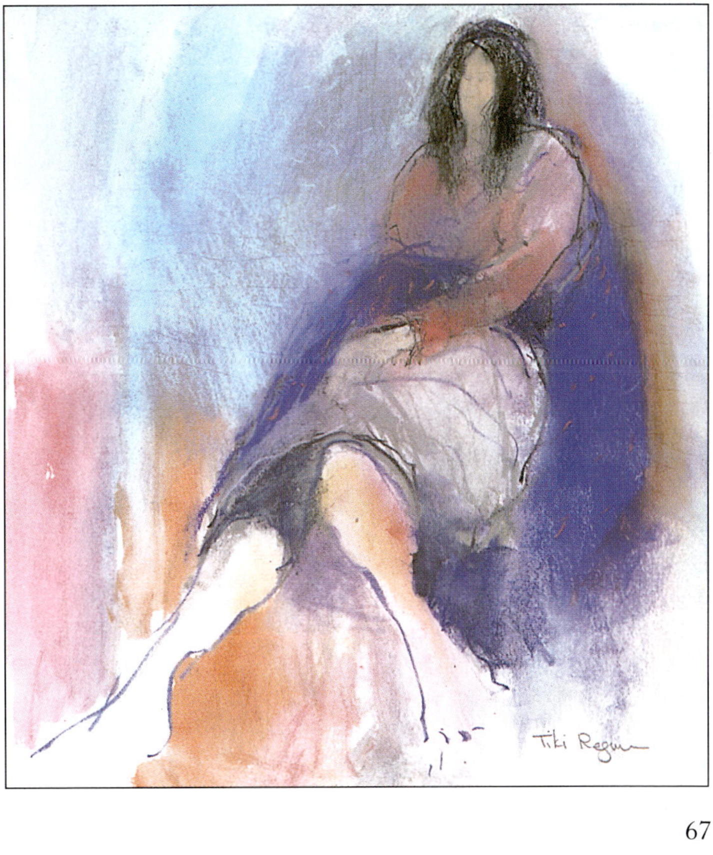

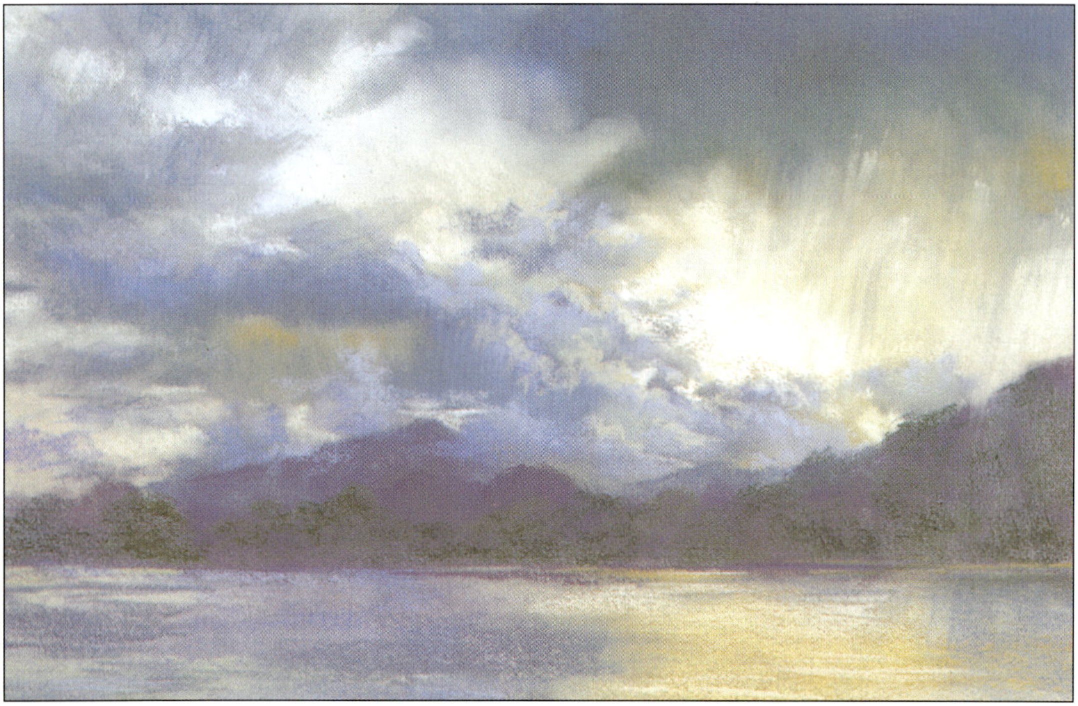

Clouds and Rain

YOU WILL NEED

- ✔ *Sheet of smooth grey pastel paper, 25½ x 19¾in (65 x 50cm)*
- ✔ *Fixative spray*
- ✔ *Soft tissues*

Soft pastels are ideal for capturing the fleeting effects of nature, and are well suited to outdoor work, thanks to their speed and readiness of handling. In this striking study of storm clouds the artist has built up the amorphous cloud shapes by blending the pastel strokes with her fingers and dragging with a crumpled tissue.

SOFT PASTELS IN THE FOLLOWING COLOURS

- *Blue-purple*
- *Purple-grey*
- *Cobalt blue*
- *Mouse grey*
- *Salmon pink*
- *Yellow ochre*
- *Light yellow ochre*
- *Raw sienna*
- *Golden yellow*
- *Medium purple*
- *Light blue-purple*
- *Pale cream*
- *Light blue-grey*
- *Light beige*

1 With skies it is best to avoid drawing any outlines, as you want to keep the image soft and loose. Snap off short pieces of pastel and use their sides to scribble down a range of appropriate colours for the sky and landscape. Use blue-purple, purple-grey and mouse grey for the rain clouds and landscape, and cobalt blue, pink, yellow ochre, raw sienna and golden yellow for the sky and the reflection in the water.

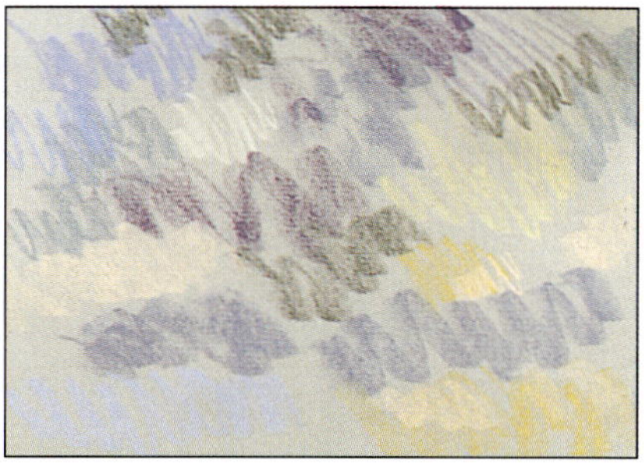

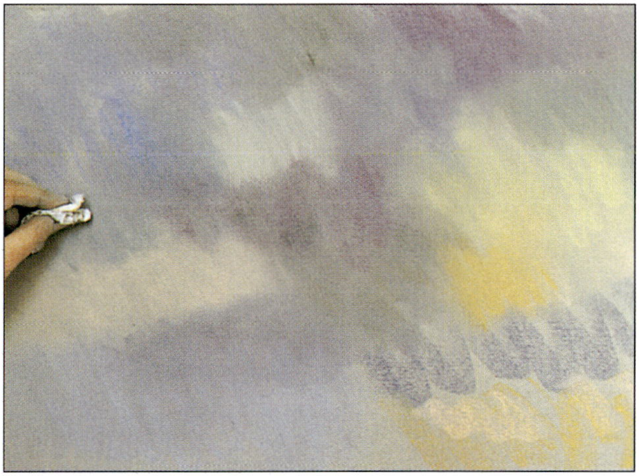

2 Use a crumpled tissue to soften and blend the pastel marks and intensify the colours. In effect, you are making a loose underpainting which will act as a guide for the colours you apply on top.

3 Block in the mountains with broad side strokes, using purple for the nearer range and purple-grey for the distant range. Blend the marks with your fingers and a crumpled tissue. Start to develop the rain clouds, working over the blended layer with side strokes of blue-grey and mouse grey. Use golden yellow and raw sienna for the lighter patches of sky, echoing the colours in the water. Use your fingers to soften and blur the clouds, dragging the colour downwards to create a sense of movement.

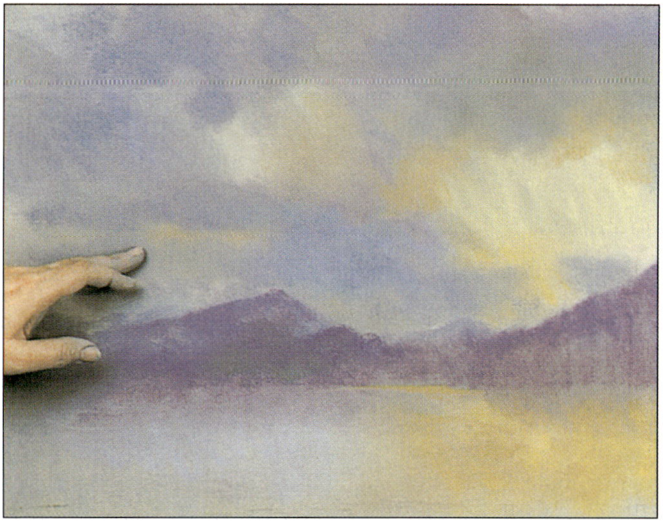

4 Step back from your picture at intervals to assess the overall effect. Continue developing the cloudy sky using blended strokes of light blue-purple. Suggest weak sunlight breaking through on the right with strokes of light yellow ochre, again blending with your fingers. Use the same colour to lighten the reflection on the water, sweeping the colour lightly across the painting with broad strokes.

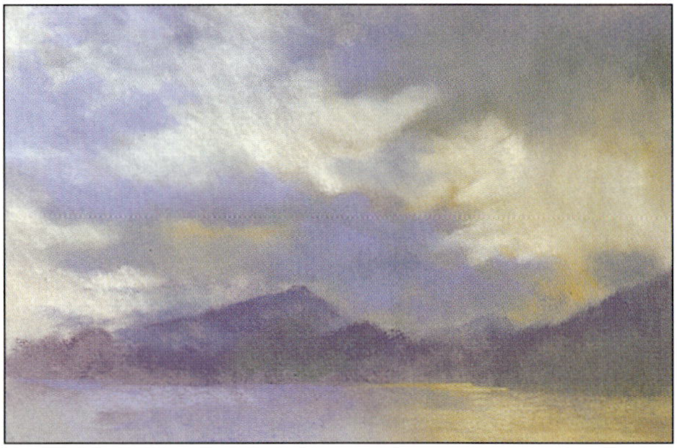

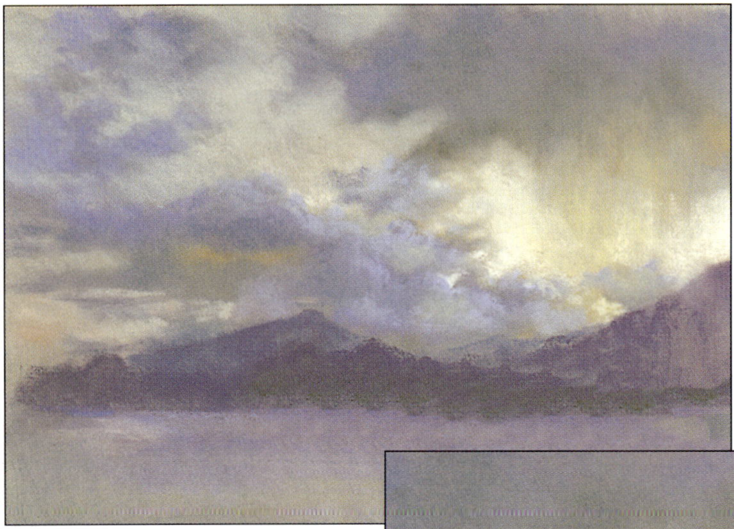

5 Introduce just a hint of pink into the sky on the left, then use a pale cream to emphasize the lighter clouds. Stroke a light blue-grey onto the light-struck tops of the clouds. Touch in some smaller clouds near to the horizon with the same colour, to help create the illusion of receding space. Blend the lower part of each stroke down into the darker clouds beneath. This detail reveals the variety of subtle marks used in the clouds. Soft vaporous rain clouds are suggested with blended strokes, while the broken tops of the cumulus clouds near the horizon are created with small scumbled strokes.

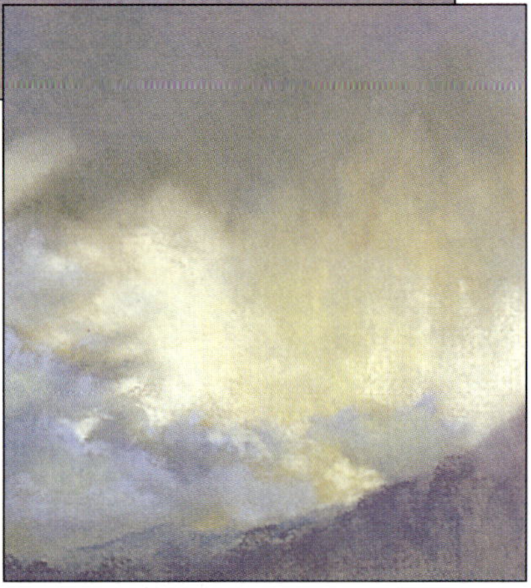

Helpful Hint

A SMALL PLASTIC TRAY – THE KIND SUPERMARKET VEGETABLES COME IN – MAKES A LIGHTWEIGHT AND EASY-TO-HOLD 'PALETTE' IN WHICH TO KEEP THE PASTELS YOU ARE USING FOR A PARTICULAR DRAWING.

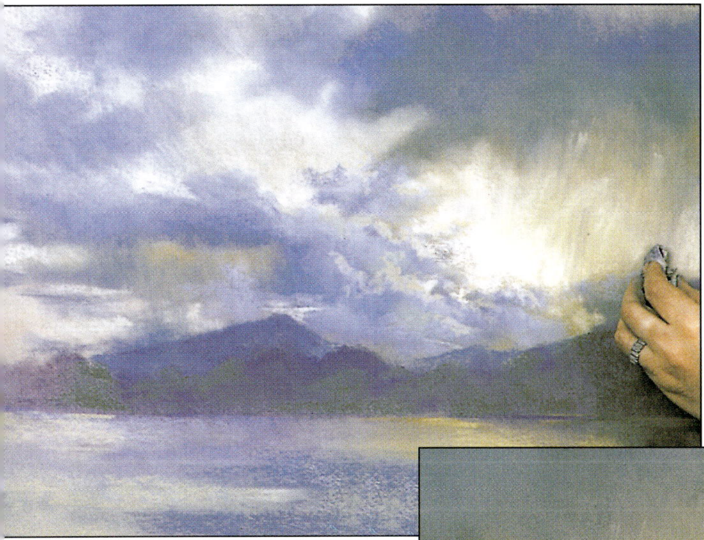

6

Use sweeping side strokes of blue-grey over the water and, where the weak sunshine is reflected on the left, just a hint of light yellow ochre. Make your strokes wider apart as you move towards the front of the picture. Touch in some loose strokes of mouse-grey to suggest the trees on the nearer mountains. Lightly scumble with a pale cream pastel to suggest feathery fragments of light cloud scudding across the sky. Add touches of light beige above the area of pale cloud on the right, then lightly drag the colour down with a tissue to give a suggestion of mist and rain (see detail left).

Helpful Hint

IF YOU HAVE A LOT OF PASTELS, STORE THEM SEPARATELY ACCORDING TO COLOUR IN A BOX OR AN ARTBIN WITH INDIVIDUAL COMPARTMENTS – IT SAVES A LOT OF RUMMAGING AROUND!

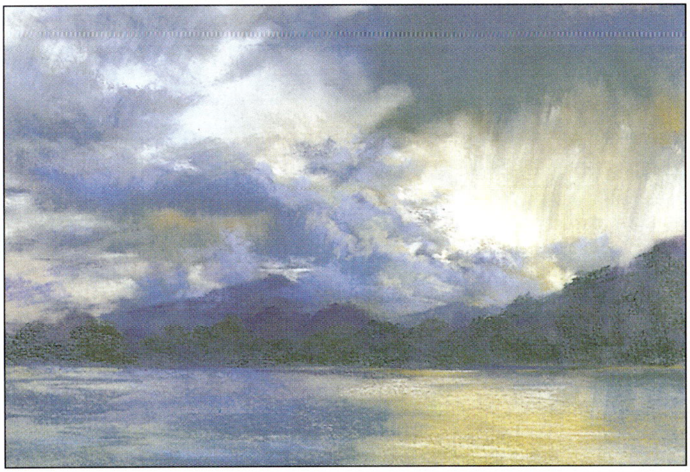

7

To complete the picture, work over the nearer hills with soft greens and purples to give them a little more definition. Feather some strokes of pale blue-grey over the distant mountains, which are partly obscured by cloud. Add the highlights on the water's surface with strokes of pale blue and pale cream.

Line and Wash

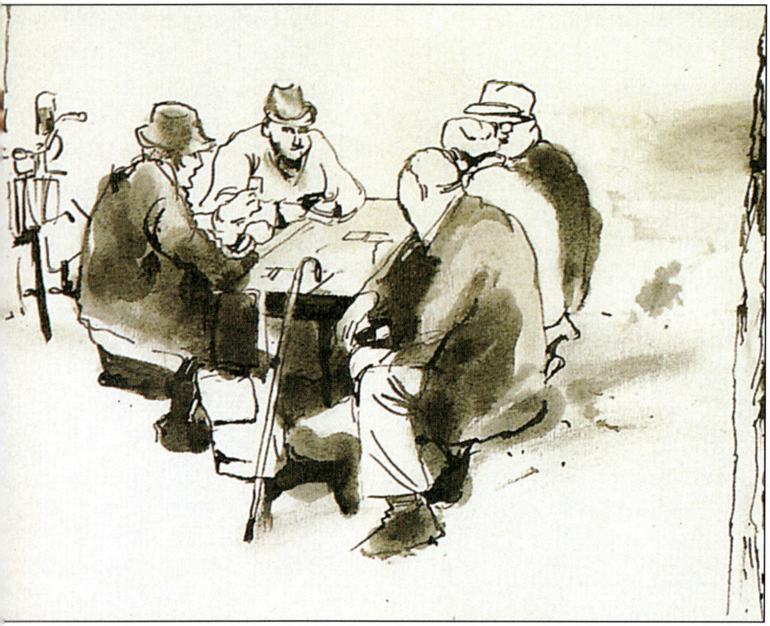

The inherent fluidity of the line and wash technique makes it ideal for portraying living, moving subjects such as figures, animals and flowers. Landscape artists, in particular, find it an invaluable method of making rapid sketches of the fleeting effects of light, or the movement of clouds.

Some of Rembrandt's most beautiful drawings were executed using the line and wash technique. With just a few brief pen lines and curving sweeps with an ink-loaded brush, he was able to capture the play of light on a figure with exquisite simplicity.

Philip Wildman
CARD PLAYERS
The essence of a good line-and-wash drawing is brevity; the secret is knowing how much to put in and how much to leave out, so that the viewer's own imagination comes into play. Rapidly executed on site, this monochrome line-and-wash drawing conveys a lot of information with great economy of means.

Line and wash is an extremely expressive and attractive technique in which finely drawn lines and soft, fluid washes work together in perfect harmony. The lines – produced with pencil or pen – give structure and lively emphasis to the drawing, while diluted washes of ink or watercolour suggest form, movement and light.

Techniques

The traditional method is to start with a pen drawing, leave it to dry and then lay in light, fluid washes of ink or watercolour on top. These washes may be either monochrome or coloured. When the first washes are dry, further washes are added to build up the dark and mid tones, leaving areas of bare paper to serve as the highlights. Alternatively, washes can be applied first to establish the main tones, with the ink lines drawn on top. Some artists prefer to develop both lines and washes at the same time.

The attraction of a line-and-wash drawing lies in its sketchy, 'unfinished' quality, suggesting more than is actually revealed. Thus the viewer is able to participate in the image by using his or her imagination to fill in the details. Never overwork a line and wash drawing – a few scribbled marks and simple, broad washes are all that is necessary to convey what you want to say.

Pens

The type of pen you choose to draw with will depend on the effect you are aiming for. It is worth experimenting with a range of different pens and brushes to discover which ones are best suited to your style of drawing. Dip pens, quill pens and reed pens, for example, produce very expressive lines that swell and taper according to the amount of pressure applied with the nib. These are ideal for making bold, spontaneous marks. In contrast, modern technical pens have very fine nibs that produce thin, spidery lines of even thickness and are suited to a more controlled, graphic style of drawing.

Brushes

Watercolour brushes can be used for lines and for washes. Don't use too small a brush as it encourages tight, hesitant marks. With a large, good-quality brush you can make sweeping washes, and it will come to a point for painting details.

Inks

It is important to choose the right type of ink for drawing the lines. If you want to overlay washes without dissolving the drawn lines, choose Indian ink, which is waterproof. If you want to be able to dissolve and blend some of the lines, choose a soluble ink instead.

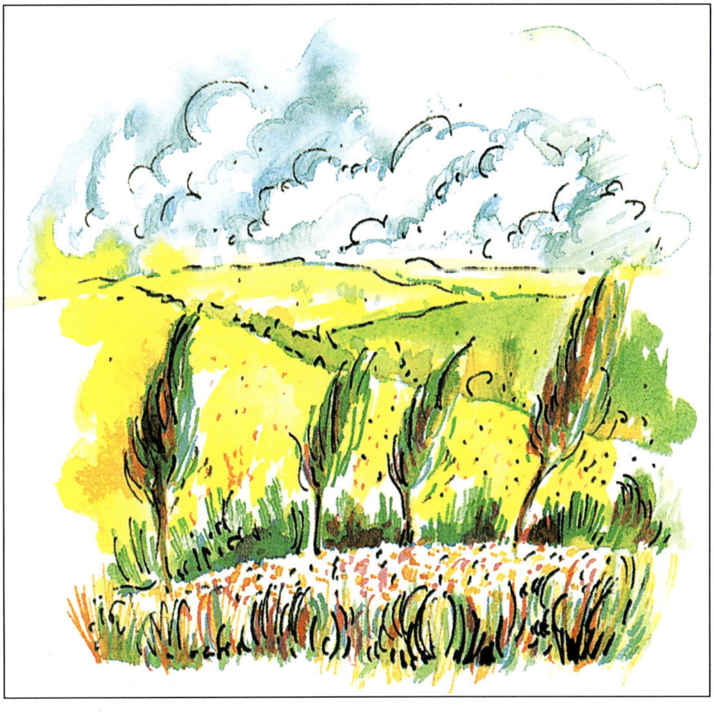

Anna Wood
TUSCAN LANDSCAPE
Based on imagination and memory, this lively drawing conveys a marvellous sense of light and movement. The artist worked intuitively, blocking in the sky and landscape rapidly with loose washes of coloured ink, leaving flecks of white paper to add sparkle. Then she emphasized the rhythms of the clouds, trees and grasses with a few dancing pen lines.

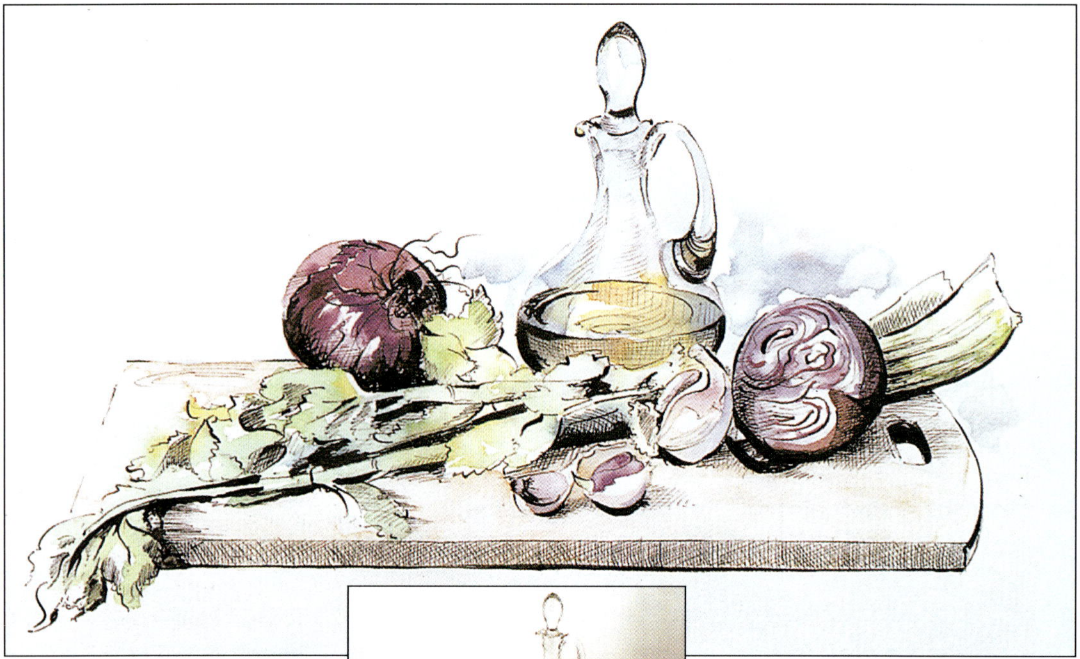

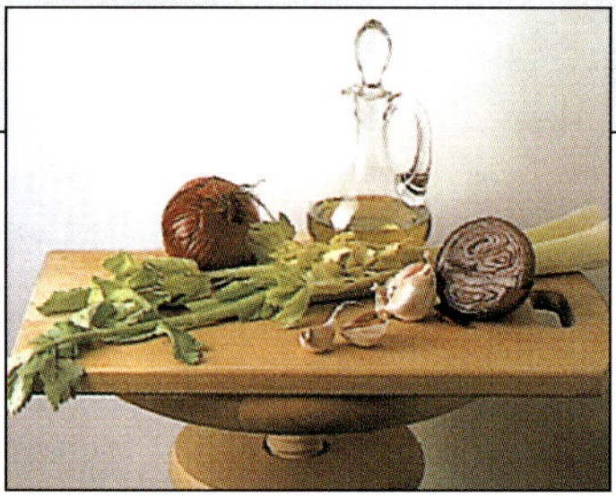

Red Onions

YOU WILL NEED

- Sheet of 90lb (190gsm) Not surface watercolour paper 15 x 22in (38 x 56cm)
- Black and brown waterproof drawing inks
- Dip pen
- HB pencil
- Eraser
- No. 2 round watercolour brush

A simple composition of fresh vegetables is the subject of this line-and-wash drawing. First, the main outlines and shading were drawn with a dip pen and ink. Then watercolour washes were applied in a free and spirited style. This combination of crisp lines and fluid washes results in a drawing that is fresh and lively.

WATERCOLOUR PAINTS IN THE FOLLOWING COLOURS

- *French ultramarine*
- *Cadmiun yellow*
- *Cadmium red*
- *Cyanine blue*
- *Burnt sienna*
- *Lemon yellow*
- *Sap green*
- *Permanent rose*

1 Using an HB pencil, lightly draw the outline of the still-life main group.

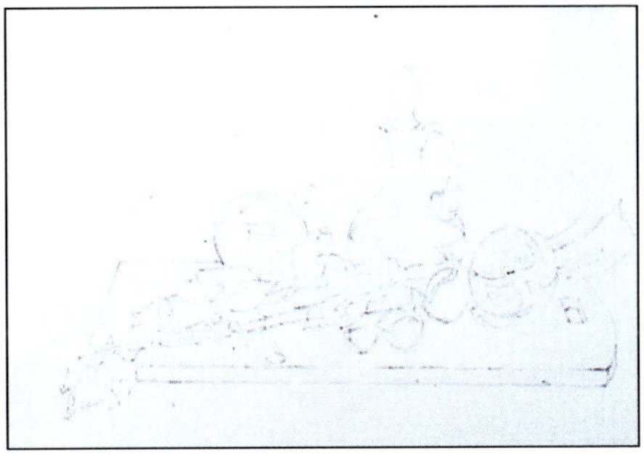

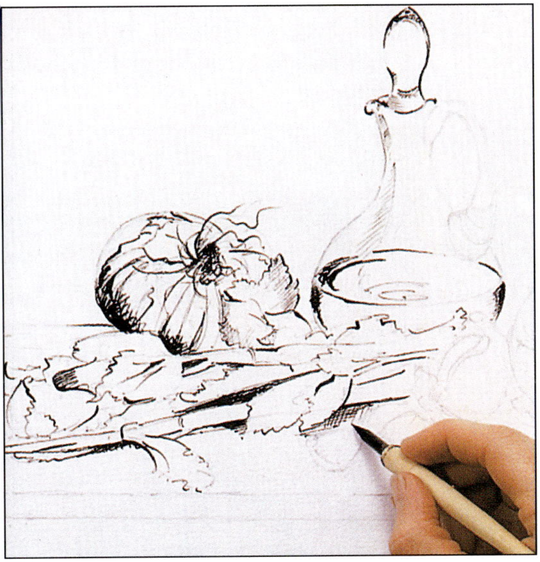

2 Mix up some black waterproof drawing ink in a container and add a little brown ink to soften the colour. Go over the pencil outlines with a dip pen and ink. Make loose, flowing lines and vary the pressure on the nib to create lines of varying thickness. Notice how the artist uses heavy lines in the shadow areas and thin, tapering lines for the light-struck areas. To darken areas and introduce tones go over the lines again to make them thicker. Some areas can be completely shaded in, but don't add too much detail or the effect will be overwhelming.

Helpful Hint

PRACTISE USING THE PEN ON A SCRAP OF PAPER UNTIL YOU FEEL COMPLETELY CONFIDENT THAT YOU CAN DRAW A STEADY LINE. GRIP THE PEN QUITE LOOSELY SO YOU CAN DRAW EXPRESSIVE, FLOWING LINES.

3 Deepen the tone of the darker shadows on the vegetables, adding horizontal and vertical crosshatched lines on top of the angled ones. In this close- up detail you can see the flowing, expressive lines produced by varying the angle of the pen nib and the degree of pressure applied. With practice you will be able to make a single line taper from thick to thin, without lifting your pen from the paper.

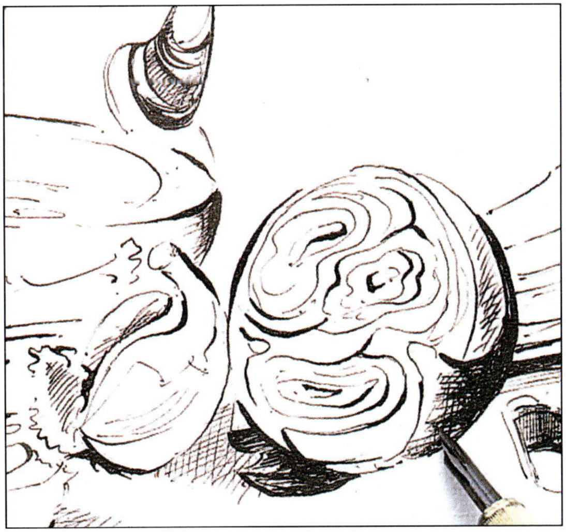

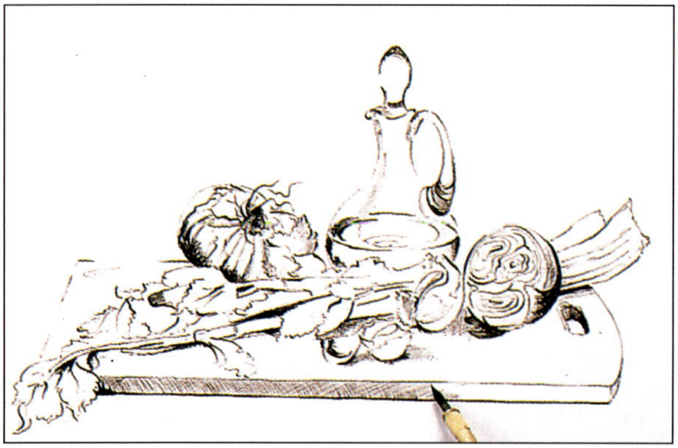

4 Suggest the shadows on the chopping board, and the shadows cast by the vegetables, using a network of lines that criss-cross each other diagonally. Again, work quickly and freely – if you are too precise the effect becomes stiff and mechanical.

5 Continue building up texture and tone throughout the drawing using hatched and crosshatched lines. Step back from time to time, to make sure you are not adding too much detail. When you have finished, leave your drawing to dry and then carefully rub out the pencil lines.

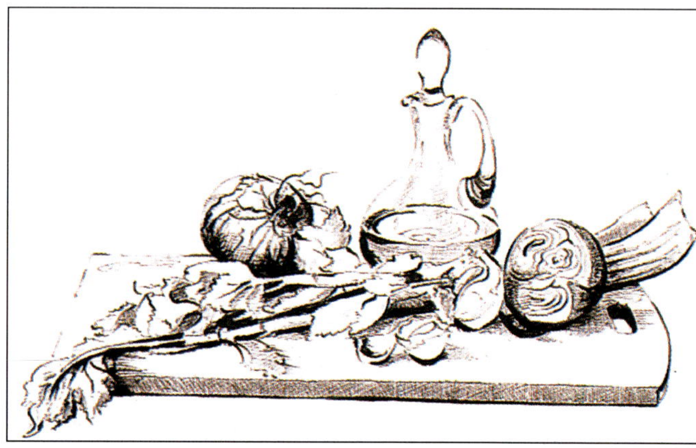

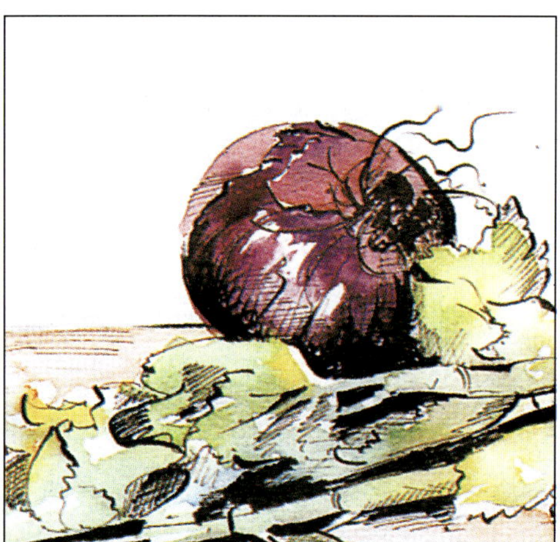

6 Now you are ready to apply watercolour washes over your drawing. First, mix burnt sienna with a little cadmium yellow and dilute it to a very pale tint with lots of water. Apply this to the chopping board with a no. 2 round brush. Paint the red onion with a mix of French ultramarine, permanent rose and a touch of cadmium red. Leaving areas of the paper bare for the brightest highlights, first apply a diluted wash over the onion, then add a heavier, darker wash for the shadow areas. This use of light and dark tones gives the effect of the rounded form of the onion. Paint the celery with pale washes of sap green and lemon yellow.

7 Paint the glass bottle with a very pale grey mixed from cyanine blue and a little cadmium red. Brush this on loosely, leaving bare paper for the brightest highlights and reflections on the glass. Now paint the markings on the cut onion, using a mix of French ultramarine and permanent rose. Add a little cadmium red to the mix for the dark outer skin.

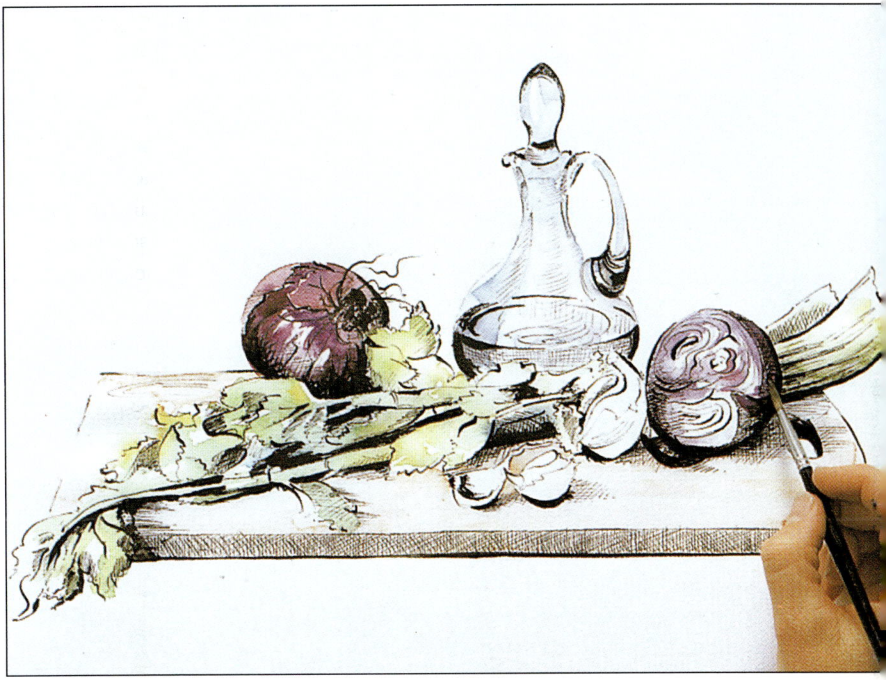

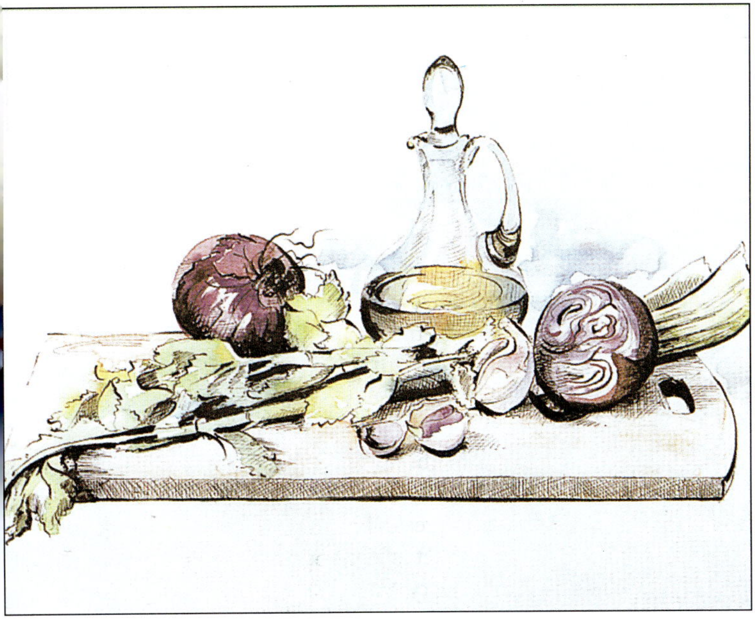

8 Using various mixtures of permanent rose, cadmium red and cadmium yellow, paint the delicate pinkish tones on the skin of the garlic cloves. Add a little ultramarine for the darker areas. For the oil in the bottle, mix lemon yellow, cadmium yellow and a little cadmium red. Finally, add a suggestion of shadow in the background, using a heavily diluted mix of cyanine blue with a little cadmium red.

Pastel Pencils

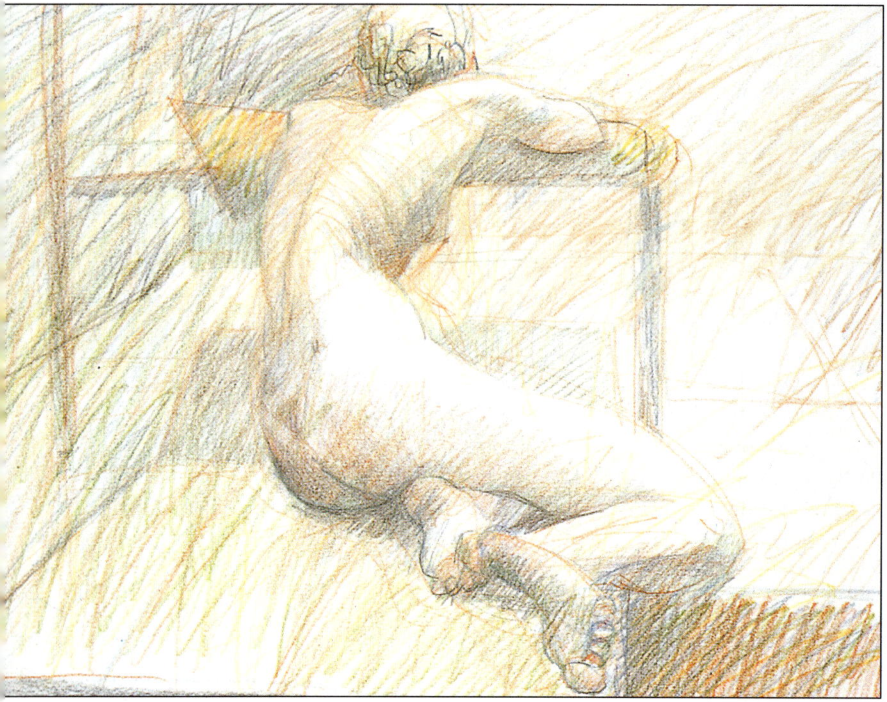

Sarah Donaldson
NUDE STUDY
Pastel pencils produce a translucent effect that is particularly suited to figure studies and portraits. Here the artist has built up the subtle hues in the skin by hatching and scribbling with a range of reds, yellows, blues and greens.

Pastels are available encased in wood, like conventional pencils, as well as in the more familiar stick form. Pastel pencils are a sort of hybrid of pastel and coloured pencil, combining many of the advantages of both.

Before committing yourself to buying a whole set of pastel pencils, it is worth testing out different brands until you find the one that best suits your drawing style. As with soft pastels, the consistency and 'feel' of pastel pencils varies from brand to brand; some are slightly harder and greasier than soft pastels, others have a line which is delicate, dry and dusty, like that of charcoal.

Pastel pencils come in a wide range of colours and are convenient to use. Apart from the advantage of keeping your fingers clean, they are also less liable than stick pastels to crumble under pressure, so that you can obtain definite marks or lines, particularly with the point sharpened.

Techniques

Many of the techniques that are used with pastel sticks are suitable for pastel pencils. The difference lies in the greater degree of control a pointed tip gives you. Because you can hone the point to any shape – blunt, fine or chiselled – pastel pencils are ideal for subjects that entail intricate work, such as flowers and architectural subjects. You can also make use of the linear qualities of pastel pencils to add crisp finishing touches to a soft-pastel drawing.

There are many different ways of 'mixing' colours on the paper surface. By using the hatching technique of laying a series of roughly parallel lines in different colours or tones you will achieve an optical mixing effect which is more vibrant than a flat area of colour. From a normal viewing distance the lines merge to give an impression of continuous tone or colour, but close up the individual marks can be deciphered.

You can also lay one set of hatched lines over another to create complex colour effects. This technique is known as crosshatching.

Alternatively, you can create smooth tones and colours by using the side of the point to build up thin layers of colour one over the other. Don't press too hard or you'll damage the paper surface and it will acquire an unpleasant sheen. The colours can be deepened and enriched by blending with your fingertip, or you can use a torchon (paper stump) for fine details.

The way you hold your pencil has a considerable effect on the marks you make. Grasp the pencil close to the point for detailed work. For broader areas of colour, hold the pencil loosely and further up the shaft, moving it backwards and forwards with a natural, sweeping movement and letting your wrist do the work.

Pastel and wash

Pastel pencils are water soluble, which means you can create a wash effect simply by 'painting' over the pastel marks with clean water and a soft brush. This technique can be useful for creating an 'underpainting' which, once dry, can then be worked over with further layers of dry colour.

Barry Freeman
WINTER LANDSCAPE
The artist used a combination of pastel pencils and oil pastels for this sketch, which he later used as the basis for an oil painting.

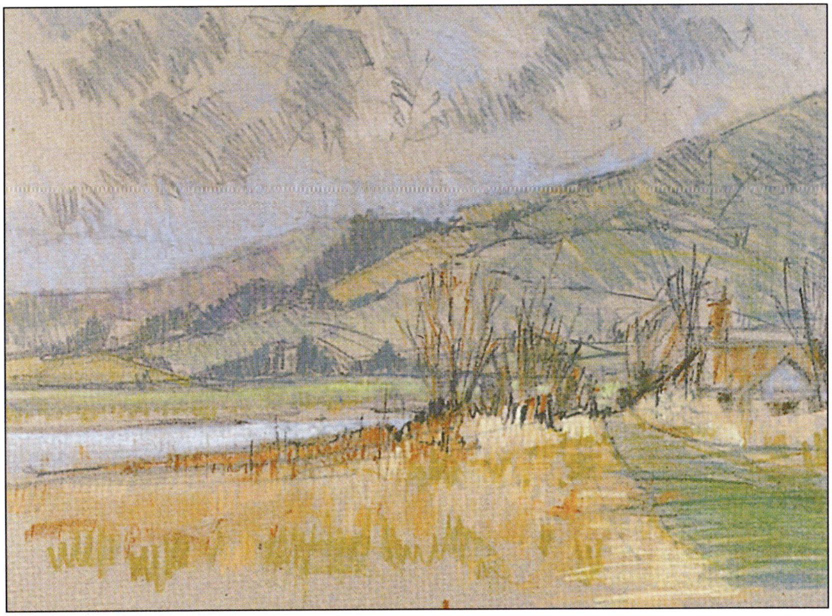

By the Sea Shore

Pastel pencils, combining the painterly qualities of pastel sticks and the linear qualities of coloured pencils, are excellent for rendering natural subjects such as these sea shells. The pale, bleached colours, reminiscent of bright sunlight on a hot day by the sea, are achieved by overlaying one colour over another with small, delicate strokes.

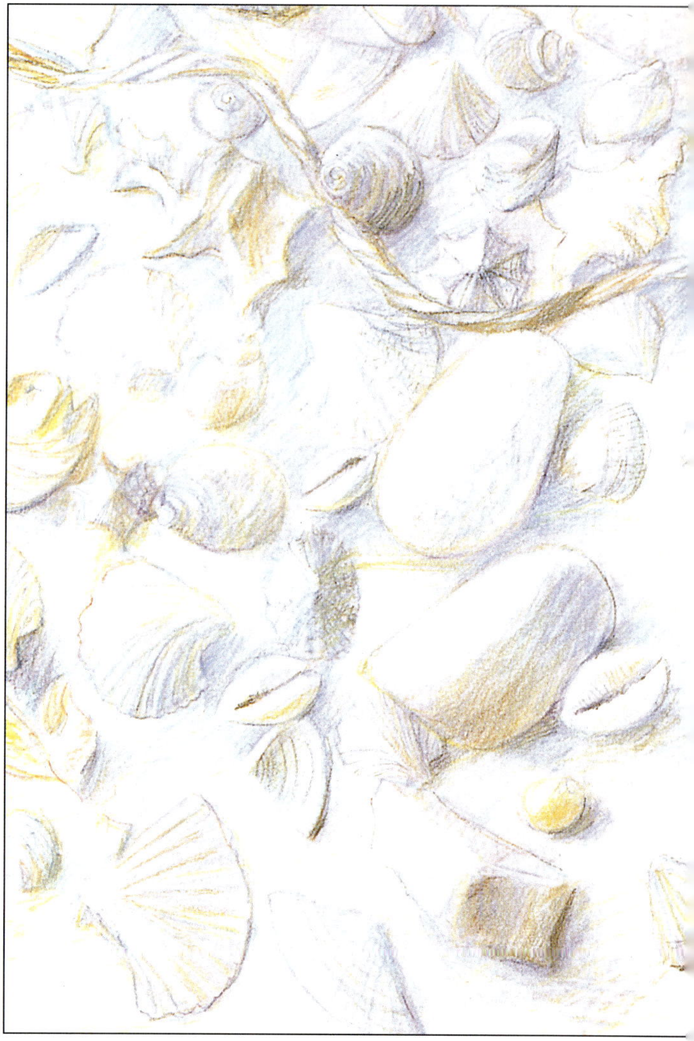

YOU WILL NEED

- *Sheet of white, rough-textured watercolour paper 14½in x 10¼in (36 x 26cm)*
- *Plastic eraser*
- *HB pencil*
- *Fixative spray*
- *Kitchen paper*

PASTEL PENCILS IN THE FOLLOWING COLOURS

- *Pink beige*
- *Naples yellow*
- *Cadmium yellow*
- *Turquoise*
- *Orange*
- *Light purple*
- *Violet*
- *Dark green*
- *Dark blue*
- *Raw sienna*
- *Dark purple*
- *Black*

1 First set out your composition, using an HB pencil to lightly draw the shapes of the shells and the piece of string. When you are happy with your sketch, carefully knock back some of the harder lines by lightly crosshatching over them with the corner of a plastic eraser to leave a faint, subtle outline. Using a soft pink-beige pastel pencil, draw over the lines of the shells as shown.

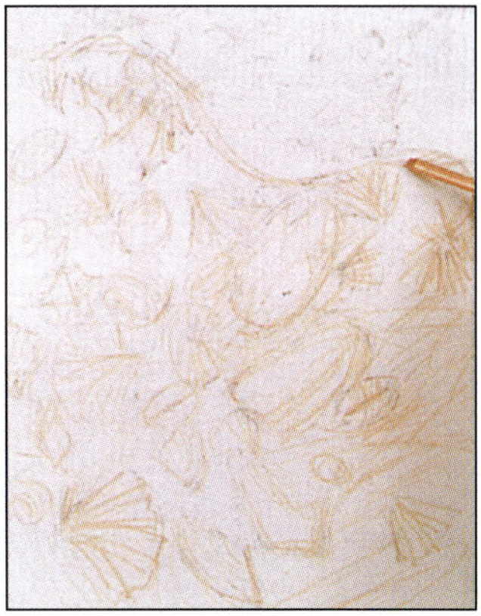

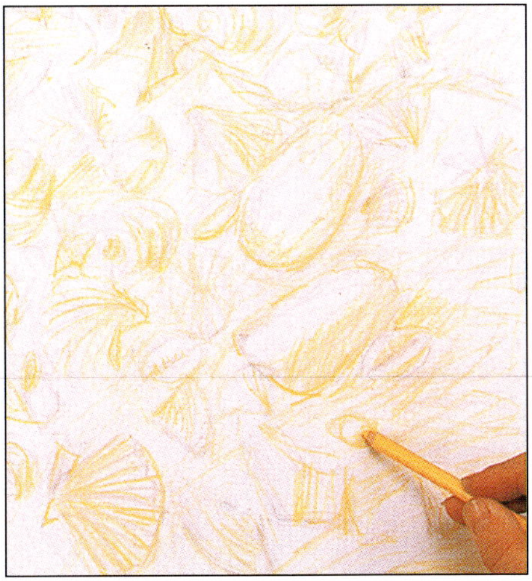

2 Start building up the colour with Naples yellow. Work over the pink-beige outlines, defining the shapes of the shells and filling in some of the shadow areas. Use light, feathery strokes and a gentle pressure on the pencil. Shade the shells with softly hatched strokes, leaving plenty of white paper showing through. Switch to cadmium yellow to define the whorls and grooves on the shells and the lines on the string.

Helpful Hint

WITH A COLOURFUL SUBJECT LIKE THIS ONE, START BY BLOCKING IN THE BROAD COLOUR AREAS OF THE COMPOSITION WITH THIN PAINT. THIS GIVES YOU A KEY AGAINST WHICH TO JUDGE SUBSEQUENT TONES AND COLOURS AND TAKES AWAY THE GLARING WHITE OF THE CANVAS.

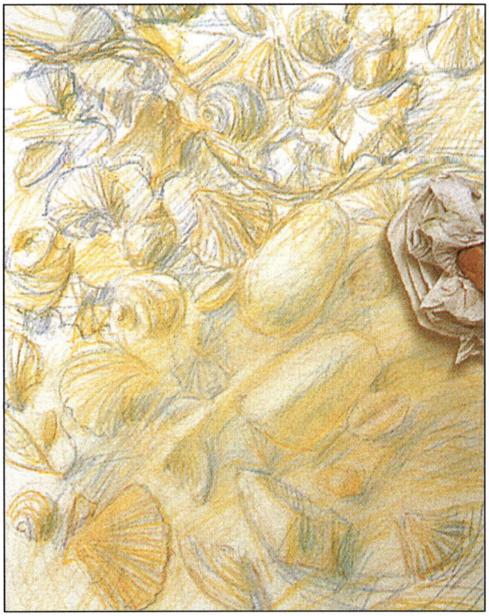

3 Start to build up form and volume on the shells and string by gently crosshatching over the shadowy areas with a turquoise pencil. Press – but don't rub – a piece of crumpled kitchen paper on to the surface to lift off excess pastel pigment. This prevents the tooth of the paper becoming clogged, allowing you to add further layers of colour.

4 Use an orange pencil to emphasize the texture and strengthen the detail on the shells. With stronger, more deliberate strokes, start to build up the shadow areas by crosshatching over the turquoise lines with light purple, still allowing plenty of white paper to show through and give translucence to the colours. Use your finger to soften any pencil strokes that appear too strong. In this detail you can see how crosshatching with different colours produces an illusion of colour mixing where the lines cross. For example, strokes of light purple and turquoise combine to create touches of violet across the picture. By using several layers of light colour instead of applying one dense layer, the fragile, ephemeral nature of the shells is captured.

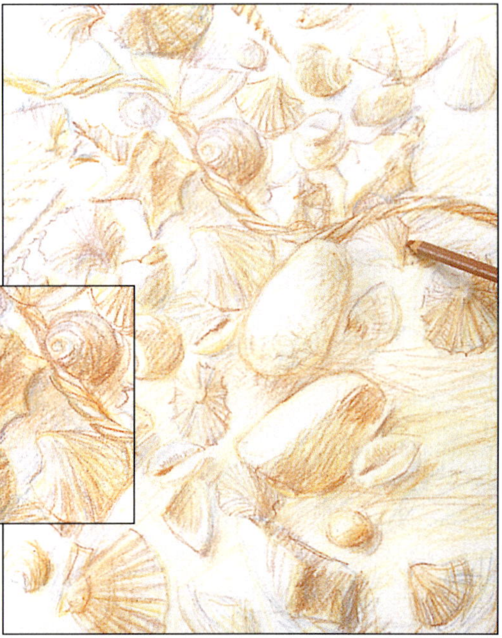

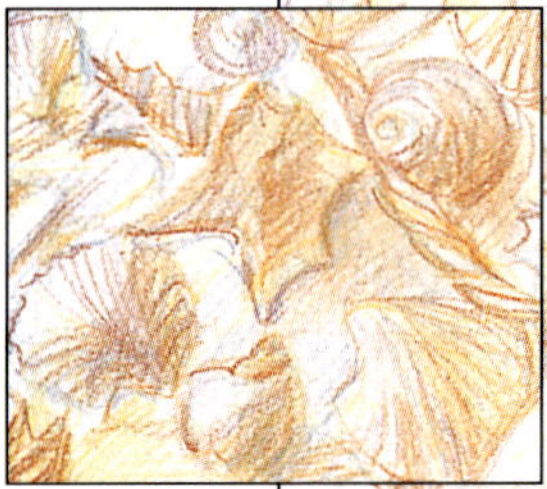

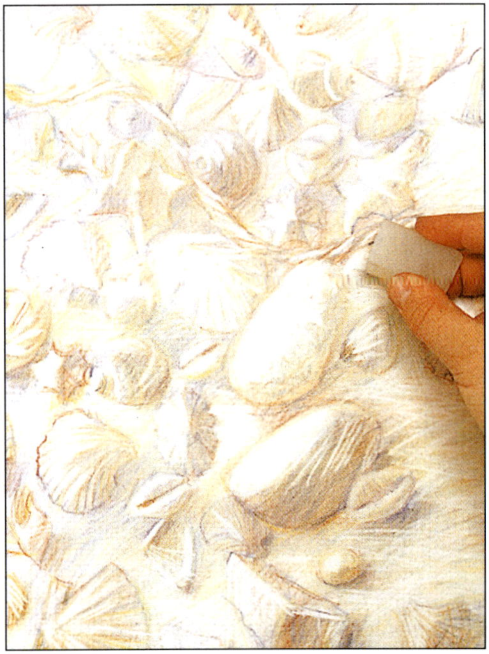

Helpful Hint

SHARPEN YOUR PASTEL PENCILS FREQUENTLY TO MAINTAIN A TRUE POINT AND KEEP THE IMAGE SHARP AND CLEAR. THE BEST WAY TO SHARPEN THEM IS WITH A CRAFT KNIFE. PENCIL SHARPENERS TEND TO BREAK THE PENCIL LEAD.

5 Knock back any excess colour by pressing gently with a piece of crumpled kitchen paper. This prevents too great a build-up of pigment and ensures that the strokes of colour remain vibrant and do not become muddy. With the point of a violet pencil, begin to define the shadows in the grooves on the surface of the shells, and deepen the cast shadows between the shells. To suggest one or two bright highlights on the shells and sand, use the corner of a plastic eraser to work across your drawing, removing areas of colour with short vertical strokes.

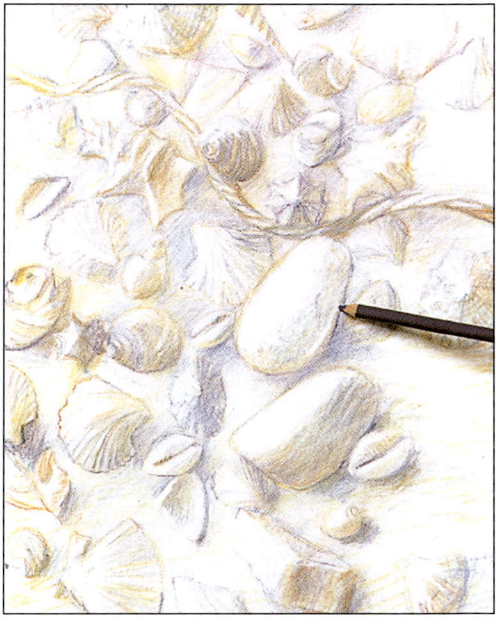

6 To convey the subtle variations of colour and texture within the shells, select pastel pencils in the colours that most closely match those of the individual shells. A dark green pencil is used to bring out the green areas in the shells, while strokes of dark blue and dark purple reinforce the stronger shadows. Work the colours into the background as well, letting the white of the paper show through and breathe air into the drawing. Create the lighter shadows with long strokes of light blue to offset the warm yellow tones most dominant in the shells. Define the grooves on the surface of each shell with raw sienna to enhance detail.

7 Pick out the edges of the shells and the grooves over their surfaces with single strokes of blue, purple and raw sienna. The marks you make should follow the lines of the shells, thereby describing the individual forms.

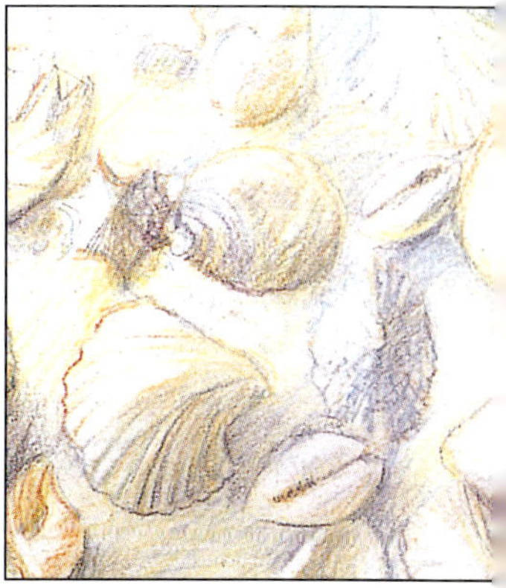

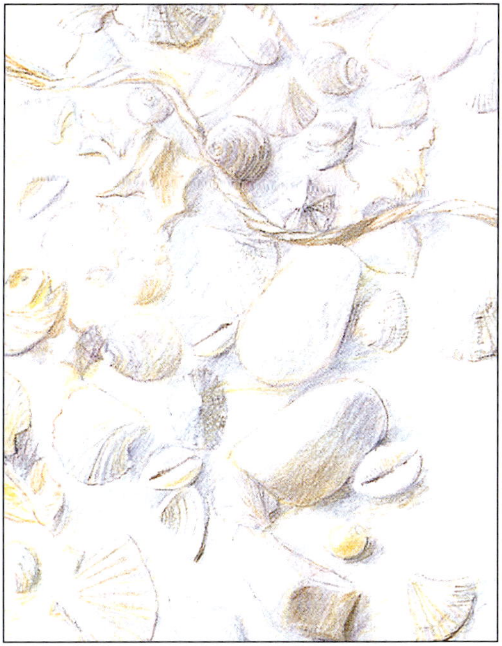

8 To finish, work a little turquoise into the shadows and, with fine black lines, strengthen some of the edges of the shells in the foreground to bring them forward in the picture plane. Stand back and assess your picture; ensure that you have achieved a fine balance of warm and cool hues that describe the form and contour of the shells. Once you are satisfied with the result, spray the whole drawing with fixative to prevent smudging.

Charcoal and Chalk

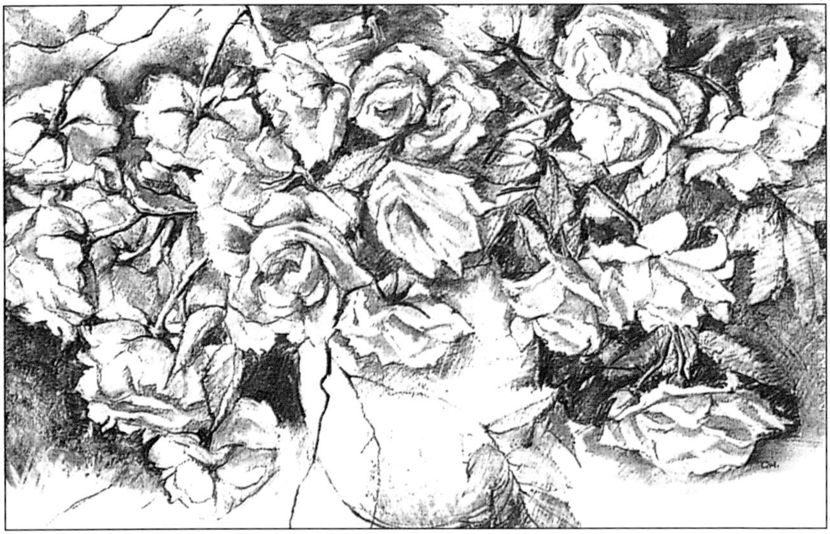

Cristiana Angelini
WHITE ROSES
This drawing proves that charcoal is capable of producing fine and delicate effects as well as bold ones. The artist worked on white paper, which serves as the highlights on the rose petals. Note the sensitive use of contrasting blended and unblended marks.

Charcoal as a drawing medium has a long and impressive history stretching back to the beginnings of art itself. It is a uniquely expressive medium with a delightful 'feel' to it as it glides across the paper. With only a slight variation in pressure on the stick you can produce a whole range of tones, from deep blacks to misty greys. The sharp corner of a broken piece of charcoal will produce strong and vigorous lines, while the side of the stick can be used to lay in broad tones. The soft, crumbly quality of charcoal makes the strokes easy to blend with your fingertip or with a paper stump, and highlights can be picked out with a putty eraser or a small pellet of kneaded white bread.

Tonal Drawings

The powdery quality of white chalk combines well with the dry, grainy nature of charcoal lines. Together they cover the entire range of tone; the charcoal can be used heavily to represent deep black, and the chalk similarly for the highlights. A range of subtle intermediate tones is produced by using lighter pressure, or by blending the charcoal and chalk together.

A light grey paper with a textured surface is the best choice for drawings in charcoal and chalk, making it easier to judge the light and dark tones against the mid-tone of the paper. Canson and Ingres papers come in a range of colours and have a matt, softly textured surface suitable for the medium.

The soft nature of charcoal and chalk makes them prone to accidental smudging. It is advisable to rest the heel of your working hand on a sheet of scrap paper laid over the drawing, and to wipe your fingertips regularly with a damp cloth. Always spray the completed drawing with fixative.

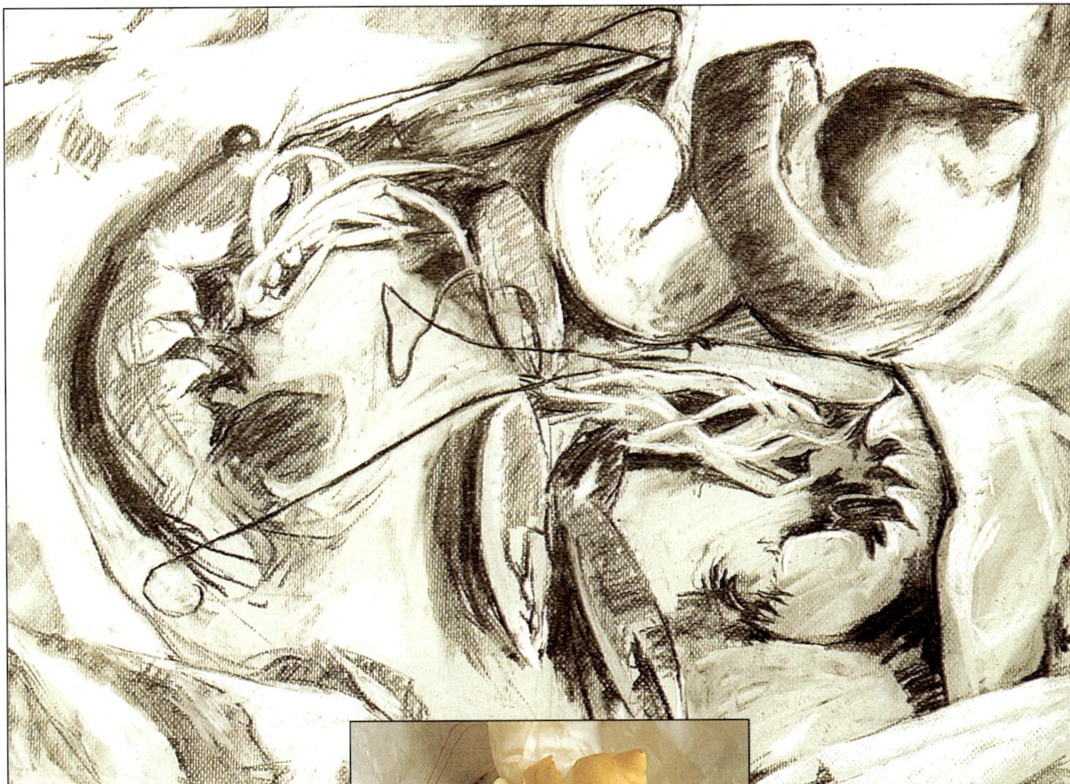

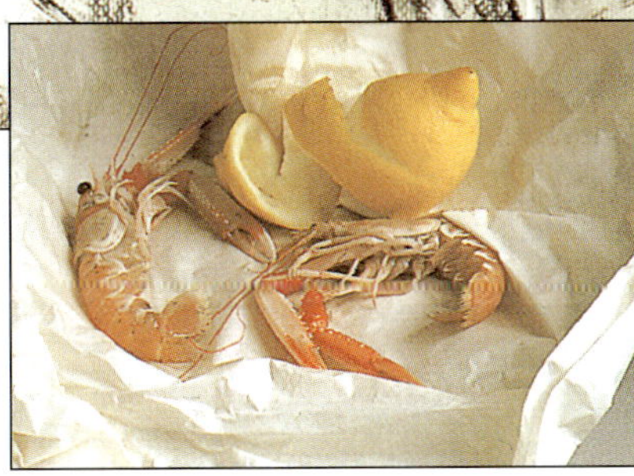

Fruits de Mer

YOU WILL NEED

- *Sheet of grey Ingres drawing paper, 21¾ x 16in (55 x 41cm)*
- *Thin and medium sticks of charcoal*
- *White chalk*
- *Kneaded eraser*

Charcoal and chalk are so immediate and responsive in use, they are almost an extension of the artist's fingers. In this lively still-life study, charcoal lines define the contours of the forms while smudges and blended tones describe volume and texture. The grey paper provides an effective mid tone, while white chalk is used for the highlights.

1 Using a thin stick of charcoal, loosely sketch the main outlines of the still life, keeping your lines light but varied in strength and thickness. Indicate the shadows on the lemon peel and in the folds of the waxed paper by drawing a dense charcoal line, then blending and fading it outwards with your fingertip.

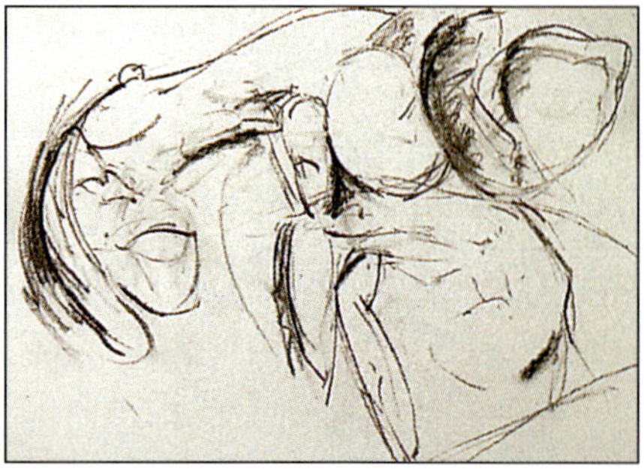

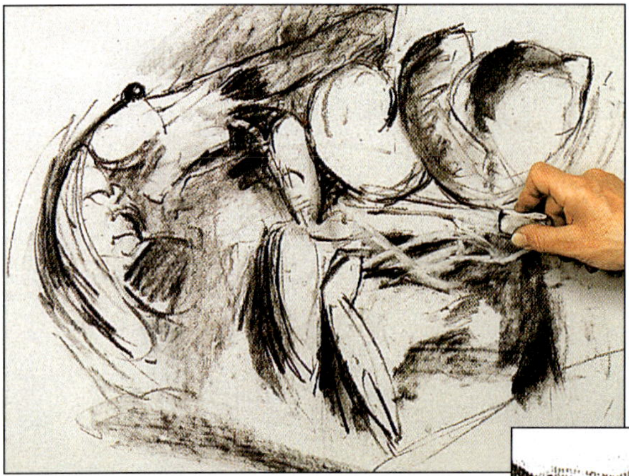

2 Use the thicker piece of charcoal to define the forms with firmer strokes. Blend with your fingertip to create rich, velvety dark tones. Snap off a small piece of charcoal and use the side to put in the mid tones with light, scribbled strokes. Don't worry about detail at this stage but concentrate on clarifying the shapes and proportions of the langoustines and the peeled lemon. To pick out the delicate light shapes of the langoustines' legs, use the corner of a kneaded eraser to 'draw' into the charcoal (see detail left).

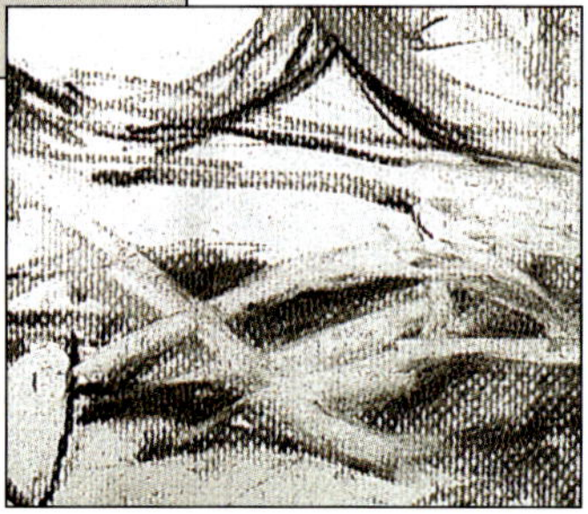

Helpful Hint

LIGHT LINES DRAWN WITH CHARCOAL ARE EASY TO CORRECT. IF YOU MAKE A MISTAKE, SIMPLY RUB THE LINES WITH A PUTTY RUBBER OR A PIECE OF BREAD KNEADED BETWEEN YOUR FINGERS AND THEN RE-DRAW

3 Continue working around the drawing, combining line with solid tones and re-defining the outlines of the subject as the work progresses. Don't finish one area at a time, but bring on all of the picture at the same rate. Build up the dark shadows on the lemon by skimming the charcoal across the paper and blending the strokes with your fingertips. Use a thin stick of charcoal to define the contours of the langoustines, using thick strokes to define the body and fainter strokes for the shadow areas.

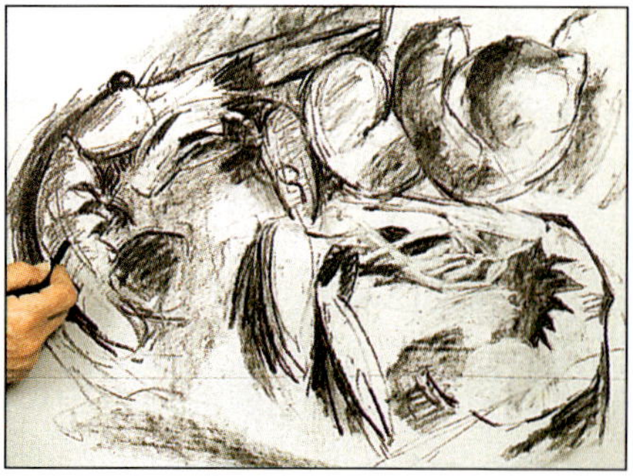

4 Now that your composition is beginning to take shape you can start working on the details. Put in more of the creases and folds in the waxed paper using the tip and side of a small piece of charcoal. Use the eraser to 'draw' the soft highlights on the paper and on the langoustines. Draw the langoustines' feelers using the sharp tip of a freshly broken charcoal stick, then strengthen the contours and the darkest areas of shadow.

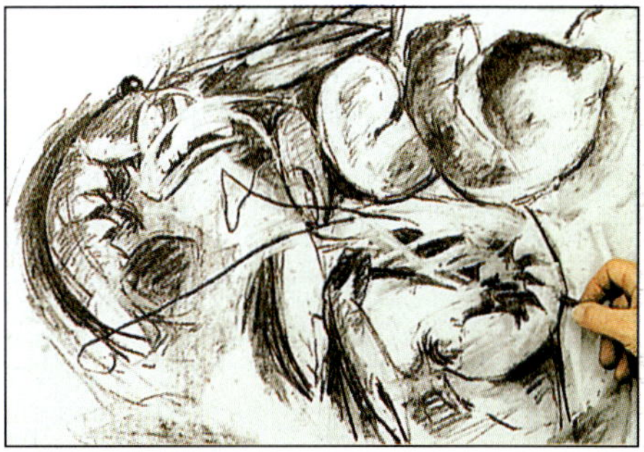

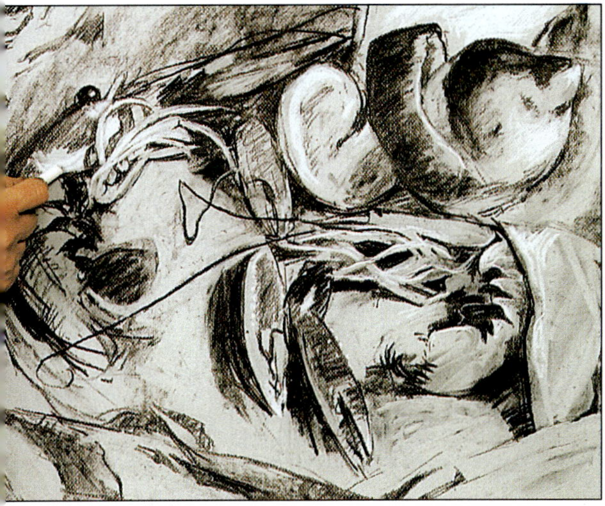

Helpful Hint

CHARCOAL IS FRAGILE AND SNAPS WHEN APPLIED WITH PRESSURE. YOU MAY FIND IT EASIER TO DRAW WITH A SHORT PIECE OF CHARCOAL THAN WITH A WHOLE STICK.

5 Now use a stick of white chalk to pick out the sharpest, brightest highlights on the langoustines, the lemon peel and the creases in the waxed paper. Vary the directions of the strokes, following the shapes made by the folds in the paper.

6 To finish, work back over the drawing adding in final touches of 'colour' with both chalk and charcoal, picking out the highlights and strengthening the contrasts. Spray your drawing with one or two light coats of fixative to prevent smudging.

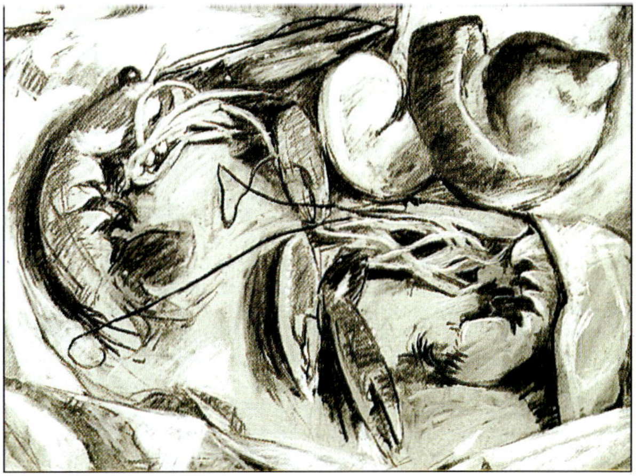

Frottage

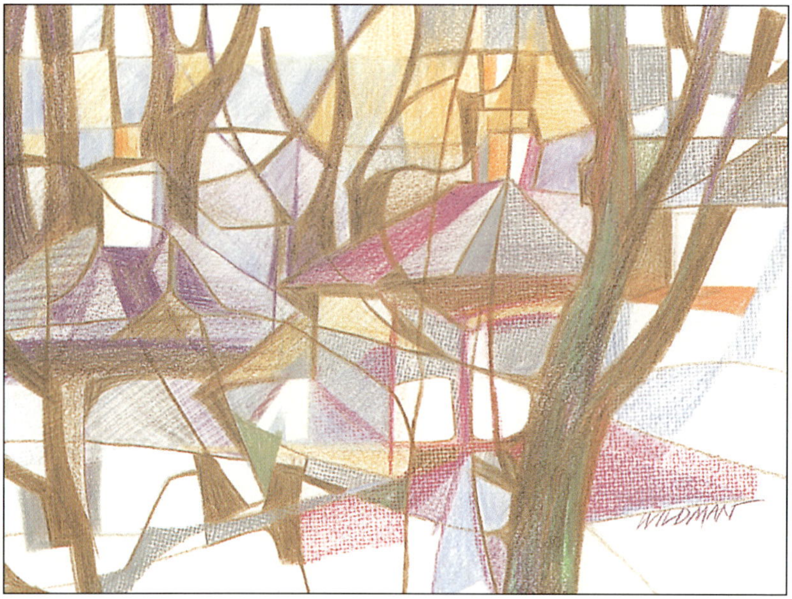

Philip Wildman
TREE STUDY
A group of houses and trees is here represented as a two-dimensional pattern resembling a stained glass window. Textural interest is provided by the use of frottage in different parts of the drawing; the paper was laid over the reverse side of a piece of hardboard and gently rubbed with coloured pencil.

This is a method of suggesting patterns or textures in a drawing by placing a sheet of paper over a surface with a pronounced texture, such as grainy wood or rough stone, and rubbing with a soft pencil, charcoal or pastel so that the texture comes through. The word 'frottage' is derived from the French word frotter, meaning to rub.

The most obvious use for frottage is in depicting a specific texture such as rock, stone or wood, and it is most often combined with freehand drawing. Frottage is also useful when you want a subtle but interesting pattern to enliven a broad area such as an empty foreground. You can also use it creatively by taking a rubbing from one object and using it in an entirely different context. You could, for example, use rubbings of leaves to represent trees in a landscape. During the early 20th century the German surrealist painter Max Ernst used frottage in this way, often combining frottage with collage to create strange, haunting images.

The patterns and effects achieved with frottage vary widely, as they are affected by both the thickness of the paper and the implement used for making the rubbing. Experiment with the technique, taking impressions from surfaces such as heavy sandpaper, coarse woodgrain, paper doilies or textured fabrics such as hessian and canvas. Interesting broken-colour effects can be obtained by making a rubbing with, say, a blue pastel, then moving the paper slightly and rubbing again with a yellow pastel to create a lively greenish hue.

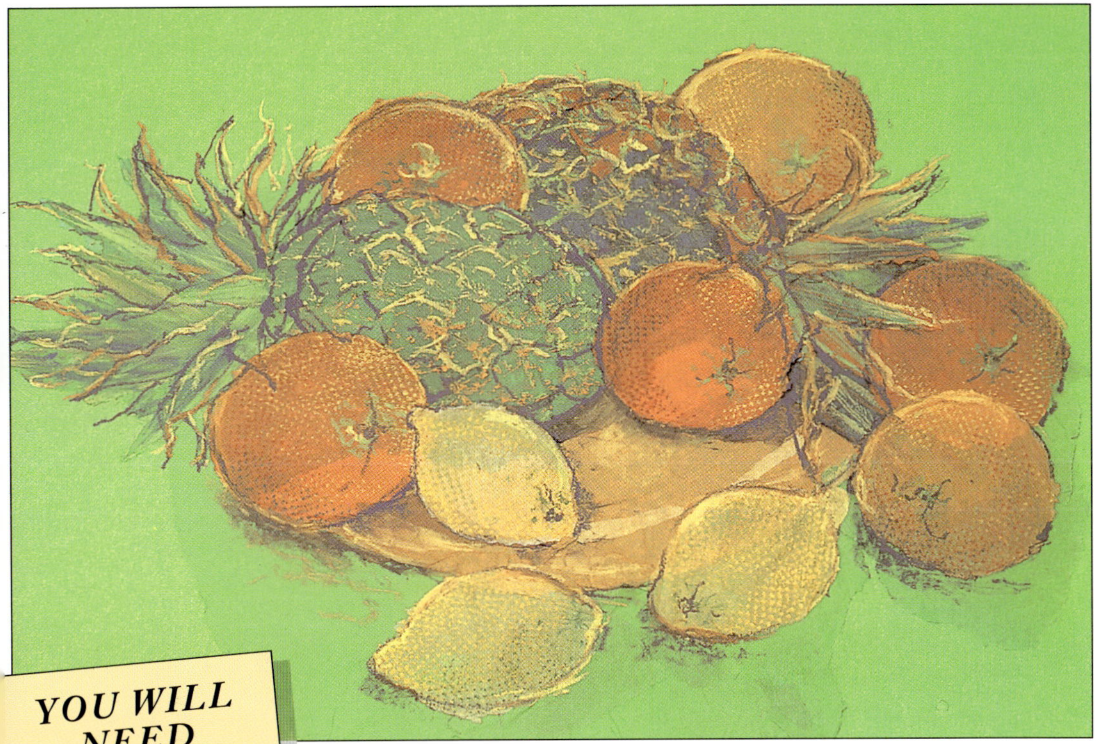

YOU WILL NEED

- Sheet of heavy card, 30 x 20in (76 x 51cm)
- Sheets of coloured tissue paper: Dark green, Bright green, Dark blue, Yellow, Light orange, Dark orange, Brown
- Pineapple
- Orange
- Lemon
- Nutmeg grater
- Can of spray mount

Citrus Fruits

Whatever your level of experience, trying out new techniques and materials will broaden your range of expression. This vibrant still life was constructed from a collage of pieces of coloured tissue paper. These were then worked over with oil pastels, using the frottage technique to suggest the various textures of the fruits.

OIL PASTELS IN THE FOLLOWING COLOURS

- *Purple*
- *Orange*
- *Light green*
- *Dark green*
- *Yellow*
- *Dark brown*
- *Reddish brown*
- *Olive green*
- *Deep aquamarine*

1 Start by making the individual collage elements from tissue paper, using the frottage technique. Firmly press a sheet of dark green tissue paper over the pineapple and gently rub over the surface with the side of a purple oil pastel. Highlight with orange, light green and dark green oil pastels to build up the characteristic colours of the fruit. Repeat with dark blue tissue paper for the second pineapple, frottaging with orange and light green pastels.

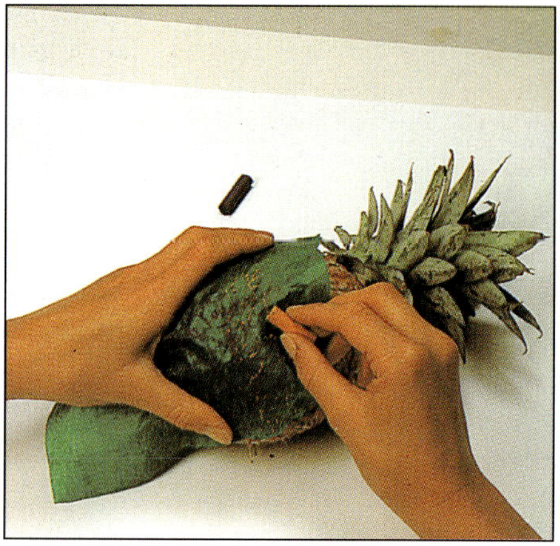

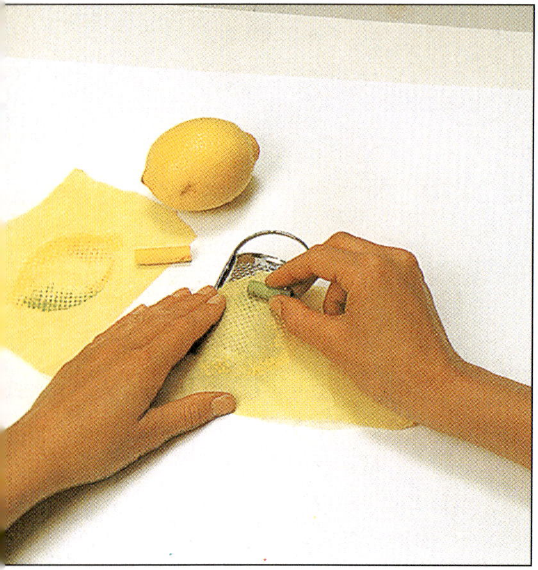

2 Now prepare three lemon-shaped cut-outs. Lay a sheet of yellow tissue paper over a nutmeg grater and draw the outline of a lemon on it, roughly life-size, using the side of a yellow pastel. Add shading with light green pastel, leaving some parts of the tissue paper untouched. Lay the tissue paper sheets aside for now.

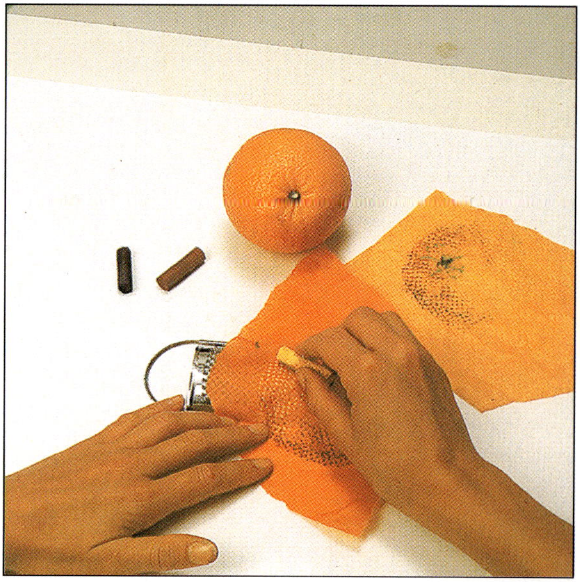

3 Prepare six orange cutouts in the same way, using light and dark shades of orange tissue paper. Frottage with purple and dark brown pastels for the shadows on the oranges, and yellow for the highlights.

4 Remove a large and a small leaf from the pineapple. These will be used to frottage the whole crown of leaves. Lay a sheet of dark blue tissue paper over a leaf and gently frottage with a light green pastel to create an outline of the leaf. Repeat using both leaves, moving the paper slightly each time to create a fan of overlapping leaves. Use more colours – olive green, reddish brown and deep aquamarine – to add interest and suggest three-dimensional form. Repeat this process for the crown of the second pineapple.

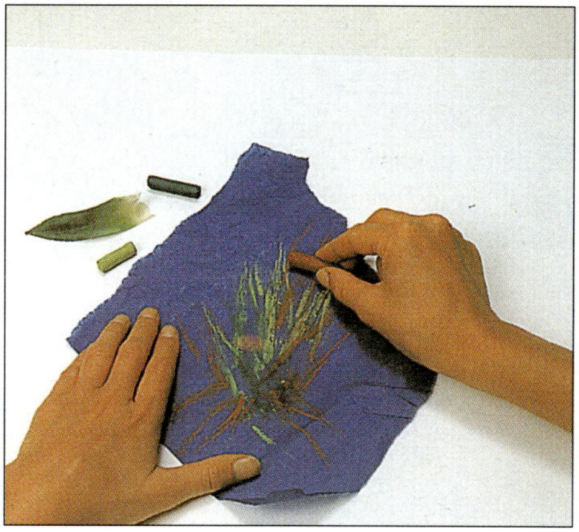

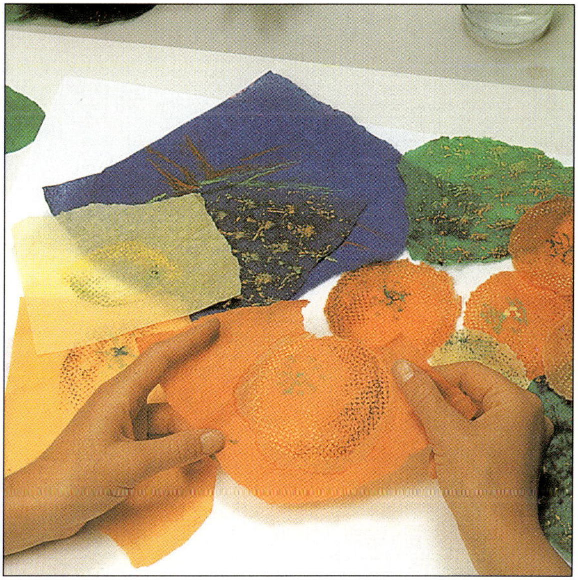

5 When you have finished frottaging the textures of the fruits, tear out the shapes ready to be assembled as a collage. If you cut the shapes with scissors they will appear unnatural and hard-edged; to create soft-edged shapes, lay each sheet of tissue over its corresponding fruit, dampen the paper around the edge of the fruit shape and then carefully tear it out.

6 Now you can assemble your collage picture. Cover the entire backing board with a sheet of bright green tissue paper, attached with spray mount. Tear a piece of light orange tissue paper to represent the wooden chopping board. Start arranging the fruit shapes on the surface, with some overlapping others. When you are happy with the composition, fix the shapes in position with spray mount.

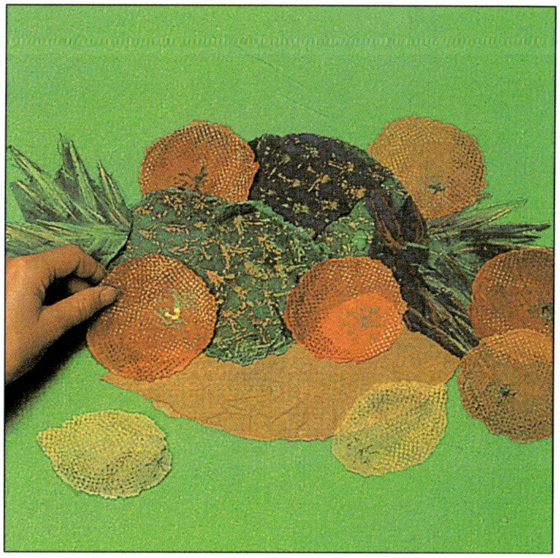

7 Continue sticking the shapes in place, adding torn strips of brown tissue for the shadows under the lemons and yellow tissue for the highlight on the chopping board. Use torn pieces of dark green tissue for the shadows cast by the arrangement on the green cloth. These shadows help to anchor the group to the table and also add colour and shape interest.

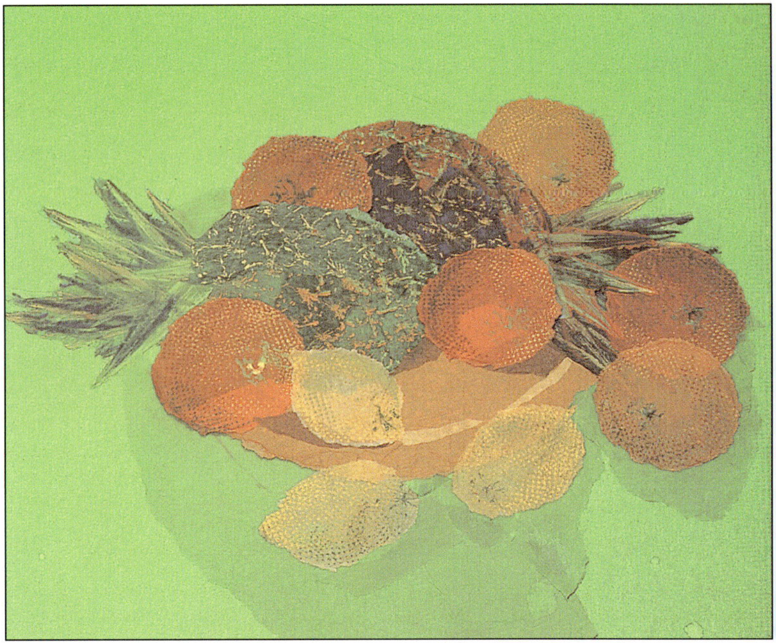

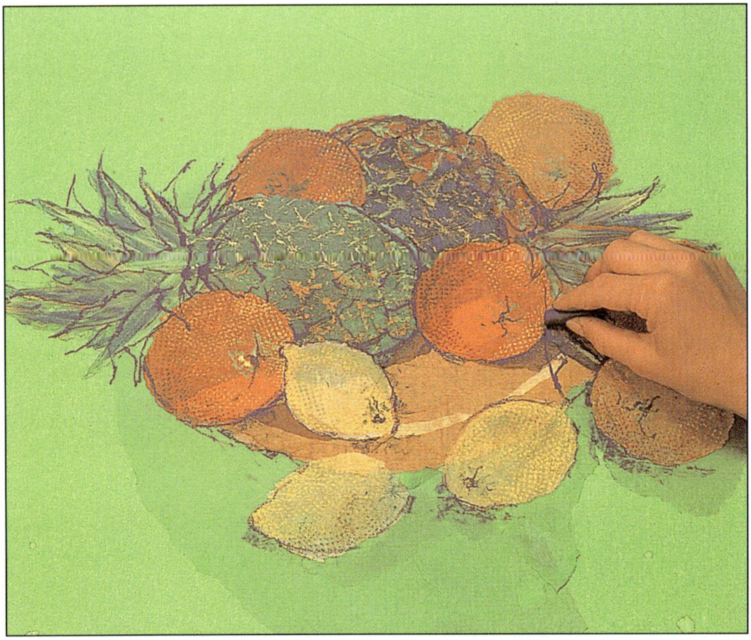

8 Using the purple oil pastel, draw around the edges of the fruits with broken lines to add definition and emphasize the shapes. Pick out some of the individual pineapple leaves, and darken the shadows immediately beneath the fruits.

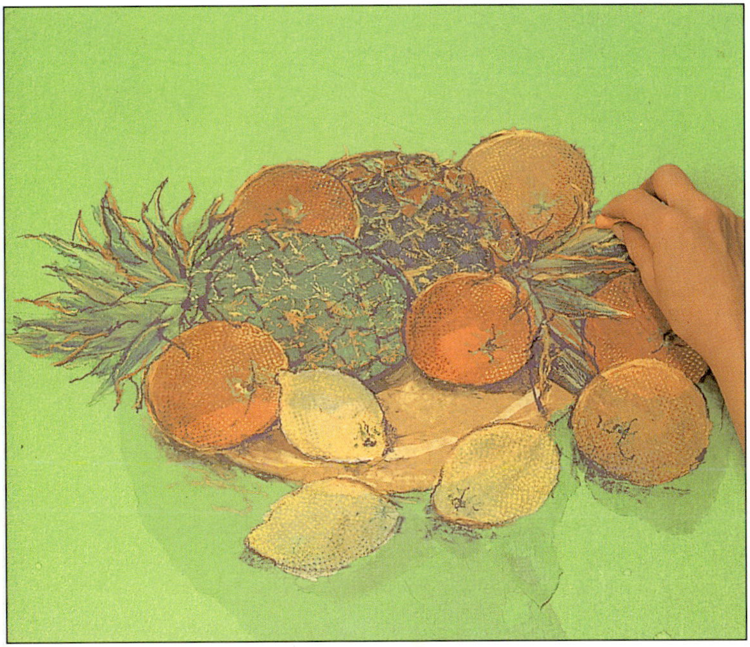

9 Switch to the orange pastel and add bright highlights to the tops of the fruits and the edges of the pineapple leaves.

Helpful Hint

TISSUE PAPER TEARS EASILY, SO WHEN GLUING HOLD THE SHAPE FIRMLY AND APPLY THE GLUE FROM THE CENTRE OUTWARDS.

10 Finally, use the yellow pastel to bring out the highlights on the knobbly surface of the pineapples and on the oranges at the back of the arrangement.

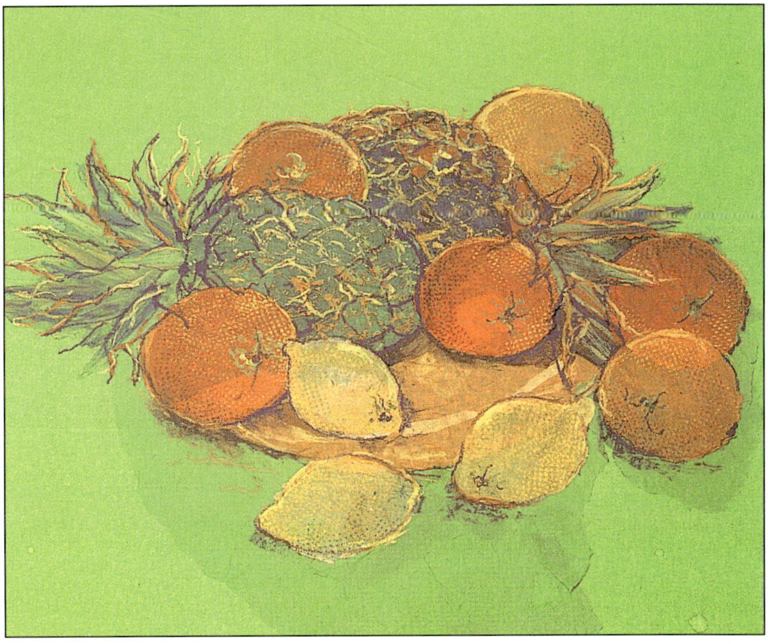

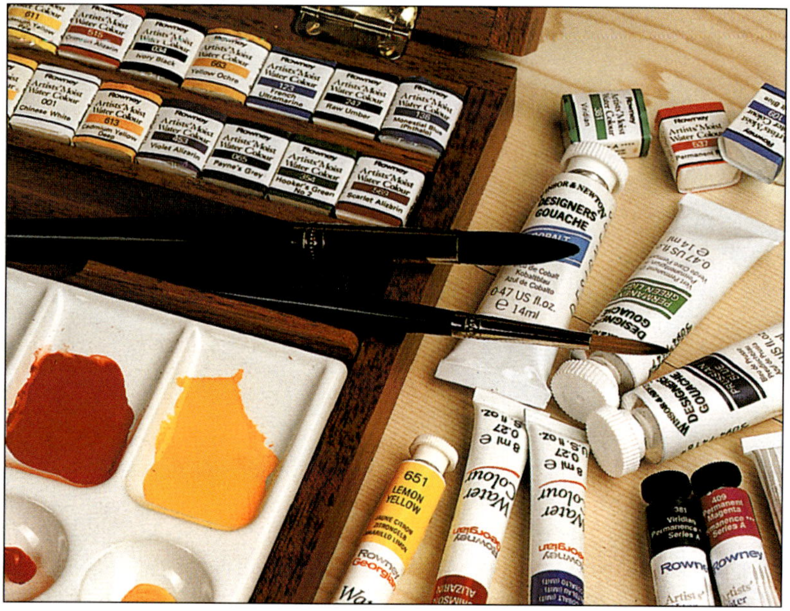
DESIGNERS GOUACHE
0.47 US fl.oz.
14ml
651
LEMON YELLOW
Rowney
Rowney

AN INTRODUCTION TO

Watercolour

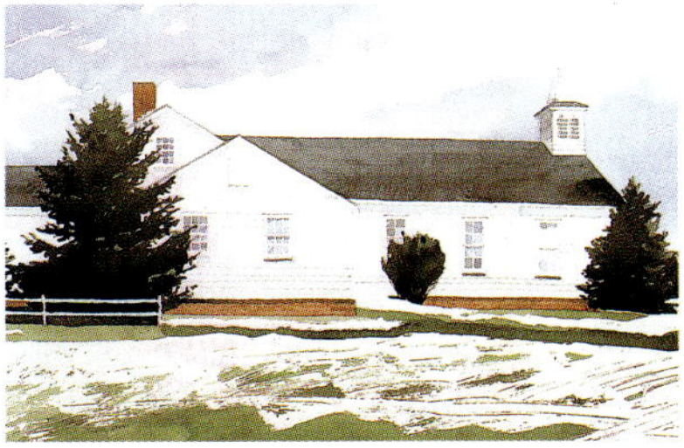

PROJECT 1

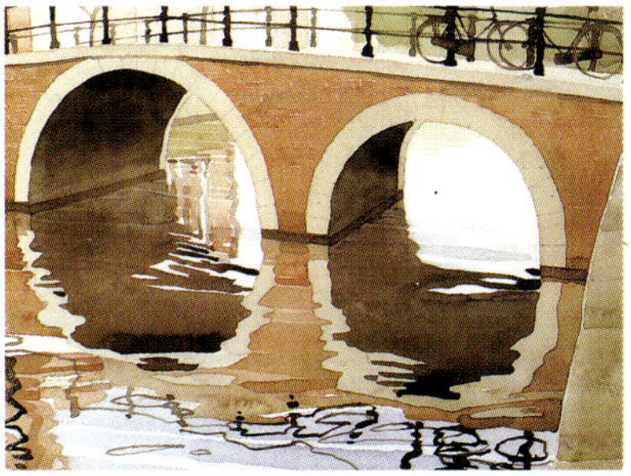

PROJECT 4

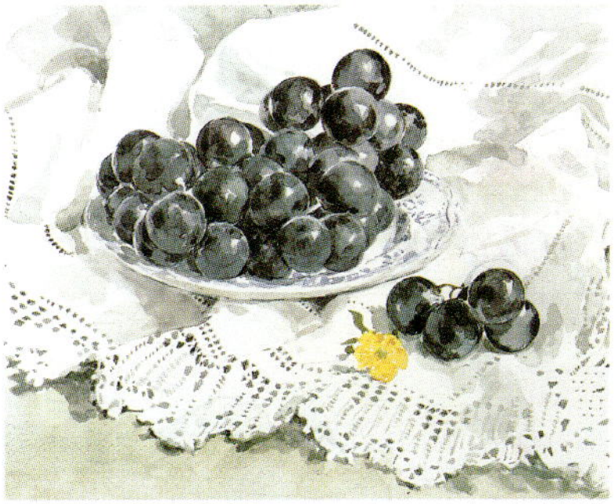

PROJECT 2

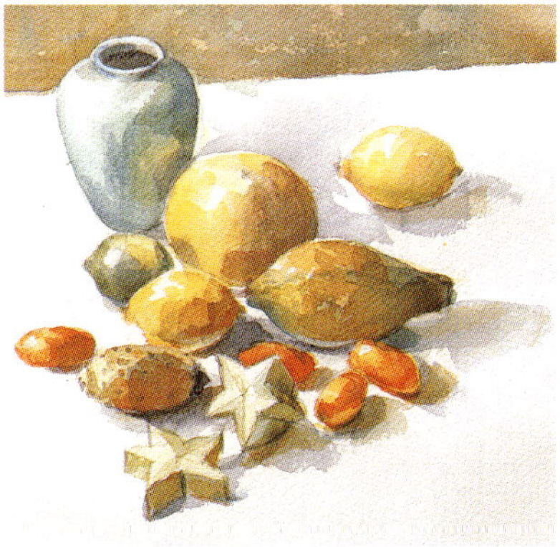

PROJECT 5

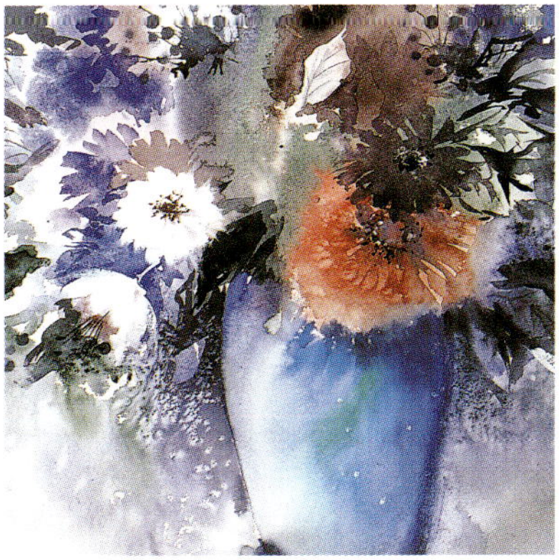

PROJECT 3

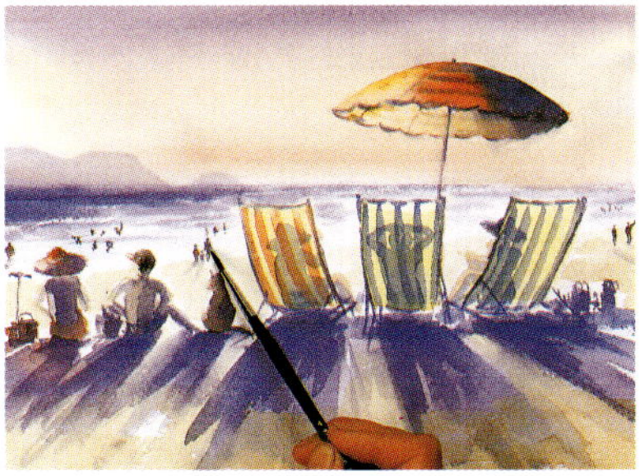

PROJECT 6

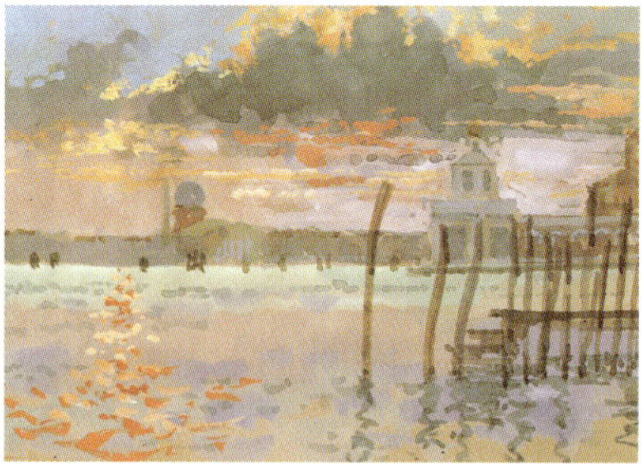

PROJECT 7

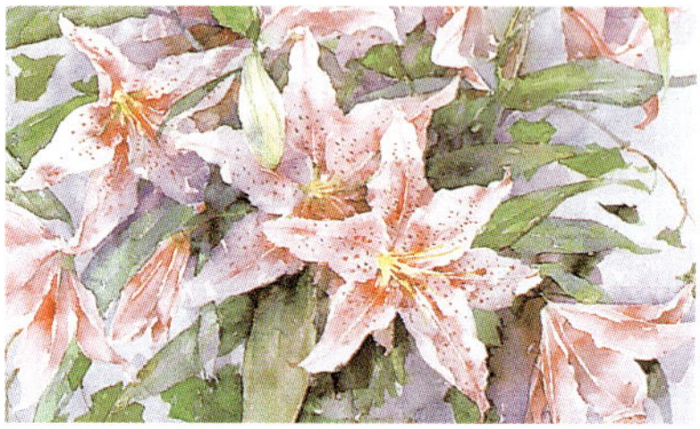

PROJECT 8

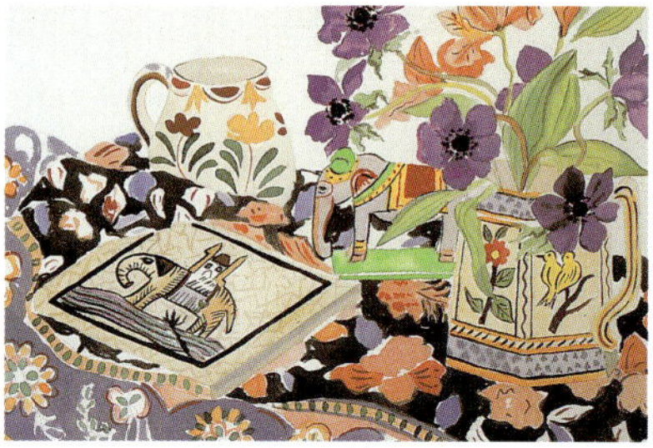

PROJECT 9

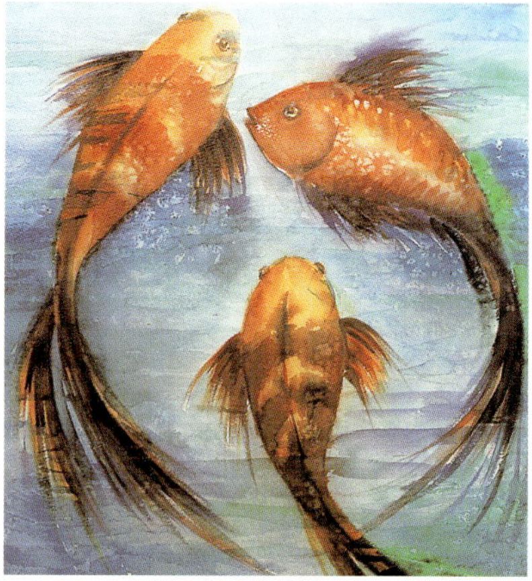

PROJECT 10

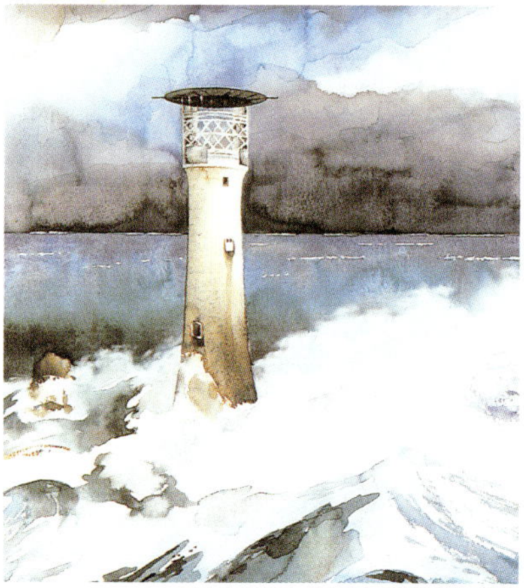

PROJECT 11

Watercolour

Watercolour

Watercolour is perhaps the most popular painting medium, with its unique delicacy and transparency capable of conjuring up the most fleeting and evanescent effects in nature. The fluidity of watercolour also makes it an exciting and unpredictable medium. For the inexperienced artist this element of uncertainty can be disconcerting at first, but a timid and cautious approach only results in a weak, dry, overworked painting. The secret of success with watercolour painting is to work boldly and with confidence. Once you learn to relax and let go of the reins, you will be delighted to find that very often the paint does much of the work for you; sometimes the most interesting and beautiful effects are achieved through a combination of accident and design. Watercolour may be occasionally irritating and frustrating, but it is never boring.

Materials and Equipment

One of the advantages of watercolour is that it requires few materials. All you need is a small selection of brushes, paints and papers and a jar of water, and you are ready to paint.

PAINTS

Watercolour paint consists of finely ground pigments bound with gum arabic and mixed with glycerine, which acts as a moisturiser. It is the translucence of the coloured washes that distinguishes watercolour from other media.

Choosing watercolour paints

There are two grades of watercolour – artists' and students'. The students' range is cheaper, but you will get better results from the artists' range, which contains finer quality pigments. The price is indicated by a series number. Some artists' colours are more expensive than others. Inorganic pigments, for example, can cost a lot more than the organic 'earth' colours.

Watercolour paints are available in tubes of thick, moist colour and in small blocks, called 'pans' or 'half-pans', of semi-moist colour.

Tubes

Tube colour is richer than pan colour and is useful for creating large areas of wash quickly; simply squeeze the paint onto a palette and mix it with water. It is best to squeeze out only a few colours at a time, keeping them well apart so that there is no danger of running together if you use too much water when mixing.

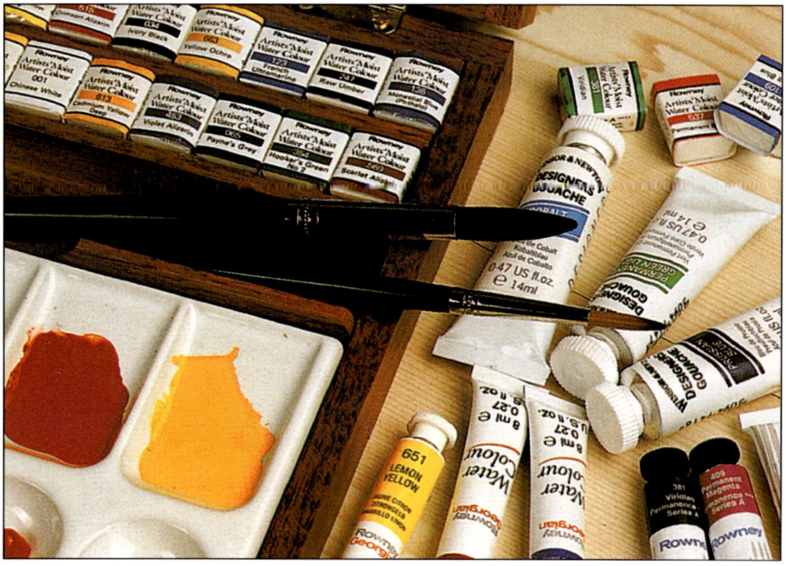

Right *A selection of tubes and pans of watercolour paint. These can be bought separately or in boxed sets of pre-selected colours.*

Pans

These small blocks of semi-moist colour can be bought individually as well as in special paint-boxes with slots to hold the pans in place and a lid that opens out to form a convenient mixing palette. They are economical to buy and useful for outdoor work as they are easily portable. However, it takes a little effort to lift enough colour onto the brush to make a large wash.

Gouache paints

Gouache is an opaque type of watercolour made by binding the pigments with gum arabic and combining them with white chalk. The paint dries to an opaque and slightly chalky matt finish, quite different to the delicate transparency of pure watercolour, but they can be diluted with water in the same way and applied with similar brushes.

BRUSHES

A common mistake beginners make when starting in watercolour is buying brushes that are too small. Because they can only make fine marks, their uses are limited. A large, good-quality brush is a better buy than several small ones because it holds plenty of paint for laying large washes and also comes to a fine point for painting fine details.

Choosing brushes

With watercolour brushes, it pays to buy the best you can afford. The better the brush, the better it performs and the longer it lasts. Cheap brushes are a false economy as they do not perform well and quickly wear out.

Sable brushes are the best choice for watercolour painting. They are expensive, but a pleasure to use, and if they are properly cared for they will last a long time. Springy, resilient and long-lasting, sable hair tapers naturally to a fine point.

Animal-hair brushes, made from ox, squirrel or goat hair, are also available. These are useful so long as a fine point is not required.

Synthetic-fibre brushes are a popular alternative to sable because they cost a lot less and are still quite springy and responsive. However, they don't hold the paint as well or last nearly as long. Also available are mixtures of synthetic and sable, which have good colour-holding and pointing properties.

Brush care

Look after your brushes and they will last you well. Never use a brush to scrub at the paint, and do not leave brushes standing in water while you work as this can ruin both the hairs

Below *There are watercolour brushes to suit all purposes – and pockets.* ***A*** *flat wash brush.* ***B*** *round wash brush.* ***C*** *round synthetic brushes.* ***D*** *flat synthetic brushes.* ***E*** *mop brushes.* ***F*** *rigger brush.* ***G*** *round sable brushes. Watercolour sponges,* ***H****, are useful for applying broad washes and for lifting out colour.*

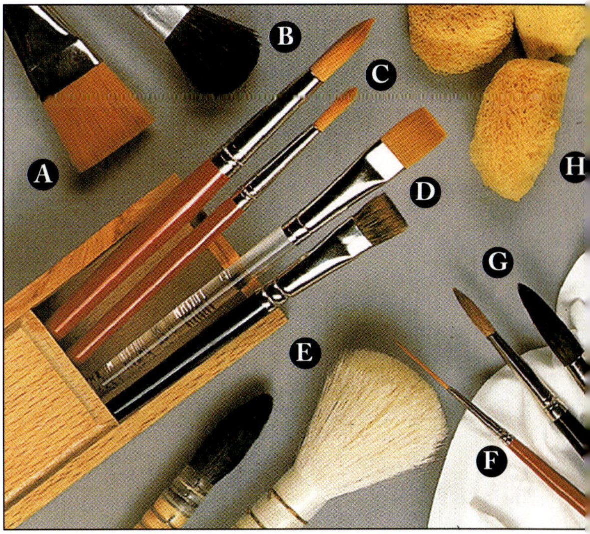

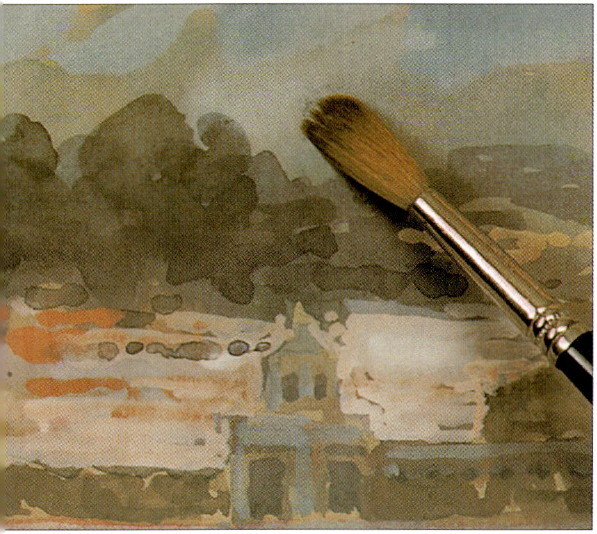

Left *When buying watercolour brushes, remember that quality is better than quantity. One good-quality sable brush, if looked after, will give you more years of service than a handful of cheap brushes.*

and the handles. Always rinse the brush in running water after use, making sure that any paint near the metal ferrule is removed. Then reshape it either by pulling it between your lips or by gently drawing it over the palm of your hand, moulding the hairs to a point. Stand your brushes, hairs uppermost, in a jar, or lay them flat. If you intend to store brushes in a box, make sure they are dry first, otherwise mildew may set in. Moths are very keen on sable brushes, so if you need to store them for any length of time, use mothballs to act as a deterrent.

Brush shapes

Rounds and flats (the flats are also called chisels or one-stroke brushes) are the main types of brush used for watercolour painting.

Rounds are bullet shaped brushes that come to a fine point. By moving the broad side of the brush across the paper you can paint broad areas of colour, and with the tip you can paint fine details.

Flats are wide and square-ended. They are ideal for spreading water rapidly over the paper to create a wash. The flat edge is useful for making clean-cut lines.

Riggers are round with very long hair. They are designed to hold a lot of paint and produce thin, fine lines.

Mops and wash brushes are designed to paint large areas quickly. Wash brushes are wide and flat, while mops have large round heads.

Brush sizes

Brushes are graded according to size, ranging from as small as 0000 to as large as a no. 24 wash brush. The size of flat brushes generally denotes the width of the brush, measured in millimetres or inches. Brush sizes are not standardized, so a no. 6 brush in one manufacturer's range will not necessarily be the same size as a no. 6 in another.

PAPER

There is a wide selection of watercolour papers on the market, varying in texture, weight and quality. Which type you choose depends very much on your personal painting style and how much you want to spend. Start by buying single sheets of various types and try them out – you will soon discover which ones suit your way of working.

Watercolour paper can be either handmade or machine-made and this difference is reflected in the price. Ordinary cartridge paper, although good for drawing, is unsuitable for watercolour painting as it lacks strength and texture.

The best-quality handmade paper is made from

cotton rag instead of the usual woodpulp. Handmade papers are generally recognizable by their irregular surface and ragged ('deckle') edges. They also bear the manufacturer's watermark in one corner. Mould-made papers are the next best thing to handmade, and are more affordable. Machine-made papers are the cheapest, but some have a rather mechanical surface grain.

Choosing paper

Watercolour paper can be bought in single sheets, but it is usually more economical to buy a spiral-bound pad. There are also watercolour blocks, which consist of sheets of pre-stretched paper gummed around the edges on all four sides; when the painting is finished and dry, the top sheet can be separated and taken off by running a palette knife along the edges.

Most watercolour paper is white or off-white, to reflect light back through the transparent washes of colour. However, tinted papers are also available, and these are often used when painting with body colour or gouache.

Paper texture

The surface texture of paper is known as its grain or 'tooth'. There are three kinds of surface:

Hot-pressed (HP) is smooth, with almost no 'tooth'. It is suitable for finely detailed work, but most artists find its surface too slippery for watercolour.

Not (meaning not hot pressed, and sometimes-referred to as 'cold-pressed') has a semi-rough

Right *Try out different types of watercolour paper until you find one that suits you.*
A *Fabriano rough.*
B *Waterford hot-pressed.*
C *Waterford rough.*
D *Waterford Not surface.*
E *Handmade paper.*
F *Wilcox (cream).*
G *Bockingford Not surface.*
H *Whatman rough.*
I *Canson Montval Not surface.*
J *Bockingford tinted (shown here in grey, cream and eggshell).*

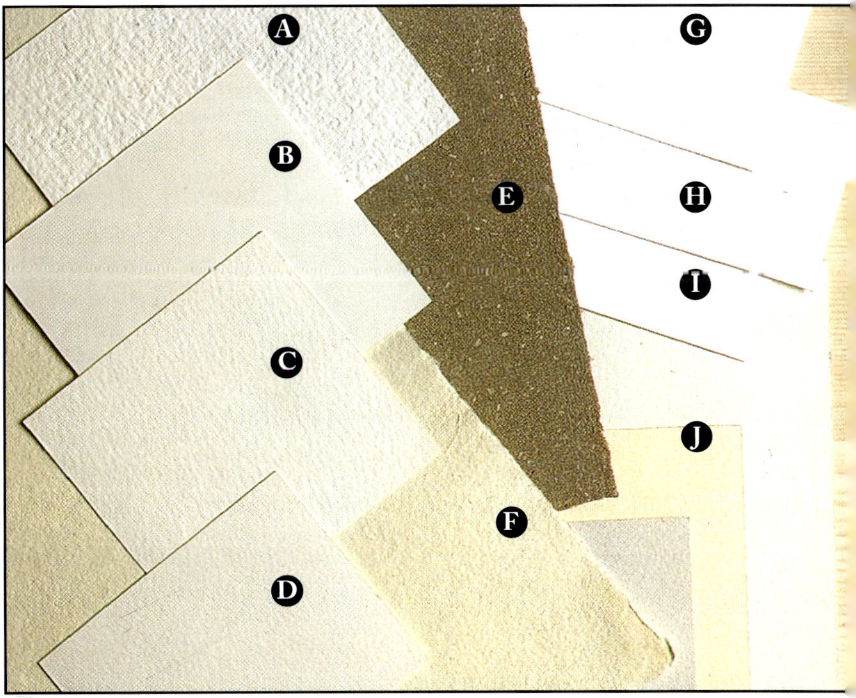

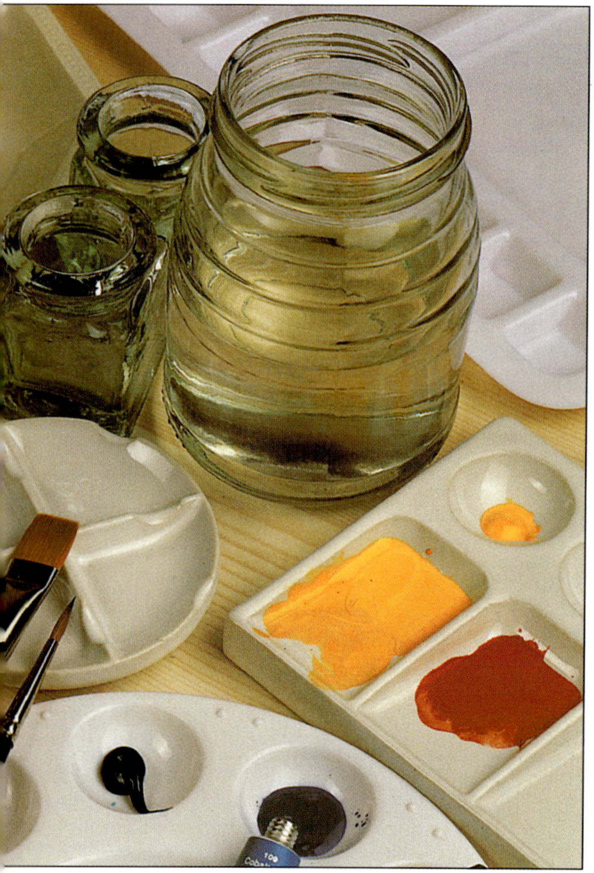

***Left** For watercolour painting you will need a palette with deep wells that hold plenty of paint. Renew your water jar frequently to keep your colours fresh and clear.*

surface equally good for vigorous washes and fine brush detail. This is the most popular type of surface for beginners.

Rough paper has a pronounced tooth which causes strokes and washes to break up. The paint sinks into the pitted surface and leaves tiny speckles of white paper untouched, causing the wash to sparkle with light.

Weight

Traditionally, the weight (thickness) of paper is measured in pounds per ream (480 sheets). The equivalent metric measure is grams per square metre (gsm). As a guide, the lightest watercolour paper is 70lb (150gsm), while a heavier paper is 140lb (285gsm). The heaviest paper weighs 300lb (640gsm).

Stretching watercolour paper

Lightweight watercolour papers – less than 140lb (285gsm) – should be stretched before use, to prevent them 'cockling' or buckling when paint and water are applied. Stretching is not usually necessary with heavier papers.

To stretch paper, immerse the sheet in cold water for a couple of minutes (use a container large enough to take the sheet without being cramped – a sink or bath is best for large sheets). This expands the paper fibres. Hold the paper up by one corner to dislodge any surplus water, then lay it flat on a wooden board. Remove any air bubbles by rubbing briskly outward from the centre, using the backs of your hands.

Stick down the edges of the paper with strips of dampened gummed brown-paper tape, cut 2in (5cm) longer than the paper on each side. Leave to dry naturally. As the paper dries it shrinks and becomes as taut as a drum. Leave the gummed paper strips in place until the painting is completed and dry. Properly stretched paper will not buckle, even when flooded with washes.

PALETTES

Watercolour palettes come in a range of shapes and sizes, and are made of either ceramic, enamelled metal or plastic. They are always white, which allows you to see the true colour

of a wash with minimum distortion, and they all have recesses or wells that allow you to mix the paint with generous amounts of water.
Slant tiles These are rectangular ceramic palettes divided into several recesses or wells, allowing several colours to be laid out separately. The wells slant so that the paint collects at one end ready for use and can be drawn out of the well for thinner washes.
Tinting saucers are small, round ceramic dishes divided into four shallow compartments, each with a useful brush-rest on the edge. They are perfect for small-scale mixing, and also useful for holding masking fluid and watercolour mediums, to keep them separate from your colour mixes.
Cabinet saucers are the same as tinting saucers, without the divisions, and come with lids.
Palette trays These are usually made of plastic and have deep wells with plenty of room in each compartment to contain large amounts of fluid paint.
Improvised palettes Ordinary cups, bowls, plates and saucers – so long as they are white and non-porous – can be pressed into service as watercolour palettes. Hors d'oeuvres dishes are particularly useful as they provide several large mixing wells.

MEDIUMS

These are jellies and pastes that you can mix with your watercolour paints to alter their consistency, transparency and finish. Used in moderation, they allow you to achieve a variety of effects that are not normally possible with watercolours, while still retaining the basic translucent quality that is so characteristic of the medium.
Gum arabic is a pale-coloured solution that increases both the gloss and transparency of watercolours.
Ox gall liquid is useful for improving the flow and adherence of watercolours.
Acquapasto is a translucent jelly that thickens the consistency of watercolours to give an 'impasto' effect.

ACCESSORIES

You will need a well sharpened pencil for drawing; a kneaded putty eraser for erasing pencil lines without spoiling the surface of the paper; soft tissues for mopping up excess colour and lifting out colour to create highlights; a natural sponge for lifting out colour and for dabbing on areas of rough-textured paint; cotton buds for lifting out small areas of colour; jars for water; a wooden drawing board; gum-backed tape for attaching the paper to the board; and masking fluid for temporarily covering areas of the paper that you don't want to cover with paint.

***Below** Some of the accessories that you may find useful for creating specific textures and effects.*

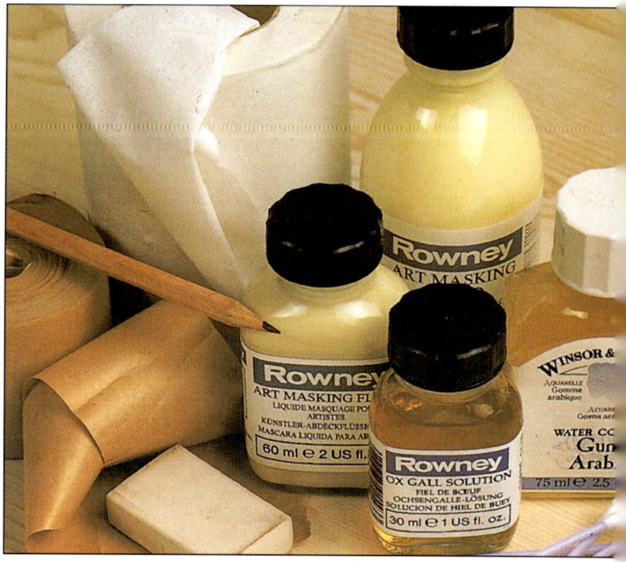

Using Masking Fluid

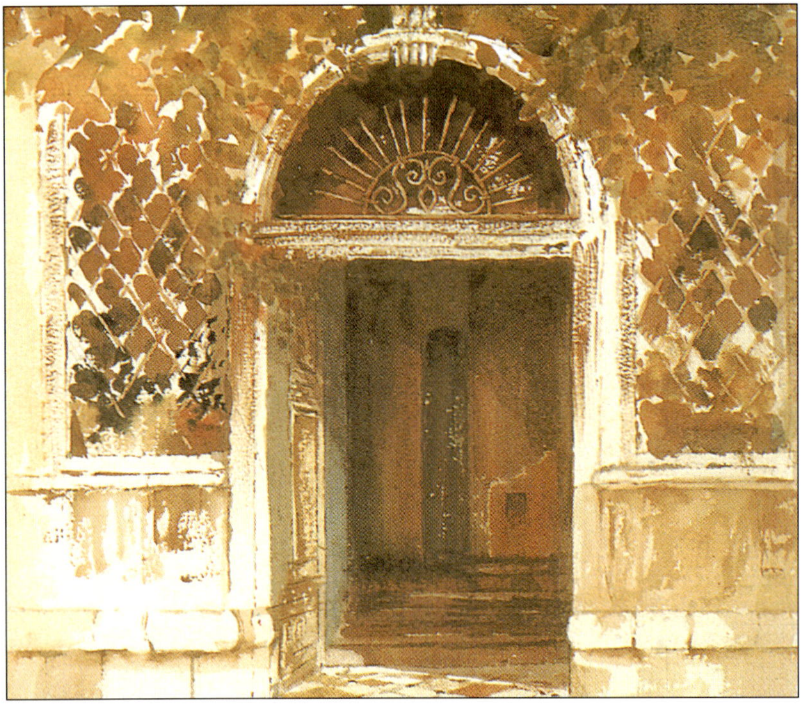

Alison Musker
RIO DI SAN LORENZO (detail)
To capture the faded grandeur of this old Venetian doorway, the artist applied ragged streaks of masking fluid to the paper before adding washes of colour on top. The paint adheres to the paper but not to the masked areas, creating a speckled pattern that suggests weathered stone and wood.

Because watercolour is a transparent medium it is impossible to paint a light colour over a dark one; you have to plan where the light or white areas are to be and paint around them. But suppose you are painting, for example, a seascape and you want to reserve small flecks of white paper to represent sparkling highlights on the surface of the water; attempting to apply broad, smooth washes while working around these tiny shapes can be a fiddly business. An effective solution is to temporarily seal off the white areas with masking fluid, allowing the rest of the surface to be painted over freely.

Masking fluid is a liquid, rubbery solution which is sold in bottles. Simply apply the fluid with a brush over the areas which are to remain white. Once it is dry (this takes only a minute or so) you can brush washes freely over the area without having to be careful to avoid the white shapes. When the painting is completely dry, the rubbery mask is easily removed by rubbing it off with your finger or with a clean eraser.

A word of warning – never allow masking fluid to dry on your brush as it will ruin it. Wash the brush in warm, soapy water immediately after use to prevent the rubber solution from drying hard and clogging up the bristles. It is a good idea to keep an old brush handy for applying masking fluid, or buy a cheap synthetic one specially for the purpose.

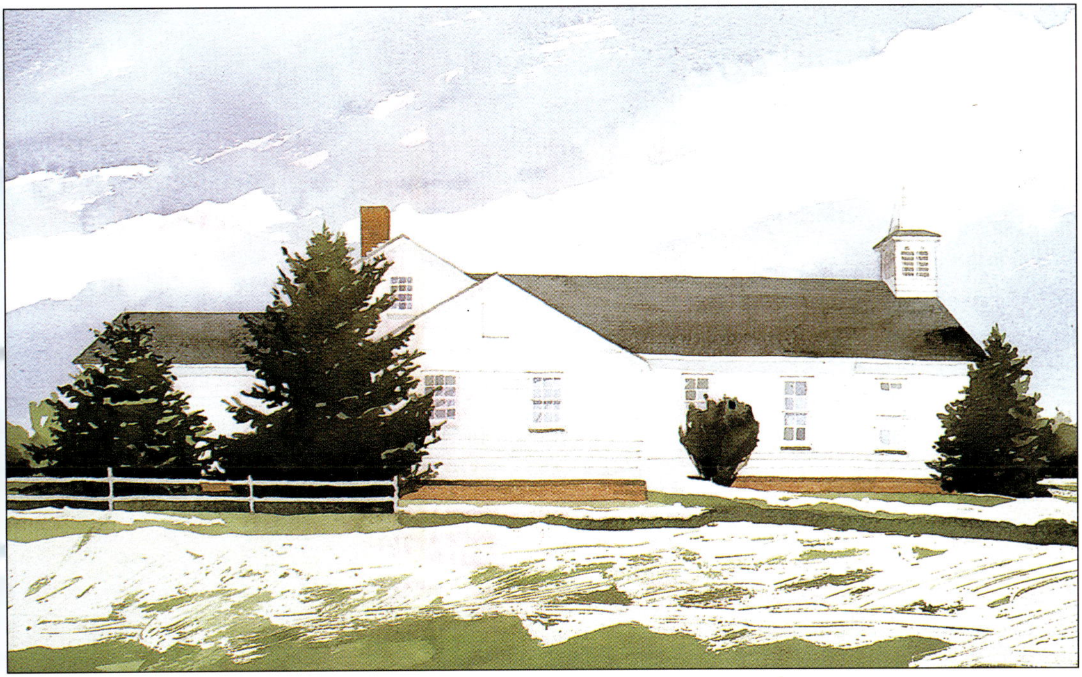

Snow in Cape Cod

Masking fluid is essential for preserving small, intricate white shapes in a watercolour wash, leaving you free to paint over the masked areas. But you can also use it to retain large areas of the paper which need to be white – as in this winter scene, where blades of grass are peeping through the blanket of snow.

YOU WILL NEED

- *Stretched sheet of 140lb (285gsm) Not surface watercolour paper, 22 x 15in (55.8 x 38.1cm)*
- *Two old brushes (one small and one large) for applying masking fluid*
- *No. 12 round brush*
- *No. 3 round brush*
- *Masking fluid*
- *HB pencil*
- *Ruler*

WATERCOLOUR PAINTS IN THE FOLLOWING COLOURS

- *French ultramarine*
- *Cobalt blue*
- *Payne's gray*
- *Yellow ochre*
- *Brown madder alizarin*
- *Raw umber*
- *Sap green*

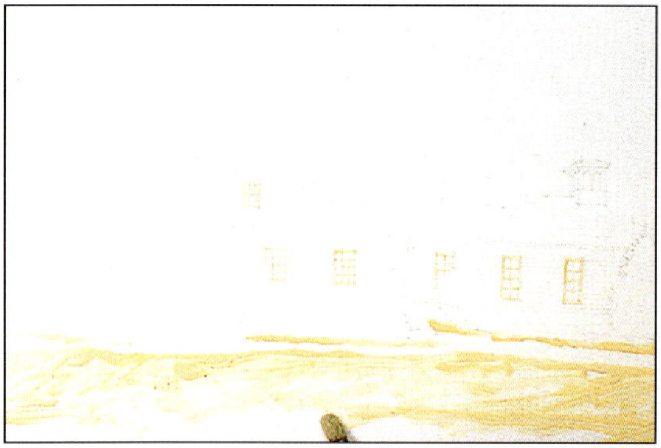

1 Sketch out the scene with an HB pencil. If necessary, use a ruler to help you draw the horizontal lines of the wooden clapboarding on the front of the house. Mask out the window frames, using a small brush to apply the masking fluid. For the large patch of snow in the foreground, use a larger brush to apply masking fluid with broad, uneven diagonal strokes. Leave small gaps between the strokes; when painted, these will represent patches of grass peeping through the blanket of snow. Leave the masking fluid to dry for approximately 10 minutes.

2 For the sky, mix a bright blue wash made up of cobalt blue heavily diluted with water. Apply this with broad, diagonal strokes using a no. 12 round brush, leaving patches of untouched paper to represent the clouds. Soften some of the cloud edges with a damp brush. Paint the glass in the windows with the same wash, using a no. 3 round brush.

Helpful Hint

TO AVOID THE RISK OF DAMAGING YOUR BEST WATERCOLOUR BRUSHES, USE OLD BRUSHES, OR CHEAP SYNTHETIC ONES, FOR APPLYING MASKING FLUID.

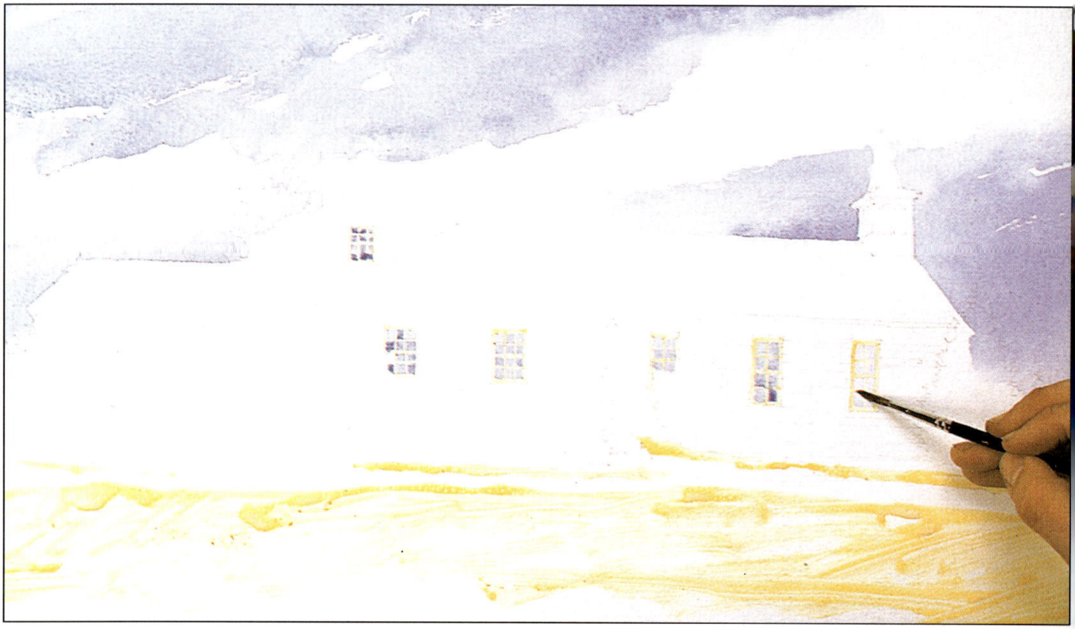

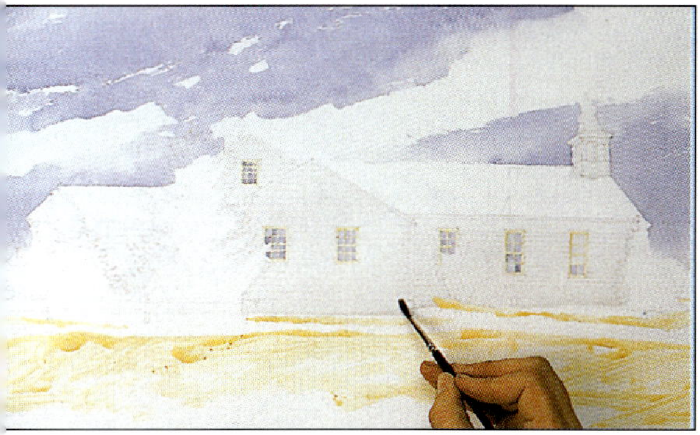

3

Mix a very light, watery wash of Payne's gray warmed with a touch of yellow ochre and apply this to the front of the house and the bell tower on the roof with a no. 3 round brush.

4

For the brick detailing at the base of the house walls mix a light wash of brown madder alizarin and yellow ochre. Use the same colour mix to paint the chimney on the left. Paint the roof with a diluted wash of Payne's gray.

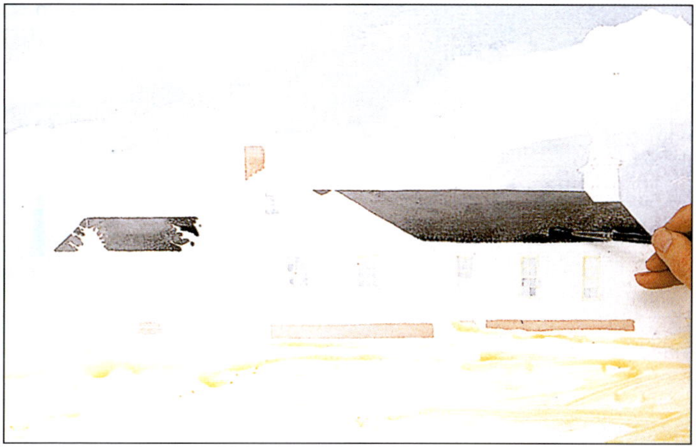

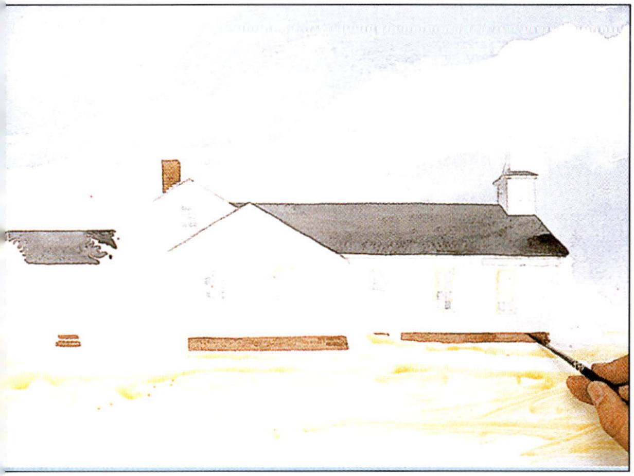

5

Paint the gable ends and the shadows on the bell tower with Payne's gray. For the shadows under the roof and under the windows use a pale blue-grey mixed from French ultramarine with just a little Payne's gray. Suggest the pattern of the brickwork on the walls and chimney using a mixture of brown madder alizarin and yellow ochre, darkened with a touch of raw umber. Apply the paint with short horizontal strokes, leaving tiny gaps to show the pattern of the bricks.

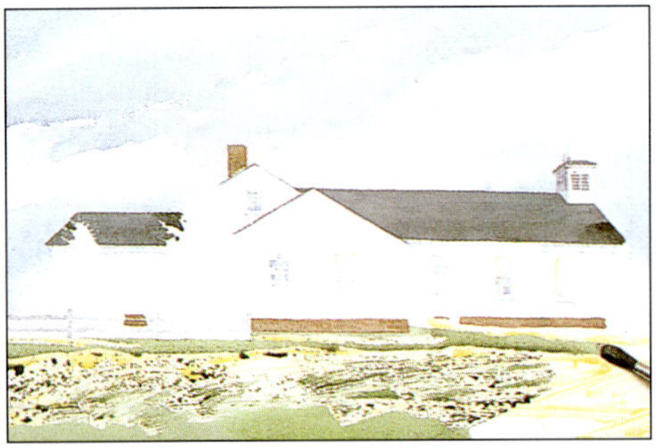

6 Mix a dark wash of Payne's gray and add some texture to the roof with a series of fine, closely spaced horizontal lines. Paint the fence with a heavily diluted wash of Payne's gray warmed with a little raw umber. Use the same wash, but less diluted, to pick out the windows on the bell tower. For the grass in the foreground, prepare a wash of yellow ochre, sap green and raw umber. Using a no. 12 round brush, apply the wash over the masking fluid using broad brushstrokes. The masking fluid will resist the paint, protecting the paper underneath. Leave until thoroughly dry.

7 Paint the fir trees in the foreground with sap green, raw umber and Payne's gray, changing the proportions of the colours in the mix to give variation to the greens. Use the tip of the brush to create the effect of leaves and thin branches. Notice how the foliage is darker towards the base of the trees glimpsed through the fencing. For the trees in the distance, use raw umber and a touch of sap green. Leave the painting to dry.

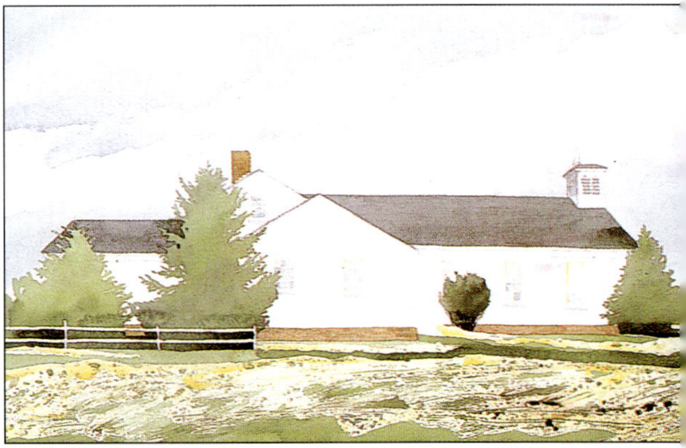

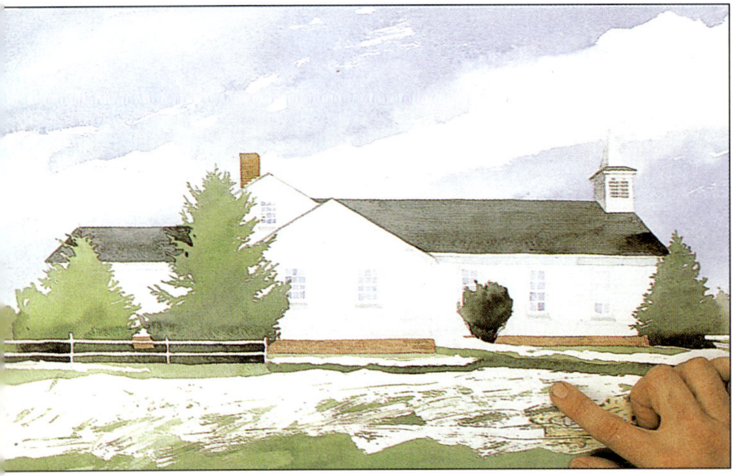

8 When the painting is completely dry you can remove the masking fluid. Rub firmly over the masked areas with your fingertip (make sure your hands are clean and free from grease) until the rubbery mask comes away, revealing the white paper beneath. Here you can see how the green paint has settled in the gaps left in the mask in step 1, giving the effect of patches of grass in the melting snow.

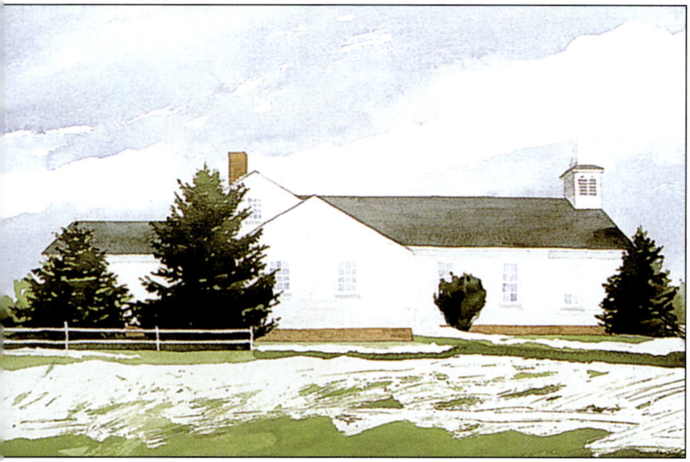

9 Use the same wash, but with a little cobalt blue and a lot more water added, to touch in the dark reflections in the windows. To finish, pick out the top edge of the brick detailing with a darker mix of the same wash. Leave the painting to dry thoroughly, then define some of the lines between the clapboard panels using an HB pencil.

Helpful Hint

IF YOU MAKE A MISTAKE WHEN APPLYING MASKING FLUID, SIMPLY WAIT FOR IT TO DRY AND THEN RUB IT OFF WITH YOUR FINGERTIP OR AN ERASER AND START AGAIN.

10 To complete the painting, mix a dark wash of sap green, raw umber and Payne's gray and work back over the trees with the no. 3 round brush, leaving some of the lighter green wash showing through.

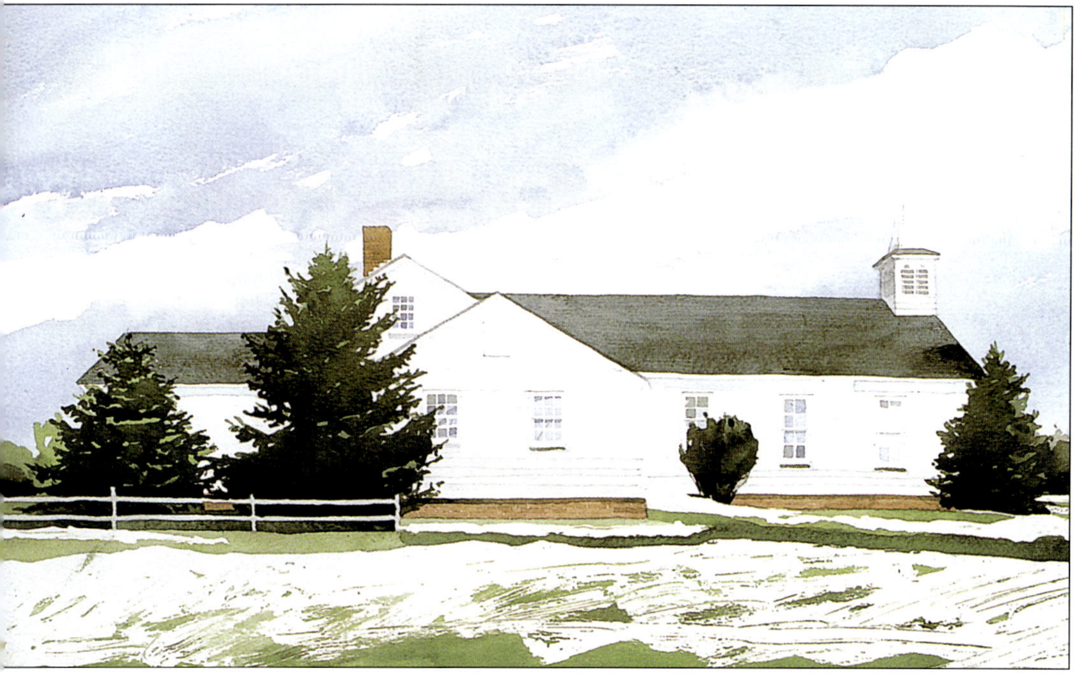

Working Light to Dark

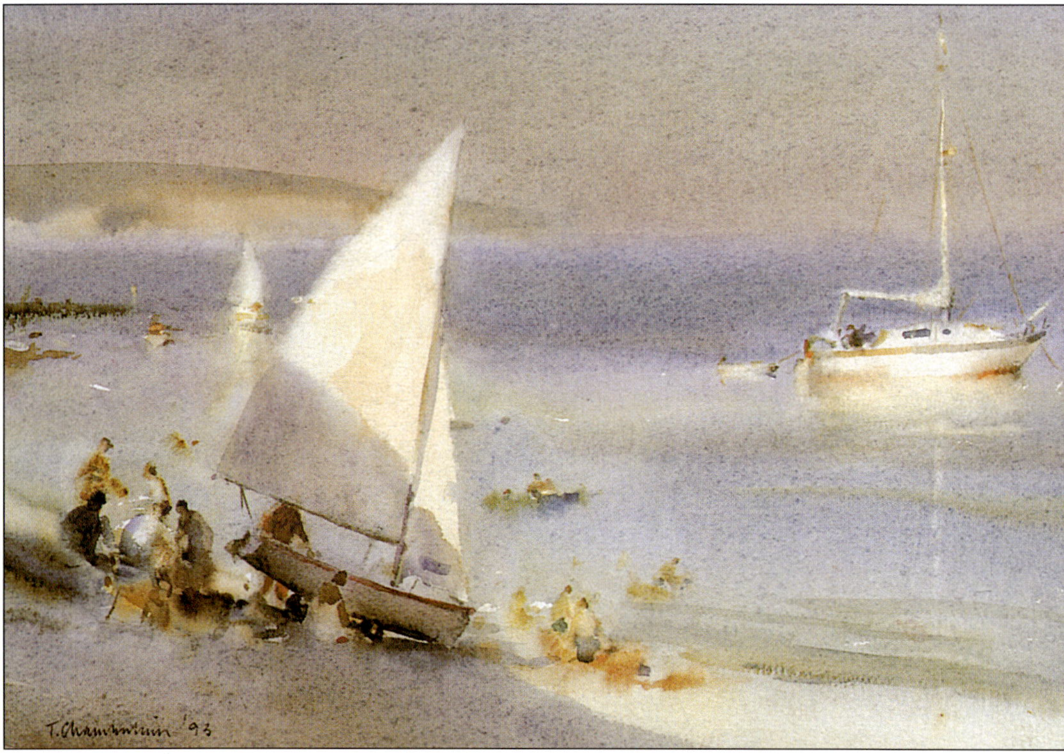

Trevor Chamberlain
SHADED BEACH, BEER
The impression of sparkling light in this painting is achieved by brushing thin, transparent washes onto dampened paper and letting them settle undisturbed. Light reflects off the white paper and up through the colours, giving them a marvellous luminosity.

With an opaque medium such as oil paint you can build up dark and light areas in any order. But because watercolour is transparent, light colours cannot be applied over dark ones; if you make a colour too dark in the first instance, it is difficult and messy to correct afterwards. The best method is to start off with the lightest of washes and build up gradually in a series of further washes to the density you require, leaving uncovered any areas that are to be left as white highlights.

The process of overlaying transparent washes results in richer, more resonant passages than can be achieved by painting with a single, flat wash of dense colour; light seems to reflect through each layer of colour, almost giving the appearance of being lit from within.

Drying

This technique requires a little patience because it is essential to allow each layer of paint to dry before applying the next; if you do not, the colours will simply mix and the crispness and definition will be lost. You can use a hairdryer to speed up the process, but avoid using it on really wet paint as it could blow your carefully placed wash all over the paper.

Testing colours

The characteristic freshness and delicacy of watercolour is lost if there is too much over-painting. Always test a colour on scrap paper before committing it to the painting, then apply it quickly, with one sweep of the brush, so that it does not disturb the paint below. A few layers of colour applied with confidence, will be more successful than colours muddied by constant reworking.

Reserving white areas

Working from light to dark means you have to establish where the lightest areas are at the outset and preserve them as your painting progresses. It is possible to remove paint by lifting out with a damp brush or sponge, but you can rarely retrieve the pristine whiteness of the paper with this method because the pigment usually sinks into the fibres of the paper and leaves a faint stain. It is wise therefore to start with a light pencil drawing to establish the correct position and shape of the highlights to be reserved. Small or awkwardly shaped highlights which are too difficult to work around can be preserved by masking them out with masking fluid prior to painting.

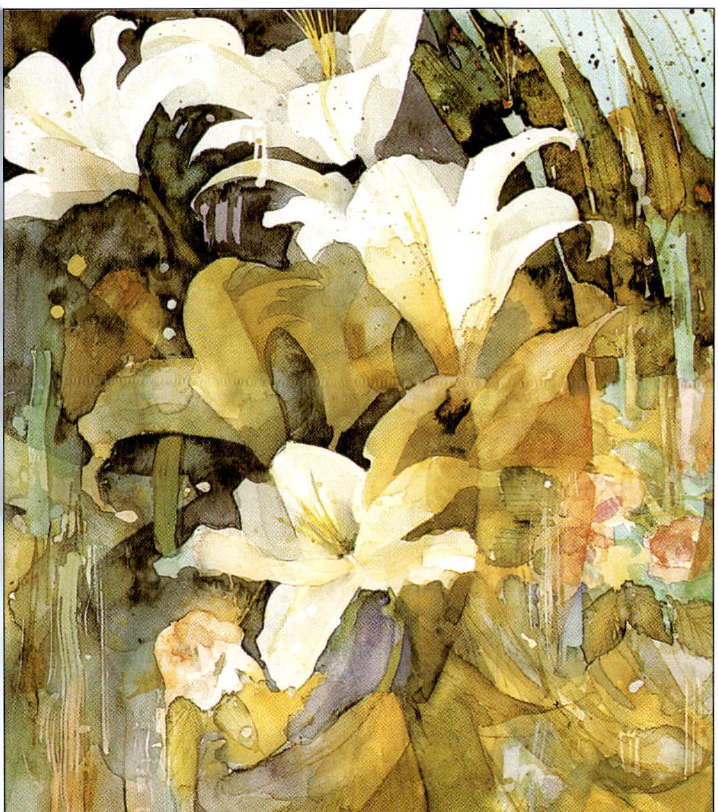

Shirley Trevena
WHITE LILIES AND PINK ROSES
Surrounded by dark tones in the background, these pure white lilies appear particularly striking. If you look closely, you will see that in fact the 'white' petals consist mainly of very thin translucent washes of warm and cool grey; white paper is reserved only for the brightest highlights.

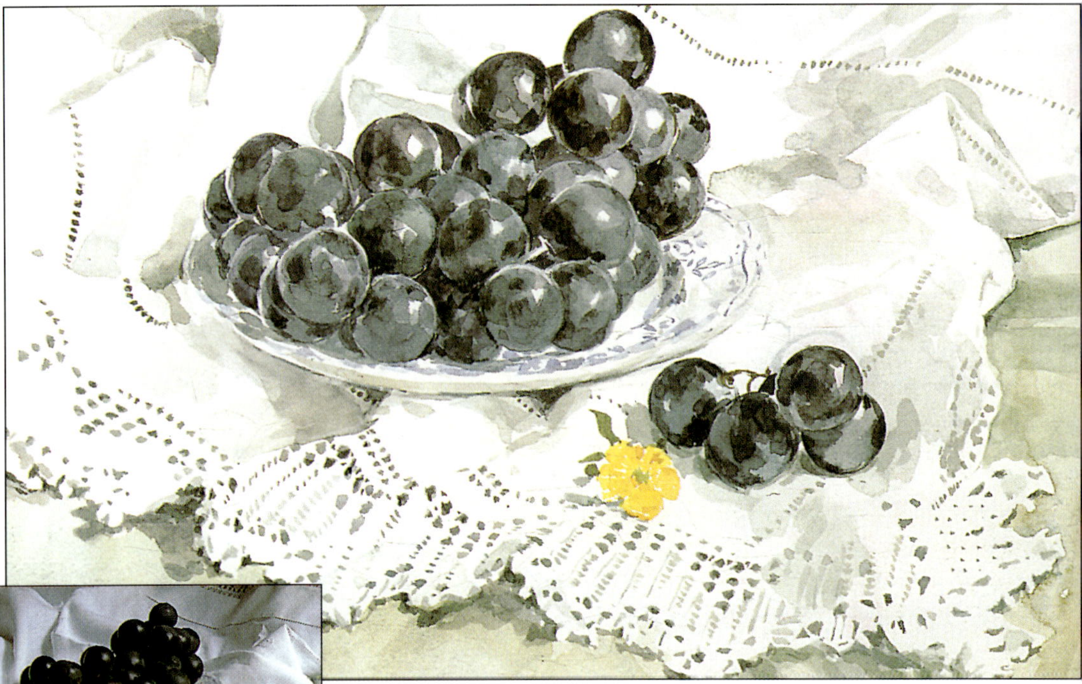

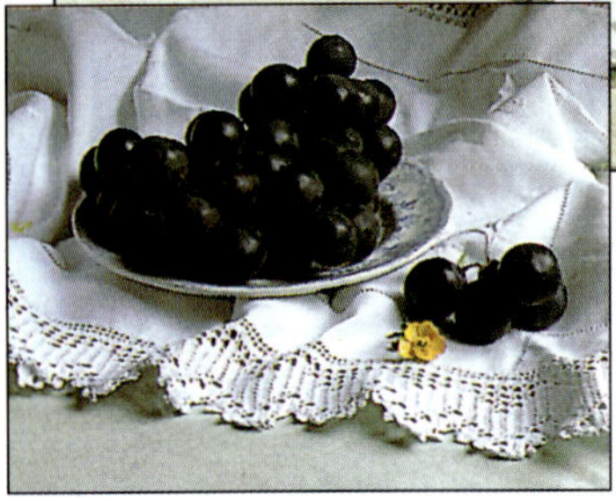

Black Grapes, White Lace

YOU WILL NEED

- Sheet of 140lb (285gsm) Not surface watercolour paper 17 x 13.5in (43.2 x 34.3cm)
- No. 3 round brush
- No. 5 round brush

Working from light to dark is the classical method of building up a watercolour painting. In this demonstration you will learn how to apply overlapping strokes and washes of transparent colour in order to create a convincing impression of three-dimensional form.

WATERCOLOUR PAINTS IN THE FOLLOWING COLOURS

- *Raw sienna*
- *Prussian blue*
- *Alizarin crimson*
- *Sap green*
- *Cerulean*
- *French ultramarine*
- *Cadmium lemon*
- *Cadmium yellow*
- *Viridian*
- *Raw umber*

1 Use a dilute mix of raw sienna and French ultramarine to position the plate and the main folds in the cloth with a no. 3 round brush. Mix a thin wash of ultramarine, Prussian blue, alizarin crimson and a spot of sap green to make a grey-purple and start painting the grapes, leaving white paper for the light parts. Build up the darker tones with overlaid washes, adding a little cerulean blue in places. Add more Prussian blue and alizarin crimson to the wash and paint the dark shapes between the grapes.

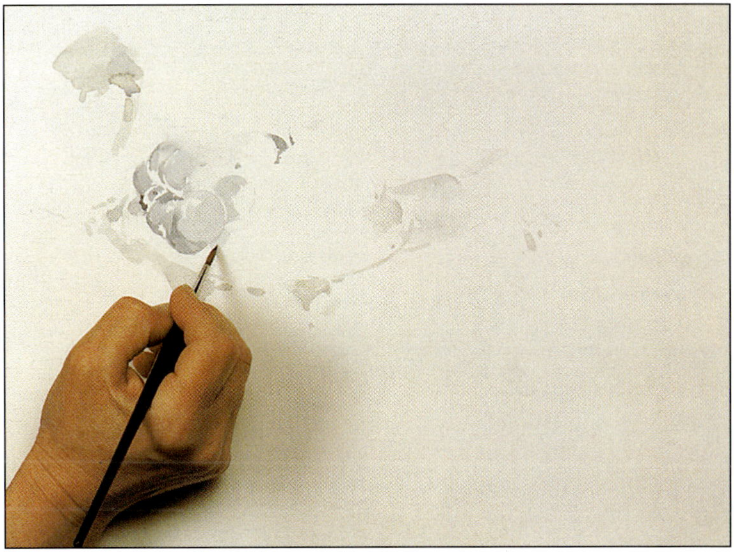

Helpful Hint

IF YOU MAKE A MISTAKE, FLOOD THE AREA WITH WATER AND THEN BLOT OFF THE OFFENDING PAINT WITH CRUMPLED TISSUE OR A CLEAN BRUSH.

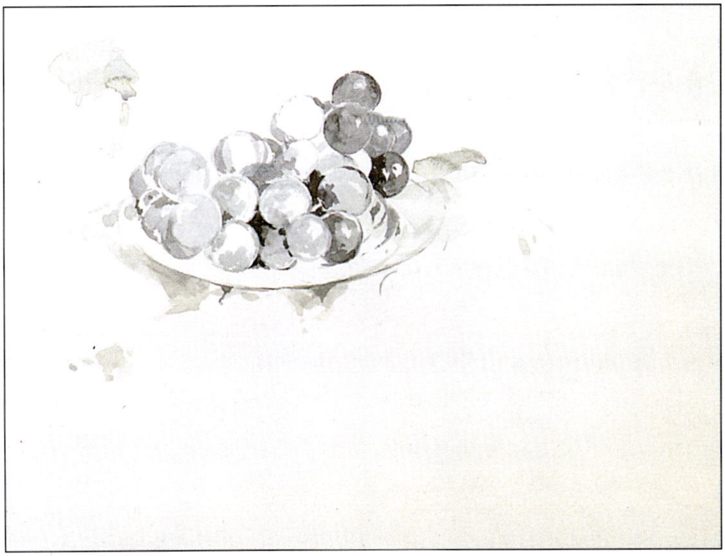

2 With the same light and dark washes used in step 1, continue to define the rounded forms of the grapes. Work methodically from light to dark, painting carefully around the sharpest highlights. Define the outline of the plate and deepen the shadow beneath it with a thin mix of Prussian blue, ultramarine, raw sienna and a touch of alizarin crimson. Soften the edge of the shadow using a damp brush.

3 Continue building up the darks on the grapes, deepening the grey-purple mix with a little raw sienna in places. This method of working from light to dark is very effective – the grapes look luscious enough to eat! Now pick out the pattern on the plate with cerulean blue and give more definition to the rim with the same grey-blue wash used earlier. Loosely outline the stray group of grapes on the cloth with the same pale wash used in step 1. In the detail (right) we see how the artist models the forms of the grapes with small, curved brushstrokes applied wet-on-dry. With the dark tones in place, the small flecks of bare paper read as bright, shiny highlights.

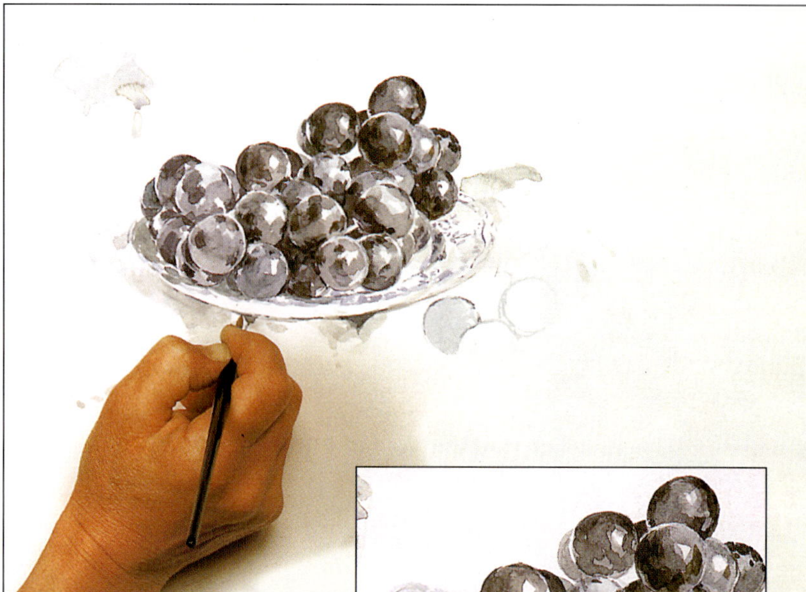

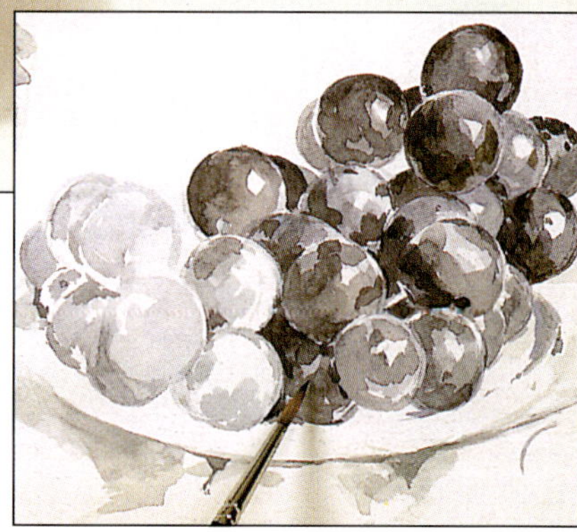

4 Continue painting the grapes in the foreground, using the same colour mixes used for the main bunch and leaving tiny white highlights. Now mix up a very dilute wash of raw sienna, ultamarine and a little burnt umber and put in more of the folds in the cloth with the no. 5 brush. Define its lacy edging by painting the shadows it casts. Use a darker version of the same wash to pick out the tiny decorative holes in the cloth with the tip of the no. 3 brush.

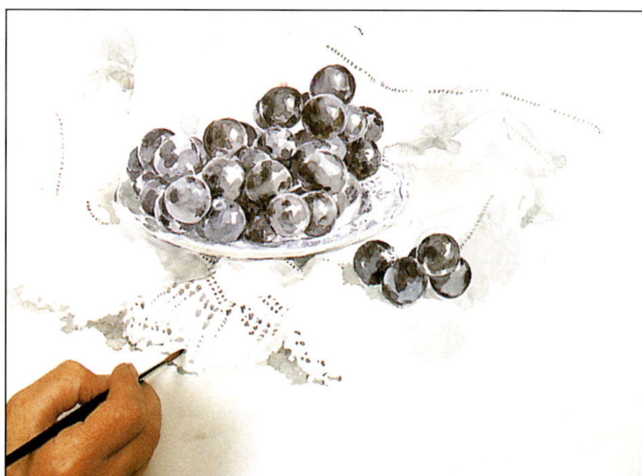

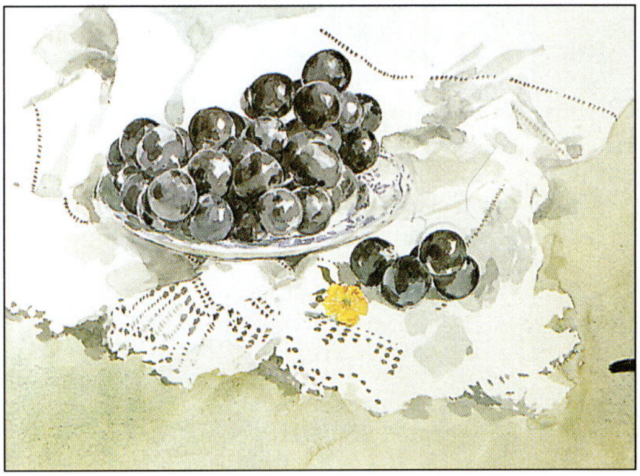

5 Paint the buttercup with mixtures of cadmium lemon and cadmium yellow, leaving tiny flecks of white paper for the highlights on the shiny petals. Paint the leaves and stem with sap green, alizarin crimson and just a touch of viridian. Apply clean water over the area of the green cloth using the no. 5 brush. Mix a light wash of sap green, cerulean and cadmium yellow and brush this onto the wet paper with broad, sweeping strokes.

6 Switch to the no. 3 brush and add the darkest tones to the small group of grapes with a dark blue-purple mix of Prussian blue, raw sienna, cerulean and raw umber. Paint the stalk with a darker version of the green used for the buttercup stalk. Go back to the lace, working on the edge in the foreground. Vary the sizes and tones of the holes to describe the folds in the fabric and the soft shadows falling across its surface.

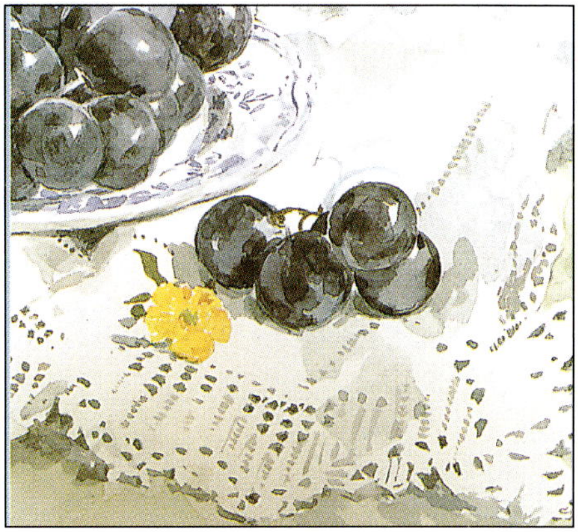

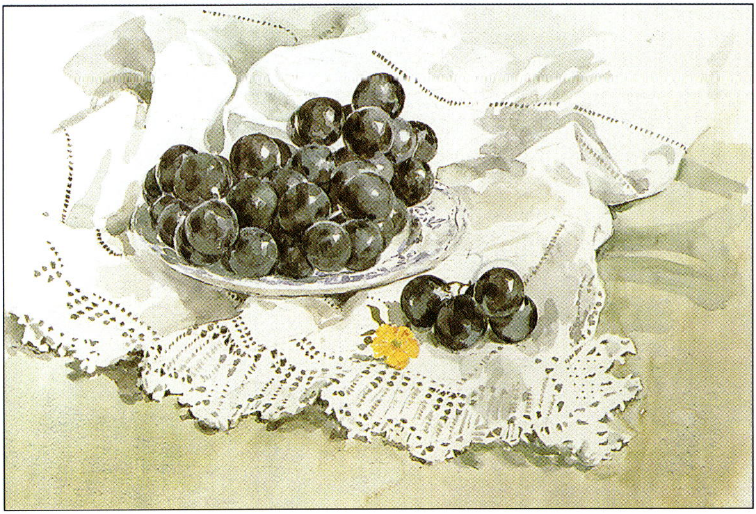

7 To finish, darken the shadows round the edges of the lace cloth using a mix of Prussian blue, raw sienna and just a touch of alizarin crimson. Use the same wash but with more water added to go over the shadows in the cloth to emphasize the shadowy folds in the fabric.

Painting Wet-in-Wet

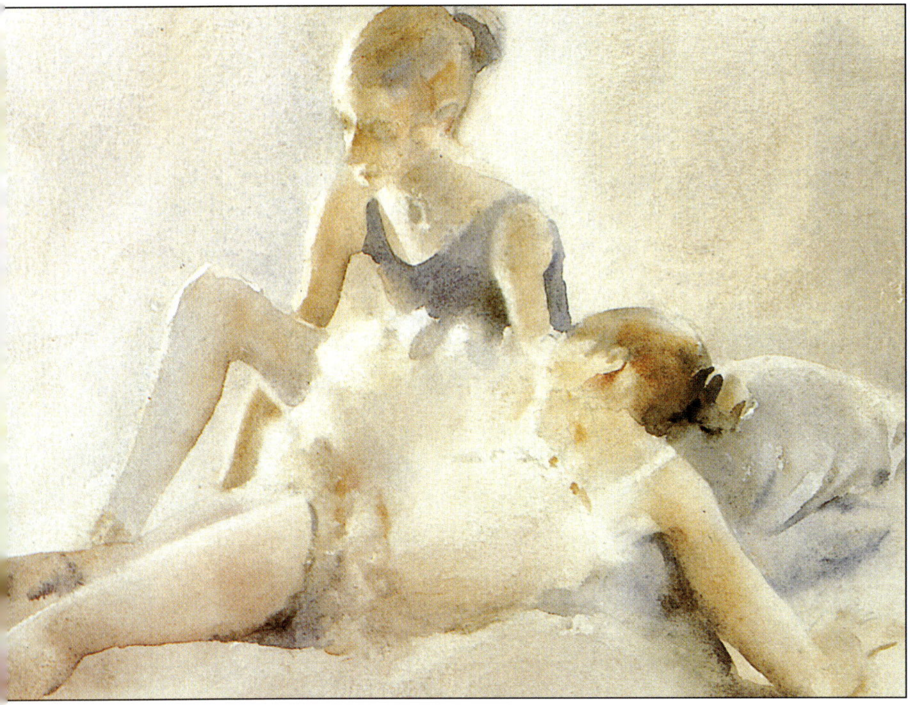

Trevor Chamberlain
BEFORE BALLET CLASS
In this charming study soft, diffused washes perfectly capture the gauzy, semi-transparent fabric of the ballet dancers' tutus.

Wet-in-wet is one of the most beautiful and expressive techniques in watercolour painting. When colours are applied to a wet or damp surface they merge gently into each other and dry with a soft, hazy quality. This is particularly effective in painting skies and water, producing gentle gradations of tone that evoke the ever-changing quality of the light.

Subjects

The wet-in-wet technique is particularly effective when painting large expanses of soft colour, for example in skies and misty landscapes, producing gentle gradations of tone and hue that capture the ever-changing quality of outdoor light. When painting delicate or hazy subjects such as flowers, fruits and distant landscape elements, wet-in-wet allows the colours to blend naturally on the paper without leaving a hard edge.

Preparation

For this technique it is best to use a heavy-grade paper (200lb/410gsm or over) which will bear up to frequent applications of water and paint without wrinkling. Lighter papers will need to be stretched and firmly taped to a board. Moisten the paper with water using a large brush or soft sponge. Blot off any excess water with a tissue so that the paper is evenly damp, with no water lying on the surface. Tilt the board at a slight angle so that the colours can flow gently down the paper; if it is laid flat there is a danger of washes creeping backwards and creating unwanted marks and blotches, known as 'blooms'.

Painting method

Working wet-in-wet requires confidence because you can only control the paint to a certain extent. Large brushes work best as they hold plenty of paint and enable you to lay in broad sweeps of colour. Charge your brush fully and work quickly and lightly, allowing the colours to spread and diffuse of their own accord. A common mistake when working wet-in-wet is to dilute the colour too much, with the result that the finished painting appears weak and insipid. Because the paper is already wet you can use quite rich paint – it will soften on the paper but retain its richness. You must also compensate for the fact that the colour will dry lighter than it appears when wet.

Make sure you mix plenty of paint – there is nothing more frustrating than running out of colour halfway through and having to stop to mix some more!

Michael Chaplin
THE ITALIAN ALPS
This is another example of the skilful use of the wet-in-wet technique, used in a robust manner to capture the atmosphere of mist and rain in the mountains.

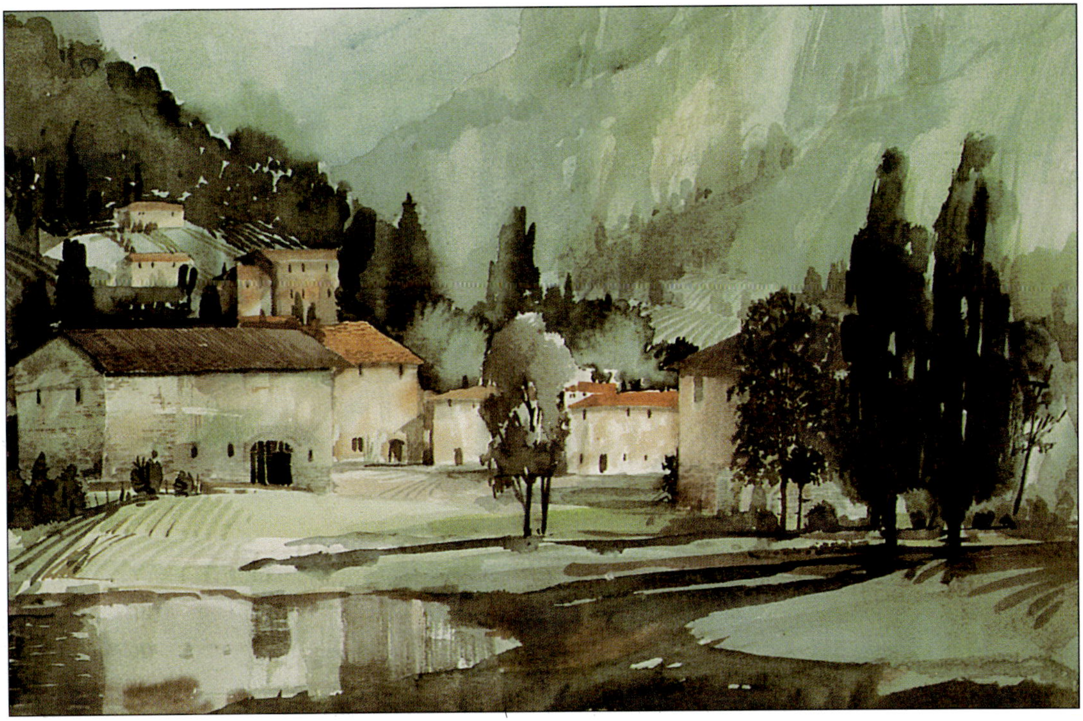

Flowers in Blue Jar

This delightful jug of flowers is more a lyrical impression of the subject than a literal interpretation. The artist worked rapidly and intuitively, flooding the colours onto wet paper to create softly blended, hazy colours that merge and flow into one another. It is an exciting method of watercolour painting as the results are unpredictable, but also highly expressive.

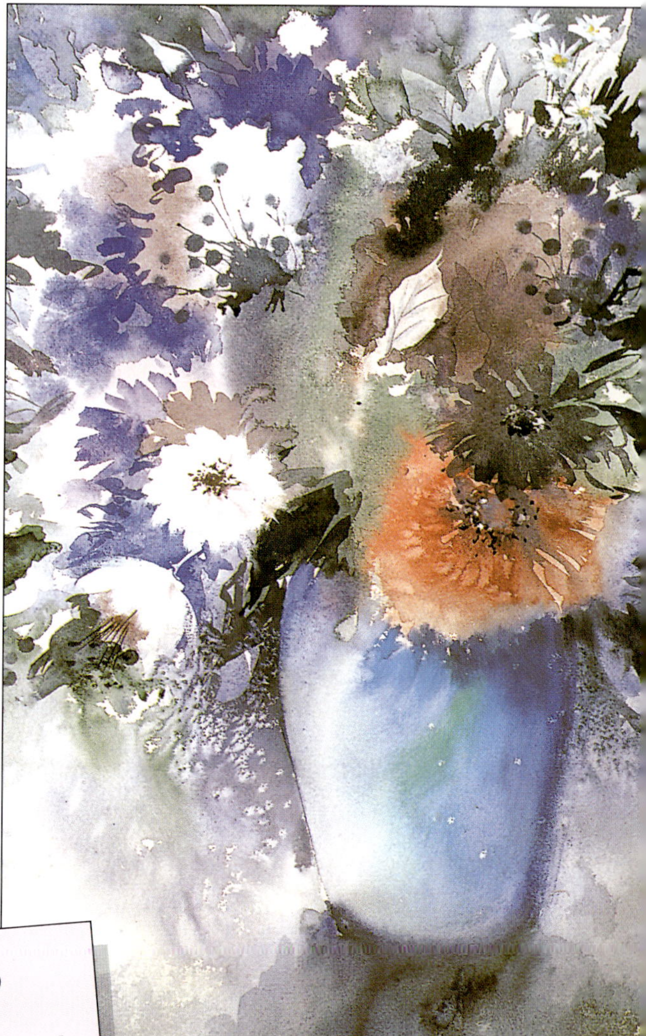

YOU WILL NEED

- ✔ *Stretced sheet of 140lb (285gsm) Not surface watercolour paper, 17½ x 22in (44.4 x 55.8cm)*
- ✔ *No. 16 round brush*
- ✔ *No. 5 round brush*
- ✔ *Drinking straw*
- ✔ *Table salt*

WATERCOLOUR PAINTS IN THE FOLLOWING COLOURS

- *Indigo*
- *French ultramarine*
- *Alizarin crimson*
- *Winsor blue*
- *Winsor green*
- *Hooker's green dark*
- *Cadmium yellow*
- *Permanent white*

1 Tilt your board at a slight angle, then wet the entire sheet of paper with clean water using a no.16 round brush. With the same brush, and working quickly, drop in separate blobs of colour to suggest flower heads. Use indigo for the blue-purple flowers, alizarin crimson mixed with a little indigo for the deep purple flowers and diluted alizarin crimson for the pink flower heads. Mix French ultramarine with indigo for the blue background areas and, for the foliage, use Hooker's green dark mixed with indigo. The colours will spread and merge on the wet surface, leaving lighter areas in between that suggest tiny white flowers.

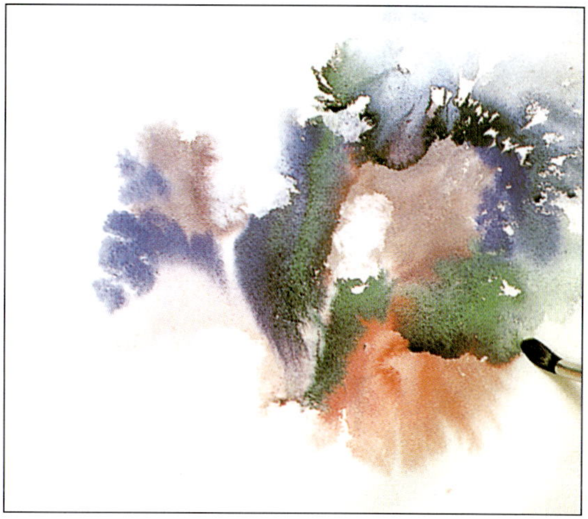

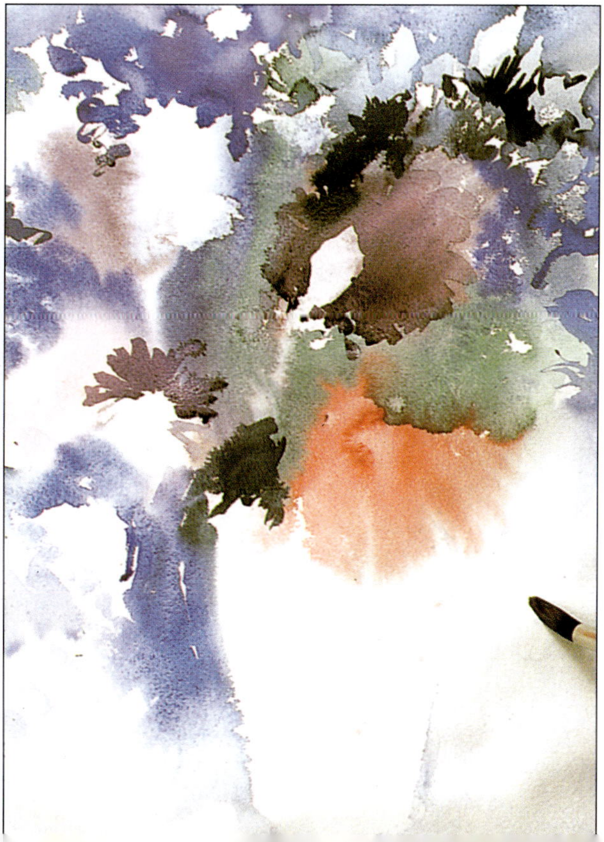

Helpful Hint

SPEED IS CRUCIAL WHEN WORKING WET-IN-WET, SO HAVE YOUR WASHES READY-MIXED IN DEEP-WELLED PALETTES OR SAUCERS BEFORE YOU START PAINTING. REMEMBER TO MIX UP PLENTY OF PAINT SO YOU DON'T RUN OUT AT AN INCONVENIENT MOMENT.

2 Move quickly across the painting, adding dabs of ultramarine, alizarin and indigo and cutting around the shapes of the white flowers. Speed is essential – the paper must be wet enough to allow the colours to spread. Don't attempt to paint the flowers realistically – let your intuition and imagination be your guide. Use the tip of the brush to give an impression of the forms of leaves and petals. Define the form of the jug by painting around it with a diluted wash of French ultramarine.

3 Put in some darks behind the group to give it definition. Use various combinations of indigo, Winsor blue and ultramarine. Mix Winsor blue and indigo and deepen the tones around the jug. With a stronger mix of the same colour, indicate the shadow cast by the jug to anchor it to the table. This detail shows the use of a clever 'trick of the trade'. Sprinkle a few grains of salt into the wet wash and leave to dry for 10 minutes. The salt absorbs the paint, leaving tiny, pale star shapes which add subtle texture and suggest small white flowers.

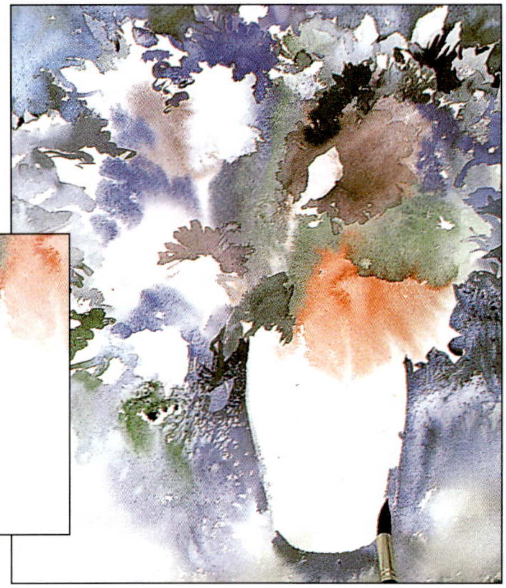

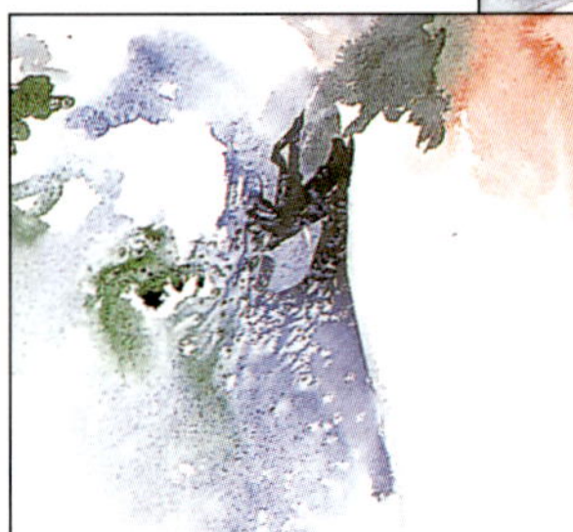

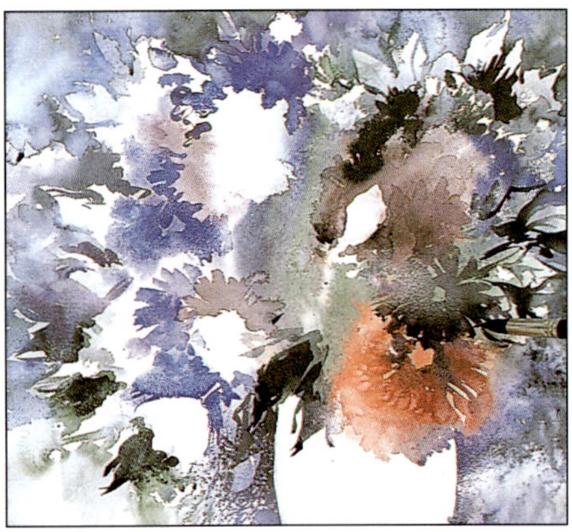

4 Brush some water over the large pink flower and drop in a darker wash of alizarin crimson and a little indigo to add tonal contrast. Describe the petals with the tip of the brush and add soft-edged highlights by sprinkling on a little salt to absorb the paint. Leave to dry, then mix a wash of alizarin and indigo and add some dark flowers and foliage for contrast.

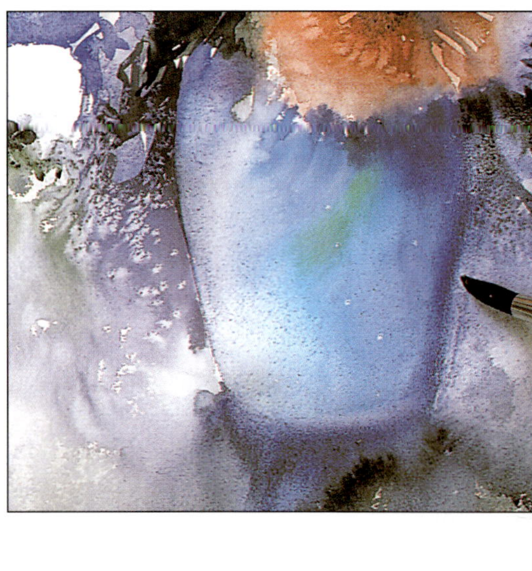

5 Paint the jar with a strong aquamarine mixed from Winsor blue and Winsor green, letting the colour fade out towards the edges. Paint the shadow on the right with ultramarine and indigo; let the colour diffuse softly into the aquamarine wash, describing the rounded form of the jar. Enrich the shadow on the table with a loose wash of ultramarine and indigo.

6

Use a mix of Winsor green, Winsor blue and indigo to suggest the dark foliage on the left edge of the arrangement with loose brushstrokes. Using the same mix, suggest a few seed heads by dabbing on the paint with your fingertip to make small blots and using a drinking straw to 'paint' the dried stalks (see detail). To create the delicate stalks carrying the seed heads, place one end of a drinking straw over the wet blots of paint and gently blow through the other end, to send tiny trails of paint spreading outwards.

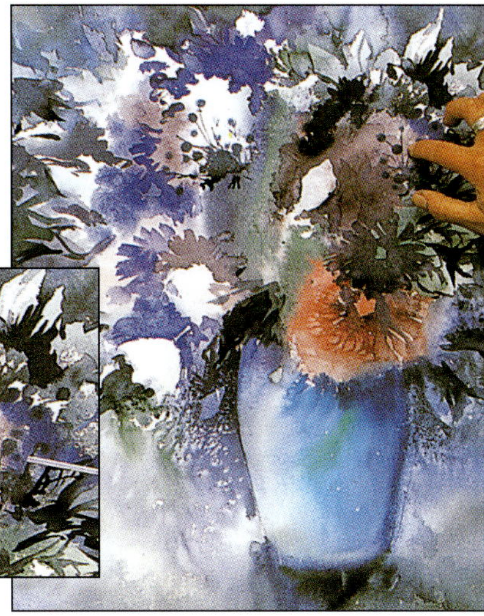

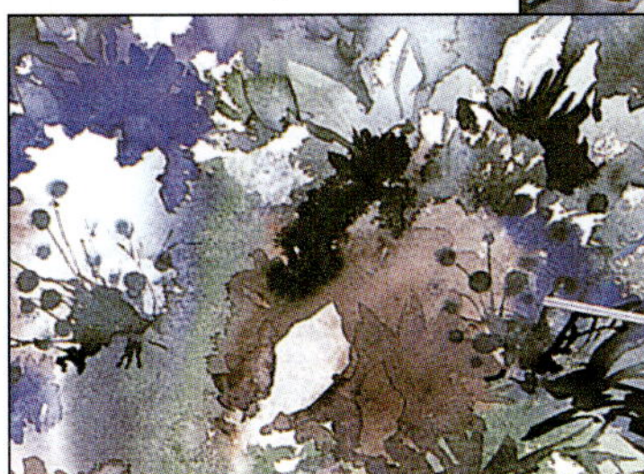

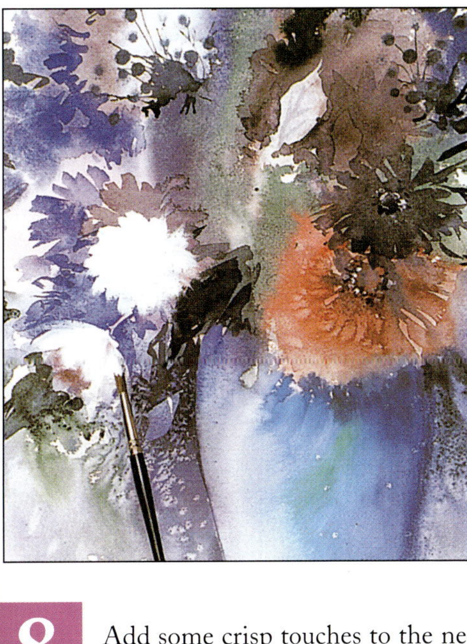

7

With a no. 5 round brush, paint the dark centres of the flowers at the front of the arrangement. Use a little white gouache paint to pick out the tiny white daisies at the top right, and to define the nearer white flowers at the bottom left. Paint the centres of the daisies with cadmium yellow.

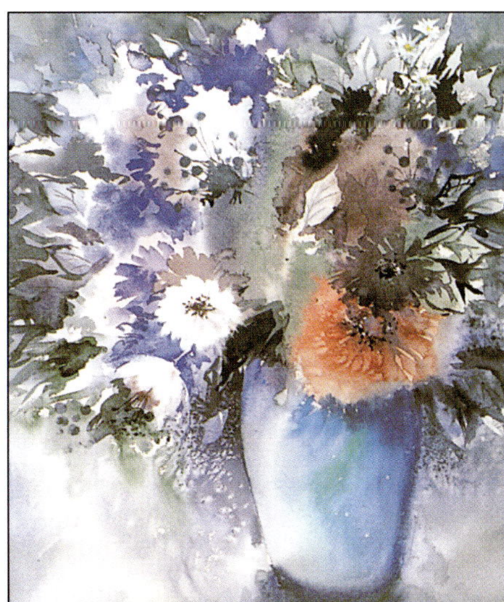

8

Add some crisp touches to the nearer flowers to bring them forward. Mix alizarin and a touch of indigo and dot in the stamens and centres of the large daisies using the tip of your brush. Finally, use a light tone of indigo to suggest veins on some of the leaves.

Painting Water

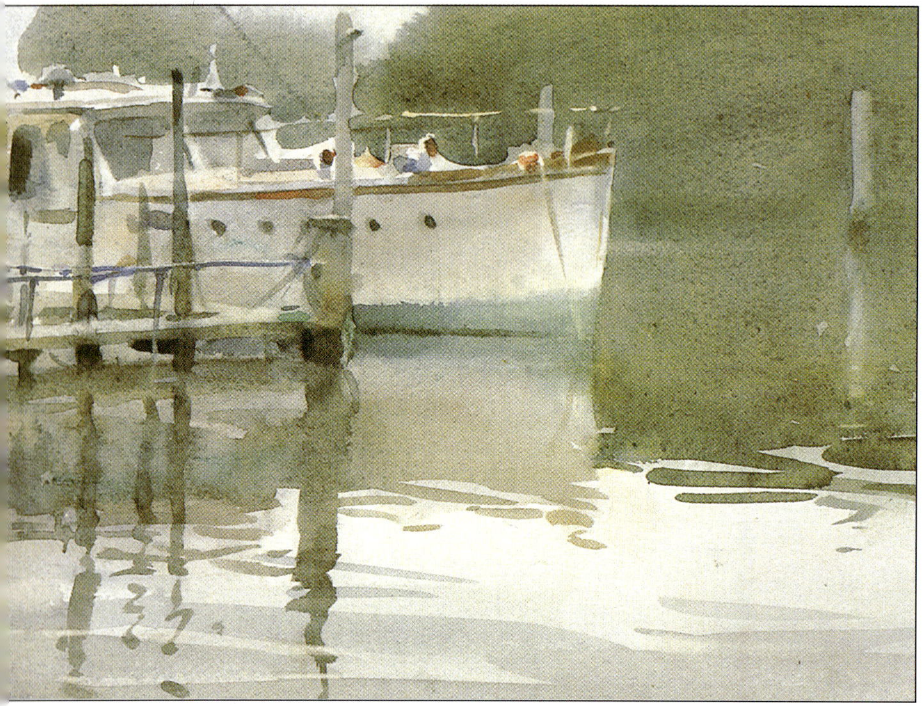

Trevor Chamberlain
THAMES REFLECTIONS
Capturing the smooth, light-reflecting surface of calm water means keeping your colours fresh and clear and letting your brush-strokes and washes settle undisturbed.

Lakes, rivers, streams and ponds are attractive but elusive subjects, being constantly on the move; ripples and eddies come and go; colours change; reflections stretch and shrink; waves break and re-form before you have a chance to put brush to paper. It is easy to become confused and end up including too much detail in your painting, with the result that the water looks more like a patterned carpet!

The secret of painting water is to seek out the major shapes of light and dark and omit all superfluous details; water looks wetter when painted simply. You've probably heard the saying 'less is more', and nowhere does this apply more readily than in the painting of water. Achieving the smooth, glassy appearance of calm water requires surprisingly little effort; often just a few sweeping strokes with a broad brush on damp paper are enough to convey the illusion.

Painting methods

Watercolour has a unique transparency and freshness which is ideally suited to painting water. Broad, flat washes are ideal for conveying the still surface of a lake or river, and a broken, drybrush stroke dragged across rough white paper is a wonderfully economical means of suggesting highlights or patches of wind-ruffled water in the distance. Masking fluid is useful here, as you can block out small highlights on the water's surface while you work freely on the surrounding washes.

Try brushing your colours directly onto dampened paper and letting them merge together wet-in-wet for a soft, diffused impression of a misty lake. Ripples and reflections can be described in a kind of shorthand with calligraphic brushmarks and squiggles, letting the action of your brush suggest the water's undulating movement.

Reflections

If you remember that reflections obey certain laws of perspective, you will find it easier to paint them convincingly. For example, you will notice that the reflection of a light object is always slightly darker than the object itself – and vice versa. An object standing upright in the water produces a reflection of the same length, but the reflection of an object leaning towards you appears longer, and that of an object leaning away from you appears shorter. When the water's surface is disturbed, reflections break up and appear longer than the object reflected. These broken reflections, too, follow the laws of perspective; as they recede into the distance they gradually appear smaller, flatter and more closely spaced.

Dennis Gilbert
ISLE OF WIGHT
Here the effect of sunlit surf is skilfully created by skimming the brush lightly over the paper to create broken strokes and leaving small flecks of the white paper unpainted.

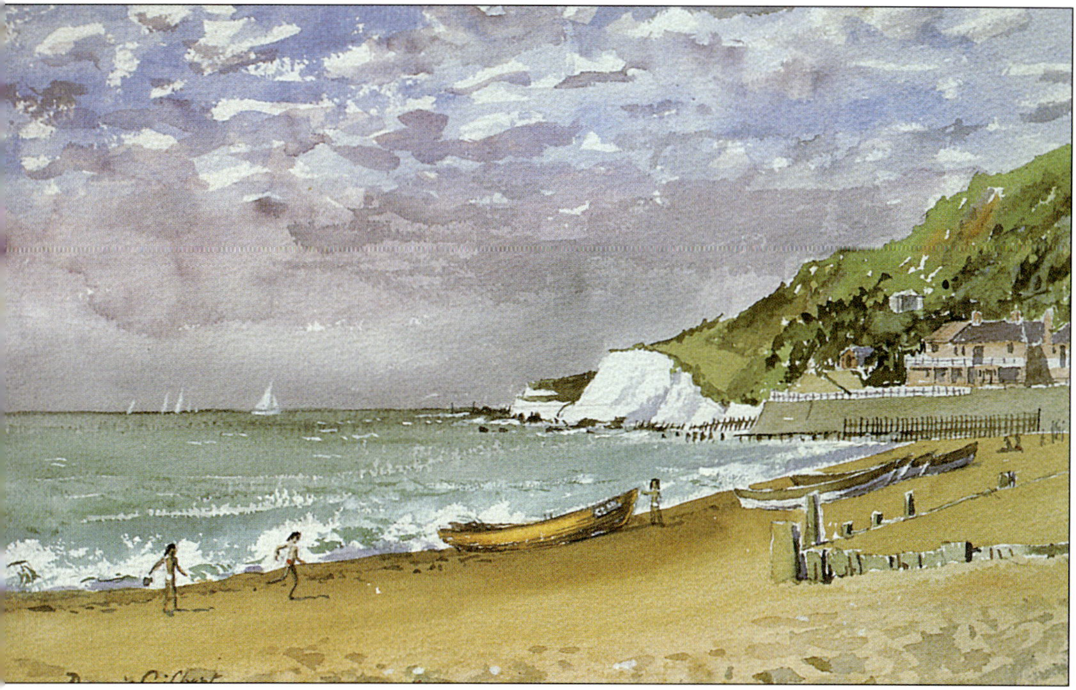

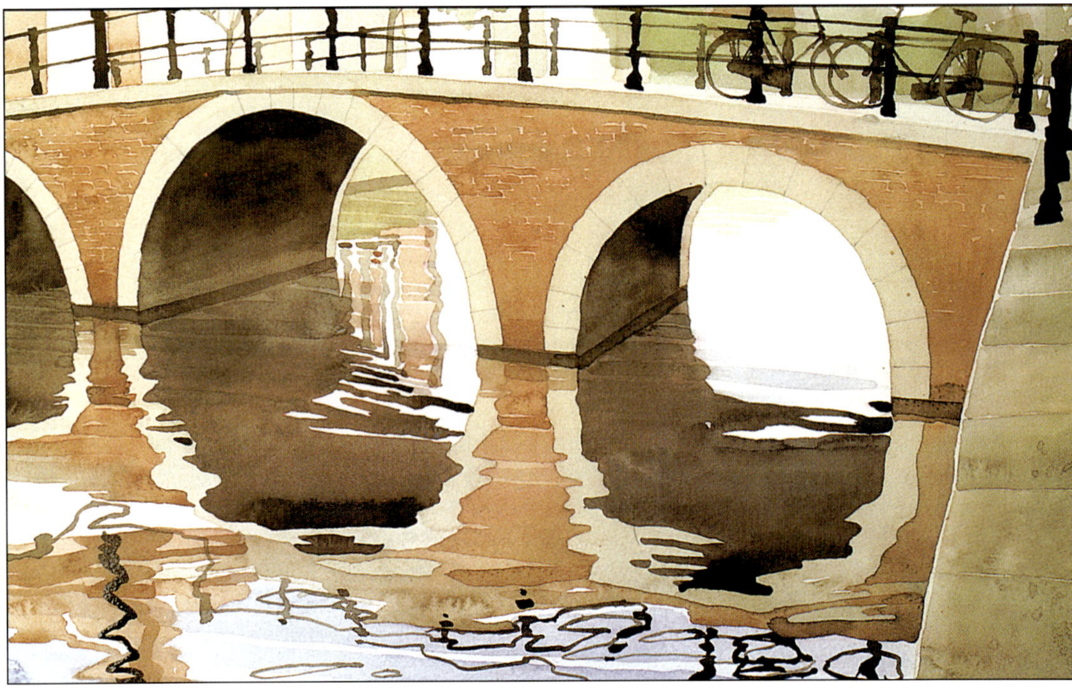

Canal in Amsterdam

In this Dutch canal scene the water's surface is ruffled by a breeze, causing the reflections to stretch and distort and form fascinating patterns. These reflections have been freely painted, with calligraphic lines and squiggles that suggest the way they are broken up by the gentle movement of the surface of the water.

YOU WILL NEED

- *Sheet of 140lb (285gsm) Not surface watercolour paper, 22 x 15in (55.8 x 38.1cm)*
- *No. 10 round brush*
- *No. 8 round brush*
- *No. 3 round brush*
- *HB pencil*

WATERCOLOUR PAINTS IN THE FOLLOWING COLOURS

- *Naples yellow light*
- *Cobalt blue*
- *Yellow ochre*
- *Raw umber*
- *Brown madder alizarin*
- *Sap green*
- *Payne's grey*

1 Lightly sketch in the main elements of the scene with an HB pencil. Mix a weak solution of Naples yellow light and apply this over the whole painting, except for the water, with a no.10 round brush. For the water, mix an equally weak solution of cobalt blue. Leave to dry.

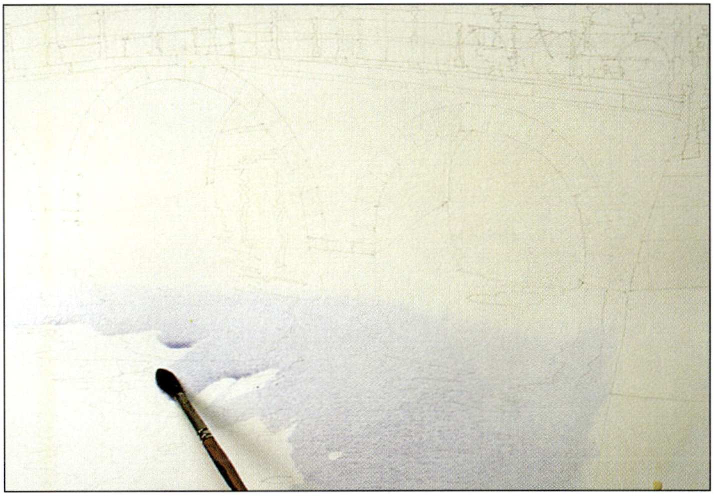

Helpful Hint

REMEMBER THAT WET WATERCOLOUR LOOKS DECEPTIVELY STRONG AND WILL DRY LIGHTER. IF YOU USE TOO LITTLE PIGMENT WITH TOO MUCH WATER, YOUR PAINTING WILL LOOK INSIPID.

2 Paint the lightest tones on the stone bridge and its reflection in the water with a mixture of yellow ochre and raw umber. Use the same colour for the stone ledge on the far right of the picture. Leave to dry.

3 Mix a slightly darker wash of raw umber and yellow ochre and, using a no. 8 round brush, paint the stone detailing along the top of the bridge. Then paint the detailing around the arches, dragging the colour down into the water with wavering strokes to describe the reflections. Leave to dry.

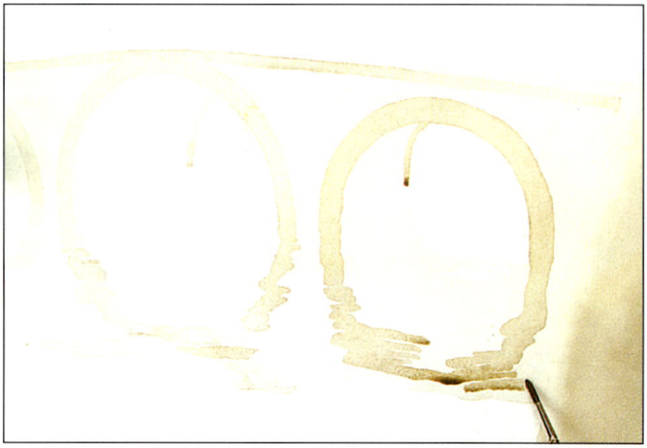

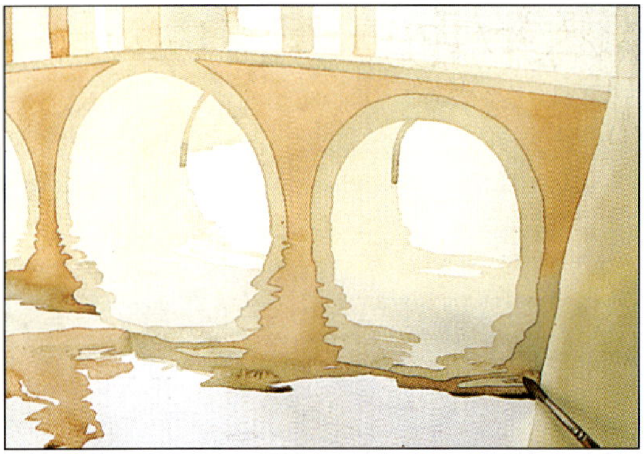

4 Mix a wash of brown madder alizarin and raw umber to make a warm, pinkish brown for the brickwork on the bridge and its reflection in the water. Again, use smooth, wavering strokes to show how the reflections break up on the rippling surface. Using the same wash, and the wash used in step 3, suggest some of the details of trees and buildings in the background, glimpsed over the top of the bridge.

5 Using a no. 3 round brush, paint the grassy bank behind the arch on the left with a pale tone of sap green and raw umber. For the reflections seen through the same arch use a wash of sap green, raw umber and brown madder alizarin. Paint the dark shadows inside the arches with a mix of brown madder alizarin and Payne's gray. Drag the washes down into the water, then pull some of the wet paint out at the edges to create the broken reflections, as shown.

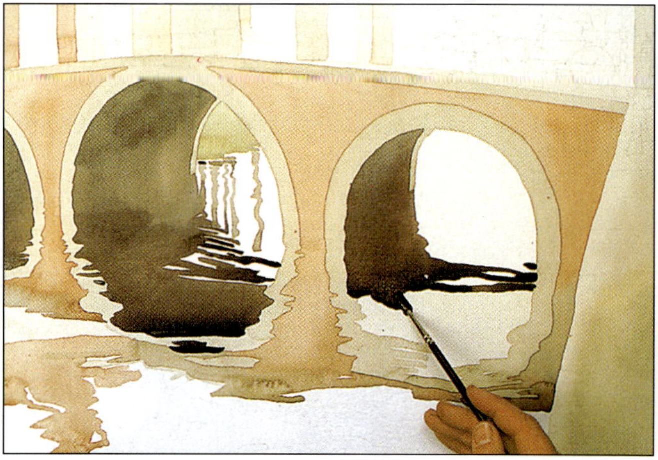

6

Paint the delicate shapes of the trees in the background using a mixture of sap green and a little raw umber for the foliage and raw umber for the trunks and branches. Dilute the colours to a pale whisper, otherwise the trees will jump forward and look as if they are sitting on top of the bridge instead of behind it. Then mix raw umber and yellow ochre for the stone slabs on the ledge on the right. Note how the slabs become cooler and lighter in tone as they recede into the distance.

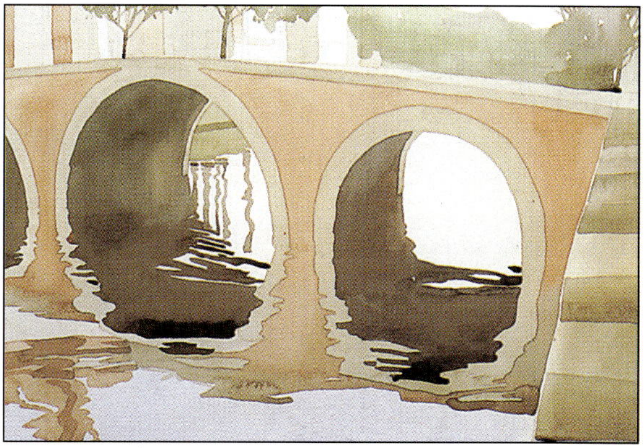

Helpful Hint

ALWAYS LET ONE WASH DRY BEFORE PAINTING OVER IT. IF YOU ARE IMPATIENT AND ATTEMPT TO PAINT ON TO A DAMP WASH YOU MAY CREATE STREAKS AND RUNS THAT RUIN THE EFFECT OF SMOOTH, CLEAR WATER.

7

Mix a deeper version of the wash used in step 4 and use this to suggest the pattern of the brickwork on the bridge. Apply the paint with short, horizontal strokes, leaving tiny gaps between them. Use the same wash to darken the reflection of the bridge in the water. Leave the painting to dry.

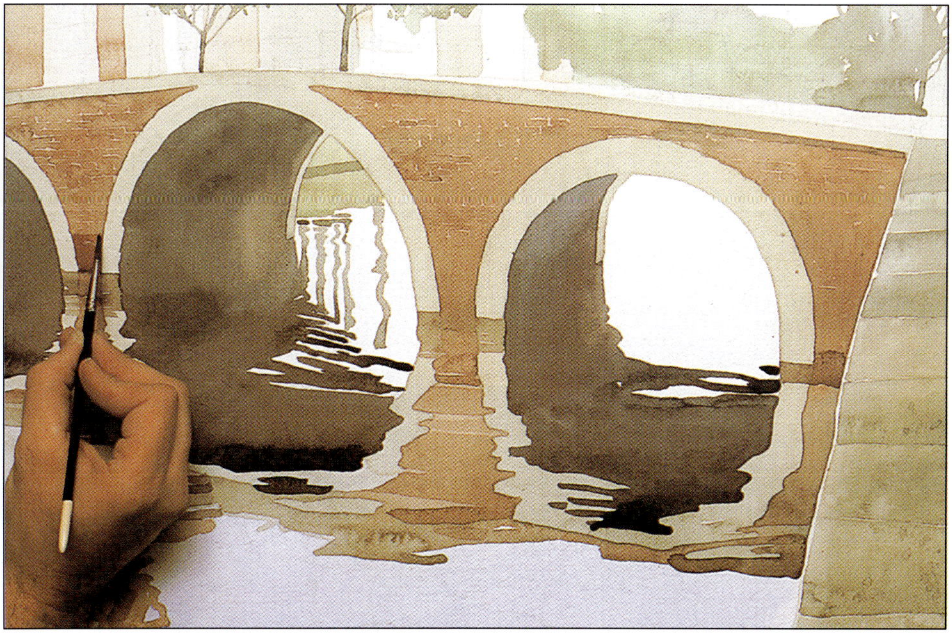

8 Draw pencil lines to define the individual stone slabs around the arches. Build up the forms of the background trees using different strengths of sap green and raw umber. Work back over the dark areas inside the arches using the same mix you used in step 5, darkened with more Payne's gray. Resume work on the reflections beyond the lefthand arch with brown madder alizarin and raw umber.

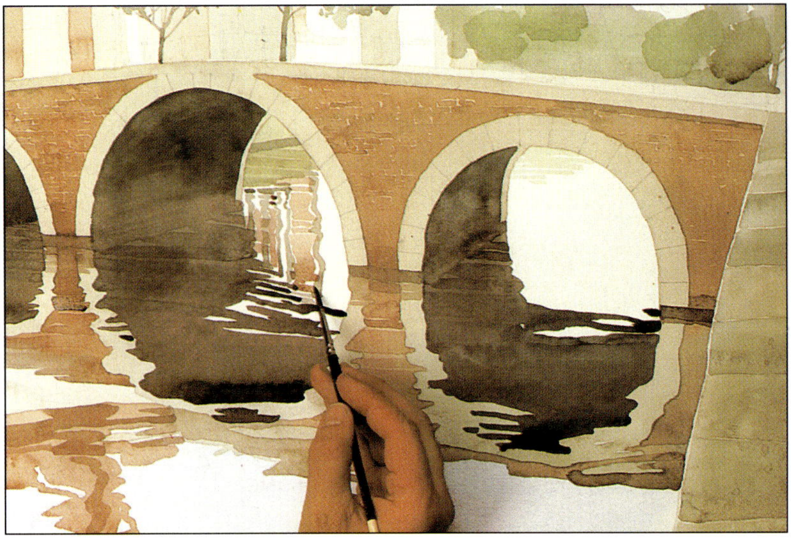

Helpful Hint

ALWAYS HAVE TWO JARS OF WATER WHEN WORKING IN WATERCOLOUR – ONE OF CLEAN WATER FOR LOADING BRUSHES AND WETTING THE PAPER, AND ONE FOR RINSING BRUSHES WHILE YOU WORK.

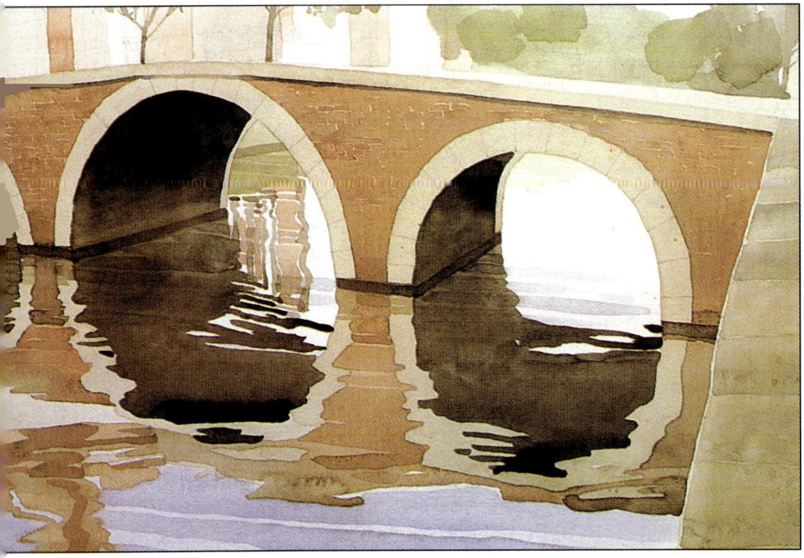

9 Mix brown madder alizarin and raw umber and paint the shadow under the stone ledge along the top of the bridge. Then mix a darker wash of brown madder alizarin and Payne's gray for the dark lines at the base of the bridge, just above the water line. Paint the darker ripples in the blue water with brushstrokes of cobalt blue, slightly deeper in tone than the original wash, to suggest the reflection of the sky.

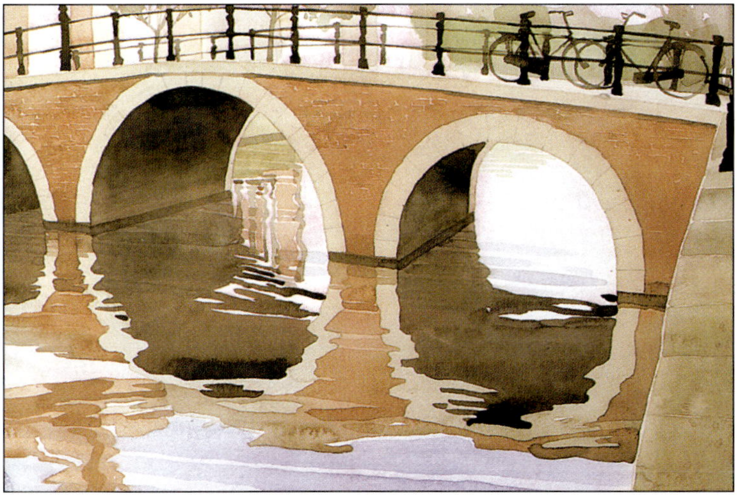

10 Make a dark, brownish black from Payne's gray and raw umber and use the tip of your brush to paint the delicate shapes of the railings. Dilute the wash to a pale grey for the railings on the far side of the bridge, and for the bicycles.

11 Complete the painting by putting in the reflections of the bicycles and the railings using the mixes used in step 10, but warmed slightly with a little brown madder alizarin. Use fluid, calligraphic strokes applied quickly and confidently, to suggest the distortions created by the movement on the water's surface.

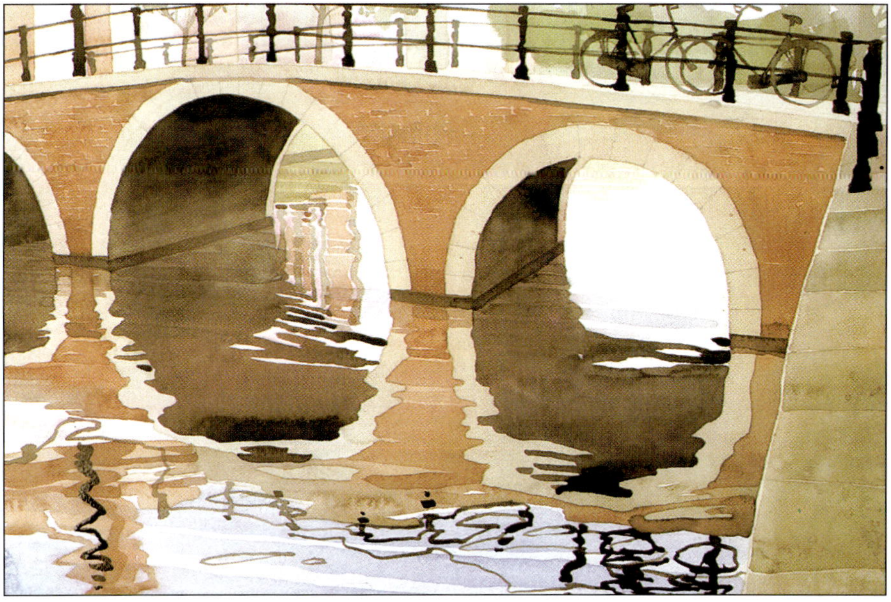

Using Gum Arabic

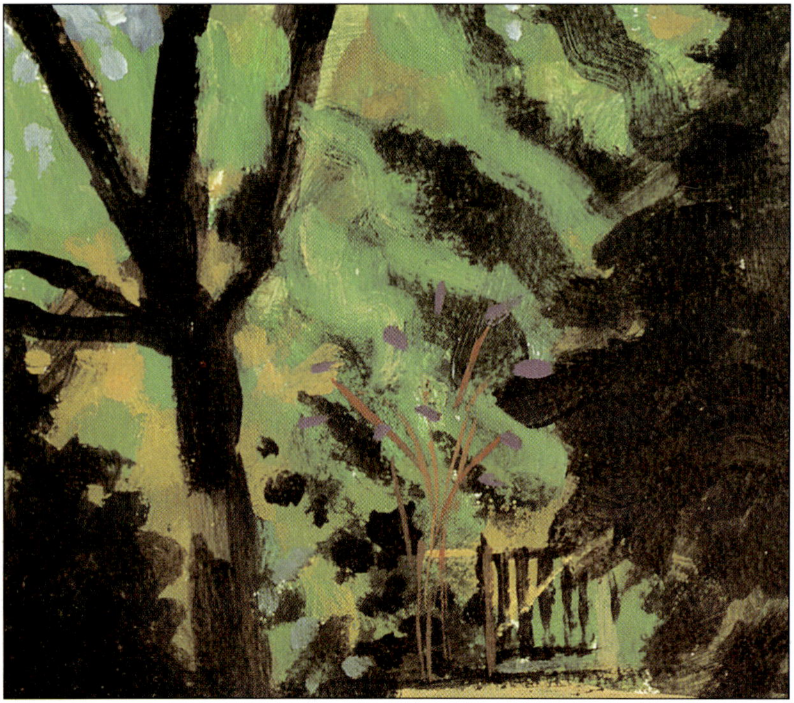

Sarah Donaldson
THE GARDEN GATE
In this rapidly executed watercolour sketch the addition of gum arabic adds richness and texture to the paint so that the lively brushwork is enhanced.

Gum arabic is derived from the sap of tropical acacia trees and has been used for centuries as a binder in the manufacture of watercolour paints. It can also be obtained as a bottled liquid for use as a painting medium. When added to watercolour paint in the palette, it enlivens the texture of the paint and enhances the vividness of the colours.

Because it also slows down the drying time of the paint, gum arabic can give greater versatility to your watercolours allowing you to keep the paint fluid on the surface for longer, work into it and create textural effects.

Paint mixed with gum arabic can be dissolved easily even when dry, because the gum suspends the pigment and prevents it from soaking into the paper. This makes it particularly useful if you want to lift out colour to create highlights. Add just a tiny drop of gum arabic to the dilute paint in your palette, or add some to the water in your jar. Don't use too much, otherwise the paint becomes slippery and jelly-like.

Gum arabic can also be used as a kind of varnish. Once the finished painting is thoroughly dry you can brush a thin layer of diluted gum arabic over it which dries with a slightly glossy surface which imparts a rich lustre to the colours. It should never be used undiluted, however, as it will crack in time.

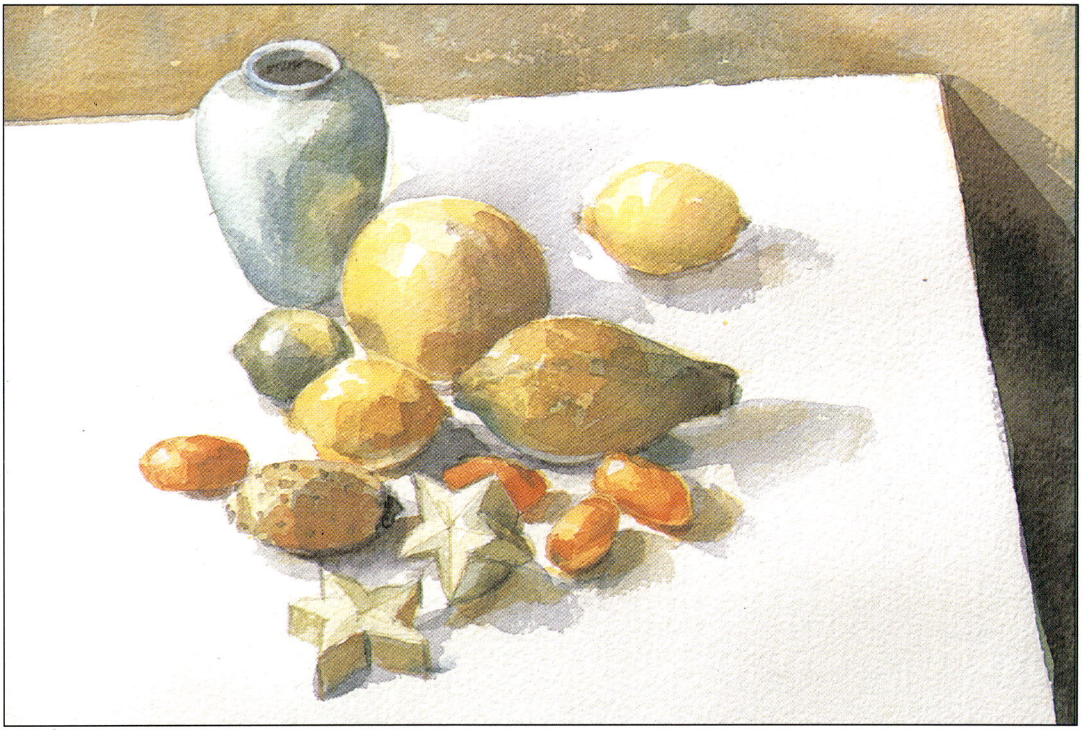

YOU WILL NEED

- Sheet of 140lb (285gsm) rough watercolour paper 12 x 9in (30.5 x 22.8cm)
- Ox gall
- Gum arabic
- Medium-sized Oriental brush
- No. 4 round brush
- HB pencil

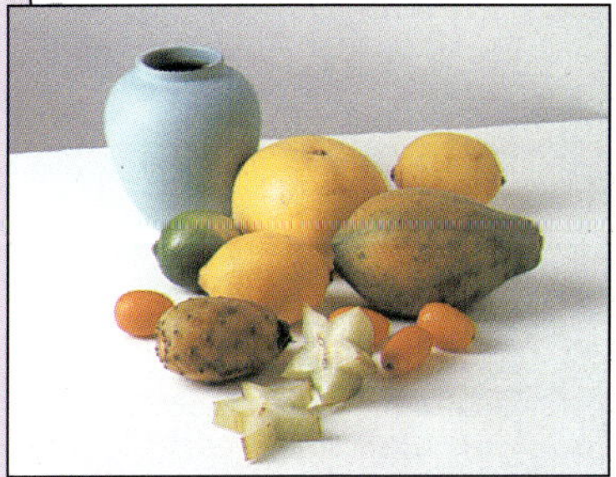

WATERCOLOUR PAINTS IN THE FOLLOWING COLOURS

- *Cobalt blue*
- *Prussian blue*
- *Aurora yellow*
- *Rose madder*
- *Chinese white*

Tropical Fruit

In this still life, transparent washes of colour have been worked over one another in order to build up a strong sense of form in the fruits. The addition of gum arabic and ox gall gives a new dimension to the paint and an opportunity to develop texture and tone

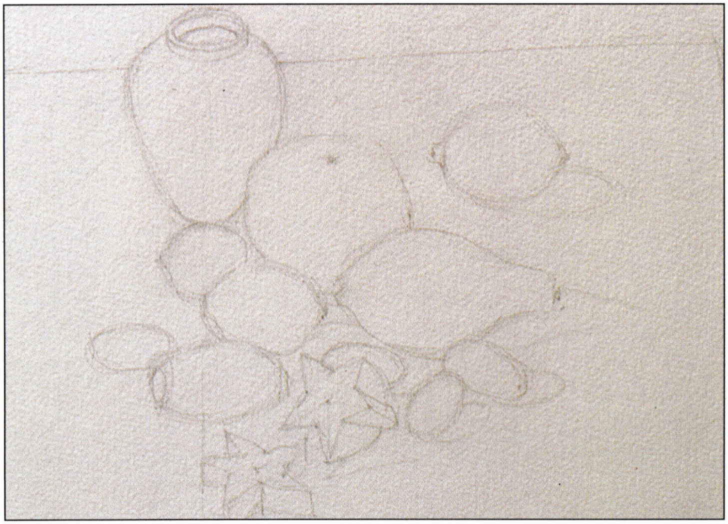

1 Sketch the main outlines of the composition using an HB pencil, but don't add any detail at this stage. Ensure that the fruits are in correct proportion to each other and that the composition is well set out in relation to the edges of the paper; here, the artist has chosen an overhead viewpoint to create a striking composition, with the top of the vase just breaking the edge of the table top.

Helpful Hint

ORIENTAL BRUSHES ARE GREAT FOR WATERCOLOUR PAINTING AS THEY HOLD PLENTY OF PAINT FOR LAYING WASHES, YET COME TO A FINE POINT FOR DETAILS.

2 Block in the background area with a pale wash of aurora yellow, applied loosely with a medium-sized Oriental brush. Add a patch of the same colour on the vase to suggest the reflection of the grapefruit on its shiny surface. Then block in all the fruits, leaving patches of white paper for the highlights. For the kumquats, add a little rose madder to the wash to make a pale orange. For the blue-green tones of the vase, mix a well-diluted wash of Prussian blue and cobalt blue, leaving a small patch of bare paper for the highlight.

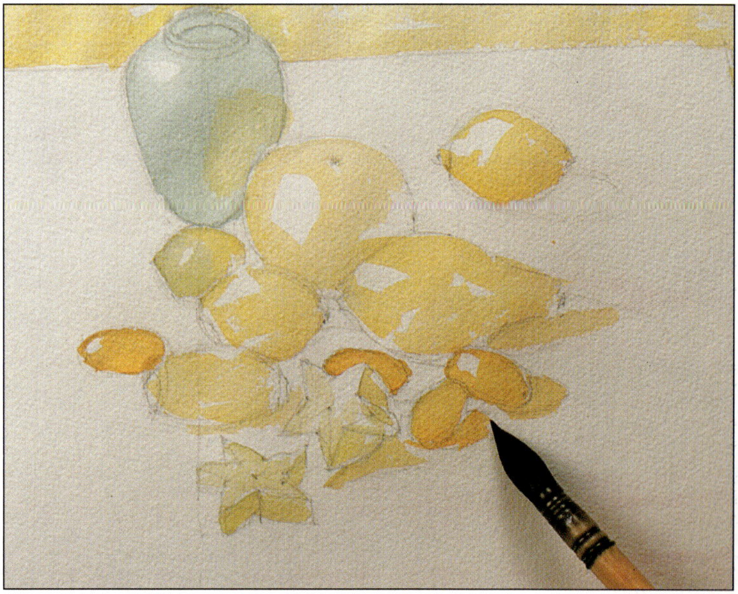

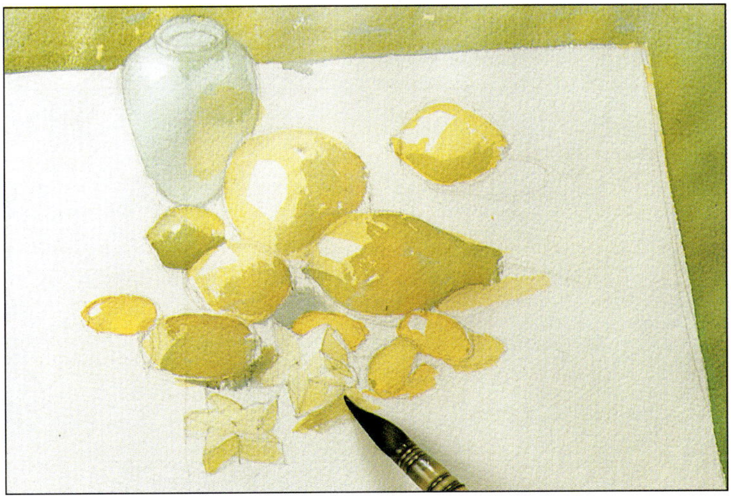

3 When the first washes have dried, start to model the rounded forms of the vase and fruits with darker tones. Apply thin washes of cobalt blue mixed with aurora yellow to add greenish tones to the grapefruit, lemon, starfruit, lime and prickly pear, concentrating on the shadow areas. Loosely wash the same colour over the background, then paint the shadows beneath the fruits.

Helpful Hint

OX GALL IS ANOTHER USEFUL WATER-COLOUR PAINTING MEDIUM. IT IS A PALE-COLOURED LIQUID WHICH INCREASES THE FLOW OF WATERCOLOUR PAINTS. AS WITH GUM ARABIC, USE IT SPARINGLY.

4 Introduce warmer tones to the fruits with various mixtures of aurora yellow, rose madder and a little cobalt blue, adding wash over wash in the shadows to build up three-dimensional form. Brush a small amount of ox gall over the back-ground area, then brush in some of the same warm colours, letting them blend wet-in-wet with the previous wash. This unifies your painting by linking foreground and background. With a no. 4 round brush, deepen the cast shadows with cobalt blue and Prussian blue.

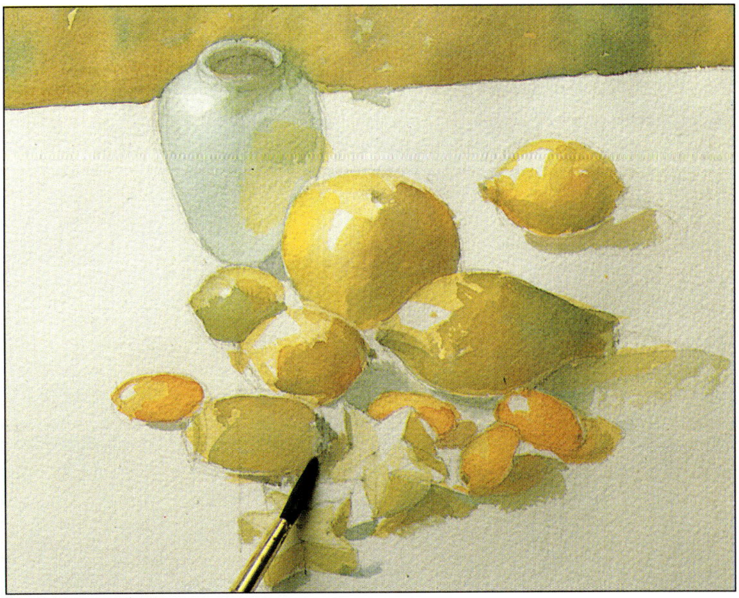

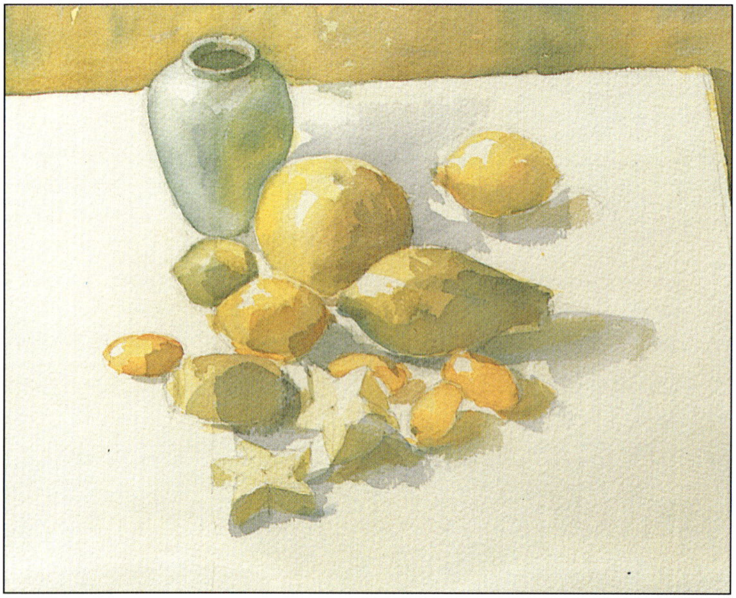

5 Gradually add more pigment to the basic washes and work on the darker tones in the group, adding variety to the range of tints in the painting and giving a sense of light hitting the subject from the side. Notice how the objects pick up and reflect the colours around them: the reflection of the grapefruit in the vase, for example, and the subtle tinge of yellow in some of the shadows.

6 Concentrate on the shadows, building up transparent layers of colour one over the other. Mix a brushful of gum arabic with the paint for the darker tones; this adds body to the paint, enabling you to apply it in distinct brush strokes to suggest form and texture. It also gives the dark tones depth and luminosity, preventing them from becoming muddy. Leave to dry, then use a little of the grey shadow mixture to suggest the knobbly texture of the prickly pear.

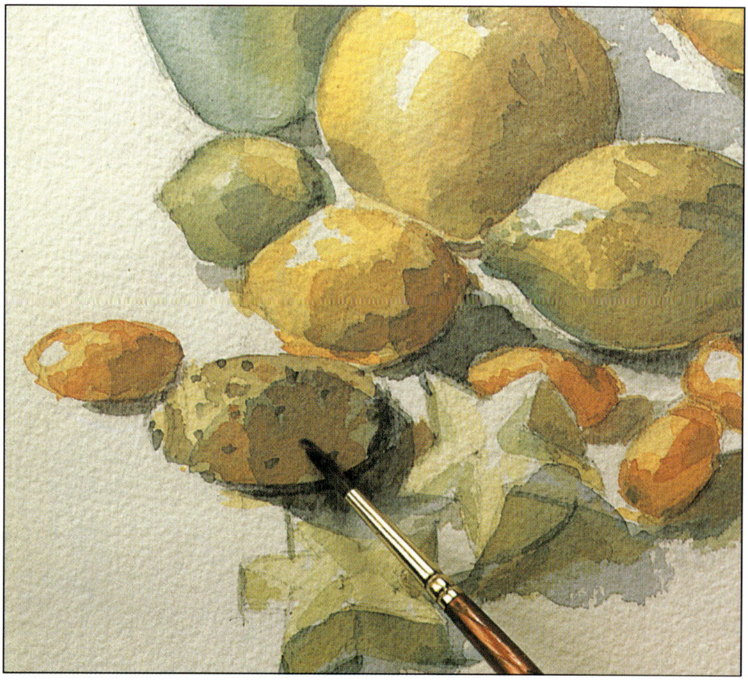

7 Develop the darks and mid tones that describe the rounded form of the vase with transparent overlays of cobalt blue and Prussian blue, adding aurora yellow for the greenish tones. Add a little rose madder to the wash, plus some gum arabic to make the paint thicker and more controllable when painting small details. Use this to strengthen the small areas of deep shadow where the objects overlap. Mix a strong solution of rose madder and aurora yellow to strengthen the warm shadows on the kumquats.

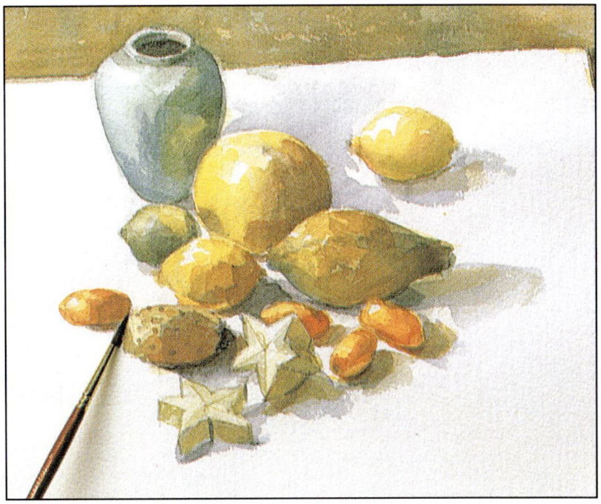

Helpful Hint

TO GIVE A SENSE OF DEPTH TO THE PICTURE, USE SLIGHTLY STRONGER TONES AND COLOURS FOR THE OBJECTS AT THE FRONT OF THE STILL-LIFE GROUP, TO BRING THEM FORWARD.

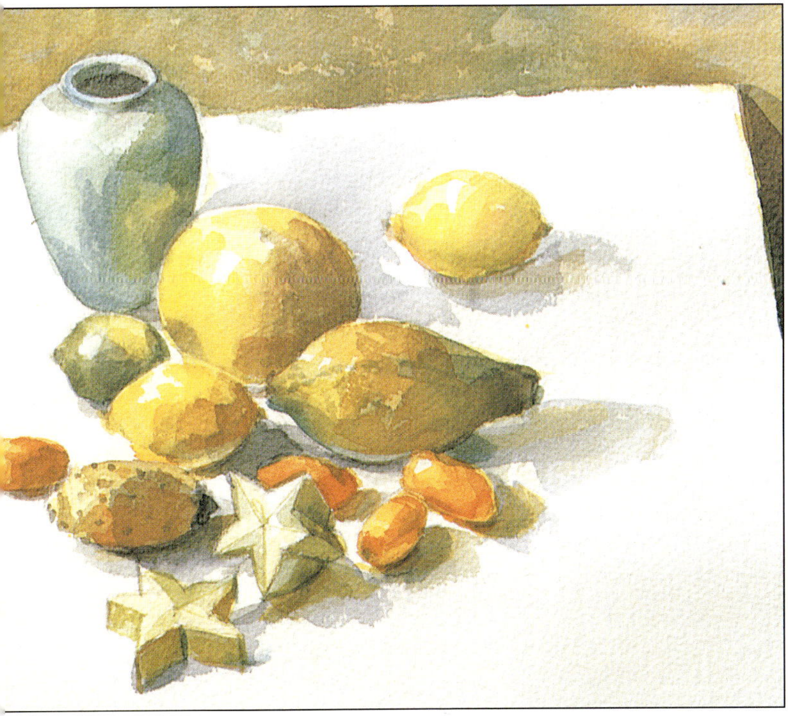

8 To complete the painting, use a little Chinese white to highlight certain areas of the subject, giving the effect of reflected light. You can also use white at this stage to correct any areas of the painting you are not entirely happy with. Stand back from the picture to check that the perspective is working and that the background objects appear to recede on the picture plane. You may want to add warmer tints to the foreground objects to bring them forward.

Complementary Colours

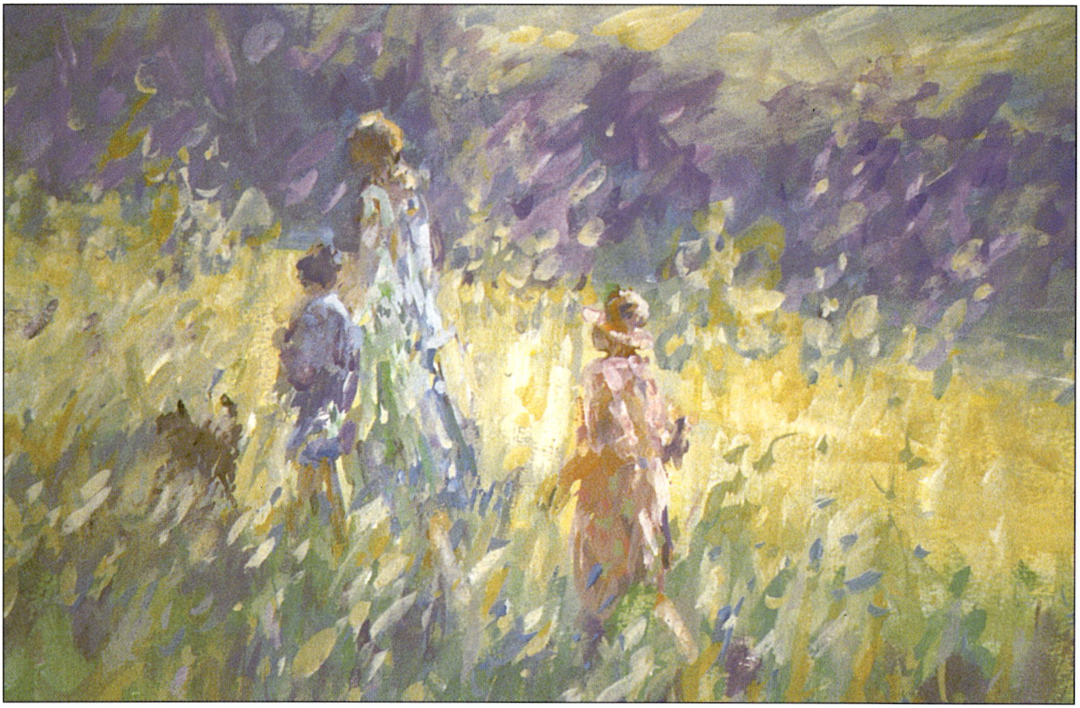

Jane Camp
SUMMER'S DAY
The effect of complementary colours need not always be bright and strident. In this lyrical scene, the complementary blue-violets and yellows give a shimmering effect of sunlight, but because the colours have been lightened with Chinese white they have a quiet harmony.

Any two colours diagonally opposite each other on the colour wheel (see opposite page) are called complementaries. For example, blue is the complementary of orange, red of green and yellow of violet. When placed side by side, two complementaries have a powerful effect on each other, the one heightening and intensifying the other. A small patch of red in a large area of green can make both the red and the green look that much brighter. Similarly, blue appears more vibrant with orange nearby. The visual impact of complementary colours is quite considerable and by controlling them carefully in your pictures you can achieve some dramatic results.

The reason this contrast between complementary colours is so effective has to do with the way the human eye works. The cones in the eye which perceive a certain colour have a natural tendency to 'search' for its complementary whenever they are stimulated. You can see this for yourself by carrying out a simple experiment. Stare at a bright red area of colour for 20 seconds, then look away to a sheet of white paper: a green after-image of the object appears. If you reverse the process and start with an area of green, you will see a red after-image. Every colour has its complementary, which can be found in the same way.

Theory into practice

You can make full use of complementary contrast to add zest to your painting. Introduce touches of red or reddish brown into areas of green foliage or grass and you make them look more lively. Complementaries placed side by side form a bright and eye-catching boundary which can be used strategically to draw the eye to the focal point of your composition. To produce luminous shadows, introduce some of the complementary colour of the object into the shadow mixture; for example, an orange will cast a shadow with a bluish tinge, while a red apple will cast a shadow that has a greenish tinge.

Neutral colours

Conversely, if two complementaries are mixed together they neutralize each other and form a whole range of greys which are far more subtle and interesting than the greys mixed from black and white. These neutral greys provide a marvellous foil for brighter, more vibrant colours. They have an inherent harmony and are never strident.

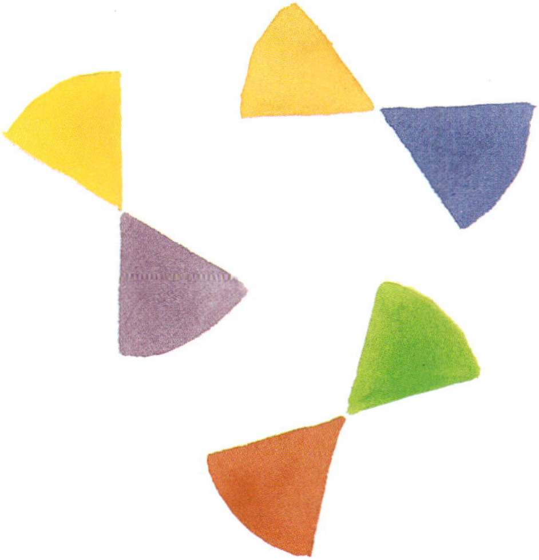

Colours that lie opposite each other on the colour wheel are called complementary colours. When juxtaposed in a painting they intensify each other.

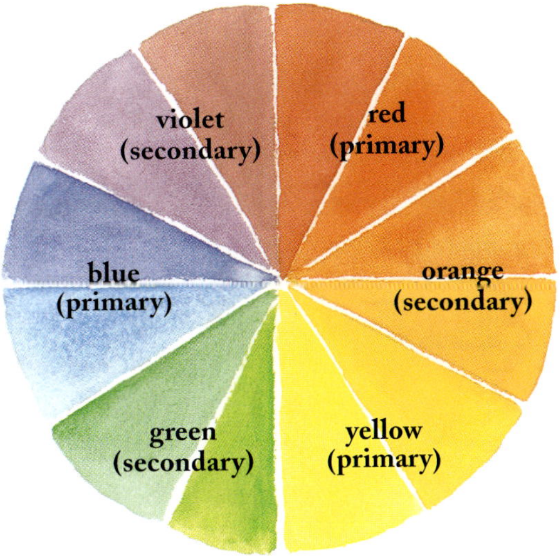

The arrangement of colours on the colour wheel helps the artist understand the relationship between the colours and the effect they have on one another when used together.

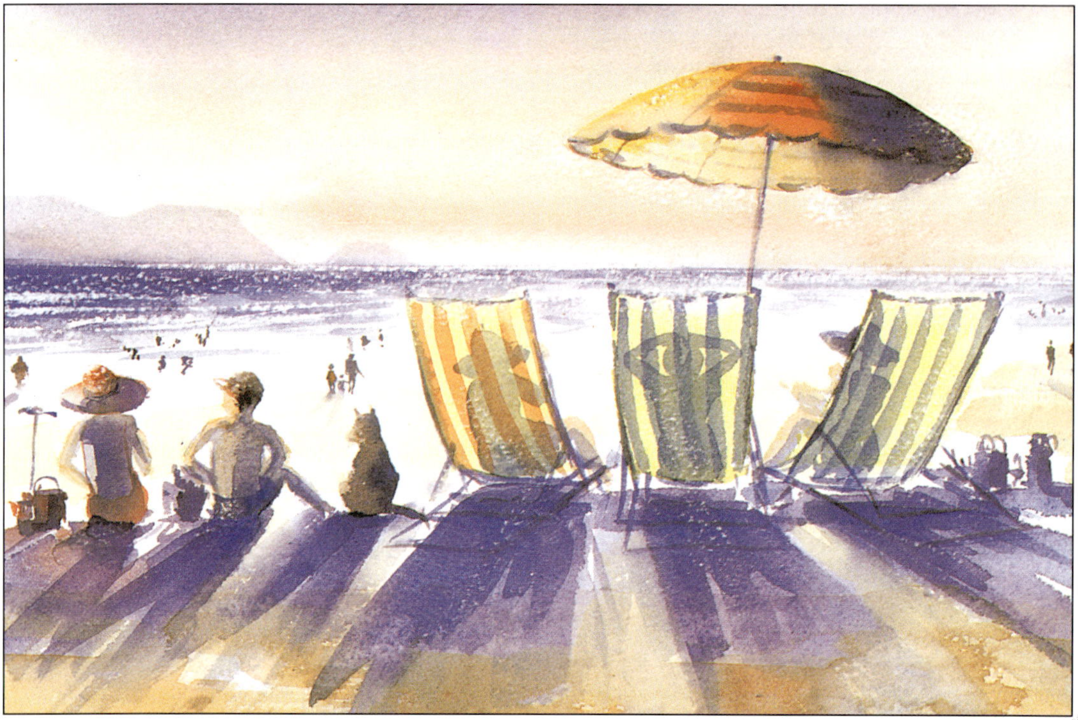

Evening Shadow

Our eyes often perceive the shadows in a scene as being the complementary (opposite) colour to that of the illuminated part. Here, the artist has exploited this effect, giving a blue-violet tinge to the shadows on the yellow beach. The violet/yellow complements are present everywhere in the painting, giving an impression of consistent, harmonious light.

YOU WILL NEED

- *Sheet of 140lb (285gsm) Not surface watercolour paper, 14 x 10in (35.6 x 25.4cm)*
- *No. 4 round brush*
- *No. 8 round brush*
- *Small piece of fine-grade sandpaper*

WATERCOLOUR PAINTS IN THE FOLLOWING COLOURS

- *Naples yellow light*
- *Cadmium red*
- *Alizarin crimson*
- *Cadmium yellow*
- *Lemon yellow*
- *Raw sienna*

1 Using thinly diluted lemon yellow, paint the shapes of the deckchairs with the no. 8 brush. Mix a pale flesh tint from thinly diluted lemon yellow and alizarin crimson. Use this to suggest the shapes of the figures and the dog on the sand as simple colour silhouettes, then jot in the figures sitting in the deckchairs. Leave to dry, then add a further wash of flesh tint to model the forms of the figures with light and shade.

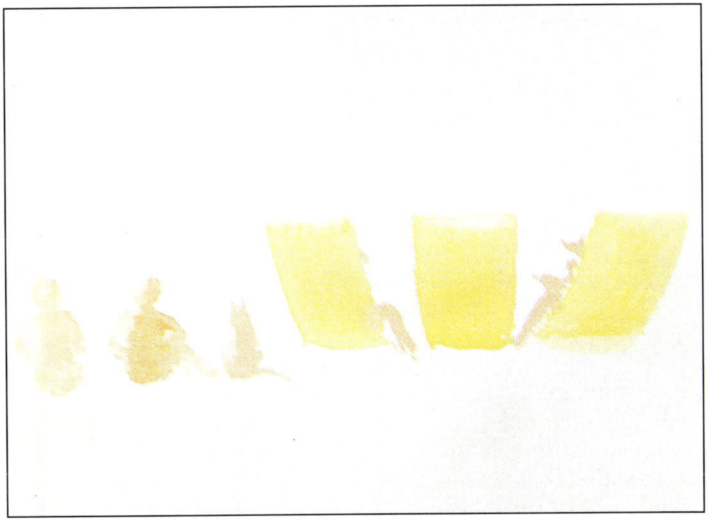

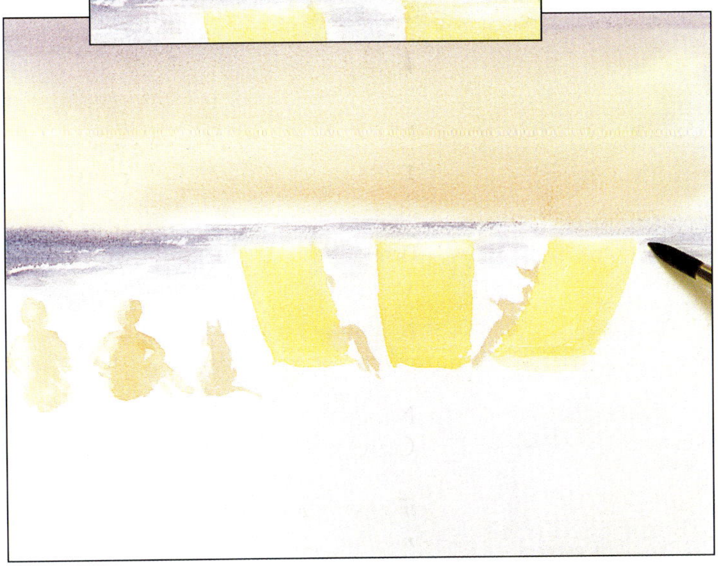

2 Paint the evening sky using variegated washes. First, tilt your board at a slight angle and dampen the sky area with water. Using a well-loaded no. 8 brush, apply well-diluted cadmium yellow to the whole area. While this is still damp, float a band of French ultramarine across the top of the paper, and a band of alizarin crimson near the horizon. The colours will gently merge together to create the effect of a hazy sky (see detail). Paint the sea with French ultramarine mixed with just a touch of alizarin crimson, fading the colour with more water in the foreground. When painting variegated washes, it takes a little practice to achieve a smooth transition from one colour to the next. The secret is to load your brush well and work quickly and confidently.

3 Paint the long shadows cast by the deckchairs and figures using French ultramarine, warmed with a touch of alizarin crimson in places. Vary the tones of the shadows, making them lighter the further they are from the objects casting them. Use the no. 4 brush and a darker tone of alizarin and ultramarine to suggest the buckets and spade, and their shadows, on the left of the picture.

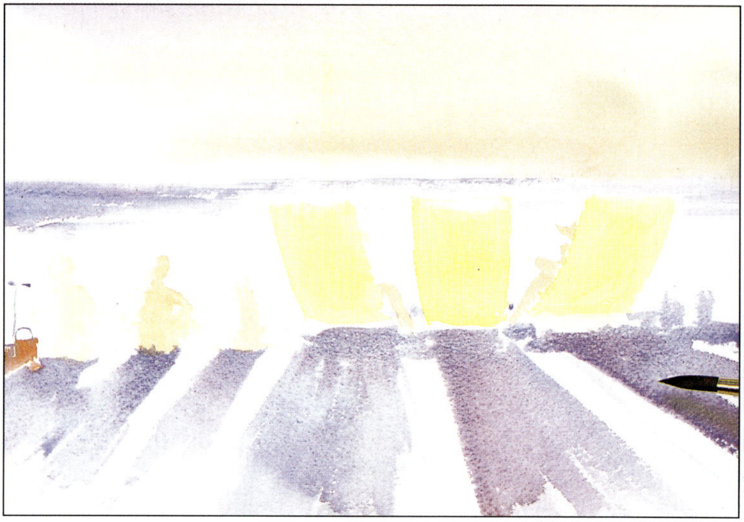

Helpful Hint

WHEN PAINTING FIGURES IN A LANDSCAPE, REMEMBER, TOO MUCH DETAIL RENDERS THEM LIFELESS AND WOODEN. AIM TO CAPTURE THEIR SHAPES AND GESTURES SIMPLY AND RAPIDLY.

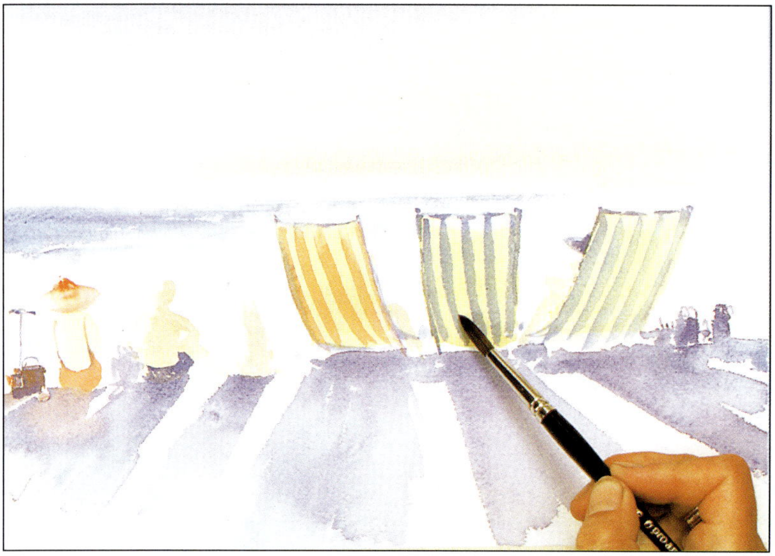

4 Now clothe the figures, painting the man's shorts with ultramarine and the woman's swimsuit and sunhat with diluted cadmium red. Let some of the red bleed into the shadow, giving the luminous effect of reflected light. Use the same colours to paint the red and blue stripes on the deckchairs, switching to the no. 8 brush.

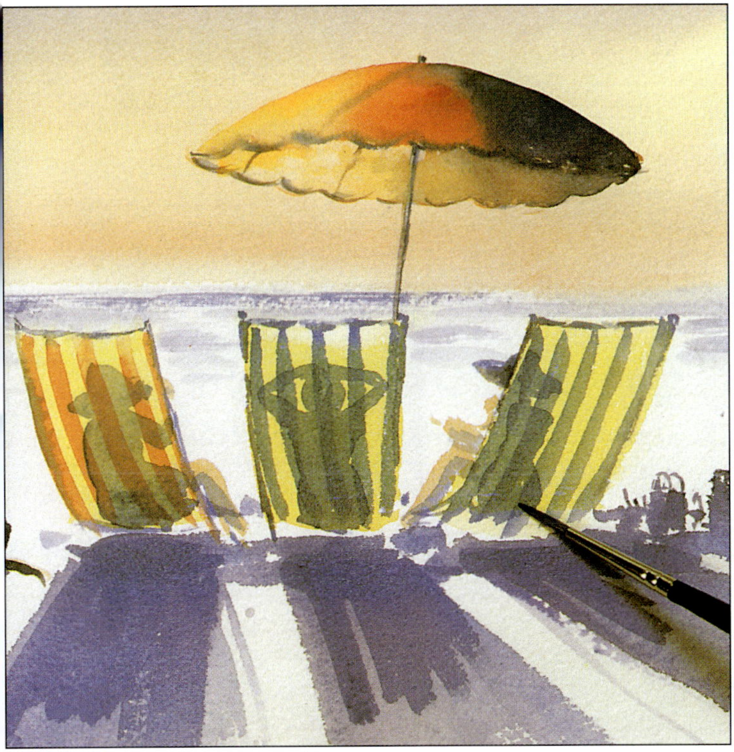

5 Switch to the no. 4 brush and paint the colourful parasol with cadmium yellow, cadmium red and ultramarine, using a mixture of all three colours to make a dark mauve for the scalloped edge and the pole. Mix a diluted wash of French ultramarine and paint the shadows of the people sitting in the deckchairs.

6 Now add more detail to the figures sitting on the sand, strengthening the shadows with transparent washes of ultramarine. Mix a dark wash of ultramarine and alizarin crimson and paint the man's hat and the dark tones on the dog.

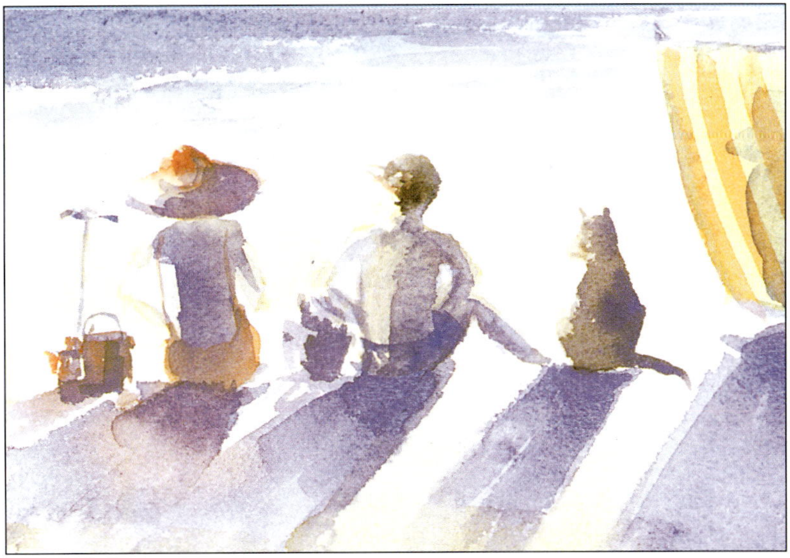

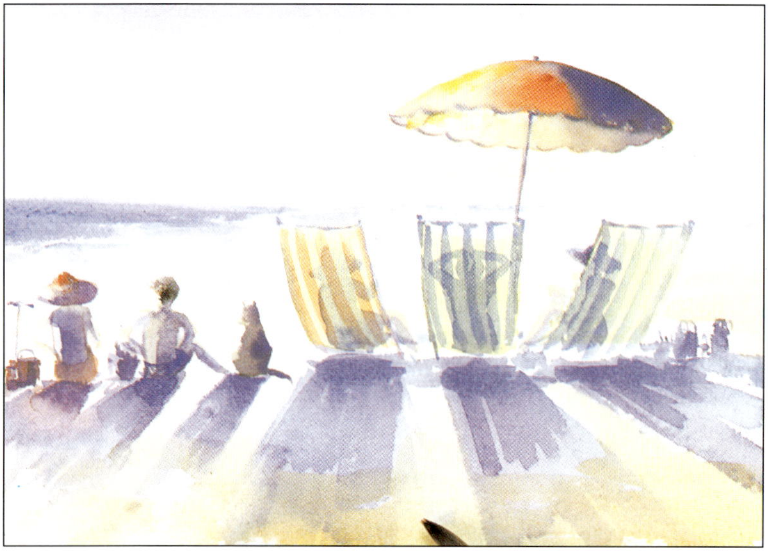

7 Mix a warm grey from ultramarine and a hint of alizarin crimson and paint the hazy tones of islands in the distance. Now paint the sandy beach with a mixture of raw sienna, cadmium yellow and just a touch of cadmium red, tickling the paint round the shapes of the figures. Strengthen the tone in the foreground with more cadmium red, washing the colour over the cast shadows.

Helpful Hint

WHEN YOU'RE WAITING FOR WASHES TO DRY, USE THE BACK OF YOUR HAND TO TEST FOR DRYNESS. IT IS A MORE SENSITIVE RECEPTOR THAN THE FINGERS AND WON'T LEAVE GREASE MARKS ON THE PAPER.

8 Sketch in a suggestion of the deckchair frames using ultramarine applied with the tip of the no. 4 brush. Add further washes of ultramarine to the cast shadows on the sand, to give an impression of double shadows. Now that the picture has developed, the sky may look a bit 'washed out'; if so, go over it again with the same colours used in step 2 and the no. 8 brush.

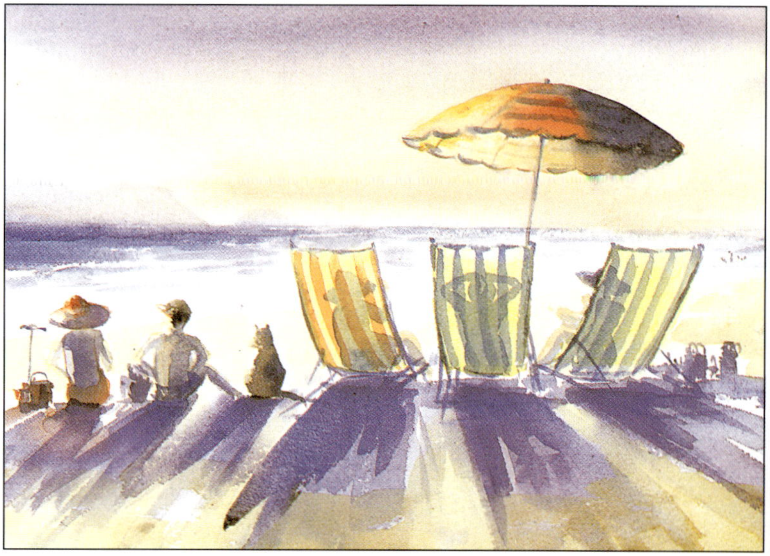

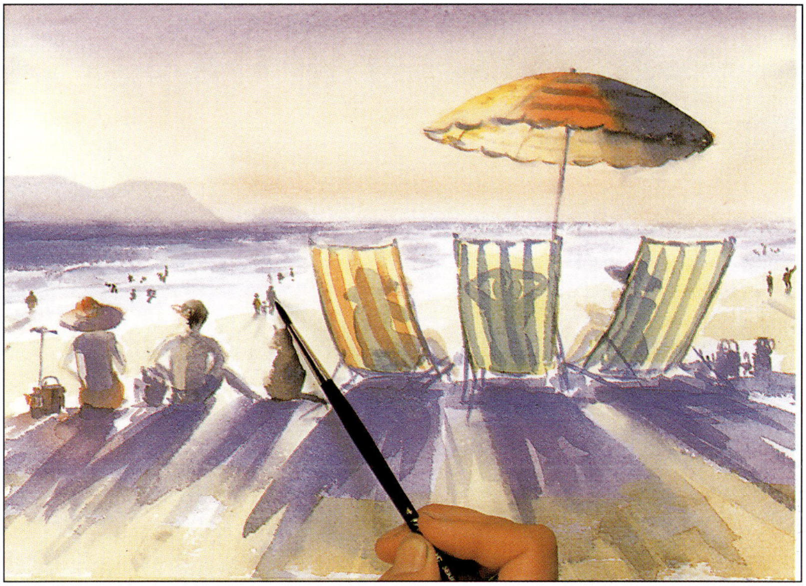

9 Use dots and dashes of French ultramarine and alizarin crimson, applied with the no. 4 brush, to suggest groups of people walking along the beach in the distance. Use smaller, sketchier marks for the figures in the water. This dimunition of scale gives the picture a strong sense of receding space. Leave the painting to dry.

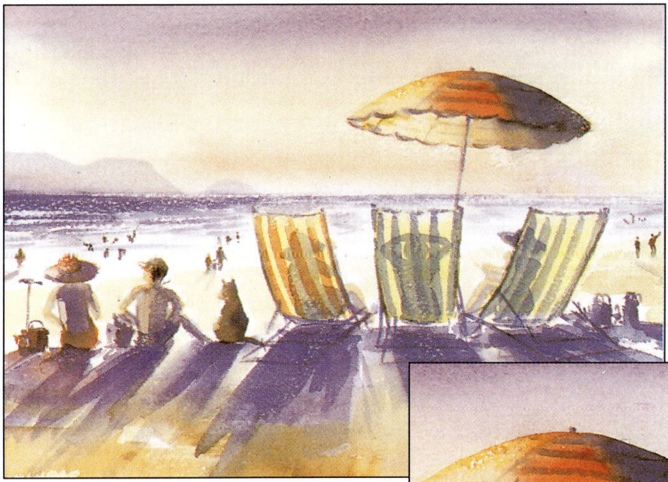

10 Check that the painting is completely dry, then add the final touch of sparkling sunlight on the distant sea. To do this, fold a small piece of fine-grade sandpaper and use the folded edge to scrape away some of the dry paint (see detail). Scrape very gently so that paint is removed only from the 'peaks' of the paper grain, leaving a series of broken white highlights. Work in one direction only, so as not to tear the paper.

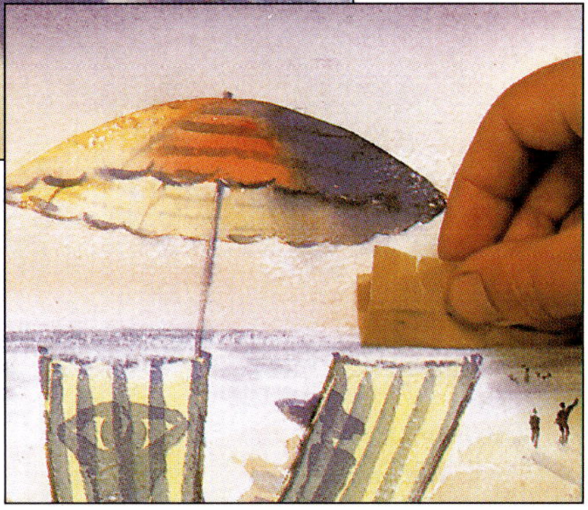

Painting Sunsets

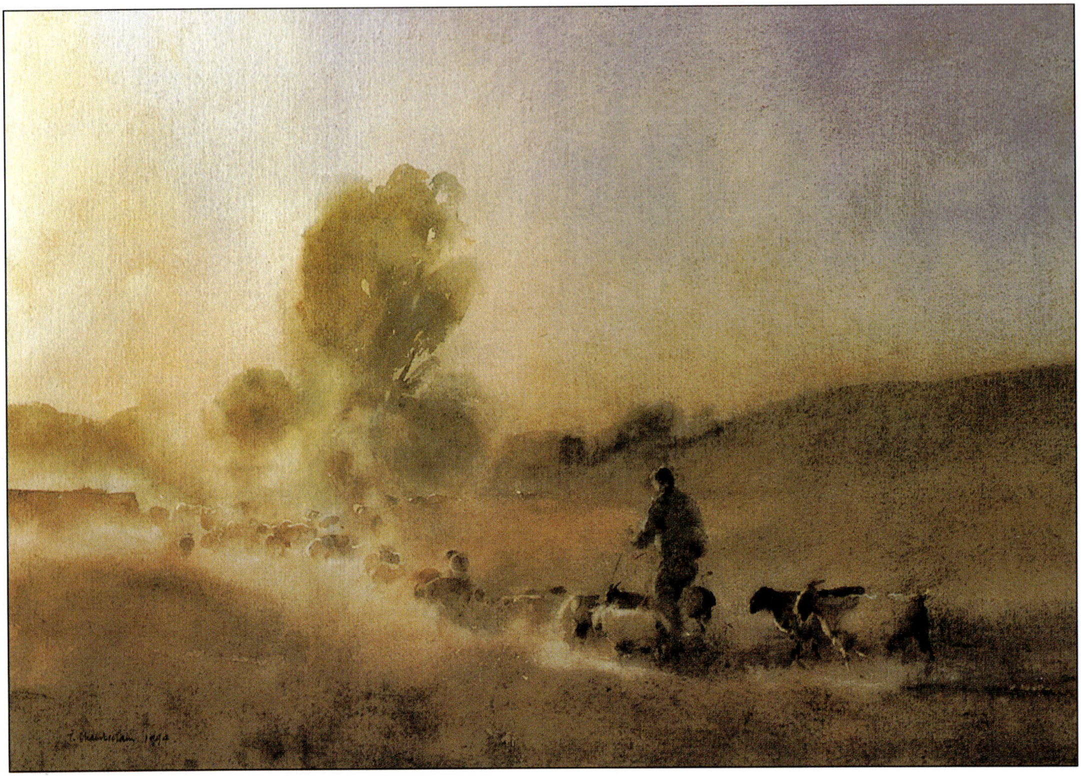

Trevor Chamberlain
DUSTY SHEEP-TRACK, EVENING
A beautiful portrayal of evening light, captured with soft, wet-in-wet washes of translucent colour on a fairly absorbent paper.

Sunsets and evening skies, with their rich, glowing colours, have long been a popular subject for artists. Anyone in search of inspiration need look no further than the work of the English artist JMW Turner, whose glorious studies of sunsets seem to glow with an inner light.

Painting outdoors

If you are painting outdoors and trying to capture the glowing effects of the evening sky, you need to work quickly as the light changes and fades rapidly at this time of day. To save time, get to your chosen spot before sunset and have all your equipment set out ready.

In this situation, the key is to simplify both colours and forms so that you can quickly convey the mood and atmosphere as it appears before you. Work on a small scale and use large brushes to apply broad strokes of transparent colour – small brushes can result in a tight, overworked image. Choose a limited range of colours to work with – you won't have time to dither over which colours to mix once the sun starts to go down.

Another approach is to make on-the-spot sketches in pastel or gouache and use these as reference for a painting to be completed at home. Work with just a few principal colours on a mid-toned paper, which leaves you free to concentrate on the lights and darks.

The sky at sunset takes on a radiant glow which even the brightest pigment colours cannot hope to match. The artist, therefore, must use cunning and skill in order to create the illusion of radiant light in his or her painting. One way to do this is by introducing cool colours as well as warm into the sky, because warm colours appear brighter and more intense when placed next to cool colours. When you interweave the warm pinks and golds of the setting sun with the cool blues and violets of the clouds, these warm and cool colours 'vibrate' against each other and create a radiant glow. In addition, the cool, shadowy tones in the darkening landscape will enhance the warmth in the sky.

When faced with a glorious sunset the temptation can sometimes be to mix too many strong pinks, oranges and reds so that when completed the sky seems to jump forward and hang in front of the landscape below. The secret of success is to use 'hot' colours sparingly. Exercise restraint with your brushwork and be selective with your colours. When painting the sun itself, for example, an orb of pale, soft colour will look subtler and more evocative than one painted in garishly bright colours.

Robert Tilling
EVENING LIGHT
Here the magical effect of a luminous evening sky reflected on still water is powerfully conveyed by paring the image down to its essential elements.

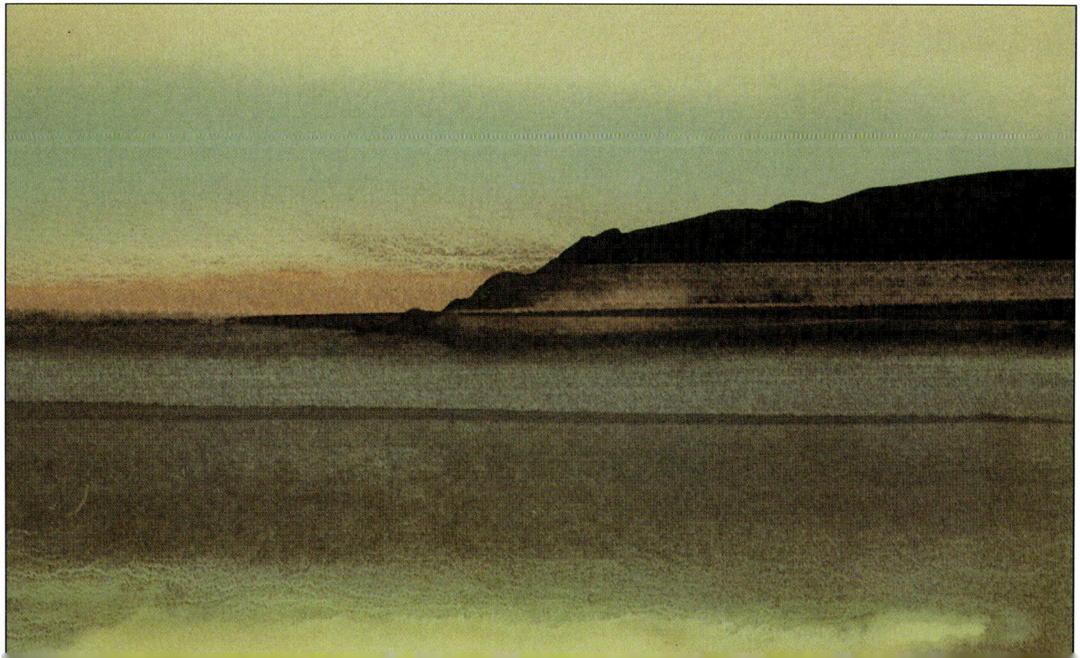

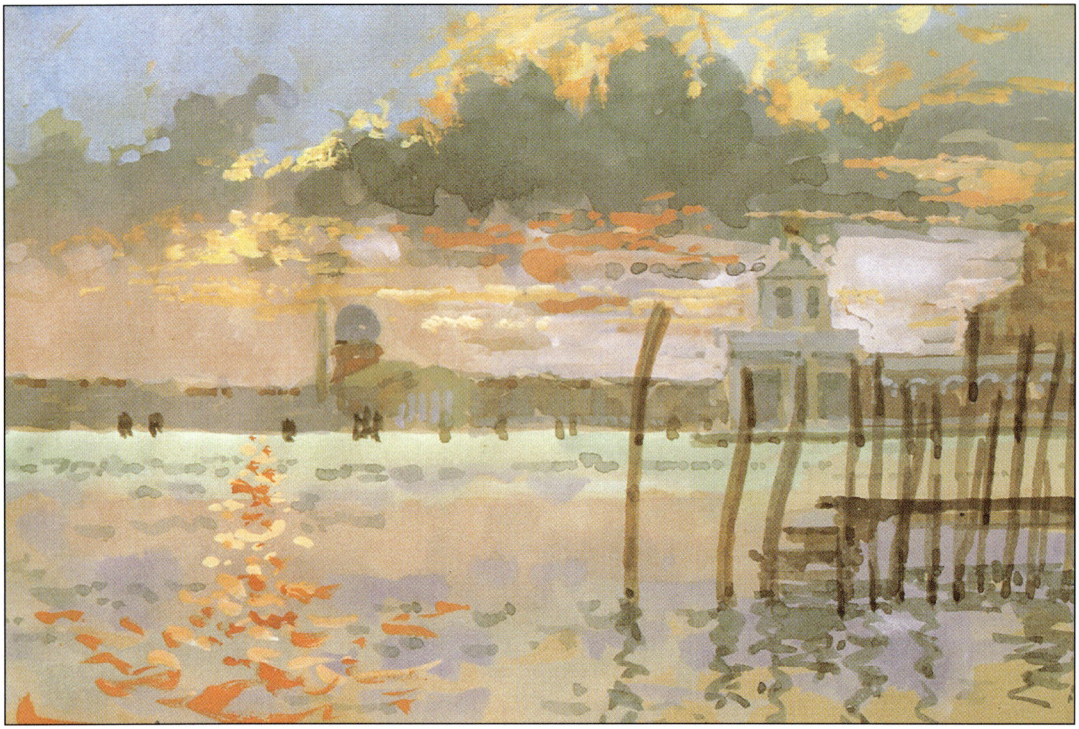

Sunset over the Lagoon

YOU WILL NEED

- Sheet of buff-coloured Ingres paper, 9 x 6½in (22.8 x 16.5cm)
- No. 10 round brush
- No. 4 round brush
- No. 1 round brush
- HB pencil

The changing hues of a sky at sunset are a richly evocative subject for the watercolour artist. This view of Venice captures that magical time of day, just before the sun sinks, when the sky takes on a luminous glow and the tones of the buildings are reduced to dark, shadowy forms.

WATERCOLOUR PAINTS IN THE FOLLOWING COLOURS

- *French ultramarine*
- *Prussian blue*
- *Cadmium yellow*
- *Cadmium red*
- *Lemon yellow*
- *Ivory black*
- *Alizarin crimson*
- *Burnt sienna*
- *Payne's gray*
- *Permanent white gouache paint*

1 Sketch in the main outlines of the composition using an HB pencil. Paint the sky with thinly diluted washes of colour applied wet-into-wet with a no. 10 brush and broad, uneven brushstrokes. Start at the top with French ultramarine, then use various combinations of ultramarine, Prussian blue and just a touch of cadmium yellow to make pale grey-blues. Add touches of thinly diluted permanent white here and there to suggest soft white clouds. Mix permanent white with a little cadmium red for the pink sky above the horizon.

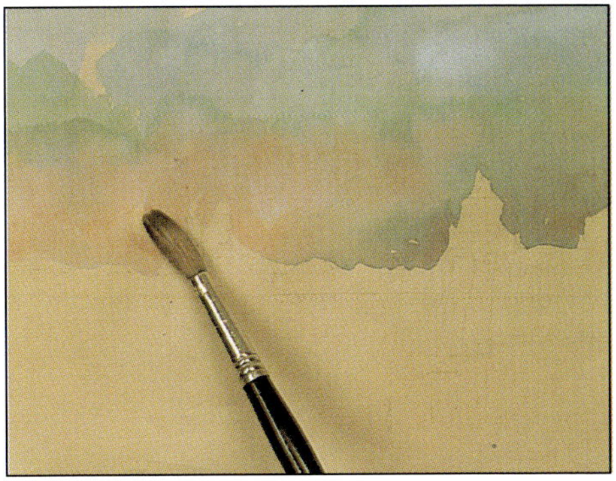

Helpful Hint

THE BUFF-COLOURED INGRES PAPER USED HERE PROVIDES A USEFUL MID TONE ON WHICH TO WORK. IF YOU PREFER TO USE NORMAL WATERCOLOUR PAPER, TINT IT WITH A WEAK WASH OF BURNT SIENNA.

2 Switch to a no. 4 brush and loosely block in the distant line of buildings. The colours used here are cadmium red, lemon yellow, burnt sienna, ultramarine and ivory black, with touches of permanent white. Mix these in different combinations and allow the colours to run into each other to achieve a wide range of tones, from purple-grey through to a warm brown.

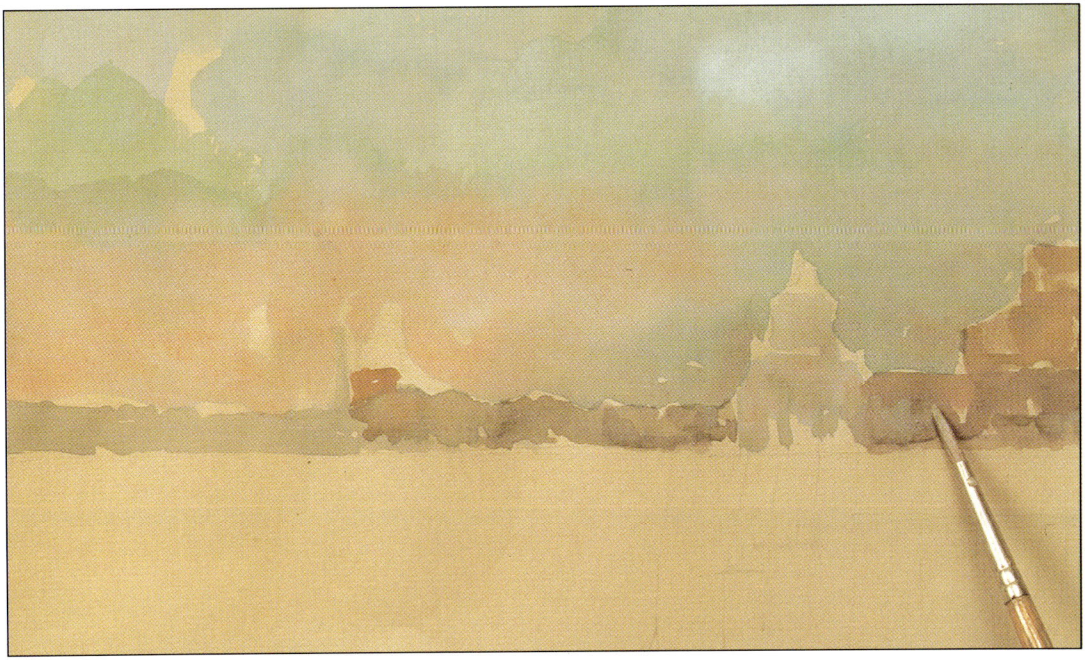

3 Let the underwashes dry, then mix a dark grey from ultramarine and black and suggest windows and doorways on the buildings. These are quite a long way distant, so don't overdo the detailing. Here you can see how loosely the paint is applied – yet there is enough detail to describe the character of the old Venetian buildings.

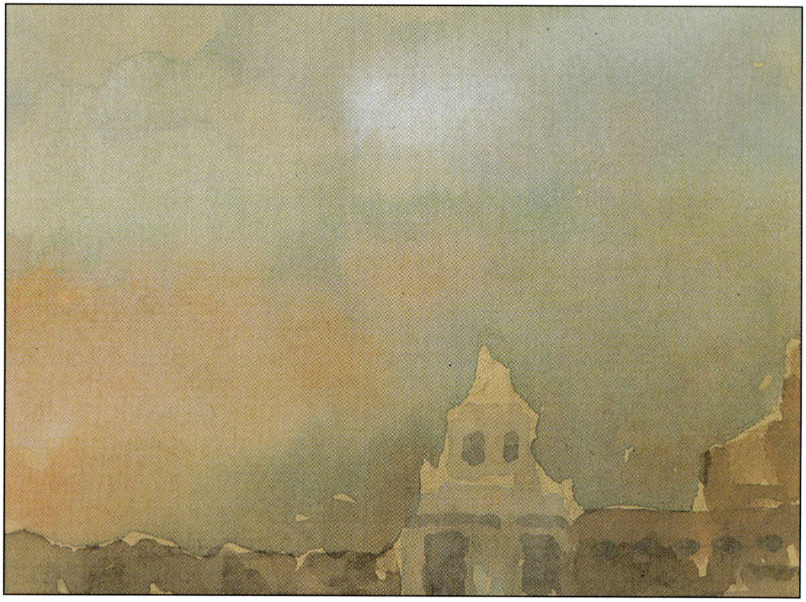

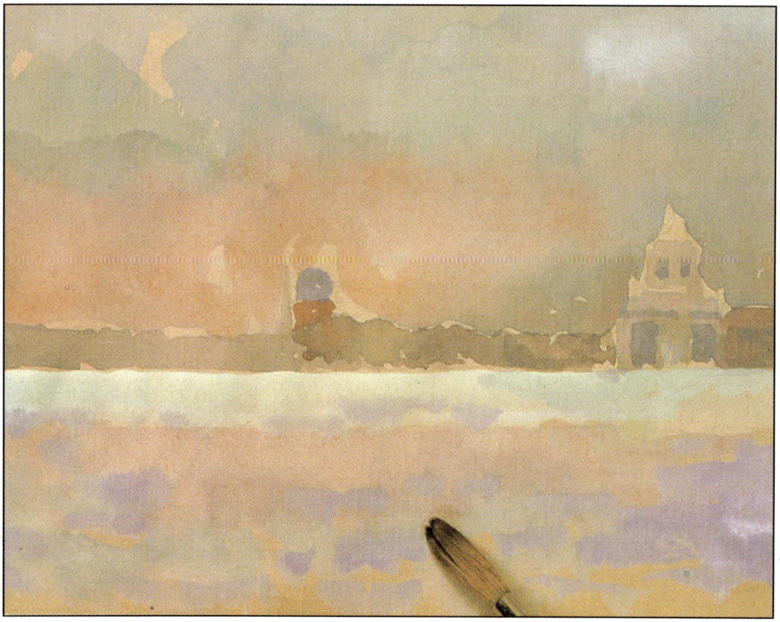

4 Now start to paint the water, starting with a thin wash of white, lemon yellow and a hint of ultramarine for the stretch of pale green water in the distance. Mix white, alizarin crimson and a touch of lemon yellow for the pink areas to show the reflection of the setting sun, and white and ultramarine for the blue areas. Apply the colours with a no. 10 brush using short, curving brushstrokes to suggest the choppy surface of the water.

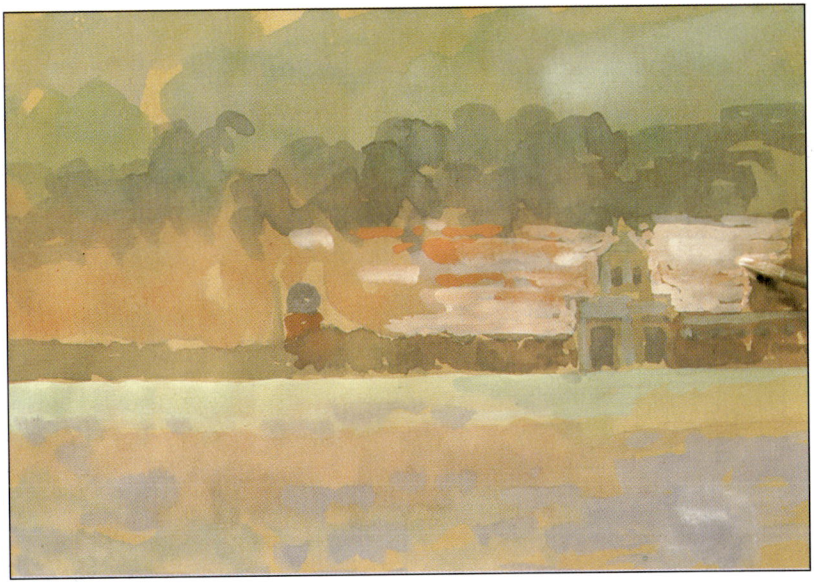

5 Check that the sky washes are dry, then mix ultramarine and alizarin and put in the dark storm clouds. Use a no. 4 brush and apply the paint wash-over-wash with lively, energetic strokes to give form and movement to the clouds. Now paint the light sky behind the buildings with narrow bands of white tinged with alizarin. Mix cadmium red and lemon yellow for the orange glow.

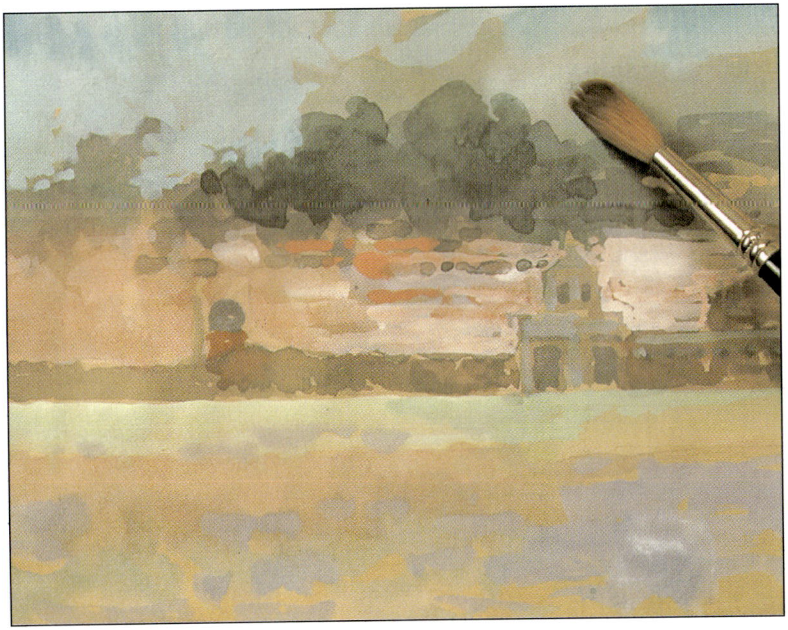

6 Build up the density of tone in the storm clouds with a darker wash of ultramarine and alizarin. Use loose, curving strokes to give the impression of movement and to give energy to the painting. Add a thin wash of white to the sky just above the buildings to lighten it. Switch to a no. 10 brush and paint the sky above the storm clouds with a loose wash of white gouache and ultramarine.

7 Now you can put in the fiery sunset colours. Mix lemon yellow, cadmium red and a little white to make a rich golden orange and, with the tip of a no. 4 brush, add touches of this colour around the lower edges of the clouds. For the yellow-tinted clouds, use flecks of lemon yellow and white, warmed with a hint of cadmium red in places. The detail (right) reveals the variety of brushwork and colour the artist has used in the sky. The airy, vaporous quality of the thin clouds at the top is described using dry paint, dragged on with a dry brush to create ragged strokes. These strokes cut into the edges of the storm clouds, giving them a more natural, broken edge.

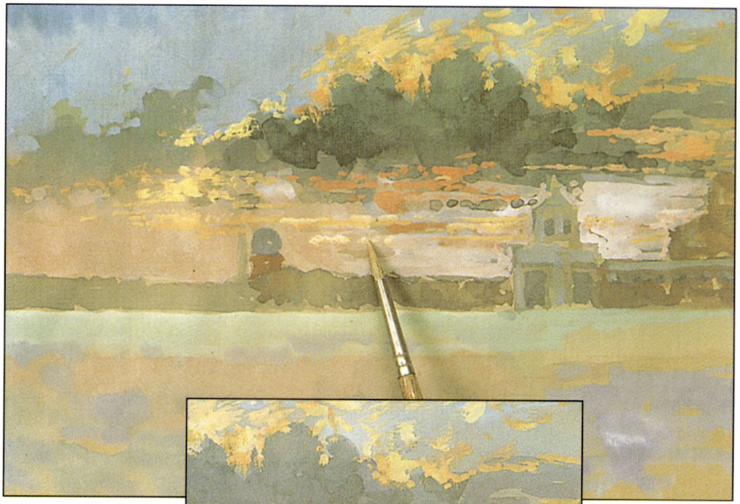

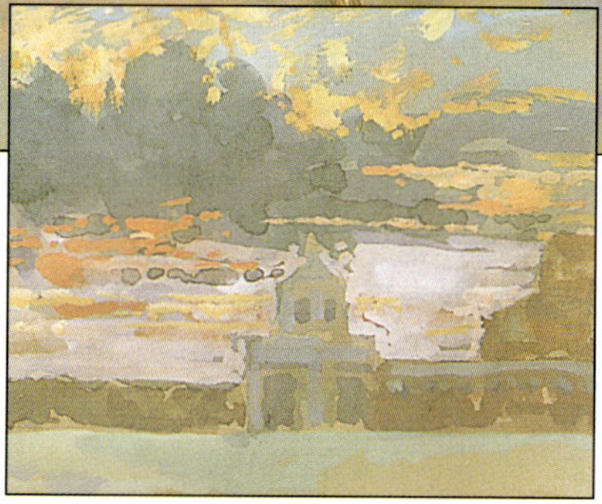

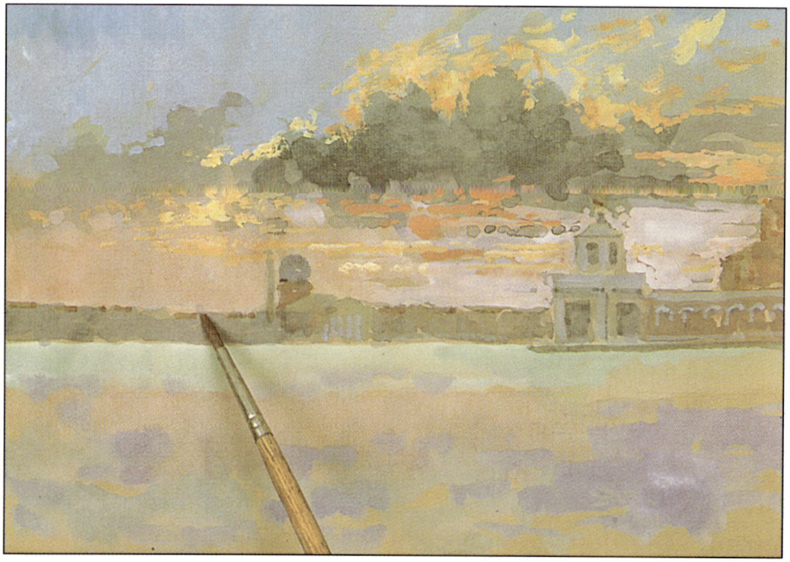

8 Deepen the tones on the distant buildings with a mixture of Payne's gray and white. Mix lemon yellow, ultramarine and white and suggest the architectural detailing on the nearer buildings on the right. Suggest the distant rooftops with thinly diluted burnt sienna.

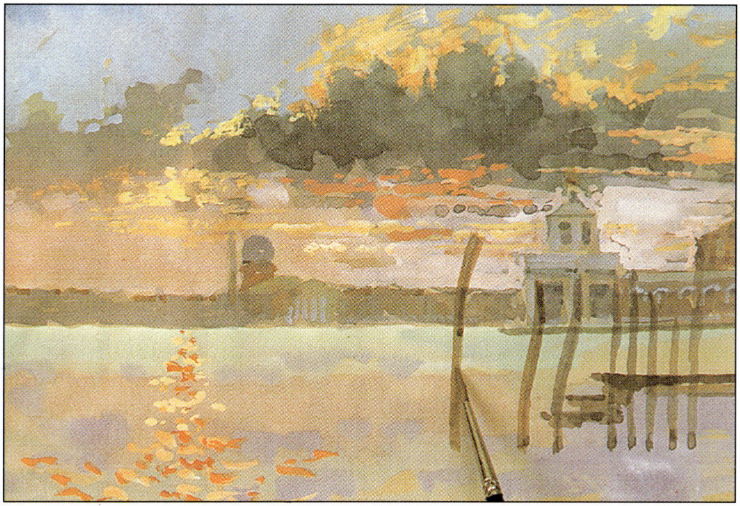

9 Switch to a no. 1 brush and paint the sun's reflection on the water with dark, medium and light tones mixed from cadmium red, lemon yellow and white. Use the tip of the brush to make rhythmic strokes that suggest the way the reflection is broken up by the moving surface. To enhance the effect of space and perspective, make these strokes smaller and more closely spaced in the distance.

Suggest the steps leading down into the water with light and dark tones of burnt sienna and black. When dry, dilute the colours with more water and paint the wooden mooring poles emerging from the water.

10 Finally, paint the reflections of the mooring poles with broken, swirling strokes, using a dark tone of ultramarine and Payne's gray. Lighten the wash with more water and use it to paint the dark ripples on the water's surface. To further enhance the illusion of receding space, jot in the groups of wooden mooring poles just visible in the distant water.

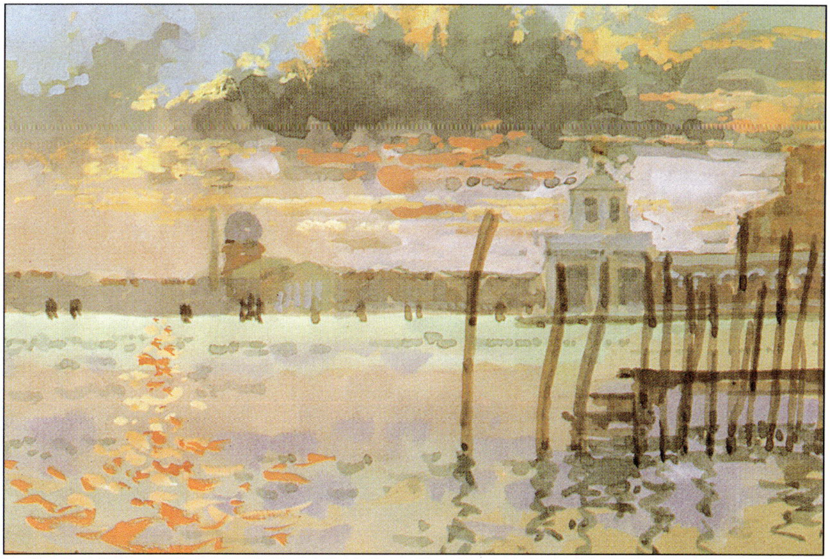

Painting Flowers

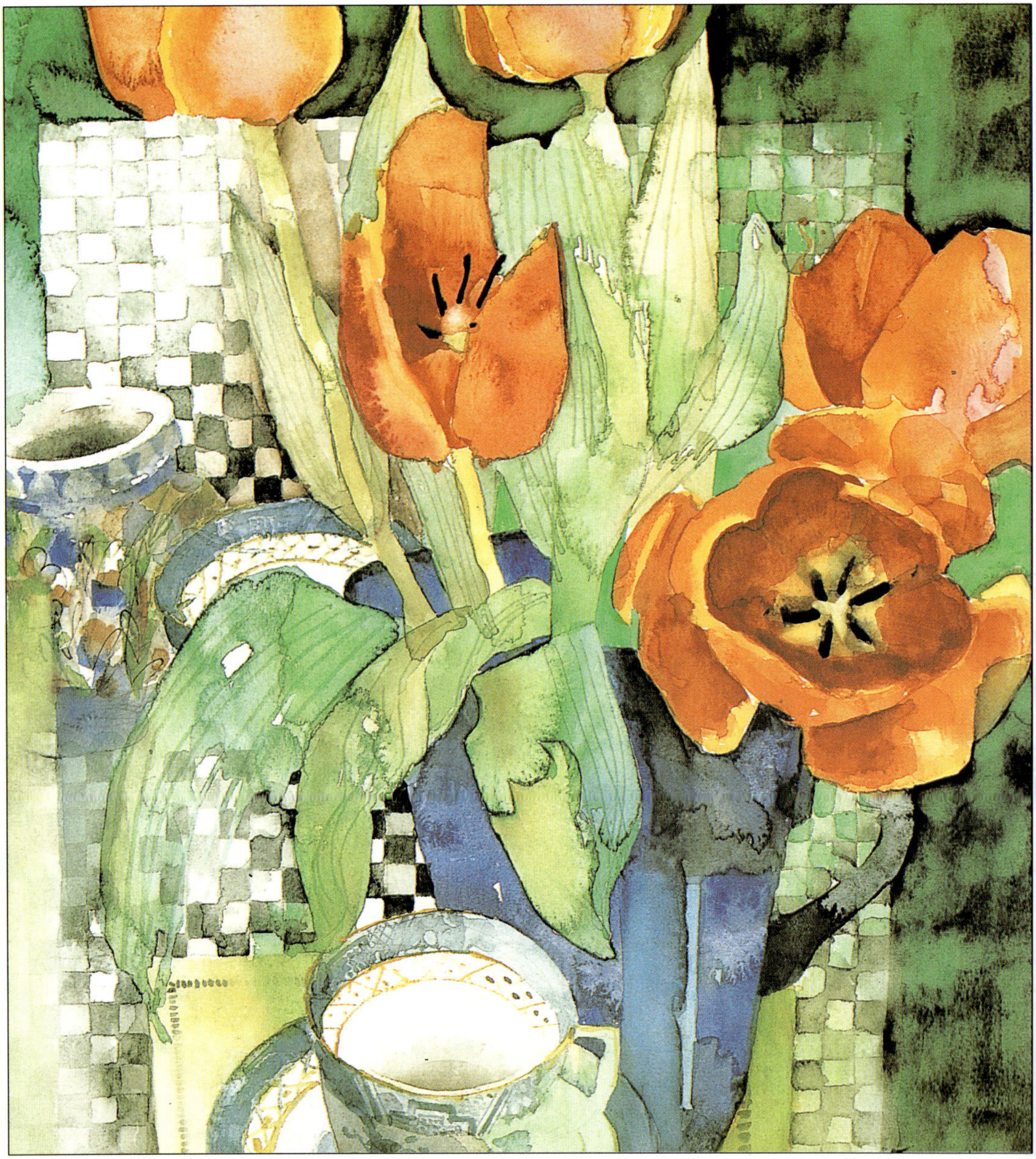

It is easy to see why flowers are such a popular painting subject. Not only are they a delight to the eye, with their graceful forms and gorgeous colours, but you can select and arrange them to your liking and paint them at your leisure – at least until the blooms die!

Setting up

Try to keep the arrangement of your flowers simple and informal – a fussy arrangement tends to look stiff and unnatural. Arrange the blooms so that they fan out naturally and gracefully, allowing some to overlap others. Place them at different heights, with some of the heads viewed from the back or in profile, just as they would appear if they were growing in a garden. Also be mindful of colour. Simple colour harmonies are usually more effective than garish multicolour arrangements.

Techniques

Try not to get bogged down in describing each leaf and flower in exact botanical detail; think of your vase of flowers as a single form in itself and establish the broad areas of colour and tone first. Starting from this base you can then build up gradually to the smaller details.

The pure translucency of watercolours makes them ideal for capturing the delicate quality of leaves and petals. Plan your approach carefully, first deciding which highlights need to be 'reserved' as white paper and then building up methodically from the palest to the darkest tones. Delicate overlapping washes can produce the effects of light shining on and through petals, and so can working wet-in-wet, allowing one colour to spread into another so that there are no hard edges. Avoid heavy applications of colour – thin, transparent washes allow light to reflect off the white paper and up through the colours.

Lost and found edges

When you paint a vase of flowers, try to convey an impression of some of the blooms being further back than others. Do this by bringing the nearer flowers into sharp focus while playing down those towards the back of the group. Pick out one or two flowers near the front and emphasize these with crisp 'found' edges. Make the flowers further back less well defined by using soft, 'lost' edges and more muted colours. Let some of the flowers touch and overlap to create the illusion of three dimensions.

Shirley Trevena
BOB'S RED TULIPS
Left: Because a vase or jug is a tall, narrow shape you will often need some additional objects to provide balance.

Sally Keir
IRIS 'WARM GOLD'
Below: Gouache paints have a vibrant light-reflecting quality that is ideally suited to painting flowers.

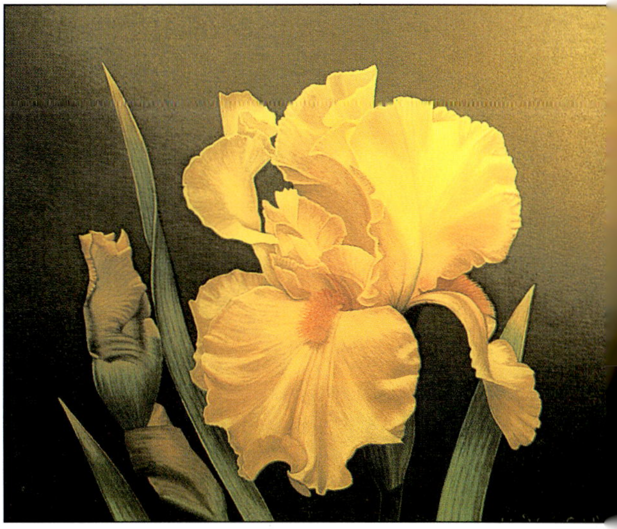

Lilies and Ivy

A huge bouquet of lilies makes a spectacular subject to paint in watercolour. The artist has taken great care with the arrangement, ensuring that the flowers, leaves and stems set up linear rhythms that lead the eye around the picture. The ivy falling in elegant curves around the vase helps to balance the weight of the flowers.

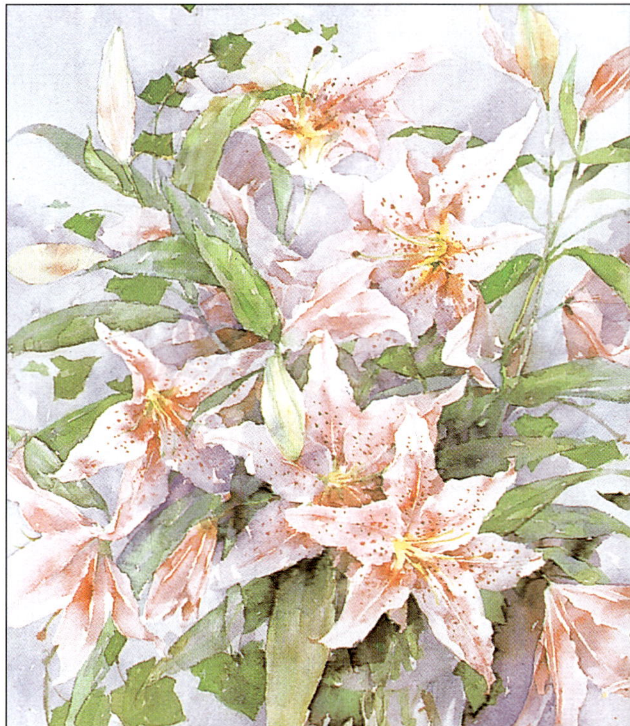

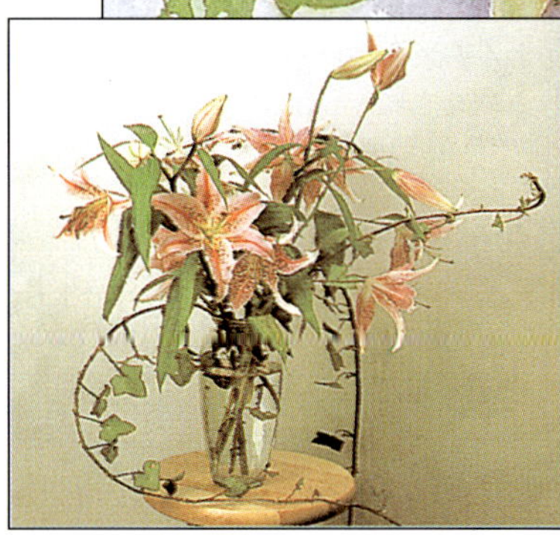

YOU WILL NEED

- *Stretced sheet of Not surface watercolour paper, 16½ x 23in (41.9 x 58.4cm)*
- *No. 3 round brush*
- *No. 6 round brush*
- *HB pencil*
- *Kneaded eraser*
- *Soft tissues*

WATERCOLOUR PAINTS IN THE FOLLOWING COLOURS

- *French ultramarine*
- *Mauve*
- *Purple madder alizarin*
- *Winsor blue*
- *Alizarin crimson*
- *Bright red*
- *Chrome yellow*
- *Sap green*

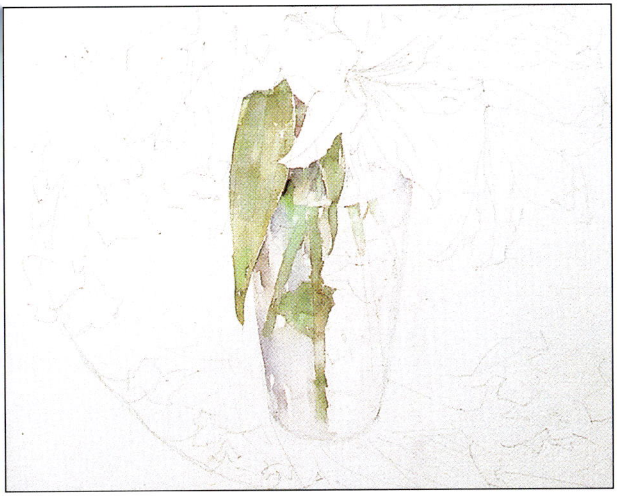

1 Make a careful outline drawing of the flower arrangement using an HB pencil. Start by working on the glass vase, using the no. 3 brush. Suggest the shadowy tones in the water with varying mixes of French ultramarine and mauve. Put on colour, water it down and spread it, then take some colour off again with a wet brush to create a range of subtle tones. For the leaves and stems use sap green and chrome yellow, cooled with hints of ultramarine and mauve. Leave to dry completely.

2 Lightly wash over the topmost lily flowers with a pale wash of carmine, leaving the centres unpainted. Then add a little mauve to give form, letting the colours merge softly on the damp paper. Apply chrome yellow to the centres of the flowers, then add a little sap green to the mix and paint the stamens. Start to paint the surrounding leaves using the same mix, adding a little French ultramarine for the darker tones. When the lily petals are dry, use the tip of the brush to add dots of purple madder alizarin for the spots on the petals.

Helpful Hint

THESE INITIAL COLOURS TOP AND BOTTOM WILL GIVE YOU SOME IDEA OF THE INTENSITY OF TONES TO BE USED WITHIN THE OVERALL PICTURE.

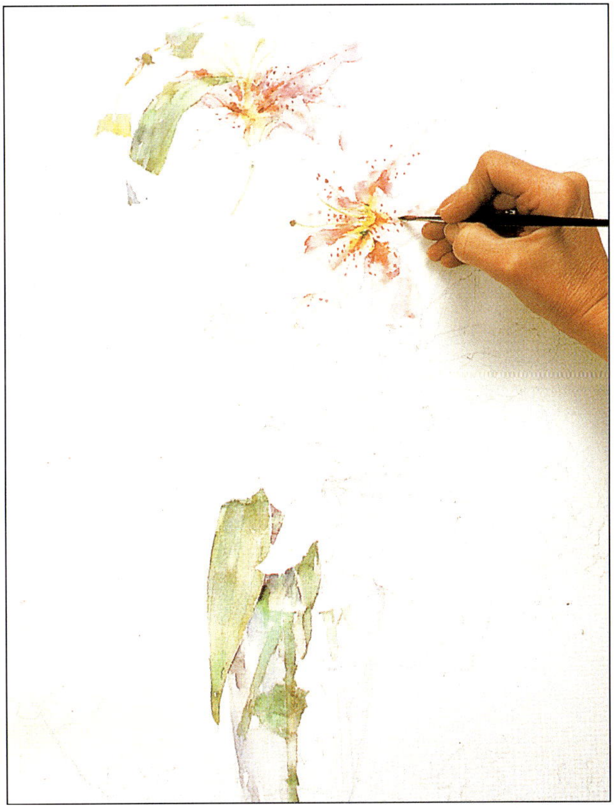

3 Work on the two unopened flowers at the top right, using the same greens mixed in step 1 for the stalks and leaves. Paint the closed flower buds with delicate washes of carmine, adding a hint of palest green from your palette. Add touches of bright red for the deeper tones. The colours will merge softly on the damp paper.

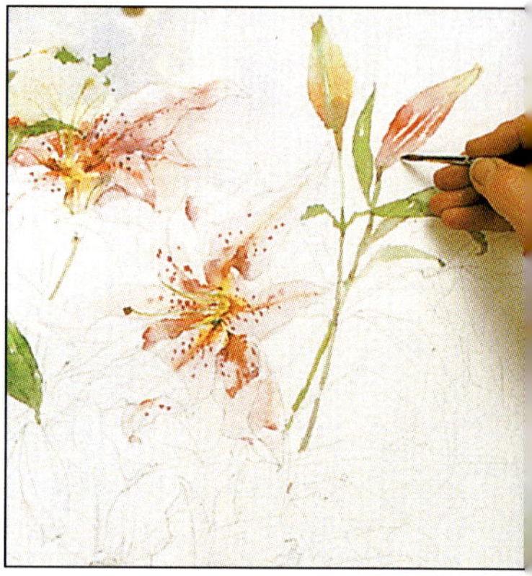

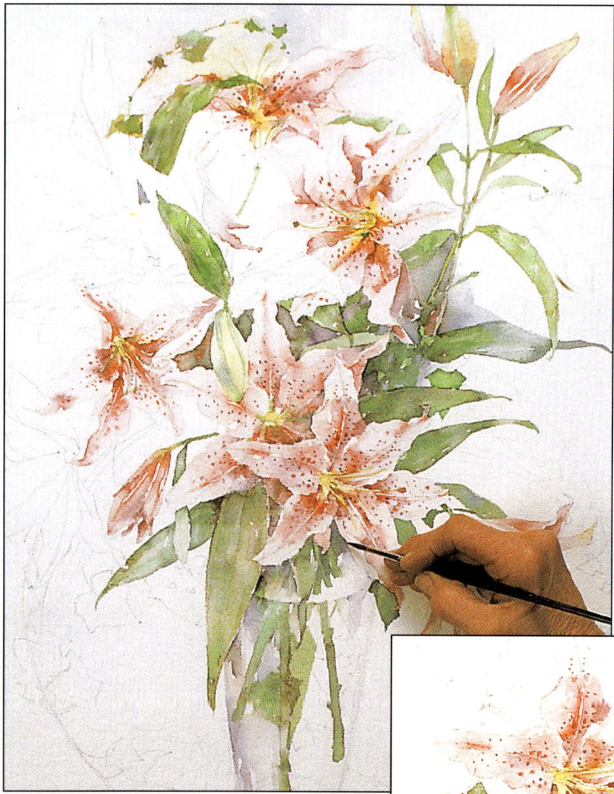

4 Continue painting in the flowers and foliage as before, working all around the picture so that the overall balance of colour and tone can be judged as you work. Mix and blend the colours on the paper, wet-into-wet, to describe the delicate forms of the petals (see detail). Strengthen your washes with more colour or dilute them with water to vary the tones and suggest the play of light on the flowers. Add some shadowy tones between the flowers and among the stems above the water in the vase with ultramarine and purple madder alizarin.

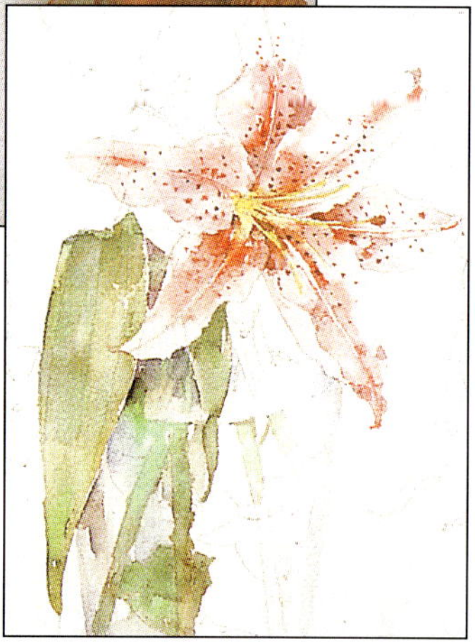

This detail of a flower (left) reveals the delicate translucency of the washes. The artist applies deeper pink hues of carmine and alizarin crimson in the centres of the flowers, washing the colour out more as she moves down the length of the petals and leaving flecks of white paper for the highlights.

5 Paint the unopened flower buds to the top left of the picture with delicate washes of chrome yellow, adding a faint blush of carmine wet-into-wet. Continue filling in the flowers and foliage around the edges of the arrangement using the same colour mixes as before. Mix a cool, bluish green with ultramarine and a little sap green and carmine for the leaves that are in shadow.

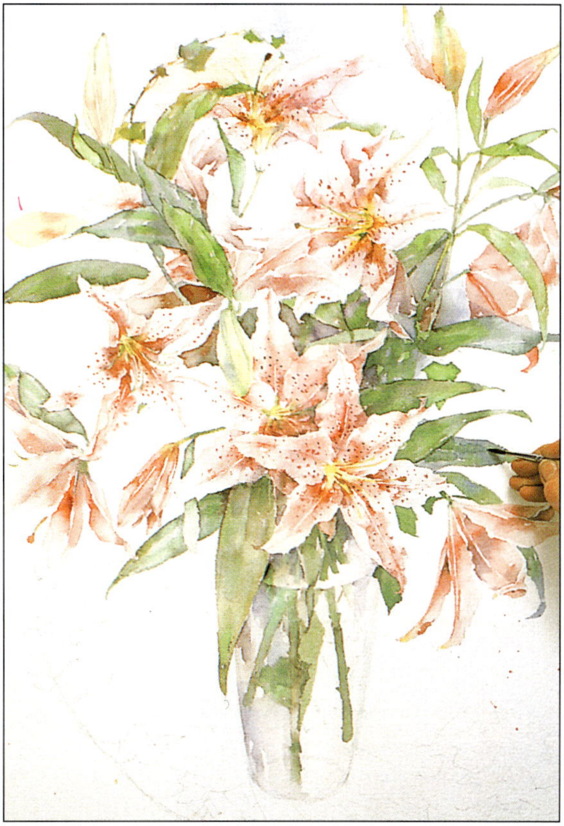

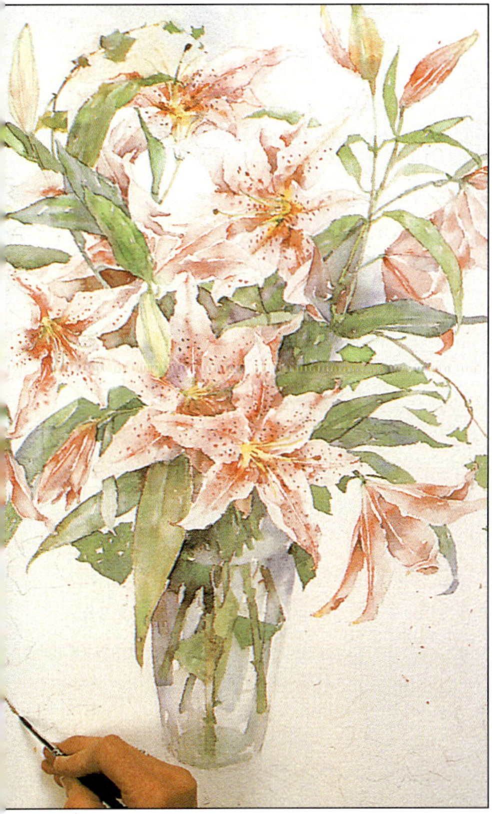

6 Develop the woody flower stems in the vase with crisp washes and glazes of sap green and carmine, adding touches of purple madder alizarin for the darker stems. Leave to dry, then work up the shadows in the water with transparent overlaid washes of ultramarine, sap green and purple madder alizarin. Lift off colour with a wet brush to lighten some of the tones. Using a tissue, blot the wash here and there around the points where the flower stems break through the surface of the water. Mix sap green and carmine for the brownish stems of the trailing ivy.

7 Paint the ivy leaves using sap green, adding a little bright red for the darker leaves. Use the no. 6 brush to paint the background around the vase with variegated washes of ultramarine and purple madder alizarin. Apply the paint loosely, leaving chinks of white paper showing through to give sparkle and suggest dappled light and shade. Dip your brush in water and lift out some of the colour so that the wash fades out almost to nothing at the extreme edges of the picture.

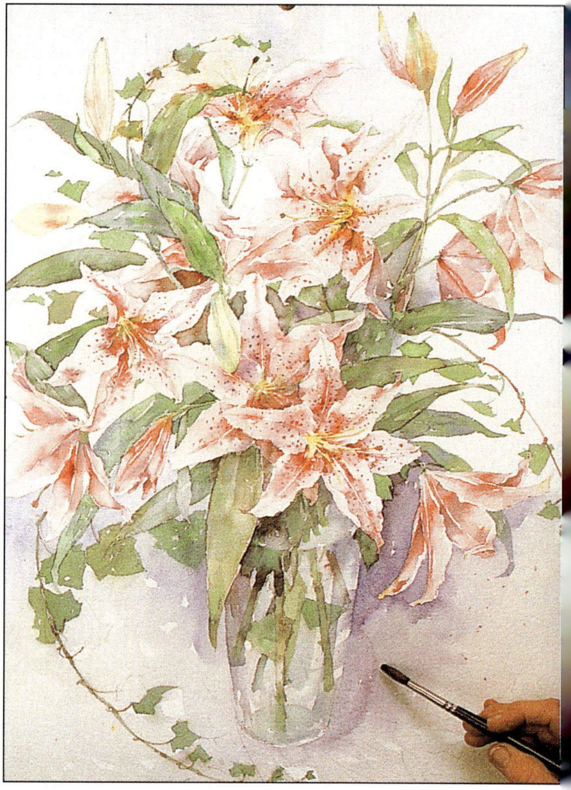

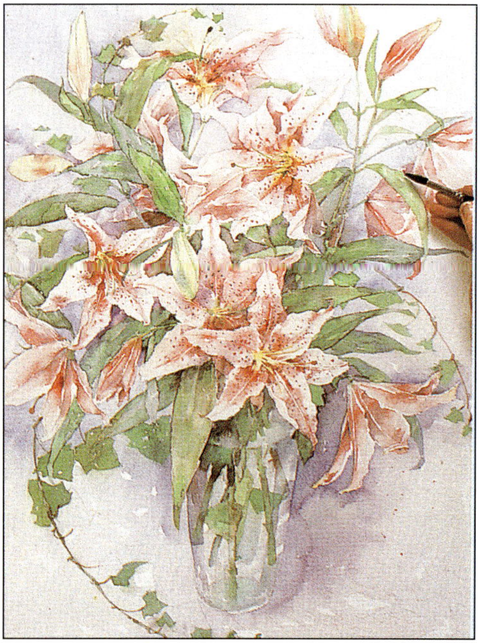

8 Now mix a watery solution of ultramarine and fill in the rest of the background, blotting off any excess colour with a tissue. Use the no. 3 brush for the intricate shapes between the flowers and stems. Add a little purple madder alizarin here and there to create subtle nuances of shade.

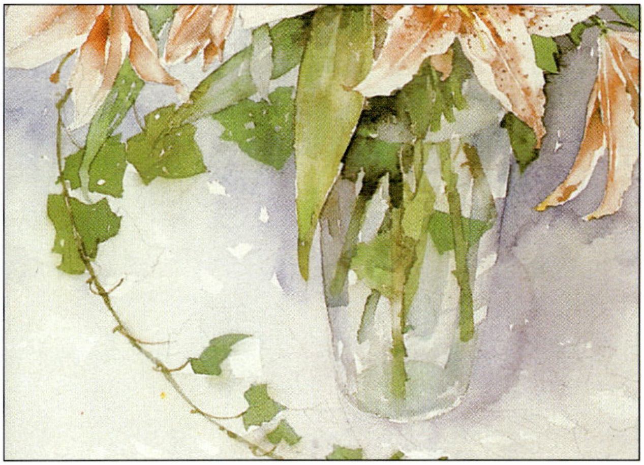

9 Suggest the shadows cast by the flowers onto the table with deeper washes of ultramarine and purple madder alizarin. Apply the paint with loose, rapid brushstrokes, leaving chinks of the pale underwash showing through. Soften some of the shadows further back with water.

Helpful Hint

DON'T WORRY IF YOU APPEAR TO HAVE USED TOO MUCH COLOUR, SIMPLY APPLY MORE WATER, WASH THE COLOUR OUT AND THEN DAB OFF THE EXCESS WITH A PIECE OF CRUMPLED TISSUE.

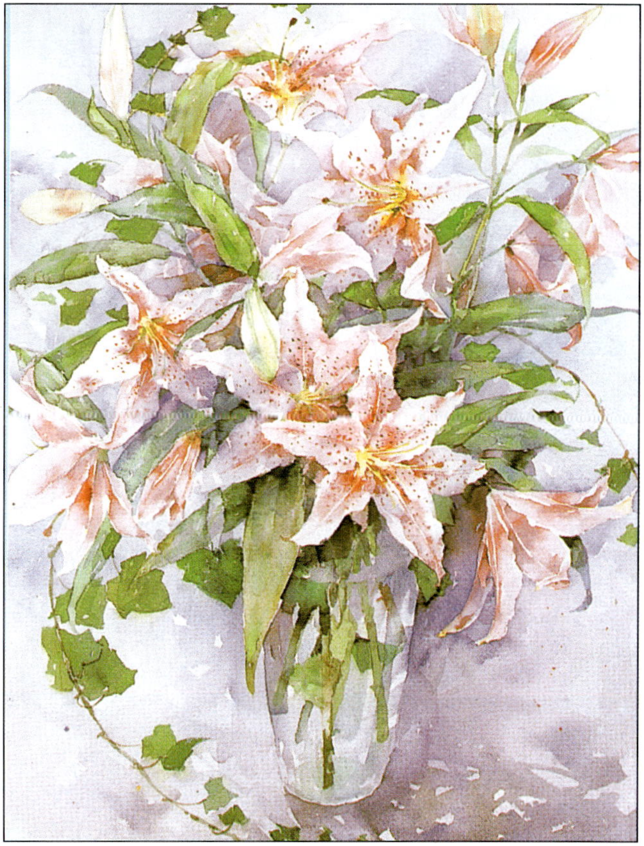

10 Use the no. 3 brush and the appropriate colours to strengthen and define any details that may have become overshadowed by the background. Darken the background behind the flowers to 'throw' them forward and give them more definition. Leave the painting to dry completely, then gently rub over the surface with a kneaded eraser to remove any of the remaining pencil lines and to soften and lighten the overall effect of the petals.

Decorative Patterns

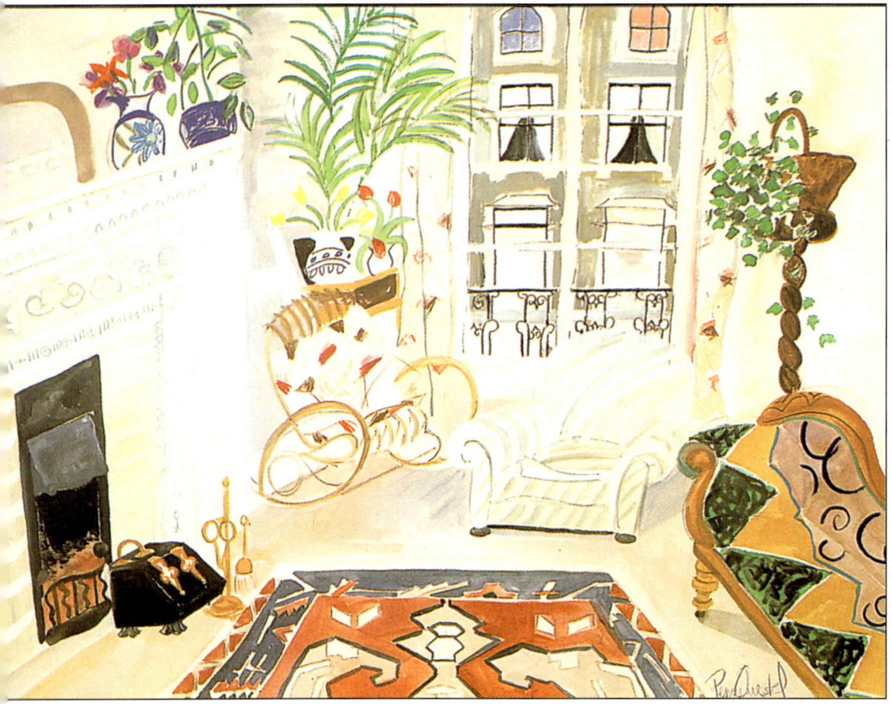

Penny Quested
THE SITTING ROOM
This delightful watercolour is reminiscent of the paintings of Henri Matisse. The artist has deliberately stylized the subject to stress the patterned quality of the objects in the room, eliminating most of the modelling in favour of all-over decorative impact.

Most still-life compositions are rendered realistically, using light, shade and perspective to produce a three-dimensional effect. Sometimes, however, it can be more entertaining to deliberately exaggerate or simplify your subject in order to create an exciting and original image – for example, treating it simply as a flat, two-dimensional pattern of shapes and colours.

Many of the domestic items artists assemble for still-life painting – containers, ornaments and fabrics – contain a wealth of colour and pattern elements which can be explored for their own sake. When setting up a decorative still life, it is important to ensure that shapes, colours and patterns combine to create a unified, harmonious effect. Think about the relationship of one object to another, and try to introduce interesting lines and rhythms that lead the eye around the painting.

Using gouache paints

The project painting which follows was painted with gouache paints, which are an opaque form of watercolour. The opacity of gouache gives strong, bright hues, and because the paint dries with a matt, smooth, opaque surface, it is ideal for this decorative style of painting in which bold, vibrant colours are placed side by side with minimal modelling.

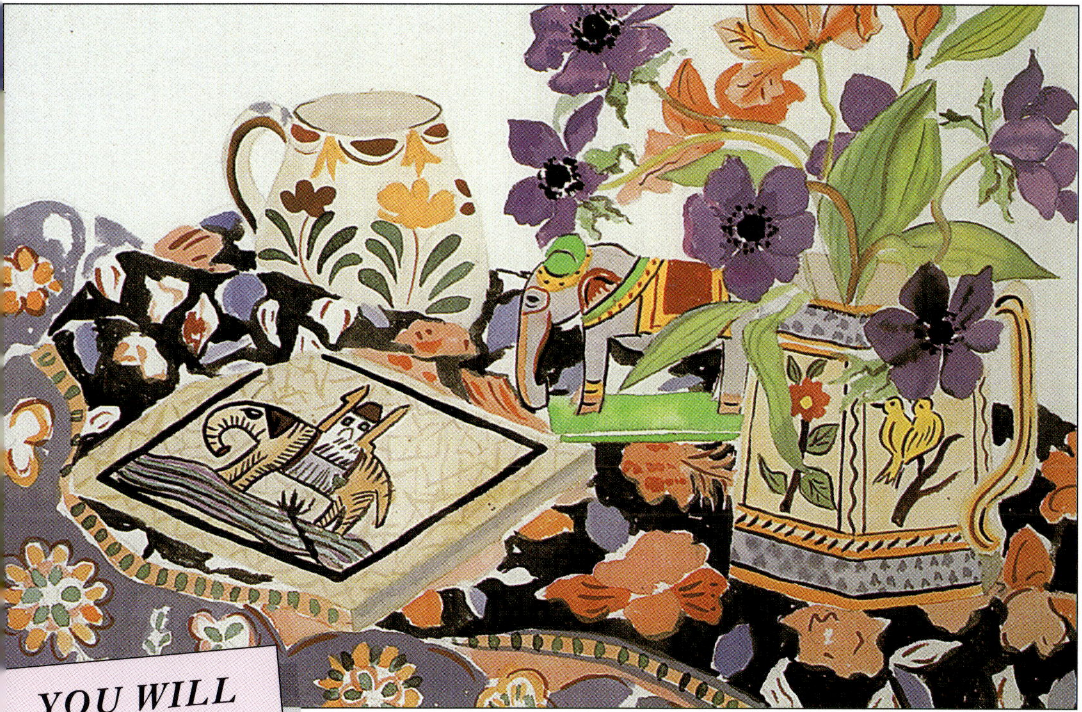

YOU WILL NEED

- Sheet of 140lb (285gsm) Not surface watercolour paper 20 x 15in (50.8 x 38.1cm)
- No. 7 round brush
- No. 3 round brush
- HB pencil

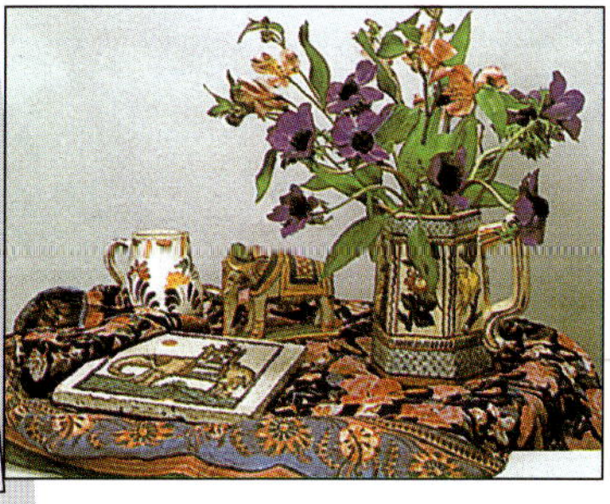

GOUACHE PAINTS IN THE FOLLOWING COLOURS

- *Indigo*
- *Brilliant violet*
- *Permanent white*
- *Prussian blue*
- *Rose malmaison*
- *Ivory black*
- *Alizarin crimson*
- *Yellow ochre*
- *Brilliant yellow*
- *Bistre*
- *Lemon yellow*
- *Winsor green*

Souvenir of India

By emphasizing bright colours and simplifying shapes, the artist has drawn attention to the decorative quality of this subject. The colours of the various objects have been carefully chosen to harmonize with and complement one another.

1 Make a careful outline drawing of the still life using an HB pencil. Make sure that your drawing adequately fills your sheet of paper, otherwise it will look as though it is 'floating'.

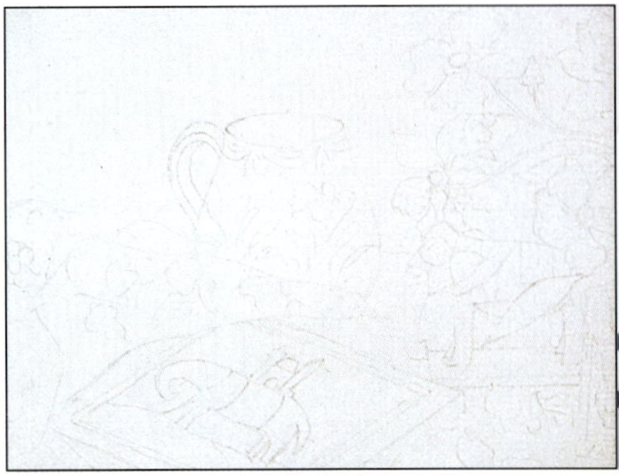

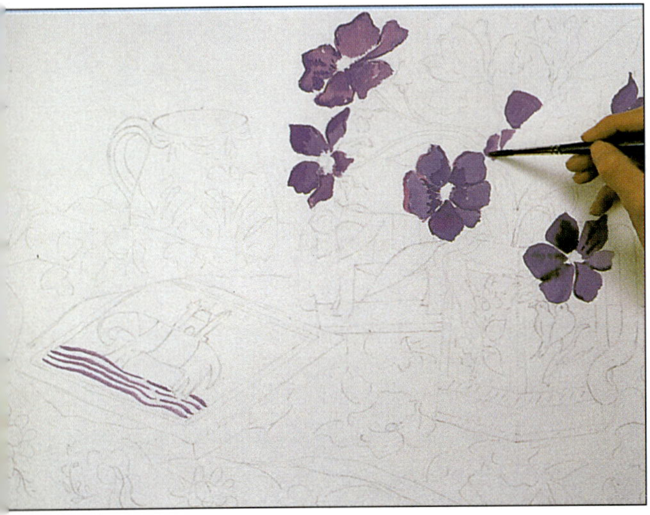

2 Begin by painting the anemones with the no. 7 brush, using a mixture of brilliant violet, permanent white and a touch of indigo, diluted with water. Use the same colour to put in the wavy pattern on the decorative tile. Add shade and tone to the petals with a mix of indigo and brilliant violet.

3 Mix Prussian blue, rose malmaison and a little ivory black to create a deep purple for the centres of the anemones. Continue working with this mixture, putting in the dark areas of the patterned scarf. You build up this picture by blocking in each individual area with paint, as if it were a two-dimensional pattern.

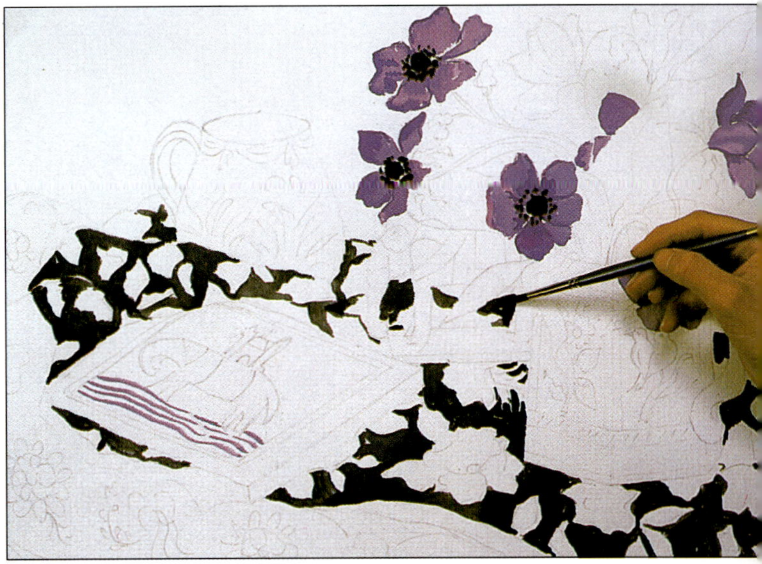

4 Mix a pale blue wash with cobalt blue, permanent white and a hint of yellow ochre for the blue bands on the tall flower vase. Add more cobalt blue to the mixture and paint the dots on the bands. Now use this mixture to paint the mid-blue areas on the scarf.

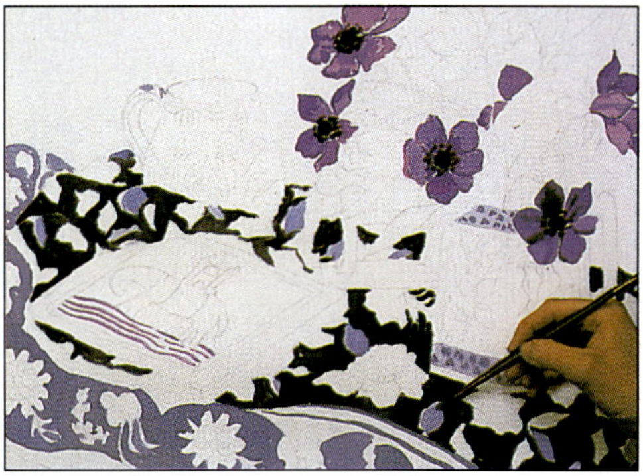

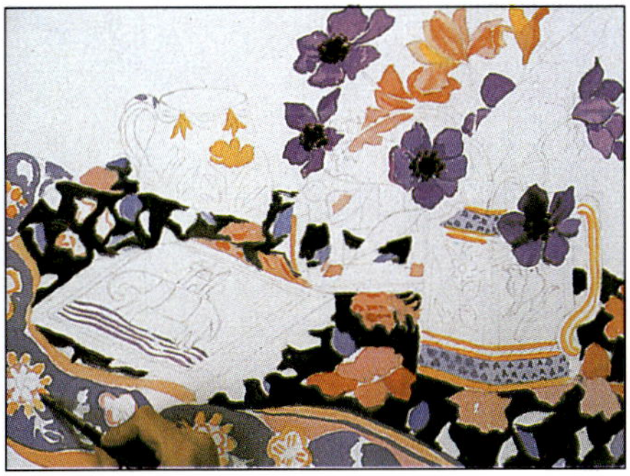

5 Use a mix of rose malmaison and white to paint the lilies, varying the amounts of white to develop the tones. Use brilliant yellow for the centres. Paint the pink patterns on the scarf and on the elephant carving with the same mixtures. Add a little brilliant yellow to the mix to make a pale orange and paint the flowers on the small vase and the orange bands on the taller vase. Deepen the mix with more rose malmaison and brilliant yellow to make a deeper orange for the floral pattern on the scarf.

6 Make a very pale, neutral-coloured wash from yellow ochre, cobalt blue and white, thinly diluted. Apply this to the small vase and the decorative tile, working around the shape of the elephant. Add a little indigo to the wash and paint the shadow inside the rim of the vase and on the edge of the tile.

Helpful Hint

SOME GOUACHE COLOURS TEND TO SEPARATE AFTER THE MIX HAS BEEN STANDING A WHILE IN THE PALETTE. SO BEFORE YOU USE A MIX, GIVE IT A STIR WITH YOUR BRUSH.

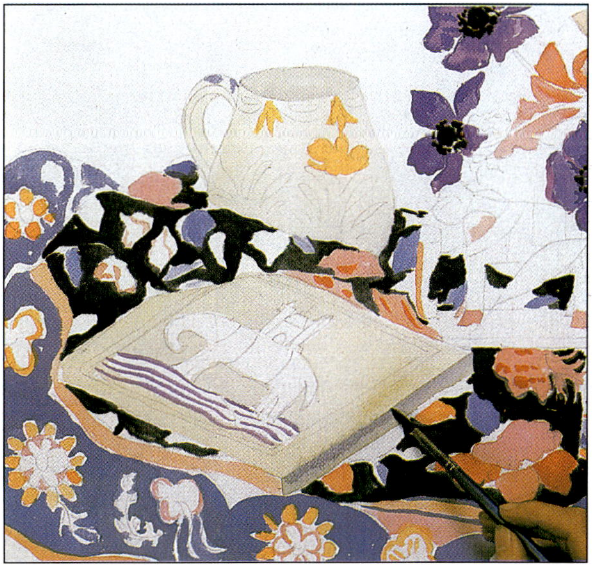

7 Switch to the no. 3 brush and use a lighter version of the same wash to paint the crackled effect on the surface of the tile with a series of criss-crossed lines.

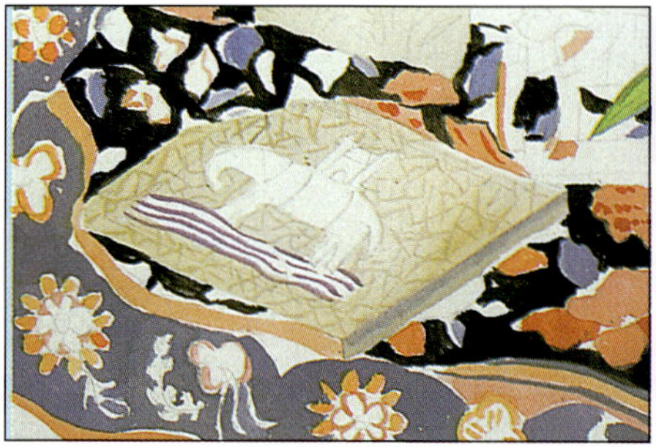

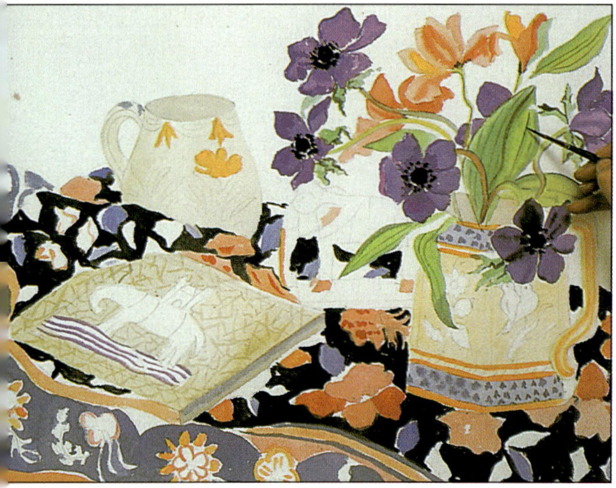

8 Mix a pale yellow with rose malmaison, brilliant yellow and white and apply this to the large vase with the no. 7 brush, leaving the birds and flowers white. Now mix lemon yellow, Winsor green, white and a touch of cobalt blue to make a pale green, and paint the stems and leaves of the flowers with the no. 3 brush. Mix in a little rose malmaison for the stems, varying their hues from green to pinkish green. Darken the wash with indigo for the shadows and the veins on the leaves.

9 Touch in the bright colours on the elephant carving with brilliant yellow and a bright green mix of Winsor green and lemon yellow. On the tall vase, use brilliant yellow on the birds and flower and mix Winsor green and yellow ochre for the leaf motif. Mix rose malmaison and yellow ochre for the elephant motif on the tile. Then mix a dark green from Winsor green and Prussian blue and paint the leaf pattern on the small vase and the green patterns on the tile and the scarf.

10 Paint the red details on the elephant carving with rose malmaison. Then add Prussian blue to the mix to make a deeper red for the flowers on the small jug and the detailing on the elephant on the tile. Use the same colour to emphasize and outline the floral pattern on the scarf with sketchy lines.

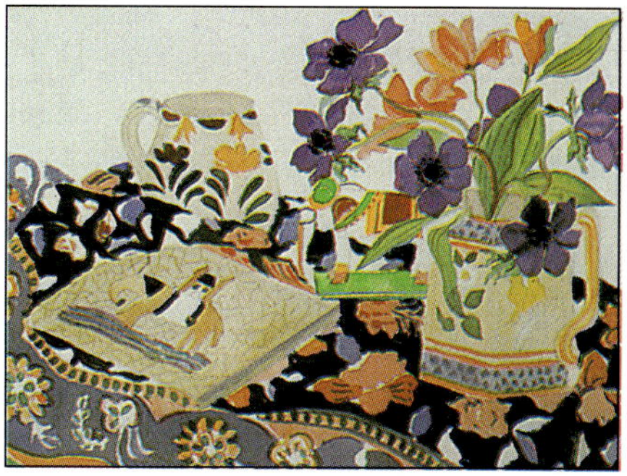

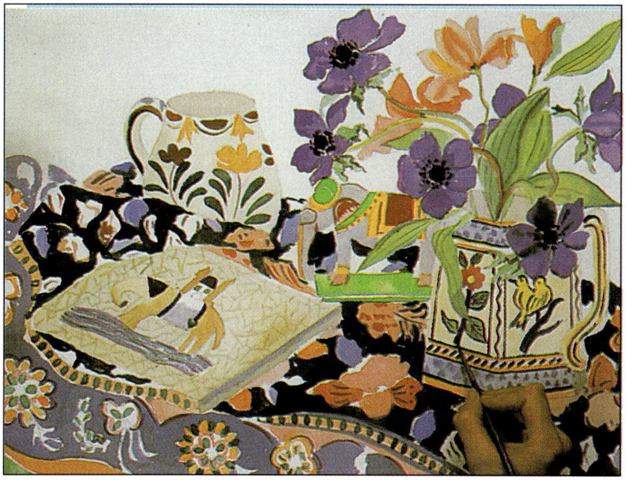

Helpful Hint

DON'T BE PUT OFF BY THE SEEMINGLY COMPLEX PATTERNS IN THIS STILL LIFE: SIMPLIFY THEM AS YOU PAINT.

11 Fill in the body on the elephant carving with a diluted grey wash of cobalt blue, brilliant yellow and white. Mix bistre with brilliant violet to make a rich brown and complete the decorative pattern on the tall vase. Use the same mix on the handle of the small vase.

12 To finish, mix Prussian blue with ivory black and paint the linear details on the tile. Outline the elephant carving with the same mixture and paint in its features and details. Stand back and assess the painting. The vibrant colours should enhance the richly patterned subject, with no one area of the painting being more important than the rest.

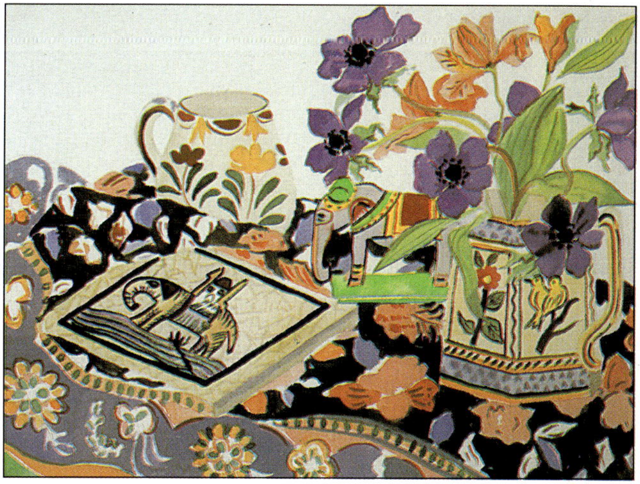

Texturing

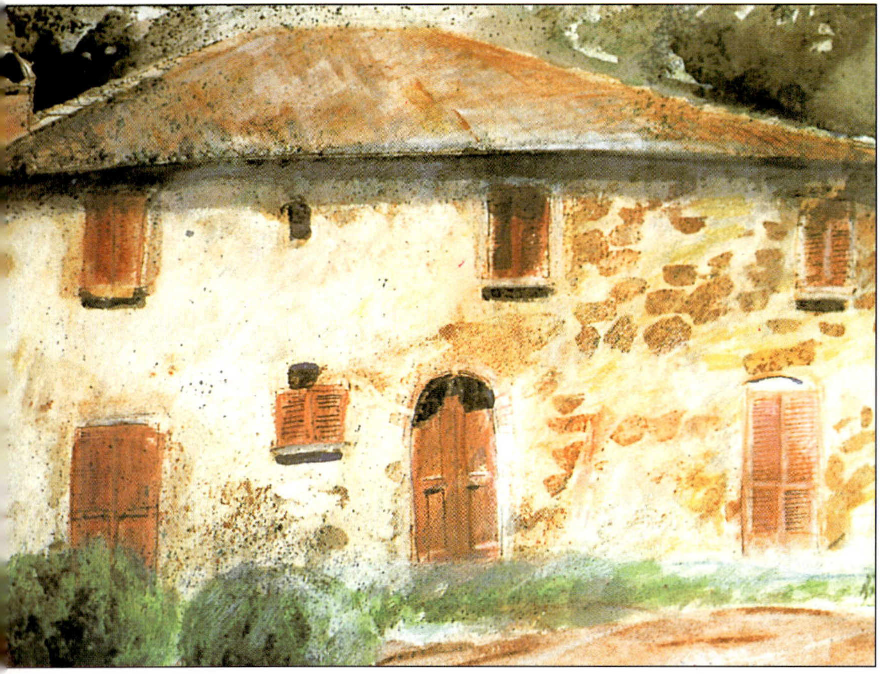

Jane Strother
ITALIAN HOUSE
There are lots of ways in which watercolour paint can be used to create textures and effects. Here, the artist has used the spattering technique to suggest the crumbling, pitted stonework of the old building. To spatter, load an old toothbrush with paint, hold it above the paper, then draw your thumbnail through the bristles to release a shower of fine droplets.

One of the more unusual techniques you can try with watercolour is texturing with plastic wrap – the thin sort used for wrapping food. This process is very simple and produces extraordinary and unpredictable effects. In our project painting the artist has used plastic wrap to create an impression of the ripples and eddies on the surface of a pond, but it could equally be used to add interest to a sky or to suggest the dappled shadows beneath a tree – the possibilities are limited only by the extent of your imagination.

The paint has to be wet for this technique to work, so have everything you need to hand so that you can work quickly. Decide on the area you want to texture and stretch a sheet of thin plastic food wrap over it. Wrap the plastic round the back of the board if necessary, to keep it taut. Using the tips of your fingers, press and squeeze the plastic so that it wrinkles up and forms ridges. With the plastic still in place, lay the board flat and leave the painting to dry. This can take anything from 30 minutes to several hours, depending on how big an area you are painting and how much wet paint you have applied.

When you think the paint looks dry, peel away the plastic. Where the paint has become trapped in the folds of the plastic, it dries with an attractive striated pattern with subtle variations in tone.

Three Fishes

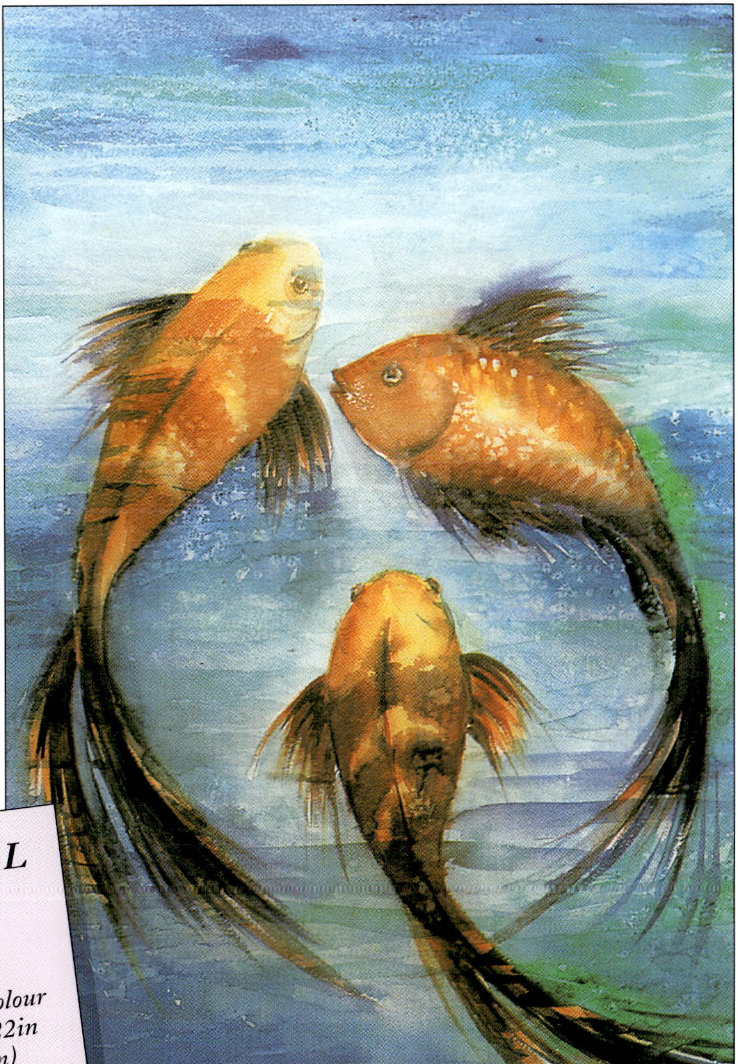

The use of unorthodox methods is fun and demonstrates the creative potential of the watercolour medium. In this delightful painting the artist exploits the fluid, unpredictable nature of watercolour, working into the wet paint with crumpled plastic wrap to create the patterns in the water.

YOU WILL NEED

- *Sheet of 140lb (285gsm) Not surface watercolour paper, 16½ x 22in (41.9 x 55.8cm)*
- *No. 16 round brush*
- *No. 4 round brush*
- *Sheet of thin plastic wrap*
- *Table salt*
- *Gum arabic*

WATERCOLOUR PAINTS IN THE FOLLOWING COLOURS

- *Winsor blue*
- *Winsor green*
- *Cadmium yellow*
- *Cadmium red*
- *Alizarin crimson*
- *French ultramarine*
- *Permanent white gouache paint*

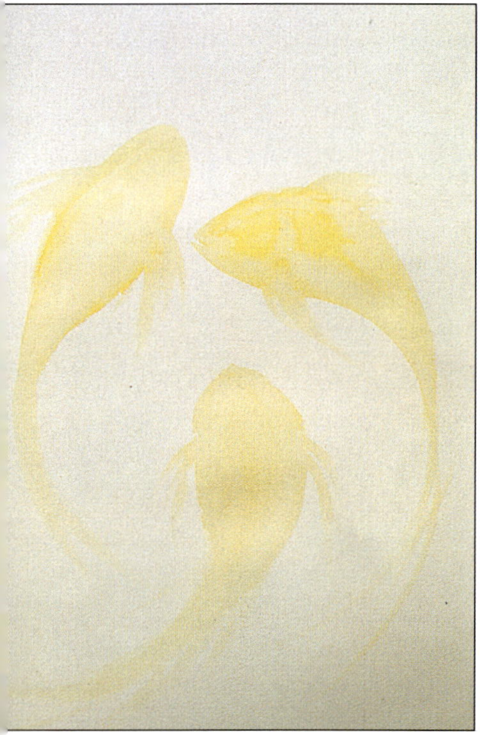

1 Mix a watery solution of cadmium yellow. Working directly onto the paper, paint the shapes of the three fishes with a well-loaded no. 16 round brush. Work quickly and confidently with just a few brushstrokes, using the belly of the brush for the wide bodies and tapering down to the tails with the tip of the brush.

Helpful Hint

IF YOU ARE UNSURE ABOUT 'DRAWING' WITH THE BRUSH, LIGHTLY DRAW THE FISHES IN PENCIL FIRST.

2 Strengthen the tones on the fishes with further washes of cadmium yellow. While the paint is still damp, mix cadmium yellow and cadmium red to make a rich orange and quickly brush this over the fishes' bodies to give them form and shading. Let the orange washes merge into the underwash, suggesting the softly rounded bodies of the fish. Use the tip of the brush and long, sweeping strokes to paint the fins and tails, lifting the brush as you near the end of each stroke to create ragged marks that suggest movement.

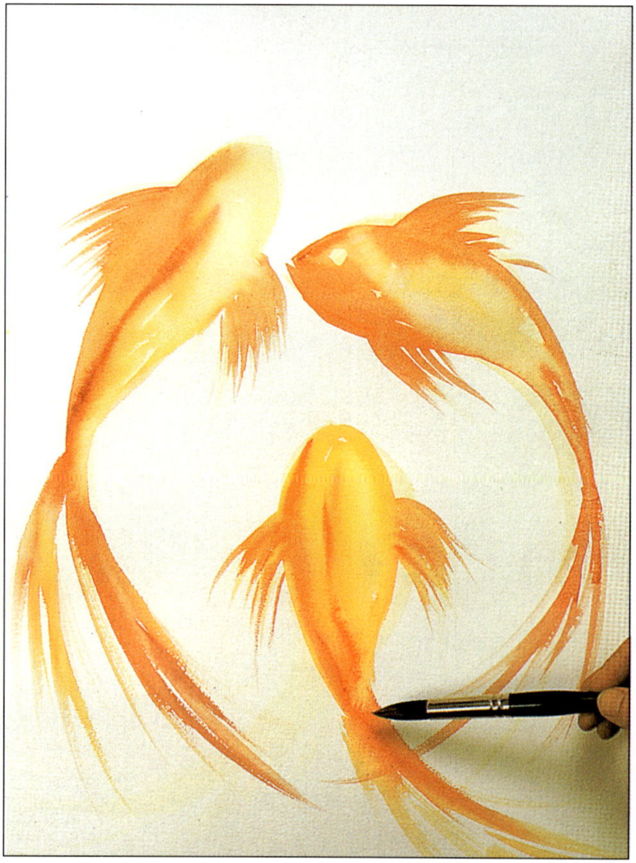

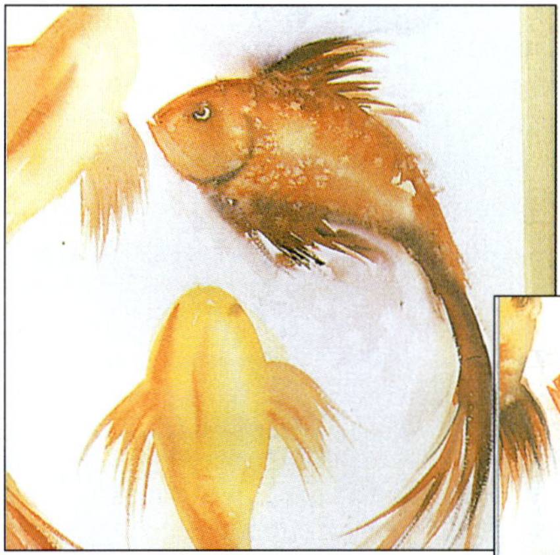

3

Develop the form of the fish on the right using alizarin crimson, darkened with French ultramarine for the deepest tones on the fins, tail and body. Define the eye and the shape of the head with the tip of the brush. While the paint is still wet, sprinkle a few grains of salt along the fish's body and leave to dry for at least 10 minutes (see inset). When dry, brush off the salt to reveal a pattern resembling fish scales. Dip the brush in clean water and work around the outline of the fish to soften the colour – this creates an impression of the fish moving through the water.

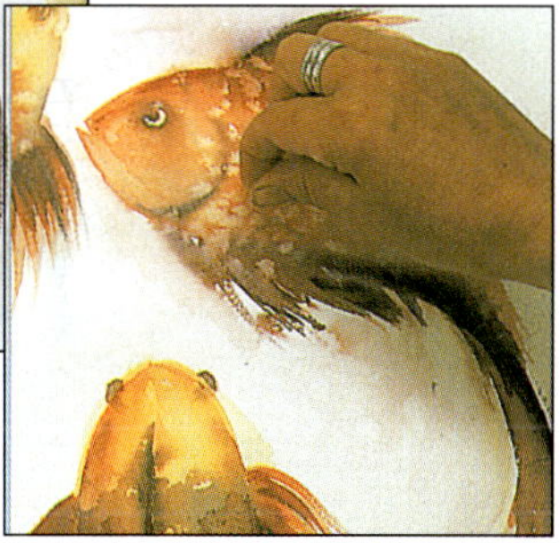

4

Work on the bottom fish with the same yellow and orange washes. Allow to dry slightly, then paint the eyes and the dark markings on the back with a mix of cadmium red and French ultramarine. Build up the mottled pattern with further washes, applied wet on dry. Then sprinkle a little salt into the wet paint and leave to dry as before.

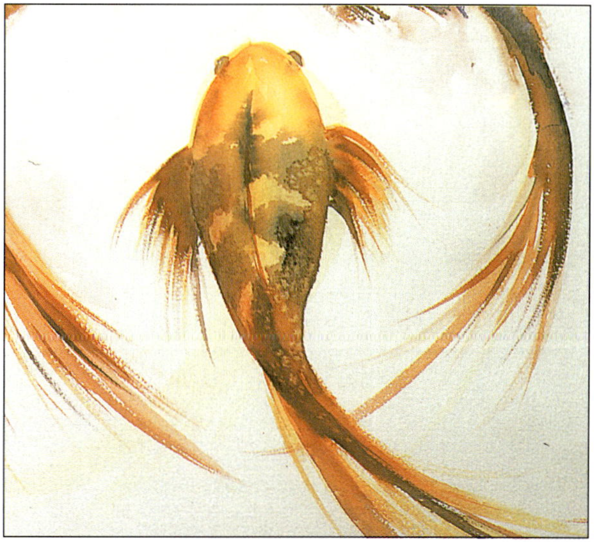

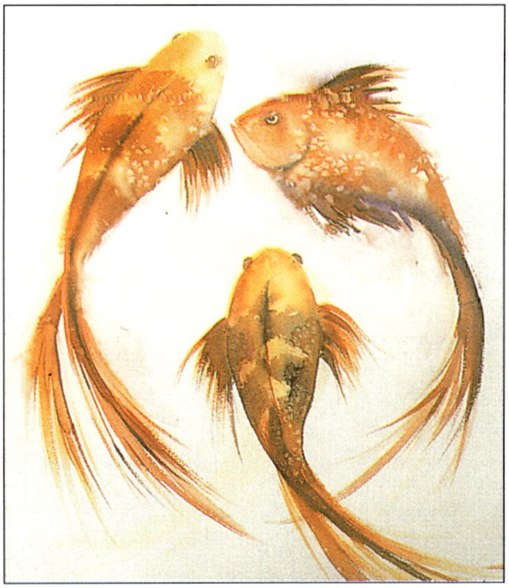

5

Now paint the lefthand fish in exactly the same way, this time mixing alizarin crimson with just a little ultramarine for the mottled markings. Again, soften the outlines in places to create a suitably 'watery' feel.

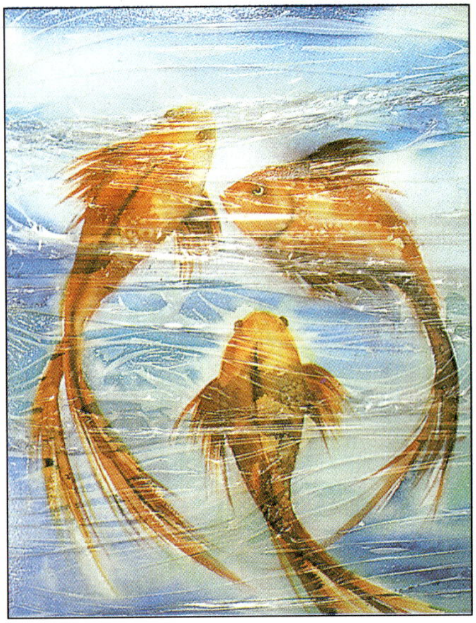

6 Now for the fun part. Apply clean water to the background around the fishes and apply broad strokes of Winsor green and Winsor blue to the wet paper to represent the water. Sweep the brush over the fishes' bodies in places, so they appear to be in the water. Sprinkle a few grains of salt near the top of the picture, and around the fishes' tails and fins. Before the paint has chance to dry, stretch thin plastic wrap horizontally over the entire picture. Pull and push the plastic with your fingers, as shown. Leave to dry for at least 30 minutes.

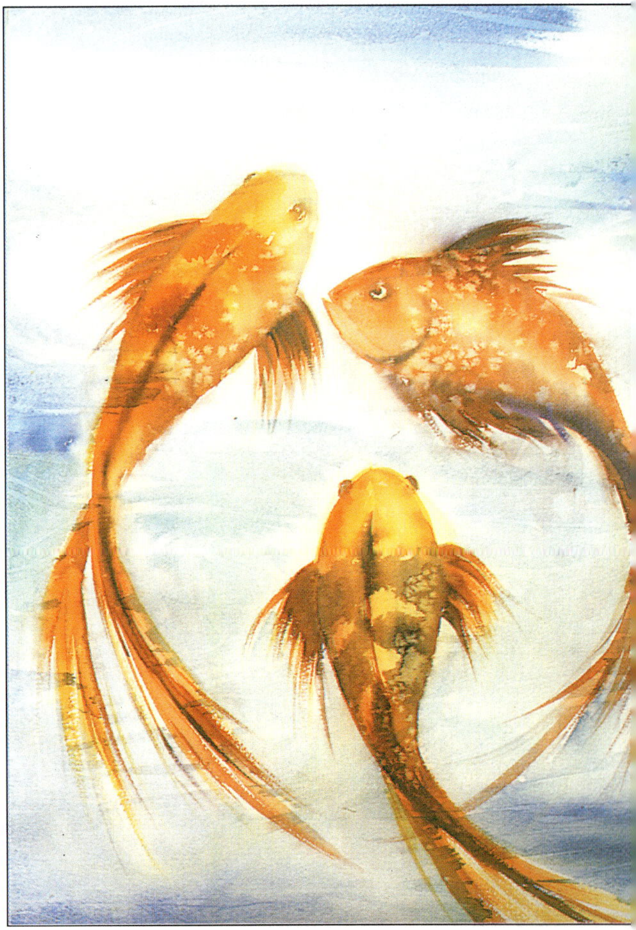

7 Peel away a corner of the plastic wrap and check that the paint is completely dry. If it is, remove the plastic wrap from the whole picture. Brush away the salt granules. Here you can see the result: where the paint gets trapped in the folds of the plastic, it dries with crisp, hard outlines that look like ripples and eddies on the surface of the water. The mottled patterns formed by the salt represent tiny bubbles in the water created by the fishes' movement.

Helpful Hint

YOU HAVE TO WORK QUICKLY WITH THIS TECHNIQUE - THE PAINT MUST BE WET WHEN YOU APPLY THE SALT AND THE PLASTIC WRAP. IF YOU'RE WORKING ON A LARGE SCALE, COMPLETE THE TOP HALF OF THE PICTURE FIRST AND THEN REPEAT THE EXERCISE FOR THE BOTTOM HALF.

8 Strengthen the tones on the fishes' tails and fins with a mixture of ultramarine and alizarin crimson. Switch to a no. 4 round brush and use the same colour to strengthen details such as the eyes, and the mouth of the righthand fish.

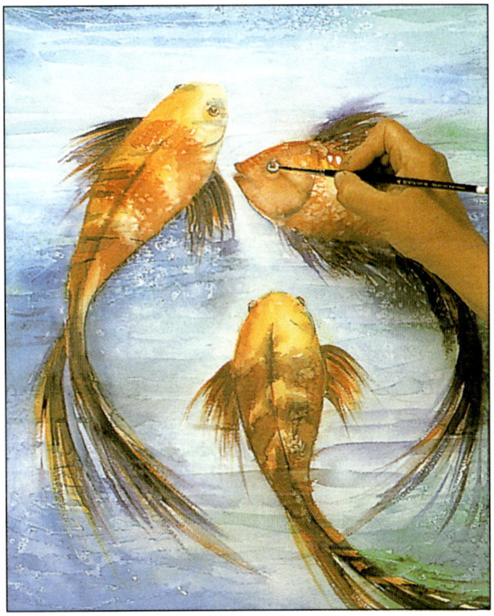

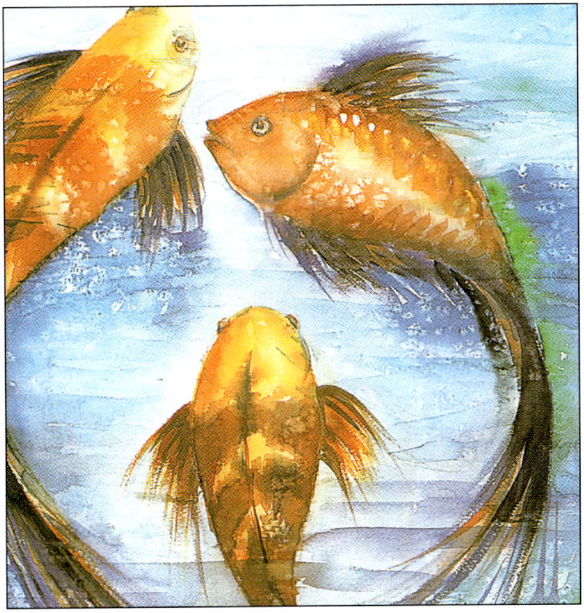

9 Build up more textural detail on the righthand fish, suggesting the scales on its belly with overlaid strokes of alizarin crimson darkened with a hint of ultramarine. Mix a warm gold using cadmium yellow and a hint of cadmium red, adding a little permanent white gouache to give it body. Add strokes of this colour along the fish's back. Allow these washes to dry, then add dots of white gouache for the highlights.

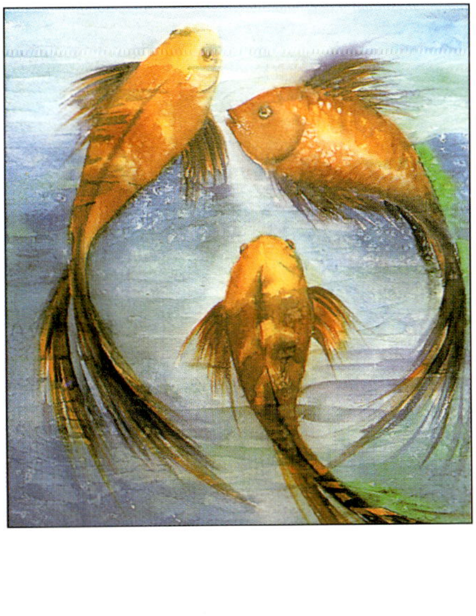

10 Leave the painting to dry completely, then brush a thin layer of gum arabic over the surface of the painting using the no. 10 brush. The gum arabic acts as a kind of varnish and gives an added brightness to the colours, appropriate to the subject.

Painting Stormy Weather

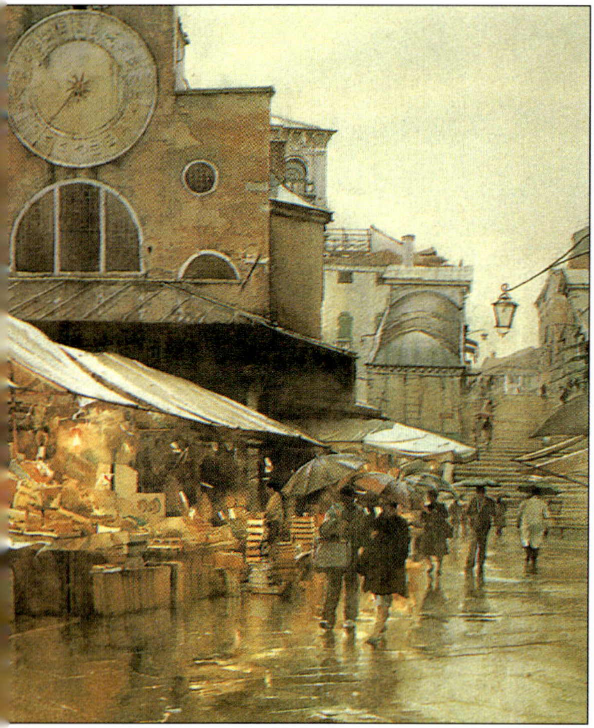

David Curtis
RAINY MORNING ON THE RIALTO, VENICE
Here the artist has made use of glistening highlights reflected on the wet ground, the rooftops and the awnings to recreate the atmosphere of a sudden rain shower.

The sheer power and drama of a storm make it one of the most challenging weather conditions for an artist to tackle. Though it is possible to recreate a stormy scene from photographs (this was the case with our project painting), there is no substitute for actually getting out there among the elements. Other senses apart from sight have a part to play in painting; if you can hear the pounding of surf against rocks, or feel the tension in the air just before a storm breaks, these qualities will come through in your painting almost without your being aware of it.

Turner was a great believer in braving the elements to paint stormy scenes on the spot. Even in a blizzard or a downpour, it is possible for less hardy souls to work directly from nature by viewing the scene from a car window, or finding some other shelter. Alternatively you could make quick, on-the-spot sketches in pencil or watercolour and use these later as reference for a painting done in the comfort of your home.

Painting methods

Storms can come and go in a matter of minutes, so you have to learn to work rapidly and intuitively, allowing the paint itself to suggest the power and drama of nature. Depict rain and swirling clouds by applying heavy washes and letting them merge wet-in-wet on damp paper. Try tilting the board at an angle so that the colour drifts down towards the horizon, giving an effect of veils of rain in the distance. When painting rapidly, wet-into-wet, your washes may settle unevenly in places; resist the temptation to eliminate every imperfection, however – blotches and blooms can be wonderfully suggestive of storm clouds and crashing waves.

By using a dry brush and dragging the colour lightly over a rough-surfaced paper you can create lively, broken strokes that convey the impression of sea foam or wisps of cloud scudding across the sky. Use sweeping, irregular strokes that reflect the violent, erratic movement of clouds and waves and encourage the eye to move freely around the picture.

Sea and Sky

In this unusual composition the brooding sky and crashing surf have been deliberately exaggerated in order to capture the powerful drama of a storm at sea. Wet-in-wet washes suggest the constant shifting of clouds, light and water.

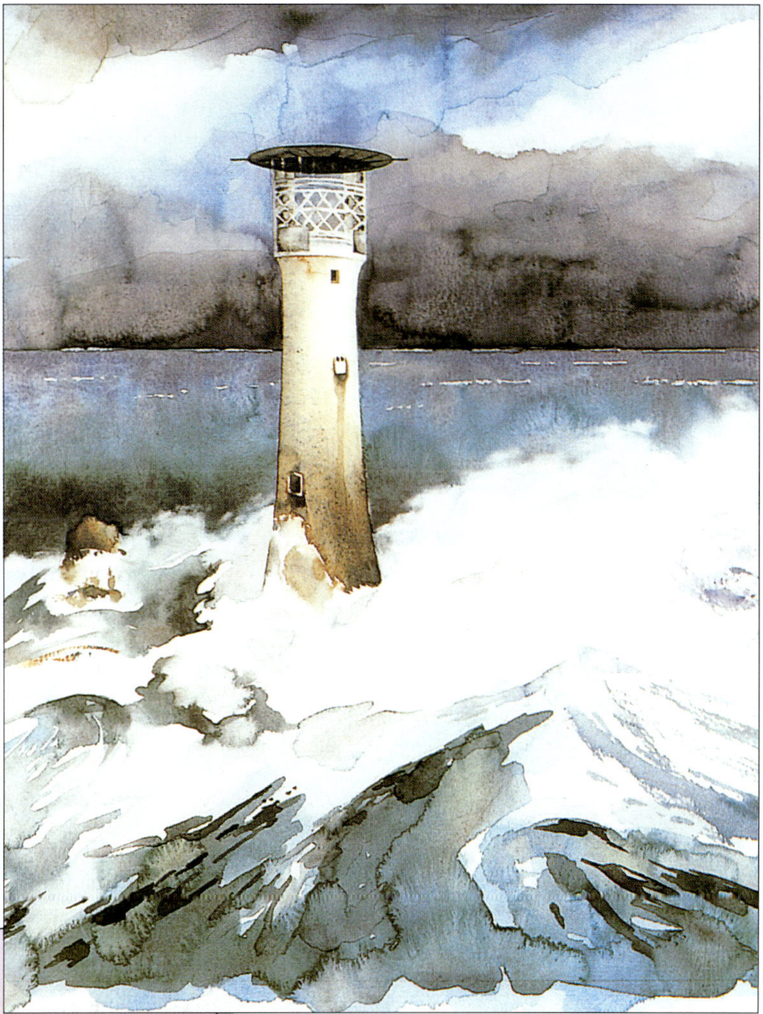

YOU WILL NEED

- *Sheet of stretched Not surface watercolour paper, 15 x 22in (38.1 x 55.8cm)*
- *Large wash brush*
- *½in (13mm) flat brush*
- *No. 2 round brush*
- *No. 0 round brush*
- *Small, old brush to apply masking fluid*
- *Masking fluid*
- *HB pencil*
- *Mixing saucers*
- *Soft tissues*

WATERCOLOUR PAINTS IN THE FOLLOWING COLOURS

- *French ultramarine*
- *Cyanine blue*
- *Cadmium red*
- *Burnt sienna*

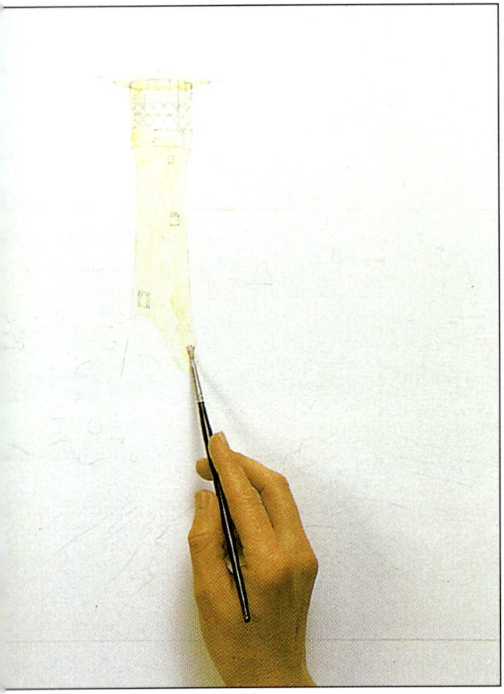

1 Use an HB pencil to sketch in the horizon line, the lighthouse and the outline shape of the foreground breaker. Use masking fluid and an old brush (use a small round one) to block out the shape of the lighthouse and the white breakers in the distance; this allows you to paint the sea and the sky with bold, sweeping strokes, without worrying about the paint running over the edges of your drawing.

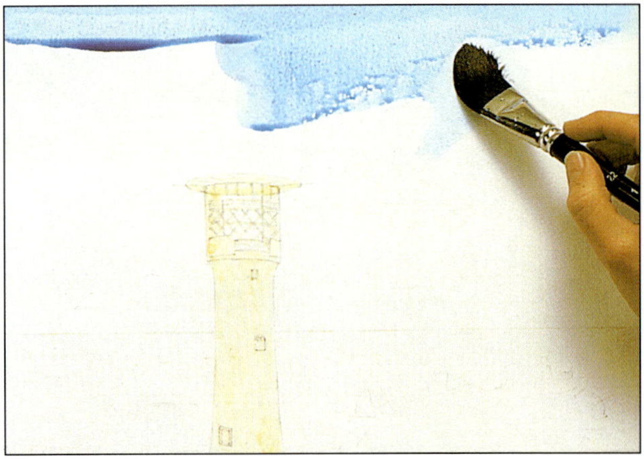

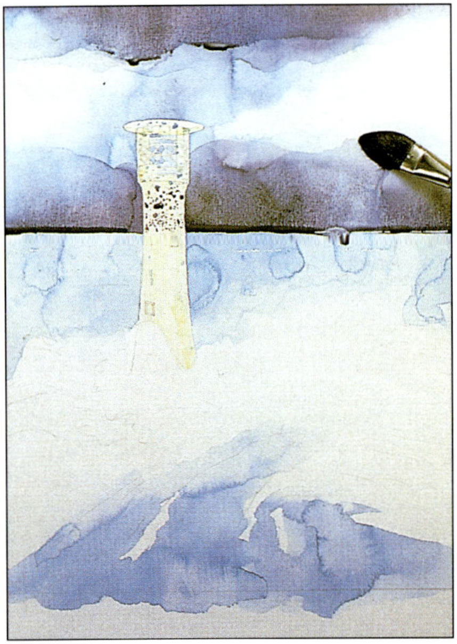

2 Mix a wash of cyanine blue and a little ultramarine, heavily diluted with water. With your board tilted at a slight angle, paint the top part of the sky using a large wash brush, working around the top edge of the clouds. If a rill of paint forms at the base of the wash, simply dry off your brush and use it to blot up the excess.

3 Work down the paper with the blue wash, painting the lower half of the sky and then the blue parts of the water. Leave the large foreground breaker white for now. Mix a watery but strong solution of French ultramarine and cadmium red and paint the heavy, purple rain clouds, spreading the paint across the paper with broad brushstrokes. Rinse your brush and blot the edges of the clouds to create soft gradations of colour that suggest mist and rain.

4 While the purple washes are still damp, add further washes in places to deepen the colour. Don't be tempted to smooth out the brushstrokes, but allow the paint to settle unevenly, creating the effect of brooding storm clouds.

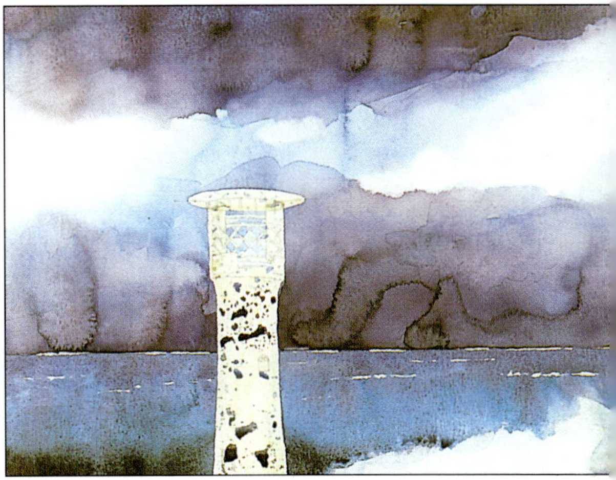

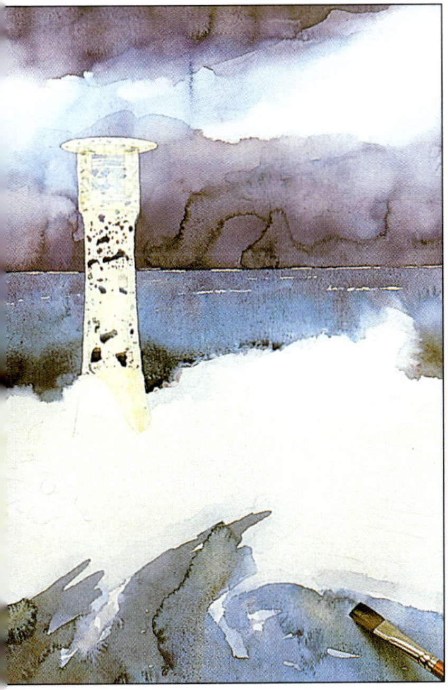

5 Mix a watery but strong solution of cyanine blue, ultramarine and touches of cadmium red and apply washes of varying tone over the distant sea with a 1/2in (13mm) flat brush. Now paint the trough of the foreground breaker, spreading the colour upwards from the bottom of the picture with rhythmic strokes to capture the upward force of the water. As with the sky, allow the paint to form into pools and curdled patterns - they add to the dynamic power and force of the wave.

6 Add more pigment to the wash to strengthen it and continue developing the dark shadows in the trough of the breaker. To show the gradation of the sea water as it turns to foam, add water to the edges of the brushstrokes to fade out the colour. The frothy foam on the crest of the breaker is produced with flecked strokes, made by using a small amount of paint on a dry brush and dragging it lightly across the paper with an upward movement. To suggest the dramatic spray as the breaker crashes against the rocks, soften the edge of the blue wash with a wet brush and gently blot with a small piece of crumpled tissue, as shown.

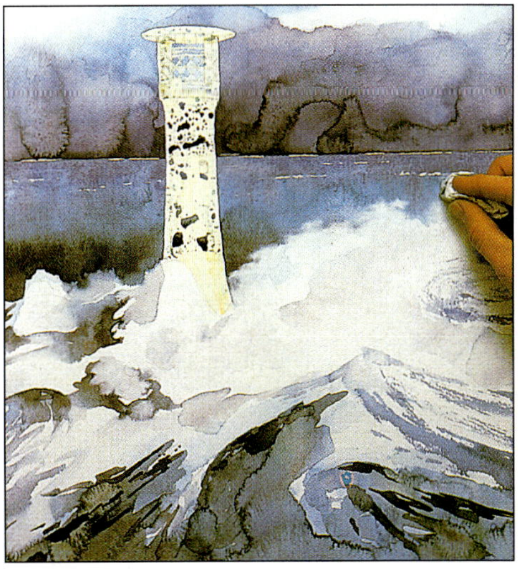

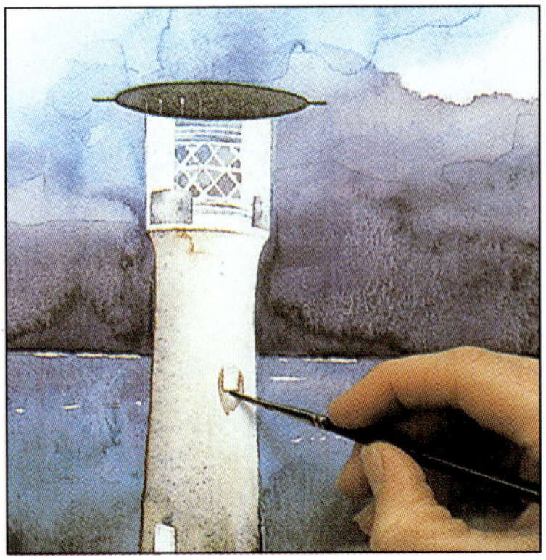

7 With the corner of an eraser, remove the masking fluid from the lighthouse and distant waves. Quickly run over the outline of the lighthouse with a clean, damp no. 2 round brush, to soften the hard edges created by the masking fluid. Now mix a dilute wash of burnt sienna and ultramarine and paint the wall of the lighthouse, starting very pale at the top and becoming darker towards the bottom. Using a no. 0 round brush, paint the detailing at the top of the lighthouse with various greys. Then paint the dark windows with a deep tone of burnt sienna and ultramarine.

8 Stand back and assess your painting so far. Here, the artist decided to accentuate the reflection of the thunderous sky in the choppy sea by adding a wash of ultramarine and cadmium red to the white waves near the horizon. This also increases the illusion of distance, with the waves becoming greyer as they recede towards the horizon.

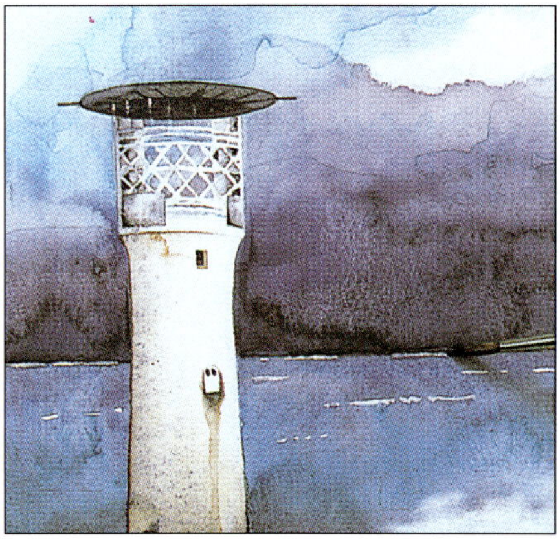

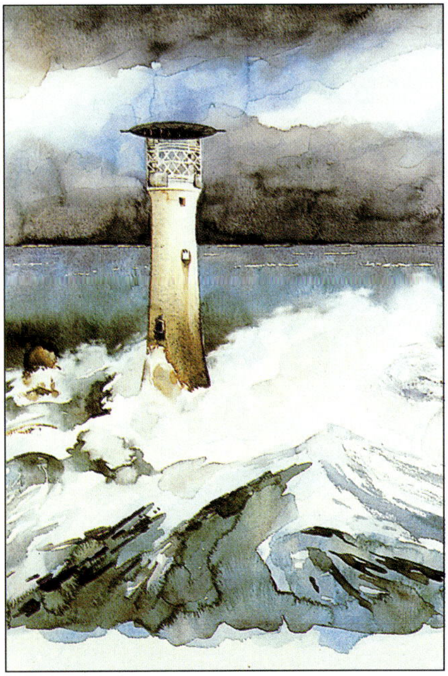

Helpful Hint

THE MARKS SEEN IN THE SKY IN STEP 4 ARE KNOWN AS 'BLOOMS' OR 'BACKRUNS'. THEY ARE USUALLY ACCIDENTAL, OCCURING WHEN YOU WORK INTO A WASH BEFORE IT IS COMPLETELY DRY; HOWEVER, THEY CAN BE USED DELIBERATELY, TO PRODUCE TEXTURES AND EFFECTS THAT WOULD BE DIFFICULT TO CREATE WITH CONVENTIONAL BRUSHWORK.

9 Finally, paint in the rock to the left of the lighthouse with a dark mix of burnt sienna and ultramarine. In the finished painting you will notice that the crashing surf in the foreground consists largely of white paper, its luminosity enhanced by the dark tones of the surrounding sea and sky.

AN INTRODUCTION TO

Oil Painting

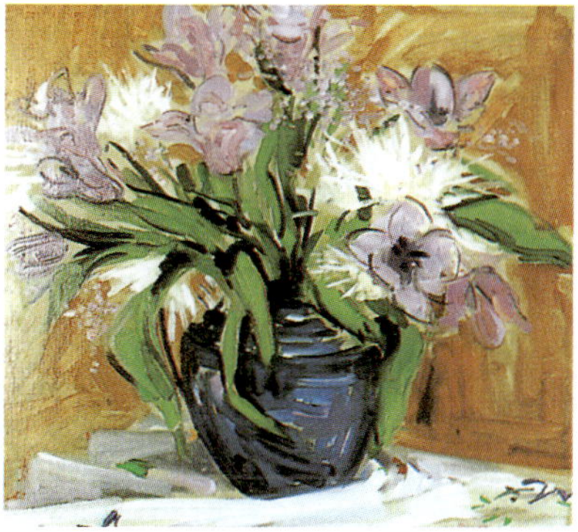

PROJECT 1

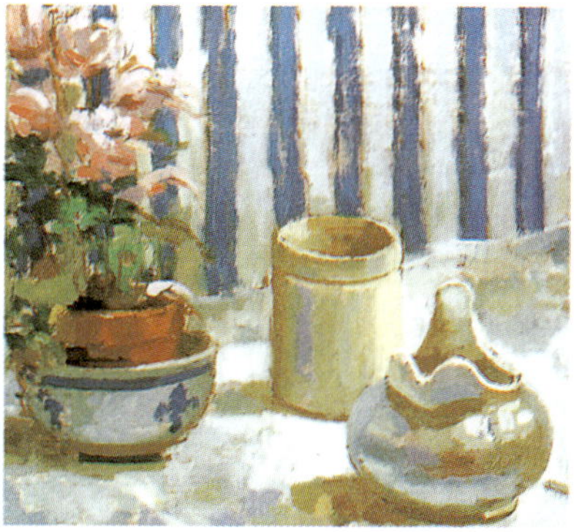

PROJECT 4

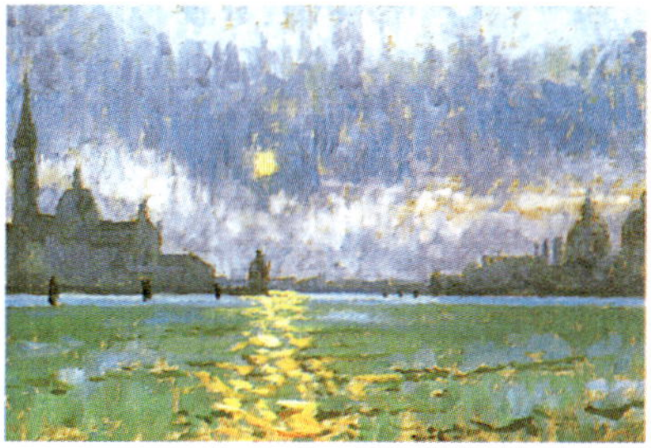

PROJECT 2

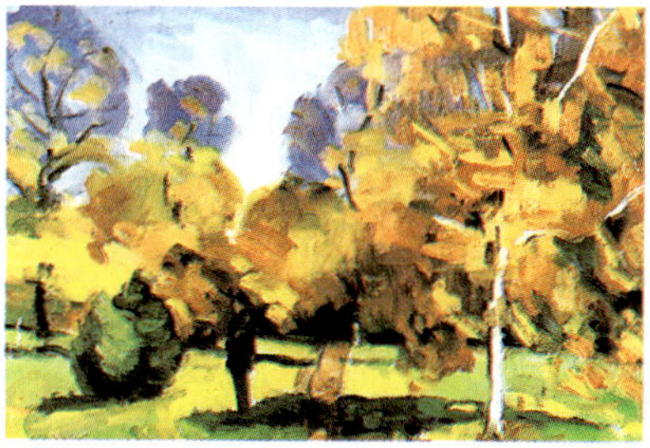

PROJECT 5

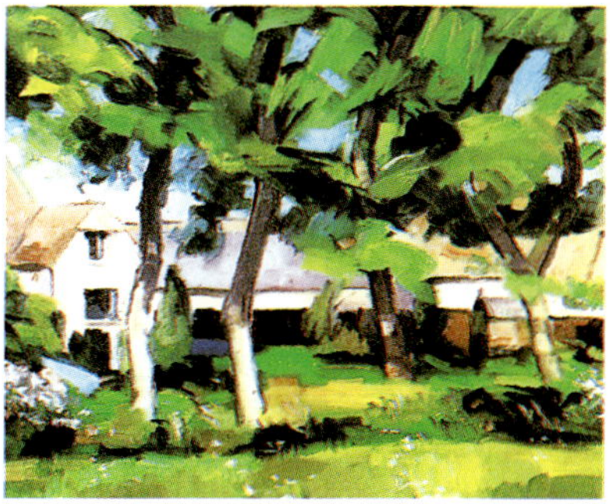

PROJECT 3

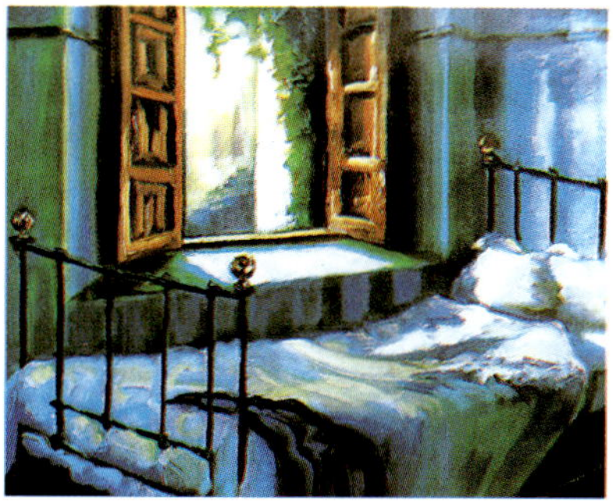

PROJECT 6

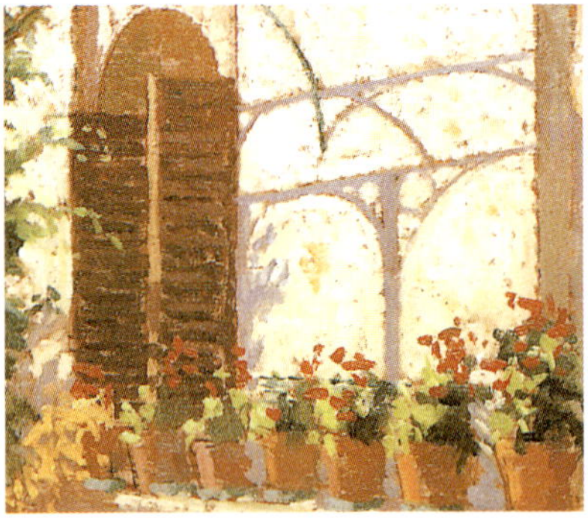

PROJECT 7

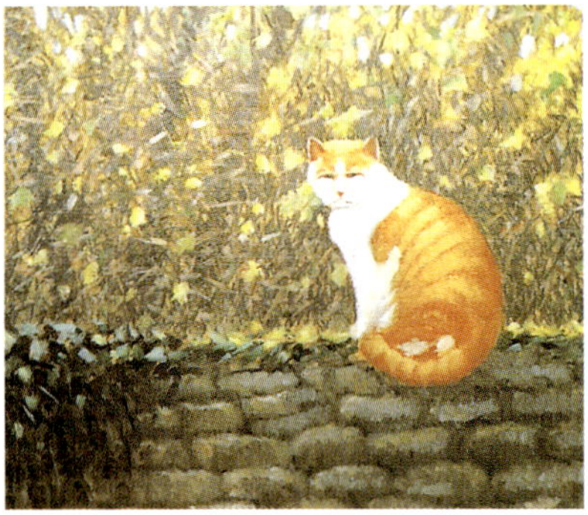

PROJECT 8

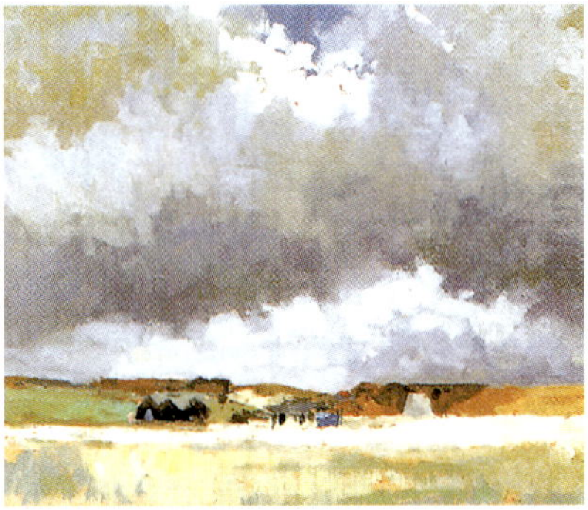

PROJECT 9

Oil Painting

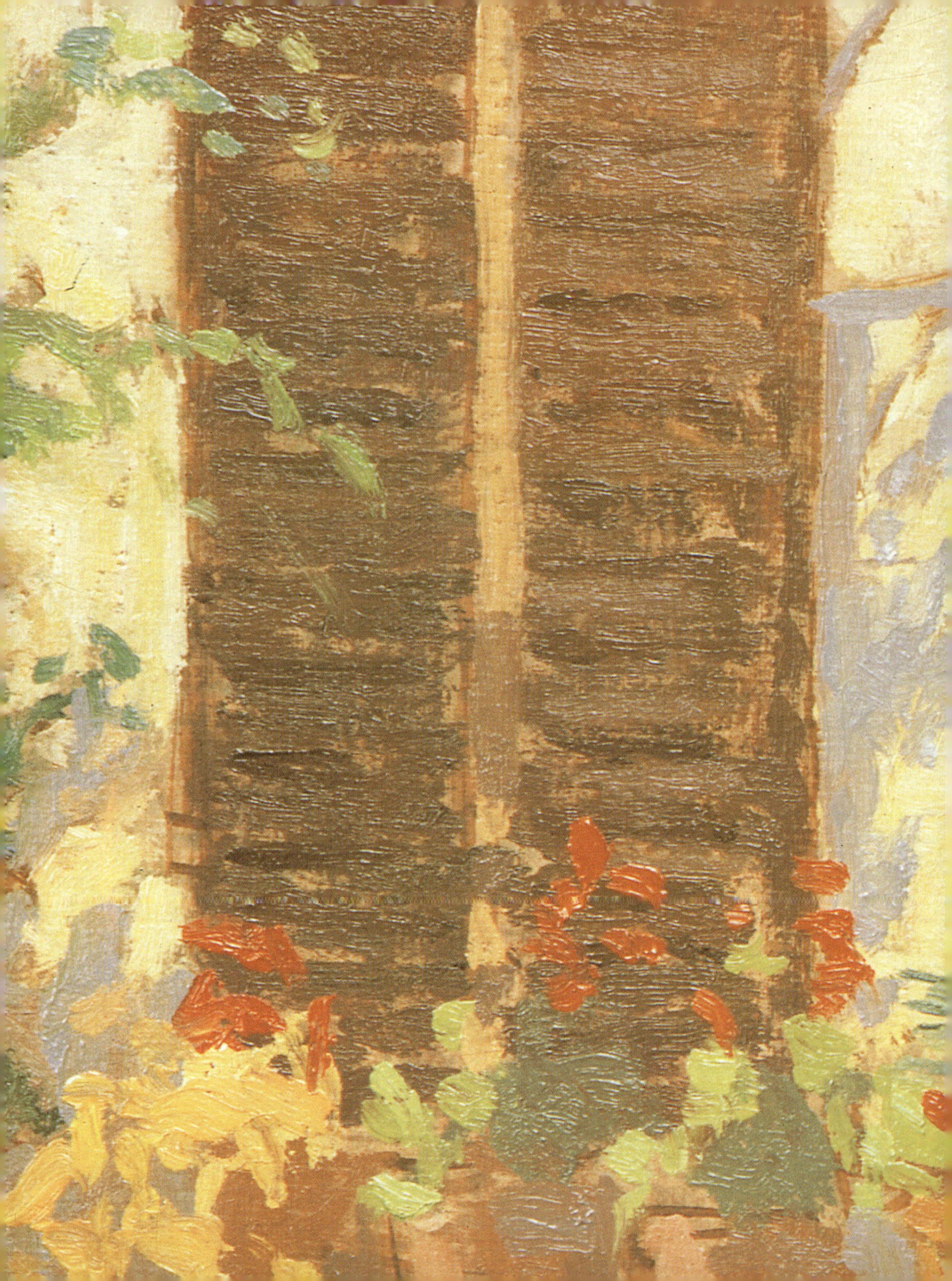

Oil Painting

Contrary to popular belief, oil paint is not a 'difficult' medium to work with. Quite the opposite; it is a perfect medium for the beginner because it is very easy to correct what you have done, either by wiping it out or painting over it. Oil paint is a flexible medium, too; its smooth, buttery consistency, coupled with its slow drying time, means that it can be manipulated freely and extensively on the canvas to produce an infinite range of textures and effects. Diluted with thinners it can be used to build delicate, translucent glazes that seem to glow with an inner light. Used straight from the tube it produces thick, rich impastos in which the texture of the paint and the mark of the brush become an integral part of the finished image.

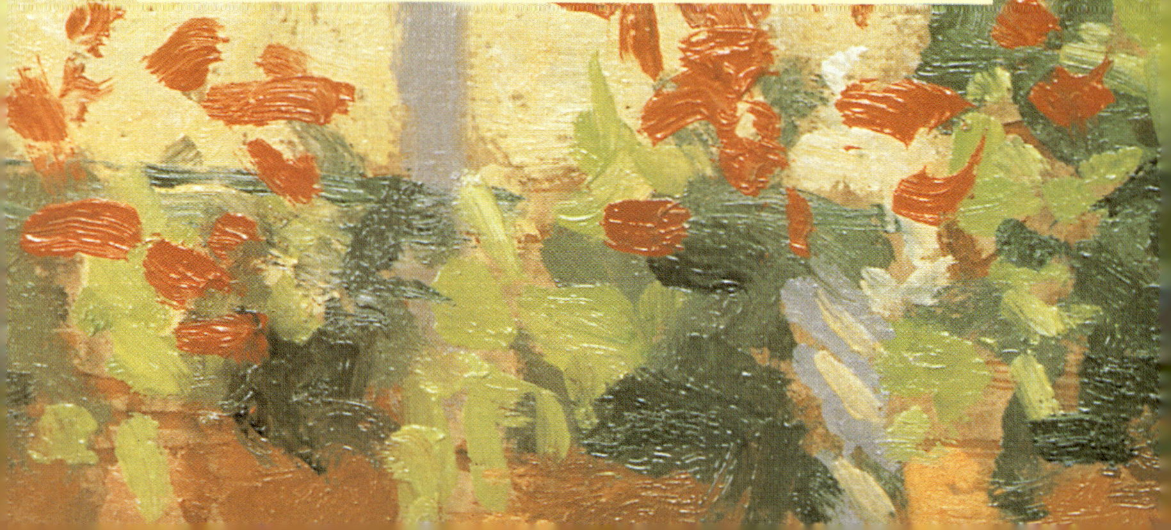

Materials and Equipment

Materials for oil painting can be expensive, so it is advisable to start out with the basic essentials and add extra colours, brushes and so on as you gain more experience.

PAINTS

Oil paints are sold in tubes and are available in two different grades: artists' and students'. Artists' colours are of better quality and this is reflected in the price. They are made from the finest pigments ground with a minimum of oil so their consistency is stiff, and the colours retain their brilliance well.

Students' colours are labelled with a trade name such as 'Georgian' (Daler-Rowney) or 'Winton' (Winsor & Newton). These paints cost less because they contain less pure pigment and more fillers and extenders; they cannot provide the same intensity of colour as the artists' range. They are, however, fine for practising with. Some artists even combine the two types, using artists' paints for the pure, intense colours and students' paints for the earth colours, which are often just as good as in the artists' range.

Artist-quality paints vary in price according to the initial cost of the pigment. They are usually classified according to a 'series', typically from 1 (the cheapest) to 7 (the most costly). Student-quality colours are sold at a uniform price across the range.

__Right__ Some of the most popular mediums and diluents available for altering the consistency of oil paint. From left to right: dammar varnish, alkyd medium, impasto medium, purified linseed oil, low-odour thinners, white spirit, distilled turpentine. At the bottom right of the picture is a double dipper, which clips on to the palette and holds oil and turpentine separately so you can dip into them as you paint.

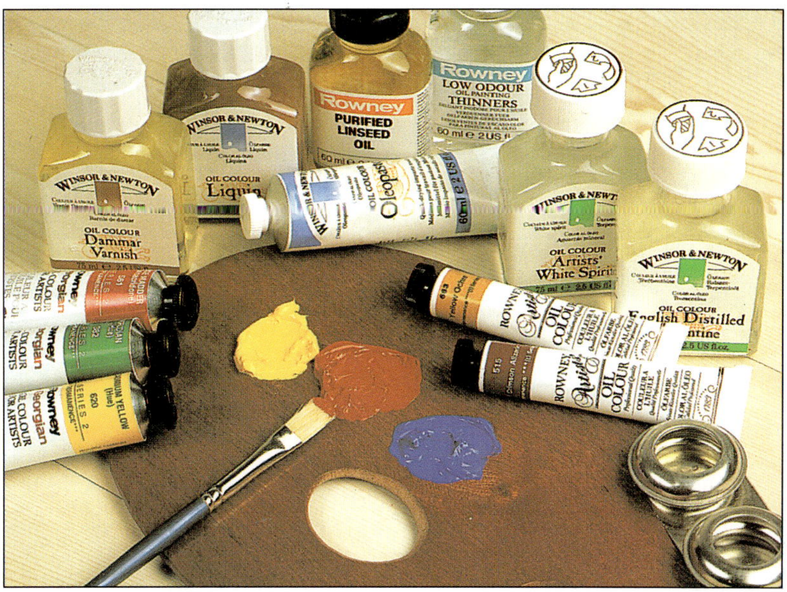

MEDIUMS AND DILUENTS

Oil paint can be used thickly, direct from the tube, but more often it needs to be diluted to make it easier to apply to the support. Paint may be thinned to the required consistency with a diluent such as turpentine or white spirit, or with a combination of a diluent and an oil or varnish – known as a medium.

Diluents

Used on its own, a diluent produces a matt finish and considerably accelerates the drying time of the paint. Always use double-distilled or rectified turpentine for painting purposes – ordinary household turpentine contains too many impurities and is not suitable.

If turpentine gives you a headache or irritates your skin, white spirit is a suitable alternative. It is also cheaper, has less odour, and stores without deteriorating. You can also obtain special low-odour thinners from art suppliers.

Mediums

There are various oils and resins that can be mixed with a diluent to add texture and body to your paint. The most commonly used painting medium is a mixture of linseed oil and turpentine, usually in a ratio of 60 per cent oil to 40 per cent turpentine. Linseed oil is used because it dries to a glossy finish that is resistant to cracking. However, be sure to buy either purified or cold-pressed linseed oil; boiled linseed oil – the sort that is sold in DIY and hardware shops – contains impurities that cause rapid yellowing. If you want a thicker mixture that dries more quickly, you can add a little dammar varnish to the turpentine and linseed oil.

Special ready-mixed painting mediums are available from art suppliers, designed variously to improve the flow of the paint, thicken it for impasto work, speed its drying rate, and produce either a matt or a gloss finish.

SAFETY PRECAUTIONS

Even small quantities of solvents and thinners can be hazardous if not used with care, because their fumes are rapidly absorbed through the lungs. When using solvents, always work in a well ventilated room and avoid inhalation. Do not eat, drink or smoke while working.

BRUSHES

Oil-painting brushes come in a wide range of sizes and shapes. Each makes a different kind

__Below__ Here is a small selection of the vast range of oil-painting brushes available. __A__ bristle brushes: fan, filbert, short flat, long flat. __B__ synthetic brushes: round, flat, filbert. __C__ mahl stick. __D__ household decorator's brush – useful for applying primer to the support.

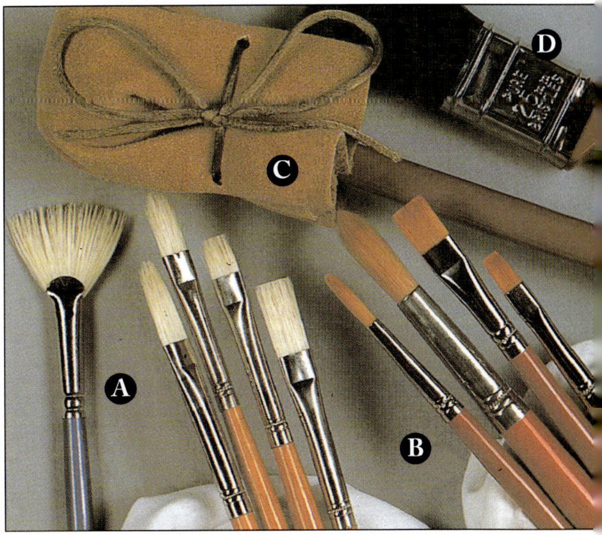

of mark, but some are more versatile than others. Through experiment you will find which ones are best suited to your own painting style.

Bristle brushes

Stiff and hard-wearing, bristle brushes are good for moving the paint around on the surface and for applying thick dabs of colour. The best quality ones are made of stiff, white hog bristles with split ends that hold a lot of paint.

Sable brushes

Sable brushes are soft and springy, similar to those used in watercolour painting, but with longer handles. They are useful for painting fine details in the final layers of a painting and for applying thinly diluted colour. Sable brushes are expensive, however, and for oil painting some artists find synthetic brushes quite adequate.

Synthetic brushes

Synthetic brushes are an economical alternative to natural-hair brushes, and their quality has improved considerably in recent years.
Synthetic brushes are hard-wearing and easily cleaned, but the cheaper ones lose their shape quickly.

Brush shapes

Rounds have long, thin bristles that curve inwards at the ends. This is the most versatile brush shape as it covers large areas quickly and is also good for sketching in outlines.
Flats have square ends and long bristles that hold a lot of paint. They are ideal for applying thick, bold colour and are useful for blending.
Brights are the same shape as flats, but with shorter, stiffer bristles that make strongly textured strokes. The stiff bristles are useful for applying thick, heavy paint to produce impasto effects.
Filberts are similar to flats, except that the bristles curve inwards at the end. Filberts are the most versatile brushes as they produce a wide range of marks.
Fan blenders are available in hog bristle, sable and synthetic fibre, and are used for blending colours together where a very smooth, highly finished effect is required.
Decorators' brushes are cheap, hard-wearing and useful for applying primer to the support prior to painting.

Brush sizes

Each type of brush comes in a range of sizes, from 00 (the smallest) to around 16 (the largest). Brush sizes are not standardized and can vary widely between brands. The brush size you choose will depend on the scale and style of your paintings. In general, it is better to start with medium to large brushes as they cover large areas quickly but can also be employed for small touches. Using bigger brushes also encourages a more painterly, generous approach.

Brush care

Good brushes are expensive, but if they are properly looked after they can last for several years. Clean your brushes at the end of every painting day, and never leave a brush soaking with the bristles touching the bottom of the container. First, remove the excess paint on a piece of newspaper, then rinse in white spirit and wipe on a rag. Wash under warm running water, soaping the bristles with a bar of household soap. Rub the soapy bristles in the palm of your hand so that the paint which has collected around the base of the ferrule is loosened. Rinse in warm water, shake dry, then smooth the bristles into shape. Leave the brushes to dry, bristle end up, in a jar. Always make sure brushes are dry before storing them in a closed container, or they may develop mildew.

PALETTES

Palettes for oil painting come in a variety of shapes, sizes and materials, designed to suit the artist's individual requirements. The best-quality palettes are made of mahogany ply, but fibreboard and melamine-faced palettes are perfectly adequate. Use as large a palette as you can, to allow your colours to be well spaced around the edge with plenty of room in the centre for mixing them together.

Thumbhole palettes

Thumbhole palettes come in a range of sizes and are designed to be held in the hand while painting at the easel. They have a thumbhole and indentation for the fingers, and the palette is supported on the forearm. There are three main shapes available: oblong, oval and the traditional kidney-shaped palette.

Preparing wooden palettes

Before they are used for the first time, wooden palettes should be treated by rubbing with linseed oil. This seals the wood and prevents it from sucking oil from the paint, causing it to dry out too quickly on the palette. It also makes the surface easier to clean after use. Rub a generous coating of the oil into both sides of the palette and leave it for several days until it has hardened and fully penetrated the grain.

Disposable palettes

Made of oil-proof paper, disposable palettes are useful for outdoor work and for those artists who hate the chore of cleaning up. They are sold in pads with tear-off sheets; some have a thumbhole.

Improvised palettes

Many artists prefer to use a 'home-made' palette which can be rested on a nearby surface. As well as saving you money, it allows you to choose any size, shape and material you like. Any smooth, non-porous material is suitable, such as a sheet of white formica, a glass slab with white or neutral-coloured paper underneath, or a sheet of hardboard sealed with a coat of paint. Old cups, jars and tins are perfectly adequate for mixing thin washes, and can be covered with plastic film between sessions to prevent the paint drying out.

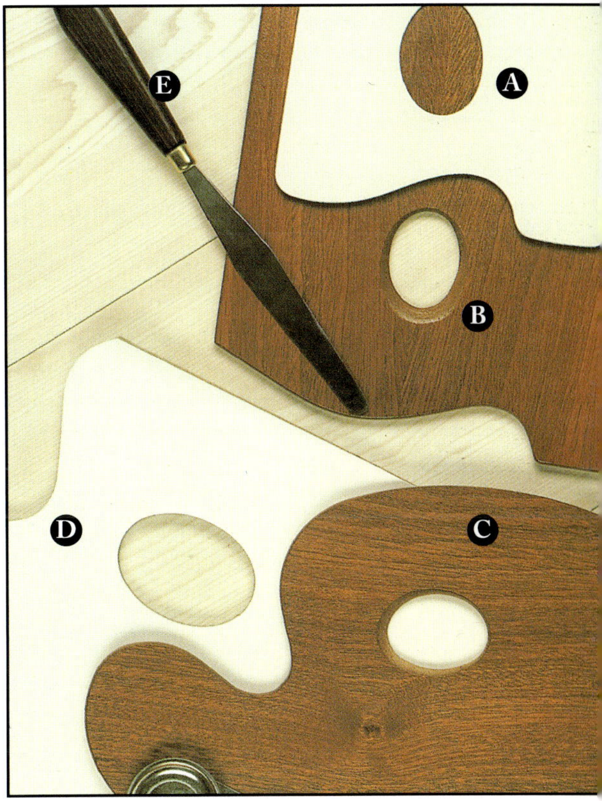

Above *Palettes for oil painting.* ***A*** *oblong melamine.* ***B*** *oblong mahogany ply.* ***C*** *kidney-shaped 'studio' palette in mahogany ply.* ***D*** *pad of tear-off disposable palettes. A palette knife,* ***E****, is used for mixing paints together on the palette. A double dipper,* ***F****, will clip on to the side of your palette.*

SUPPORTS

The support is the surface on which you paint – whether canvas, board or paper. A support for oil painting must be prepared with glue size and/or primer to prevent it absorbing the oil in the paint; if too much oil is absorbed, the paint becomes underbound and may eventually crack.

Canvas

The most popular surface for oil painting is canvas, which has a unique responsiveness to the brush and plenty of tooth to hold the paint. Canvas is available in various weights and in fine, medium and coarse-grained textures. You can buy it either glued onto stiff board, ready-stretched and primed on a wooden stretcher frame, or in lengths from a roll. Prepared canvases are expensive and it is much cheaper to buy lengths of unprimed canvas and stretch and prime your own.

The weight of canvas is measured in ounces per square yard. The higher the number, the greater the density of threads and therefore the better the quality. The two main types of canvas available are linen and cotton.

Linen is considered the best canvas. It has a fine, even grain that is free of knots and a pleasure to paint on. Although expensive, it is very durable.

Cotton Good-quality cotton canvas, such as cotton duck, comes in 12oz and 15oz grades. It stretches well and is the best alternative to linen – at about half the price. Lighter-weight

Below *Oil paint can be applied to a wide range of supports.* ***A*** *stretched and primed canvas.* ***B*** *plywood.* ***C*** *hardboard. D oil sketching paper. E linen canvas.* ***F*** *cotton canvas (both of these need to be stretched and primed).* ***G*** *cardboard.* ***H*** *prepared canvas panel.*

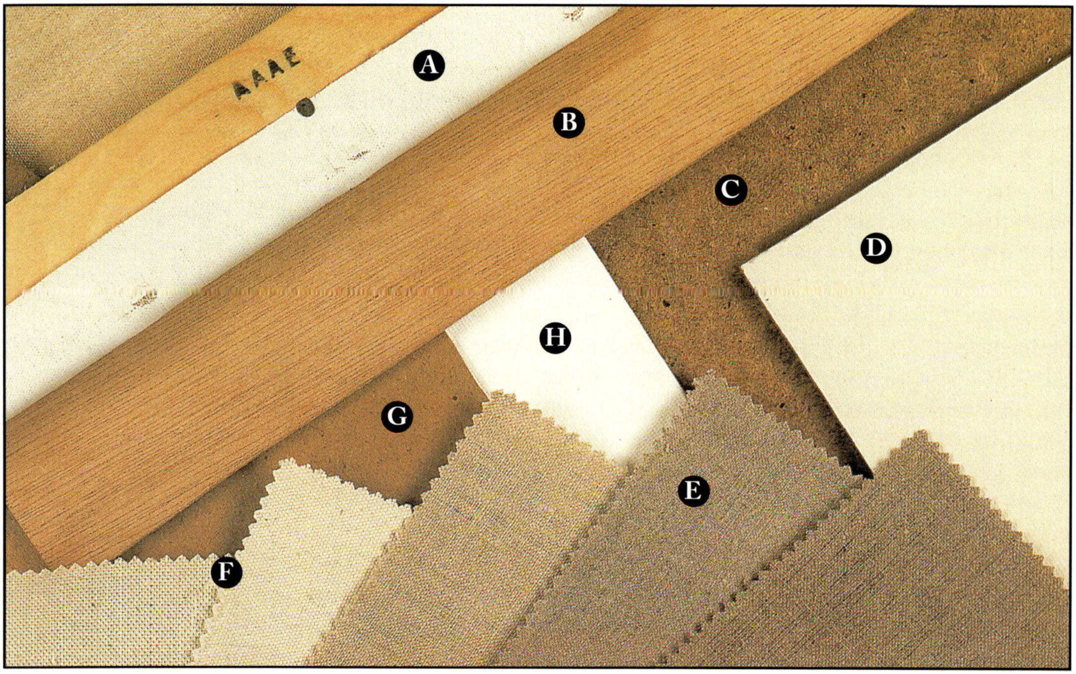

linen – at about half the price. Lighter-weight canvases are recommended for practice work only.

Boards and papers

Prepared canvas boards are relatively inexpensive and are ideal when trying out oils for the first time. However, the cheaper ones have a rather mechanical texture and a slippery surface.
Hardboard, which you can buy from builders' suppliers, is an excellent yet inexpensive support for oils. Most artists use the smooth side, as the rough side has a very insistent, mechanical texture.
Plywood, chipboard, MDF (medium-density fibreboard) are also suitable for oil painting. Prepare the board with primer if you like a white surface, or, if you prefer to work on a neutral mid-toned surface, simply apply a coat of glue size or PVA to the support.
Oil sketching paper is specially prepared for oil painting and is textured to resemble canvas weave. Available in pads with tear-off sheets, it is handy for outdoor sketches and practice work.

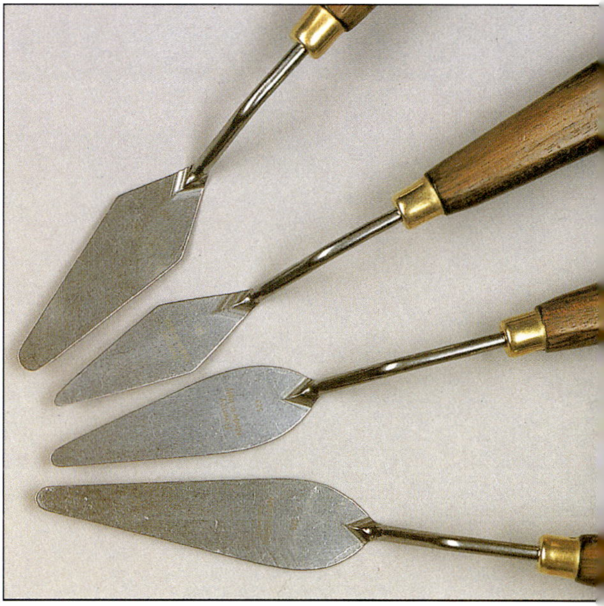

Above *Painting knives come in a range of shapes and sizes. They are not an essential item unless you intend to experiment with knife-painting techniques.*

PAINTING ACCESSORIES

Painting in oils can be a messy business, so the most essential accessories you will need are large jars or tins to hold solvents for cleaning brushes, and a good supply of cotton rags and newspaper! The following items are not essential, but some, such as palette knives, you will certainly find useful.
Painting knives have flexible blades and cranked handles, and can be used instead of a brush to apply thick paint directly to the support.
Palette knives have a long, straight, flexible blade with a rounded tip. They are used for mixing paint on the palette and for scraping paint off the palette at the end of a working session.
Dippers are small open cups that clip onto the edge of your palette to hold mediums and thinners during painting. These are not essential – you can just as easily keep small jars of painting medium on a nearby surface.
Mahl stick This is useful for steadying your hand when painting small details or fine lines. It consists of a long handle made of bamboo, wood or metal, with a rubber or chamois cushion at one end. Hold the mahl stick so that it crosses the painting diagonally, the padded end resting lightly on a dry section of the work, or on the edge of the canvas. You can then rest your painting arm on the stick to steady yourself as you paint. You can make your own mahl stick from a length of dowelling or garden cane with a bundle of rags tied to one end.

Painting Alla Prima

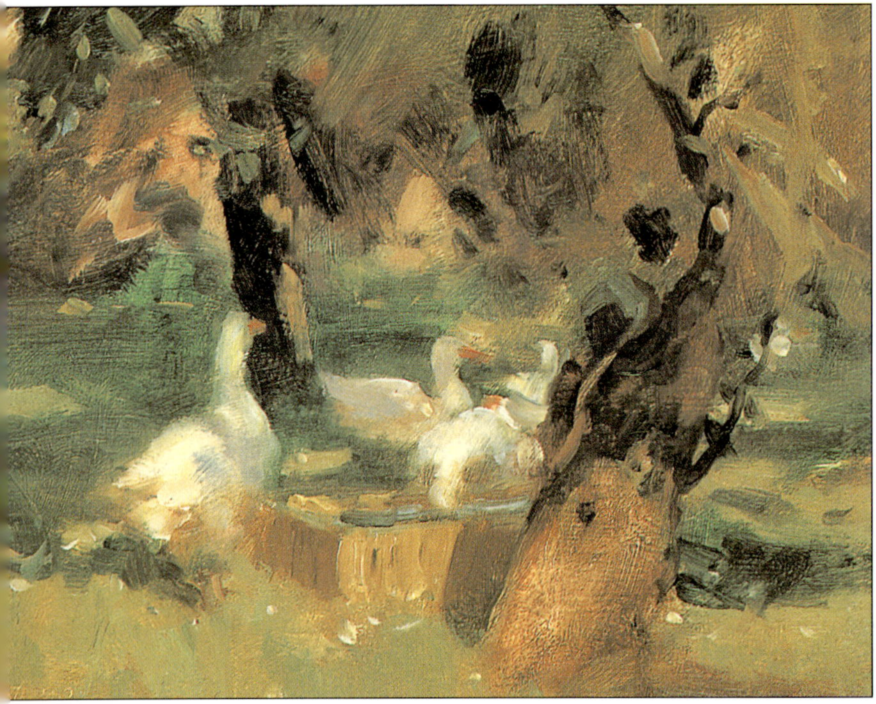

Trevor Chamberlain
ERIC'S GEESE
The artist had to work quickly to capture this delightful scene before the light changed and the geese wandered off. By using thinned paint and rapid, wet-in-wet brushstrokes, and by working on a small scale, he was able to complete the picture in about two hours.

Alla prima is an Italian expression meaning 'at the first'. It describes a technique in which a painting is completed rapidly in a single session, as opposed to the 'traditional' method of working up the image layer by layer over an extended period.

The alla prima method is often used by artists when painting outdoors directly from the subject, where speed is essential in order to capture the fleeting effects of light and movement in the landscape. In alla prima painting there is usually little or no initial underpainting, although artists sometimes make a rapid underdrawing in charcoal or thinned paint to act as a compositional guide. Each patch of colour is laid down more or less as it will appear in the final painting, or worked wet-into-wet with adjacent colours; the main idea is to capture the essence of the subject in an intuitive way using vigorous, expressive brush strokes and minimal colour mixing.

Alla prima painting requires a confident approach. It is, of course, possible to scrape away and rework unsuccessful areas of a painting, but the danger is that some of the freshness and spontaneity will be lost. It is therefore important to start out with a clear idea of what you want to convey in your painting. Make a positive statement, and don't be tempted to include any unnecessary, cluttered detail.

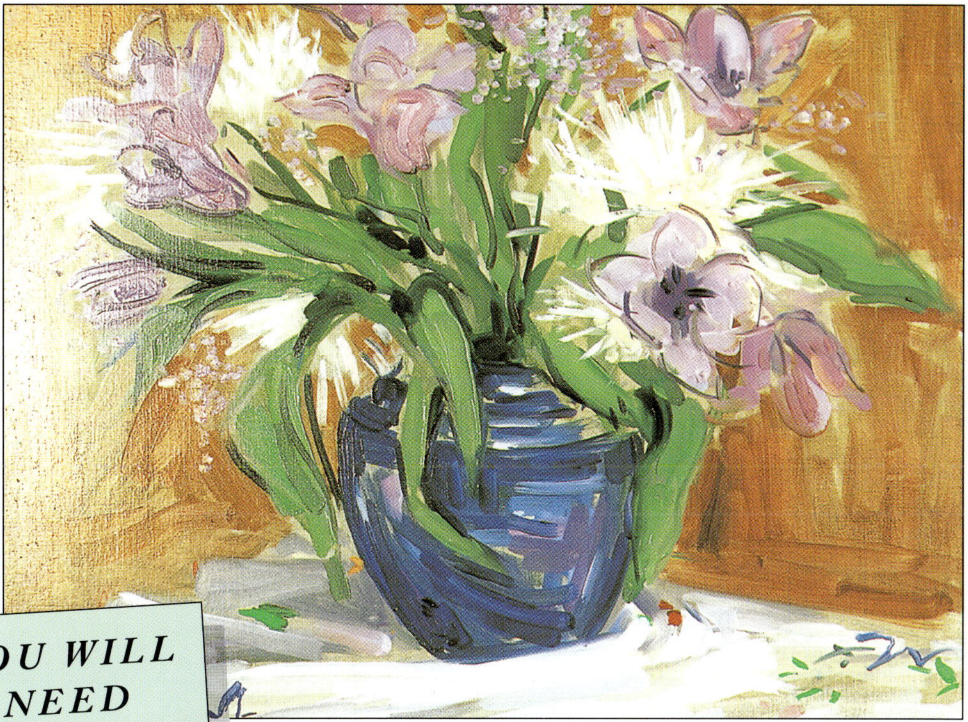

YOU WILL NEED

- *Sheet of primed canvas or board, 18 x 14in (45.7 x 35.6cm)*
- *No. 2 round bristle brush*
- *No. 2 filbert bristle brush*
- *No. 8 filbert bristle brush*
- *No. 10 flat bristle brush*
- *Turpentine*
- *Linseed oil*
- *Clean rag*

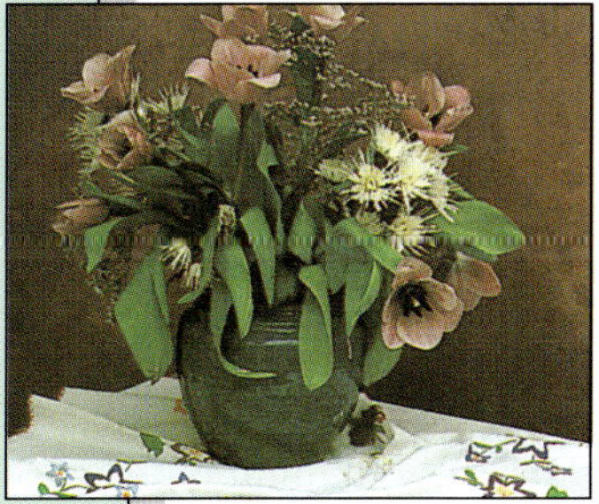

Spring Flowers

This painting was completed quickly, using a limited palette of colours. Bold, expressive brushwork gives rhythm to the composition, leading the eye around it from one area to another.

OIL PAINTS IN THE FOLLOWING COLOURS

- *Naples yellow*
- *Chrome yellow*
- *Permanent rose*
- *Cadmium red*
- *Burnt sienna*
- *Cadmium green*
- *Yellow ochre*
- *Alizarin crimson*
- *Olive green*
- *French ultramarine*
- *Cobalt blue*
- *Cobalt violet*
- *Titanium white*

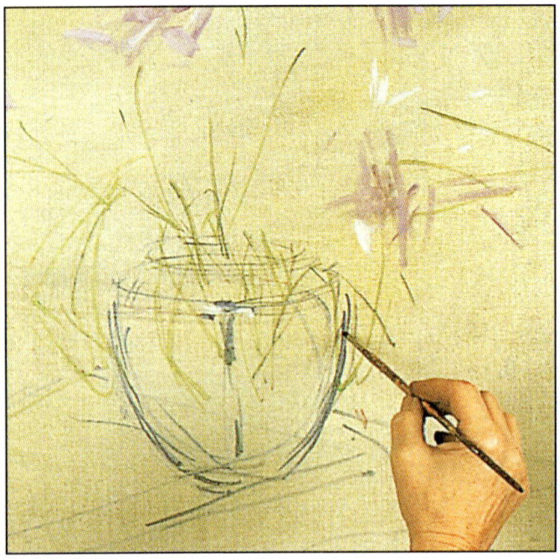

1 Prepare the canvas by tinting it the day before you start painting, so that it has time to dry. Mix yellow ochre, French ultramarine and a little cadmium green, then dilute with lots of turpentine to make a very thin wash of pale grey-green. Rub the colour over the entire canvas area using a rag dampened with a little turpentine.Using a no. 2 filbert brush, lightly sketch in the main outlines of the composition with thin paint. Use French ultramarine for the vase, cobalt violet and titanium white for the tulips and cadmium green for the stalks. Hold your brush lightly, well back from the bristles, and draw with loose, fluid lines, feeling your way around the forms.

2 Establish the lightest tones in the composition – the white daisies and the highlights on the folds of the white tablecloth – using the 'rub-out' technique: fold a clean rag over your finger, dip it in turpentine, and remove some of the base colour, down to the bare canvas, as shown

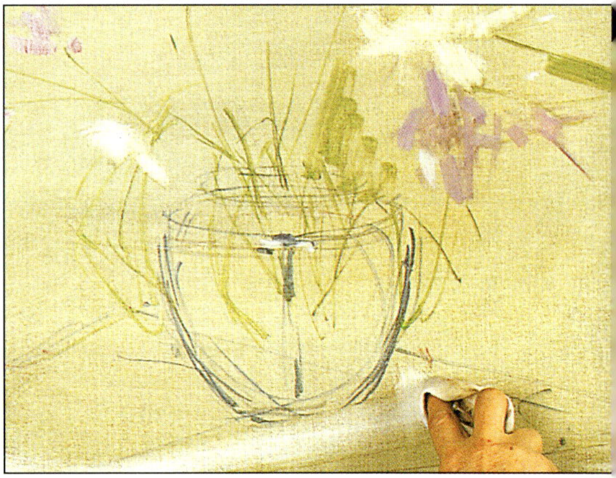

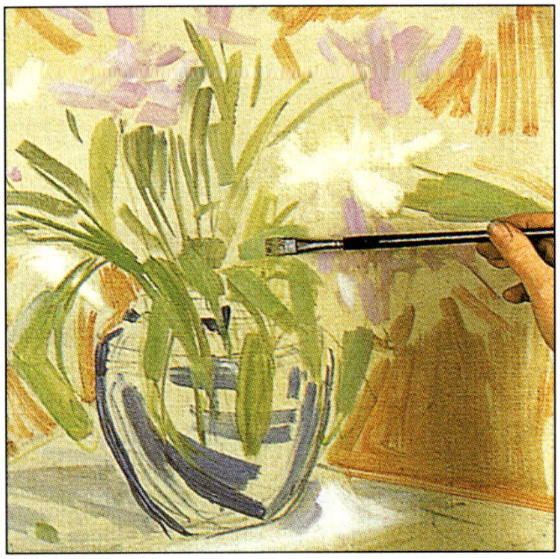

3 Now start to build up the composition as a whole, working on related areas simultaneously with small touches of thin paint. With a no. 10 flat brush, mix burnt sienna, yellow ochre and a little cadmium red to make a warm brown and loosely block in the background with broad strokes. Mix French ultramarine, alizarin crimson and white to create the shadows and folds in the tablecloth. Add strokes of ultramarine to the vase, following its curved form with your brush strokes. Paint the tulip leaves with cadmium green. For the darker leaves, add a touch of ultramarine and white to create a green with a hint of grey.

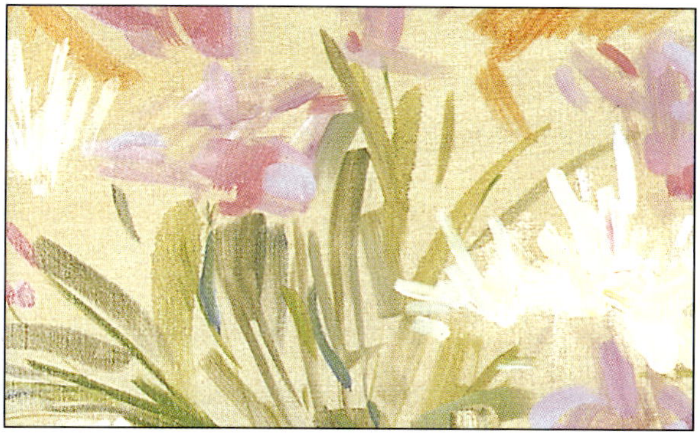

4 With a no. 8 filbert brush, work on the forms of the flowers. Use pure white, and white warmed with a little Naples yellow, for the daisies. Plot the light and dark tones of the tulips using various mixes of cobalt violet, cobalt blue, permanent rose and white. Apply the colours rapidly so you don't get bogged down in detail – concentrate instead on capturing the gestures of the petals.

Helpful Hint

IT'S IMPORTANT TO KEEP YOUR COLOURS FRESH AND UNSULLIED, SO RINSE YOUR BRUSHES FREQUENTLY IN A JAR OF WHITE SPIRIT.

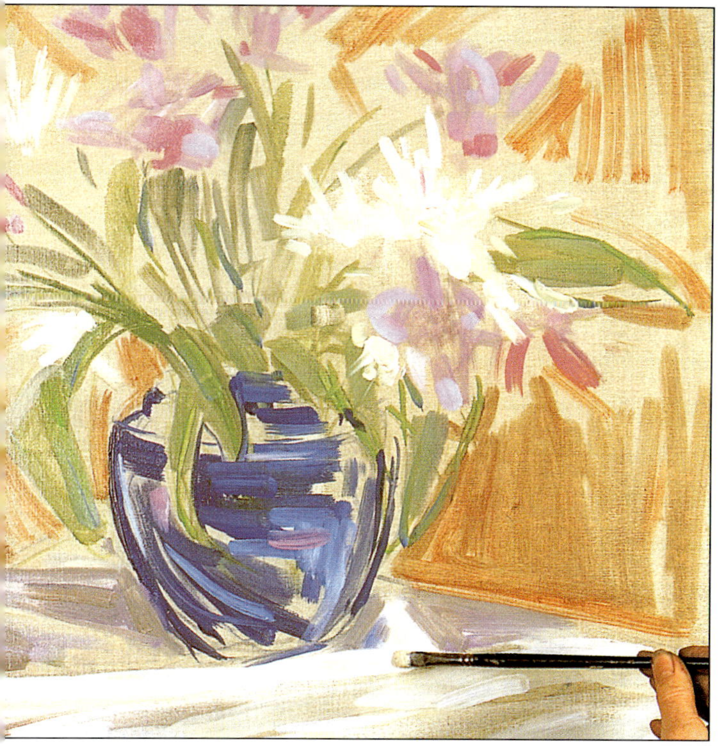

5 Now your painting is taking shape. From here on, mix your paint with turpentine and linseed oil to give it more body. Build up the reflections in the vase with French ultramarine, darkened with a touch of cobalt violet for the deepest tones, and cobalt blue and white for the highlights. Work on the folds in the tablecloth, deepening the shadows with a mix of burnt sienna and cobalt violet and adding white to the raised folds. Keep your brush moving and work on all the areas of the canvas.

6 Continue working on the vase with the same colours used in step 4. Add hints of cobalt violet to echo the colour of the tulips, and touches of pure white for the bright highlights. Let your brushstrokes describe the vase's rounded shape. Add tone and form to the leaves with a mixture of olive green and cadmium green, adding a little white for the highlights.

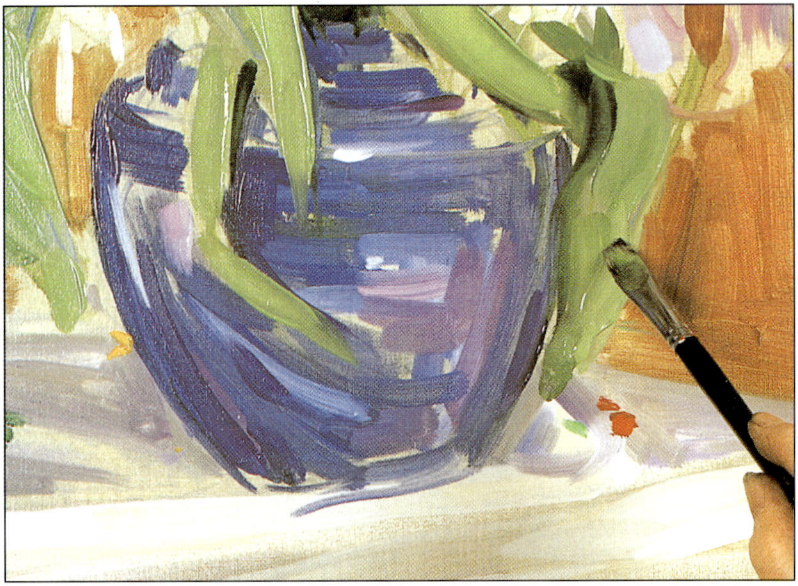

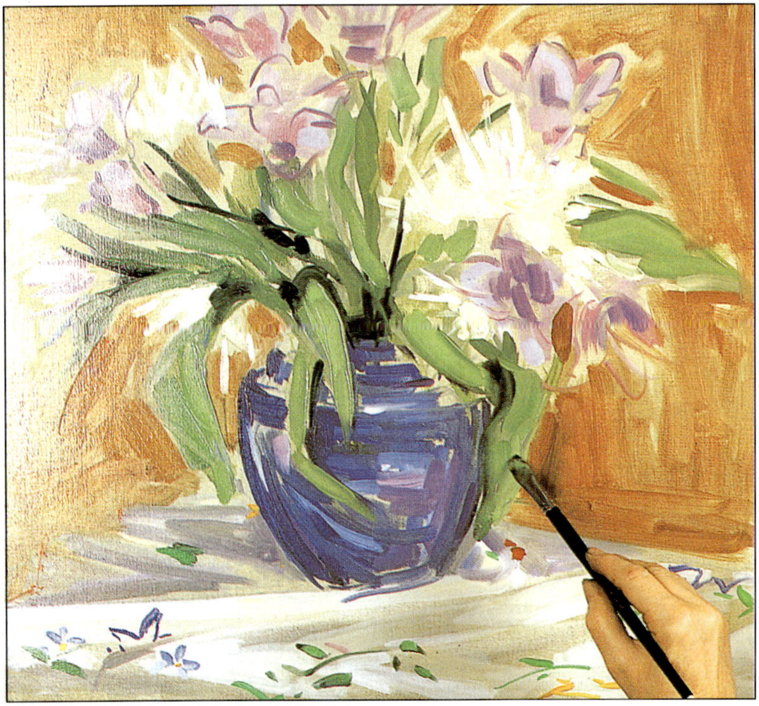

7 With a no. 2 round brush and cobalt violet, define the shapes of the tulips. With a no. 10 flat brush, fill in the background behind and between the flowers with a mix of burnt sienna, yellow ochre, chrome yellow and cadmium red. Suggest the embroidered flowers on the tablecloth using French ultramarine, cobalt blue and white for the petals, chrome yellow for the centres, and cobalt green darkened with cobalt blue for the stalks and leaves.

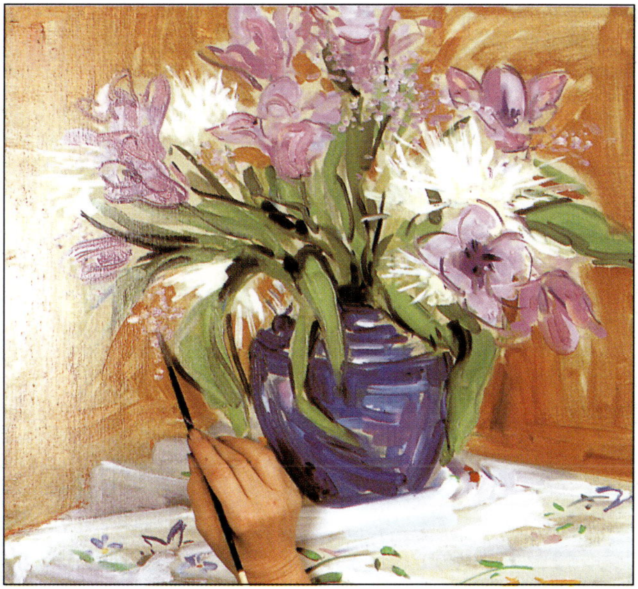

8 Add more white, mixed with a touch of cobalt blue, to the folds at the base of the vase. Using a no. 2 round brush, pick out the spiked petals of the daisies with pure white. Continue working on the tulips with mixtures of cobalt violet, cobalt blue, permanent rose and white, and touch in the stamens with pure cobalt violet. Let your brushstrokes follow the curved forms of the petals and allow the colours to mix wet-into-wet on the canvas. Mix cobalt violet and white and dot in the tiny statice flowers.

9 Stand back from the picture to see if there are any final adjustments that need to be made. Don't be tempted to add any unnecessary detail, however, otherwise you will lose the freshness and immediacy of your alla prima painting.

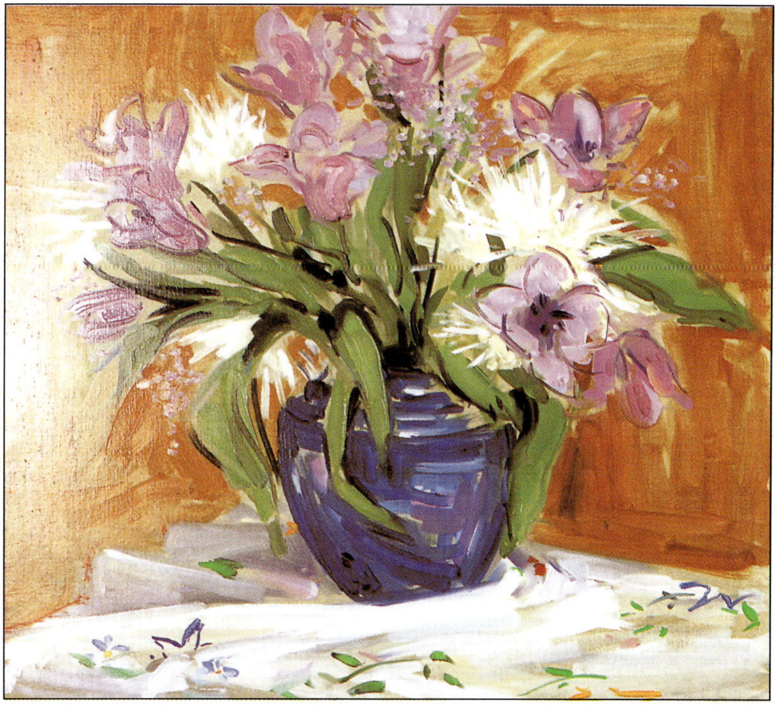

Toned Grounds

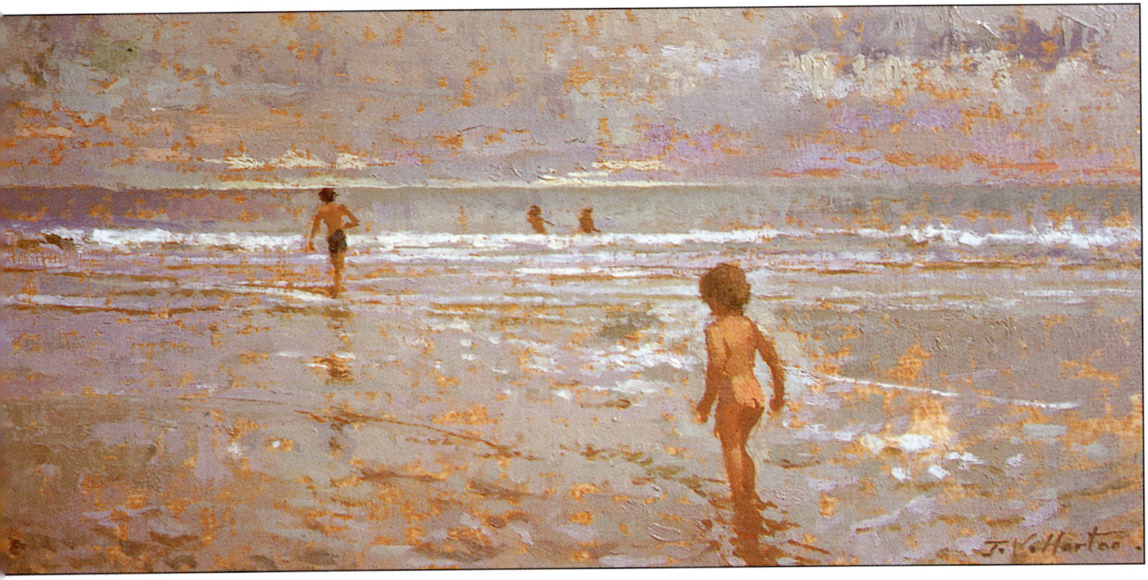

James Horton
BOYS BATHING AFTER A STORM
In this painting the artist has toned the canvas with a diluted earth colour. The toned ground breaks through the overlaid strokes, its warm colour providing a lively contrast with the cool greys of the sea and sky.

Once a canvas or board has been primed it can be given a wash of colour using thinned paint applied with a brush or a rag, and this is called a toned ground.

Toning the ground serves two purposes. First, it softens the stark white of the primed canvas or board, which can make it difficult to assess colours and tones accurately. A colour like red, for instance, may look quite dark when applied to a white canvas; but as the painting progresses that same red will be surrounded by other colours, and suddenly it looks much lighter. A neutral, mid-toned ground provides a more sympathetic surface on which to paint, and you can work out to the light and dark tones with equal ease.

Second, if patches of the coloured ground are allowed to show through the overpainting in places, they become an integral element of the painting and act as a harmonizing influence by tying the separate elements together.

Choosing the ground colour

The colour chosen for a toned ground will depend on the subject you are painting, but it is normally a neutral tone somewhere between the lightest and the darkest colours in the painting. The colour should be subtle and unobtrusive so that it does not overwhelm the colours in the overpainting. Diluted earth colours such as Venetian red, raw sienna or burnt umber work very well, as do soft greys and greens. Some artists like a ground that harmonizes with the dominant colour of the subject; others prefer a ground which provides a quiet contrast. For instance, a warm red-brown enhances the greens in a landscape, while a soft ochre adds brilliance to the blues in a skyscape.

Applying the ground

Dilute the paint thinly with turpentine or white spirit and apply it with a large brush (a decorator's brush is useful). After a few minutes, rub with a clean rag, leaving a transparent stain of colour which is ready to paint on the following day. Alternatively, some artists prefer to apply the colour vigorously, leaving the brushmarks showing.

Always make sure the toned ground is completely dry before you paint over it. An oil ground usually takes around 24 hours to dry thoroughly, but if time is short you can use acrylic paint instead. Acrylic is an alkyd-based paint which is water soluble. It dries in minutes, allowing you to overpaint in oils straight away (though you should never apply acrylics over oils as this causes the picture surface to crack. This is because oils are more flexible and slow-drying than acrylics).

The other great advantage is that acrylic paint acts as both a sealing agent and a primer, so you don't need to size and prime the canvas as you would for oils (never apply acrylics on a ground which has been sized and primed for oils, however, as this may lead to eventual cracking of the paint film).

James Horton
GRANTCHESTER, CAMBRIDGE
Here the toned ground has been chosen to harmonize, rather than contrast with, the colours in the painting. Although much of the ground is covered up, it has an important role to play, modifying the greens in the landscape and unifying the picture.

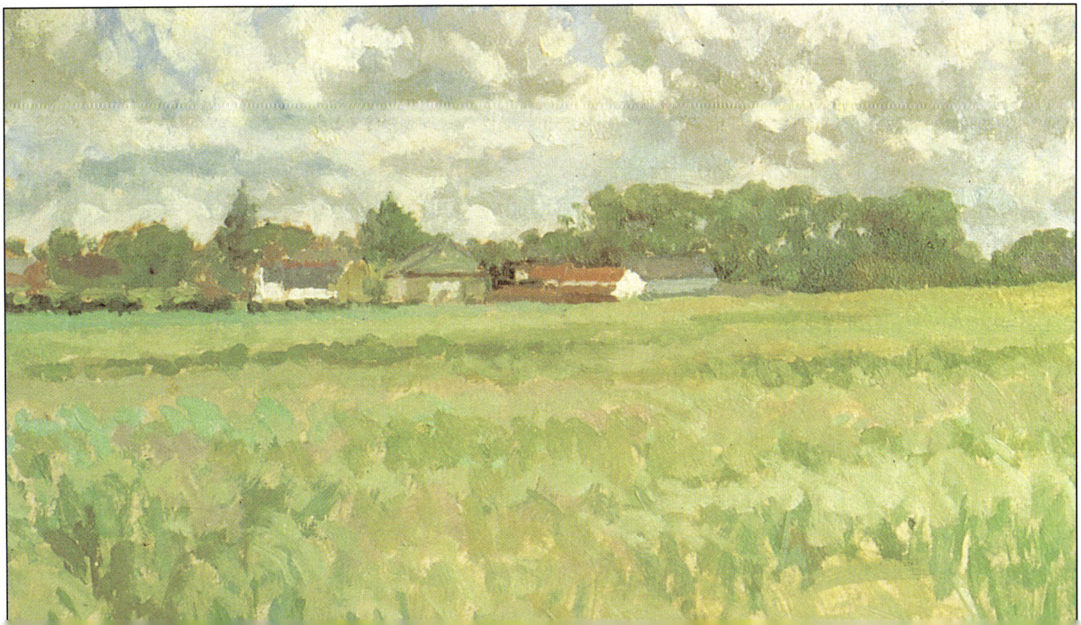

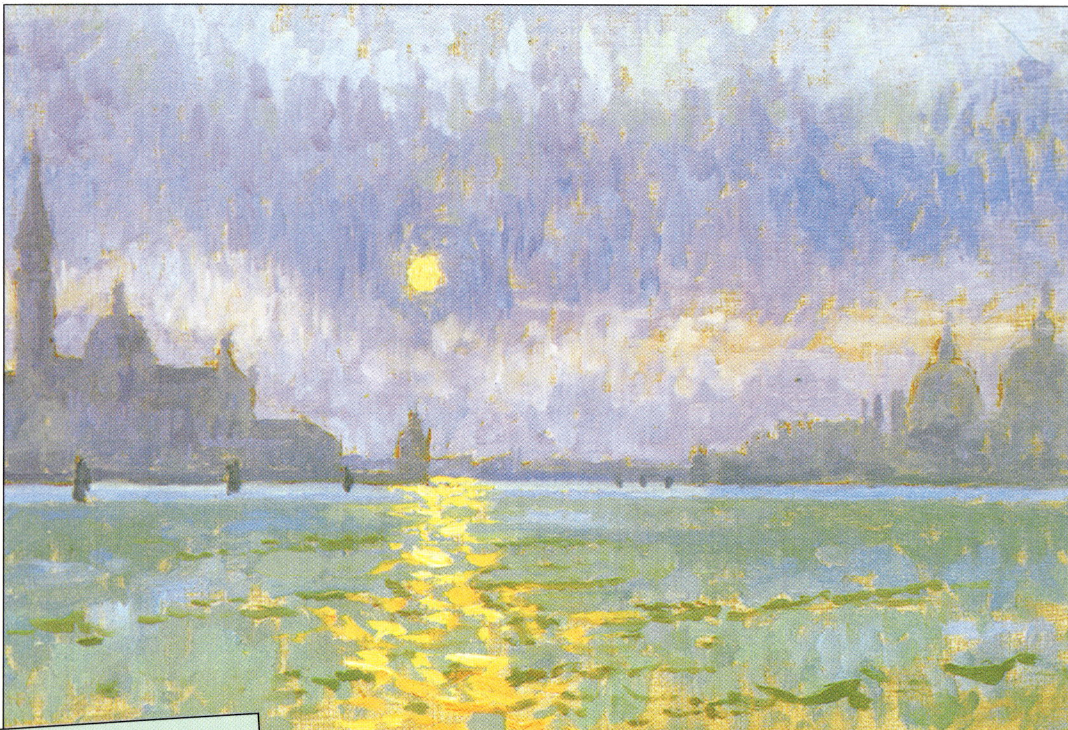

Venice, Evening

A carefully chosen toned ground can act as a mid tone and provide a link between disparate areas of colour. In this lovely painting, small patches of the umber ground remain exposed throughout the picture, their warm colour helping to unify the composition and enhancing the impression of the shimmering light of Venice at sunset.

YOU WILL NEED

- *Canvas board, 14 x 9½in (35.6 x 24.2cm)*
- *No. 2 round sable brush*
- *No. 5 round bristle brush*
- *1½in (38mm) decorating brush*
- *Turpentine*
- *Linseed oil*
- *Dammar varnish*

OIL PAINTS IN THE FOLLOWING COLOURS

- *Raw umber*
- *Burnt sienna*
- *French ultramarine*
- *Cerulean*
- *Alizarin crimson*
- *Cadmium red*
- *Cadmium orange*
- *Lemon yellow*
- *Titanium white*
- *Ivory Black*

1 Cover the whole surface of the canvas board with a transparent wash of raw umber, diluted to a thin consistency with turpentine. Use a $1^1/2$ in (38mm) decorating brush for this. The aim is to knock back the stark whiteness of the primed board and establish a warm mid tone against which you can judge the lighter and darker tones. Leave to dry overnight. Dilute raw umber and burnt sienna with turpentine and sketch in the main outlines of the scene, including the orb of the sun, with a no. 2 round sable brush.

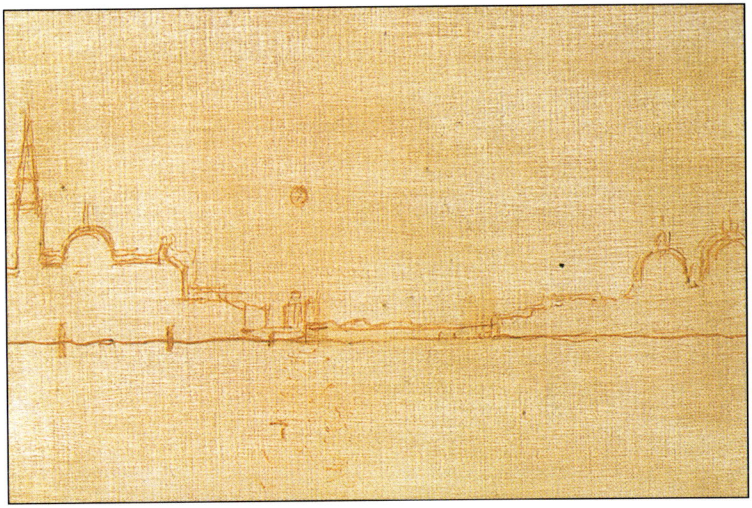

Helpful Hint

WHEN PAINTING LANDSCAPES, AVOID PLACING THE HORIZON LINE IN THE CENTRE OF THE CANVAS AS THIS EFFECTIVELY CUTS THE PICTURE IN HALF.

2 From here on, mix your colours with a little medium, consisting of equal amounts of linseed oil and dammar varnish and twice the amount of turpentine. Mix a warm grey from raw umber, French ultramarine and alizarin crimson and loosely touch in the buildings in the distance with a no. 5 round bristle brush. Then mix a vibrant, turquoise grey with ultramarine, white and a little lemon yellow and paint the upper part of the sky with random brushstrokes, letting the ground show through.

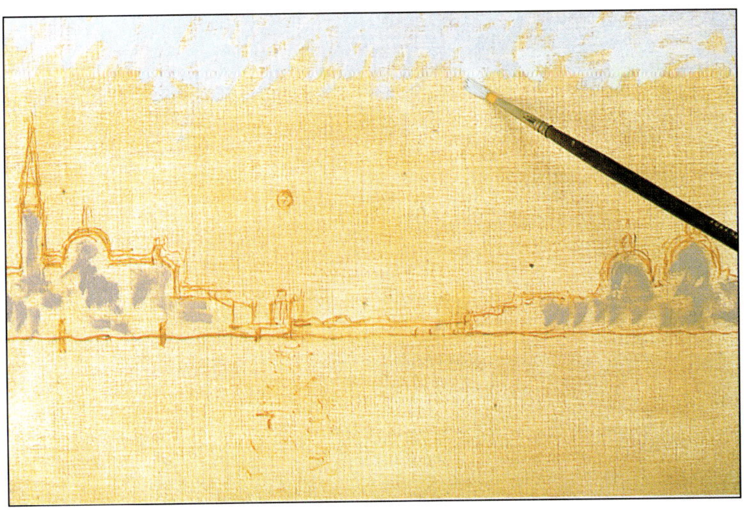

3 With the same brush, continue painting the sky, starting beneath the first band of colour with a combination of ultramarine, alizarin crimson, titanium hite and a tiny spot of ivory black. As you work down towards the horizon, add more alizarin and a little more white to the mix so that the sky gradually takes on a warm, violet hue. Again, apply the colours with loosely spaced marks, leaving plenty of the ground colour showing through.

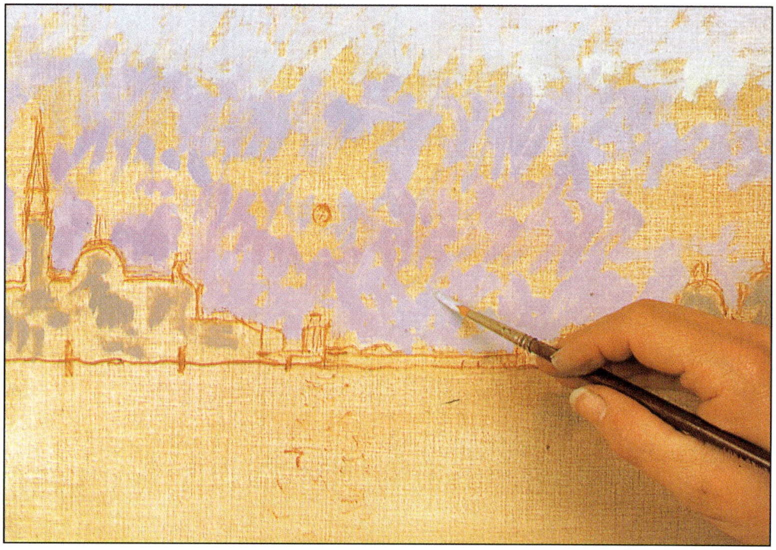

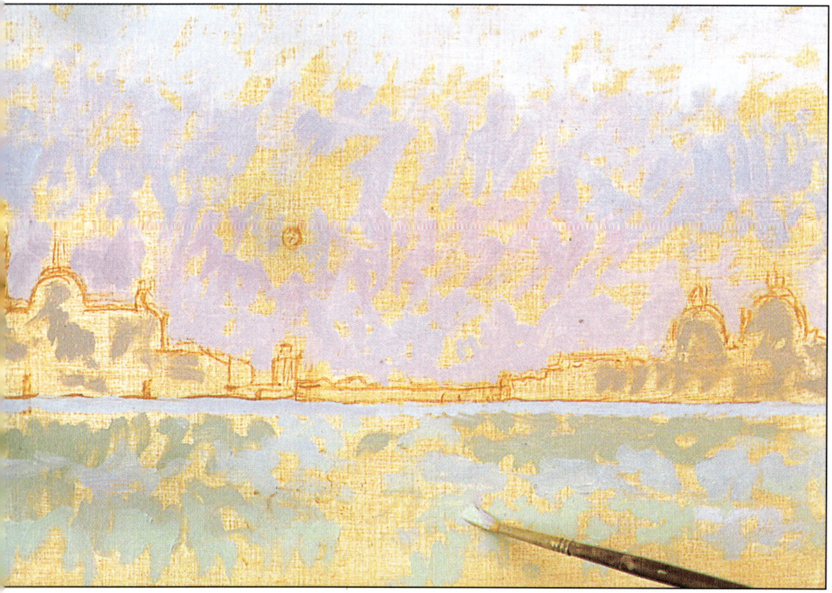

4 Start to work up the greenish tones in the water, leaving a 'pathway' for the sun's reflection. The basic colours are ultramarine, lemon yellow, cerulean and white – mix these in different combinations to give a range of greenish greys. For example, add more blue for the darker, cooler greens and more yellow or white for the lighter, warmer hues. Suggest light shining on the distant water with a band of pale green.

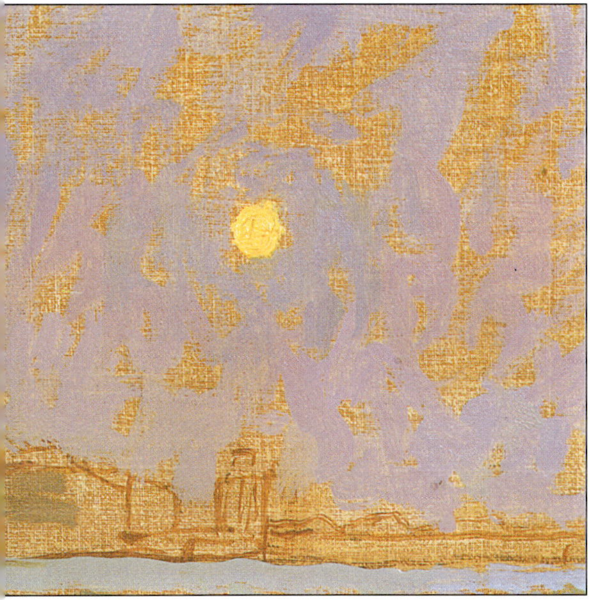

5 Mix lemon yellow, cadmium orange and white and paint the brilliant orb of the sun. Use fairly thick paint so that it catches the light. Then mix ultramarine, alizarin and white and use this to create a cool 'halo' of blue-grey around the sun, using loose strokes that follow a circular shape. This is an example of how one colour can be influenced by neighbouring colours; the yellow sun appears more brilliant in contrast with the darker tone of grey surrounding it.

6 Paint the group of buildings on the left of the picture with soft blue-violet greys mixed from various amounts of ultramarine, alizarin, black and white (make use of the greys already mixed on your palette). Instead of 'filling in' with a flat layer of paint, apply small strokes and dabs of subtly modulated colour. Allow small patches of the toned ground to show through the strokes; this gives a soft effect that suggests hazy evening light gently enveloping the scene.

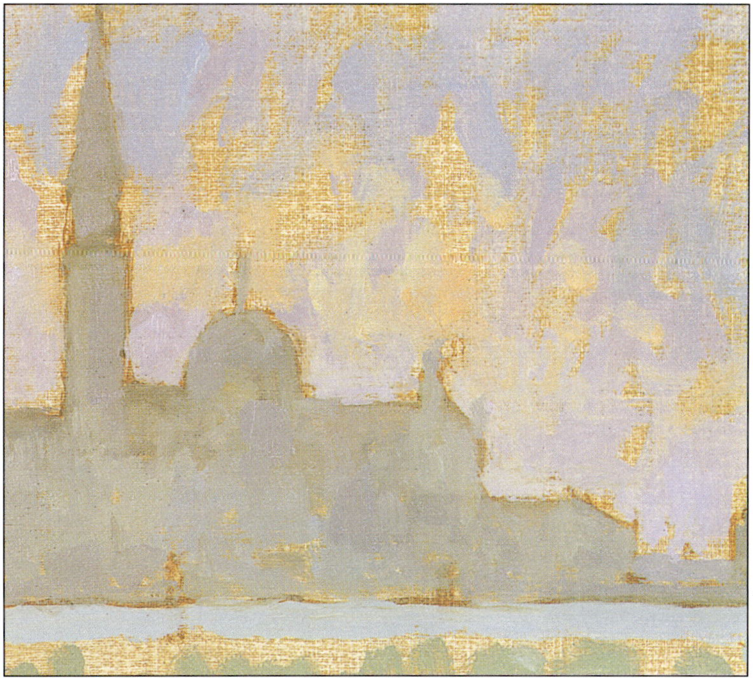

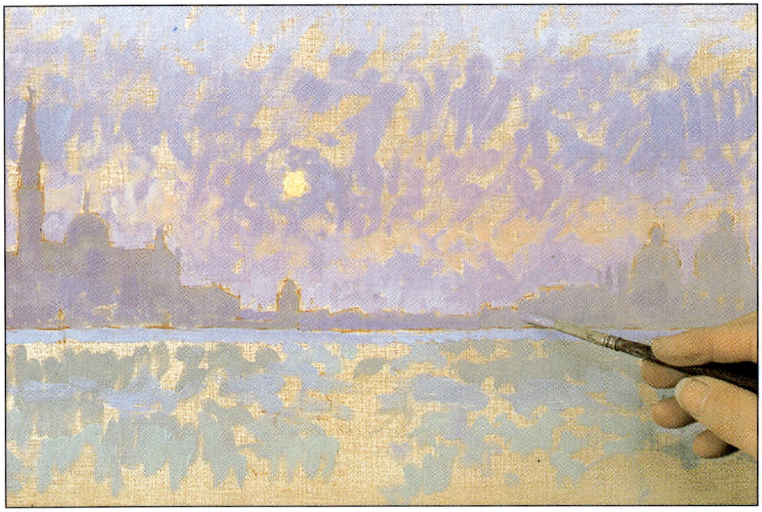

7 Suggest the soft rosy glow in the sky near the horizon with a mixture of cadmium red, lemon yellow and lots of white, applied with loose strokes. Now fill in the rest of the buildings, which lie behind those on the left. Use the same mix as in step 6, adding more white to lighten the tone and push the buildings back in space.

8 Mix lemon yellow, cadmium orange and white and paint the sun's broken reflection on the water. Use a no. 2 round sable brush to make rhythmic strokes and ticks that suggest the gentle lapping of the water. To enhance the effect of space and perspective, make these strokes smaller and more closely spaced in the distance, as well as lighter in tone.

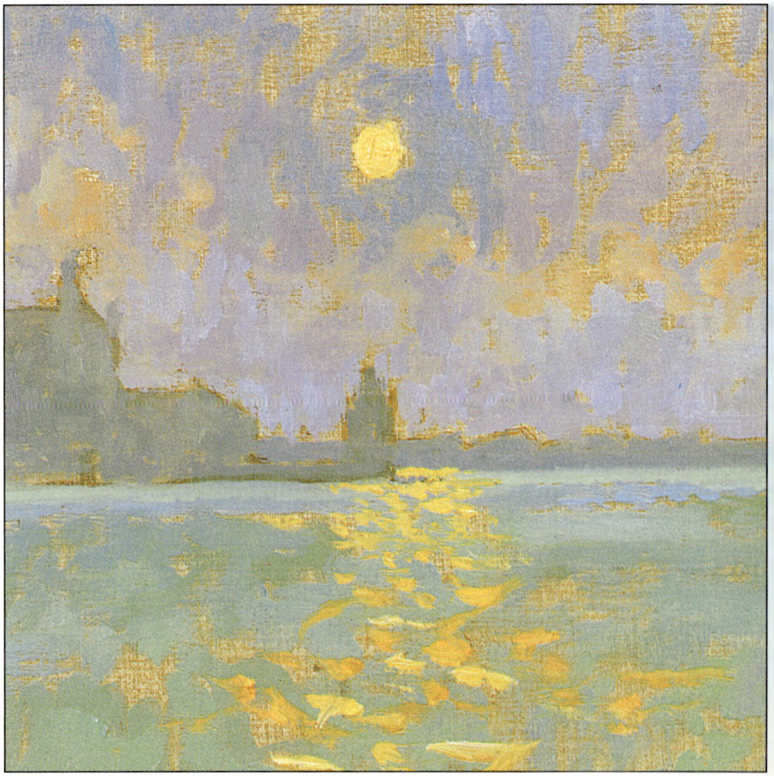

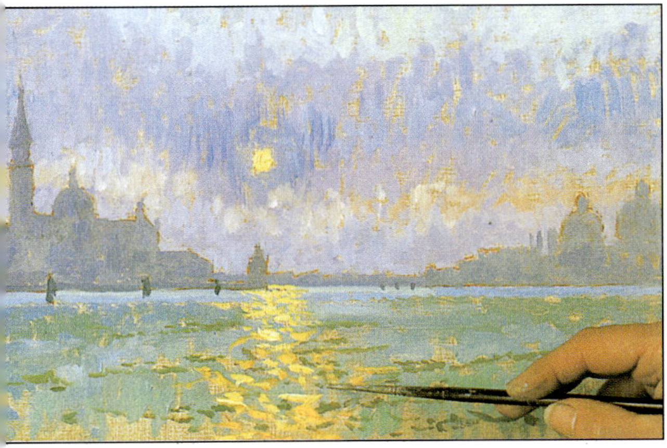

9 Mix ultramarine, alizarin and a little black to paint the tops of the wooden poles sticking out of the water, just visible in the distance. Then mix ultramarine and lemon yellow, warmed with cadmium orange, and touch in the small dark waves.

10 Look for the tonal balances of colour and make sure nothing jumps out at you – the effect should be one of hazy evening light. Any sharp divisions of colour can be softened and blended by gently hatching over them with a no. 2 round sable brush, to produce atmospheric blends and veils of colour.

Helpful Hint

WHITE IS USED A LOT IN OIL-PAINTING MIXTURES, SO IT IS MORE ECONOMICAL TO BUY A LARGE TUBE OF IT.

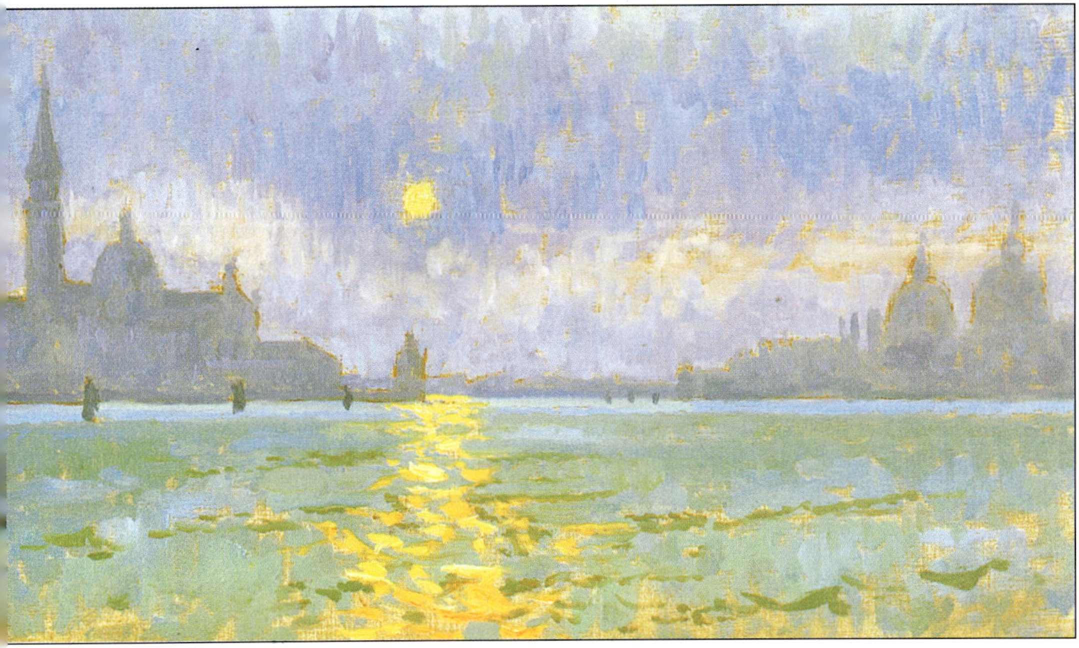

Mixing Greens

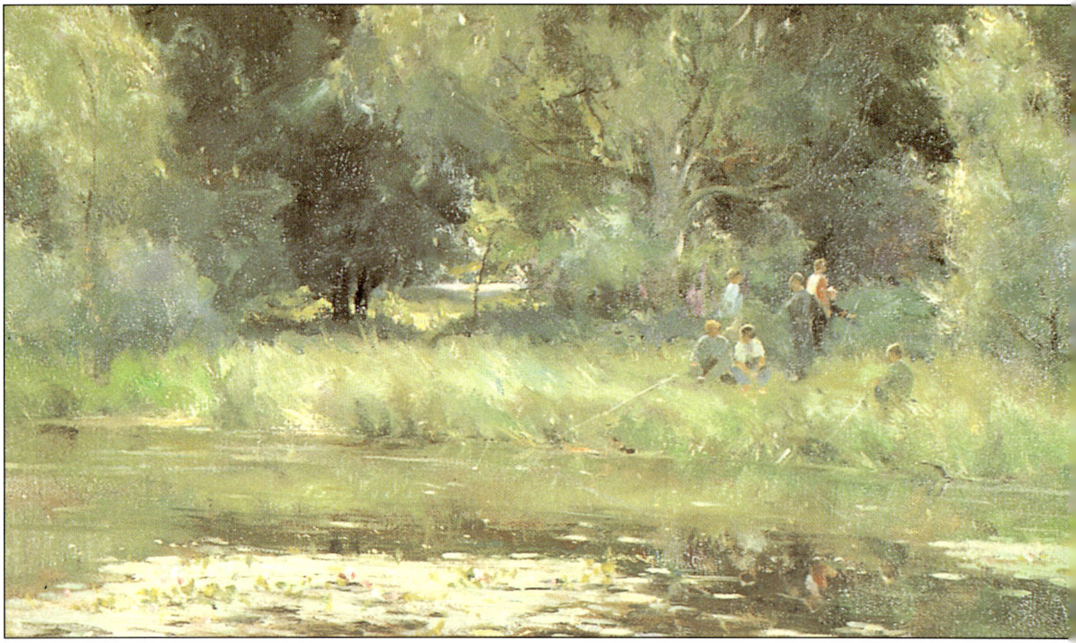

David Curtis
FISHING BY THE LAKE
A rich variety of greens is woven throughout this painting. Note how a sense of depth is created by using warm greens in the foreground and cooler greens in the distance.

Green is often the dominant colour in landscapes, but that green can vary enormously from almost blue to near yellow.

Before you start to mix paint, it is worthwhile to go out and observe the landscape, comparing the different greens to each other. On a bright day, for instance, sunlit areas of grass and foliage are a warm, yellowish green, while those greens in shadow appear cooler and bluer. And if you look towards the horizon, you will see that the greens of trees, fields and hills appear progressively cooler, bluer and paler in tone as they recede into the distance.

Where many inexperienced painters go wrong is in painting an entire landscape using ready-mixed greens straight from the tube, and simply adding white or black to make them lighter or darker. Because there aren't enough contrasts of light and dark tone and warm and cool colour, the result is a flat, monotonous painting with no feeling of light.

If you want to paint realistic landscapes, it is worth learning how to mix more lively greens, and there are two ways in which you can do this: using tube greens modified with other colours, and mixing your own greens from blues and yellows.

Modifying tube greens

There are several greens available ready-mixed in tubes, but most of them are too intense, not like the soft greens of nature. However, tube greens are excellent when modified by the addition of other colours on your palette. For example, viridian is an intense, cold green that looks unnatural in its pure state. But by adding red, yellow or orange to it, it is possible to create a whole range of life-like greens.

Mixing blues and yellows

Blues and yellows mixed together give an even wider range of rich and subtle greens that can be varied from light to dark, bright to muted and warm to cool. Such greens can be further adjusted by adding a third colour, such as a touch of red if the green is too bright and you want to tone it down a little.

Discover for yourself the value of mixing your own greens. Take three blues – cerulean, cobalt and ultramarine – and three yellows – lemon, cadmium and ochre. Add each of the yellows to each of the blues, and you instantly have nine different greens, ranging from bright, leafy hues to warm, rich tones. Start with a 50:50 mix, then see what happens when you alter the proportions of each colour in turn: adding more blue creates darker, cooler greens, while more yellow creates brighter, warmer greens. You can extend the possibilities even further by experimenting with adding touches of earth colours such as raw sienna or raw umber to make even richer greens.

Warm and cool greens

Colours are classed as being either 'warm' or 'cool' in temperature, and in general blue is regarded as cool, and yellow as warm. However, within this broad definition, some blues are warmer or cooler than others, and the same goes for yellows. French ultramarine contains a hint of red, so is warmer than cerulean; lemon yellow has a green cast, so is cooler than cadmium yellow.

Bear this in mind when mixing greens for your landscapes; if you want a cool green for painting shadowy foliage, it makes sense to choose a cool blue such as Winsor blue and a cool yellow such as lemon yellow. If you want a warm, rich green for sunlit foliage, try a blend of ultramarine and cadmium yellow. When mixing colours, bear in mind that some colours are strong and others weak. A little cadmium yellow, for instance, goes a long way, so add it in small amounts.

The colour swatches below demonstrate just some of the colour combinations that will give you a wide range of lively and expressive greens.

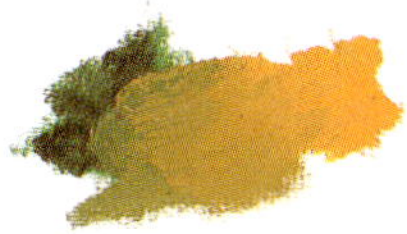

Viridian & cadmium yellow

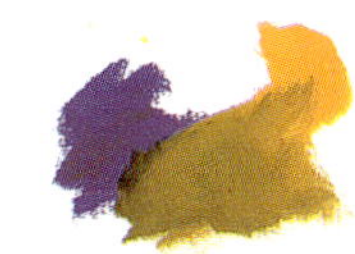

French ultramarine & cadmium yellow

Viridian & lemon yellow

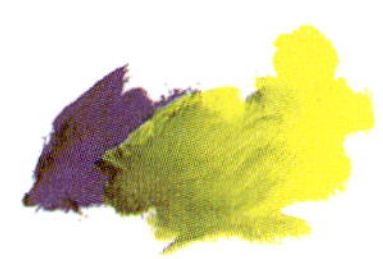

French ultramarine & lemon yellow

Sap green & cadmium yellow

Sap green & lemon yellow

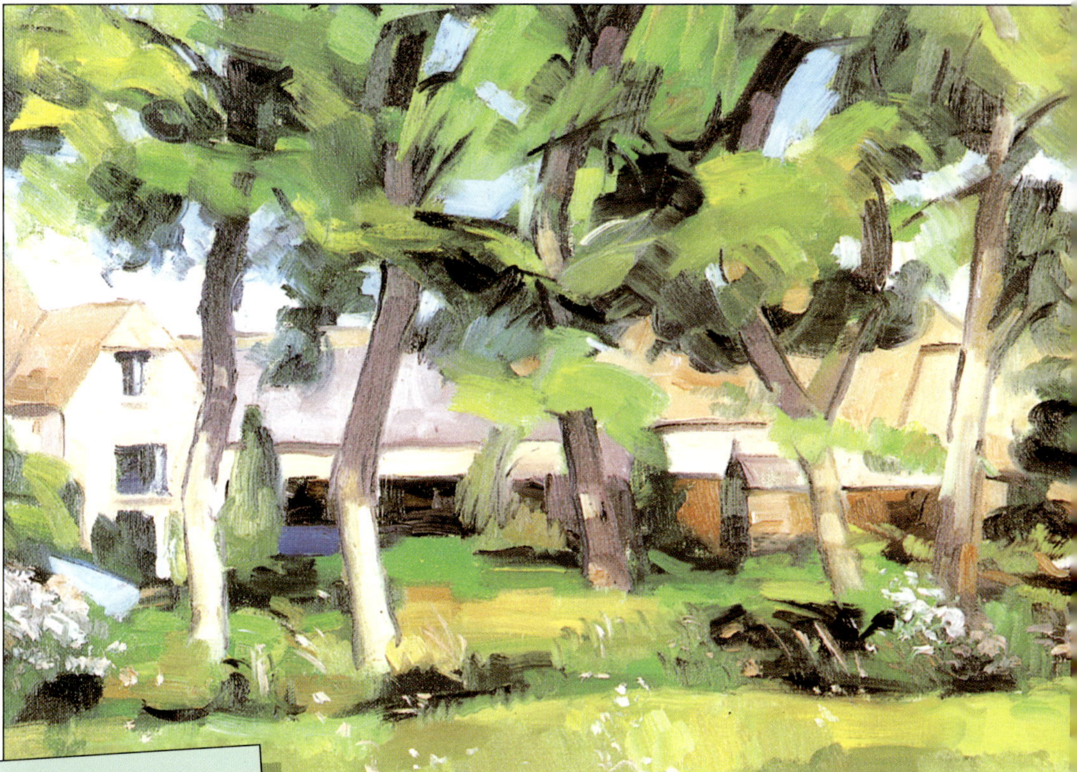

YOU WILL NEED

- Sheet of canvas board, 20 x 16in (50.8 x 40.6cm)
- Nos. 2, 5 and 10 flat bristle brush
- No. 4 filbert bristle brush
- Distilled turpentine
- Purified linseed oil
- Charcoal

A Country Scene

In this lively painting the artist has succeeded in mixing a wide range of foliage greens, from cool blue shades to vibrant yellow hues. He used a limited palette of colours, mixing greens from various blues and yellows and modifying tube greens with other colours.

OIL PAINTS IN THE FOLLOWING COLOURS

- *Lemon yellow*
- *Spectrum yellow*
- *Yellow ochre*
- *Venetian red*
- *Cobalt violet*
- *Chrome oxide green*
- *Permanent green*
- *French ultramarine*
- *Cerulean*
- *Titanium white*

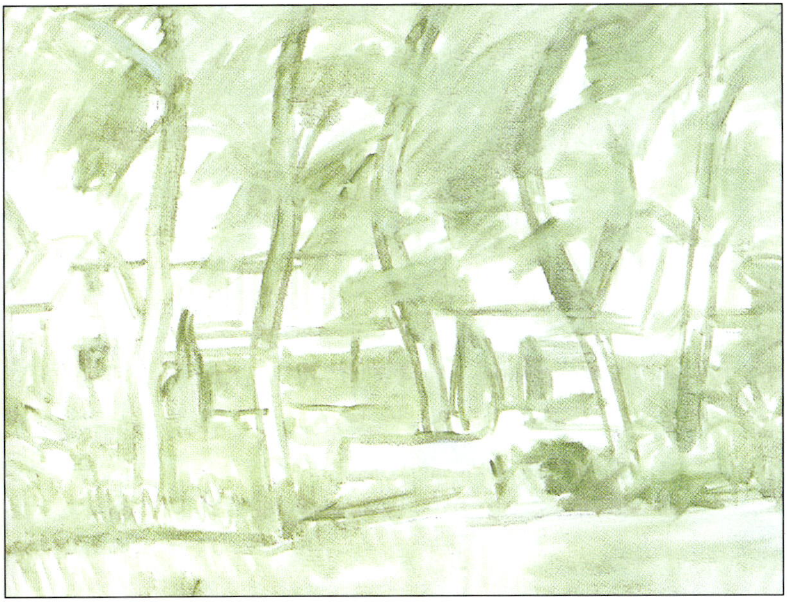

1 Sketch in the main outlines of the composition with charcoal. Dilute some chrome oxide green with turpentine so it flows easily and, with a no. 4 filbert bristle brush, loosely paint in the main areas, using the charcoal marks as a guide.

2 Mix a cool green from permanent green, French ultramarine and chrome oxide green, adding a little linseed oil to the turpentine to make the paint more workable. With a no. 10 flat brush, work across the canvas using broad strokes to block in the darkest areas in the pine trees and the cast shadows on the grass. Vary the direction of your brush strokes to convey the direction of growth of the branches.

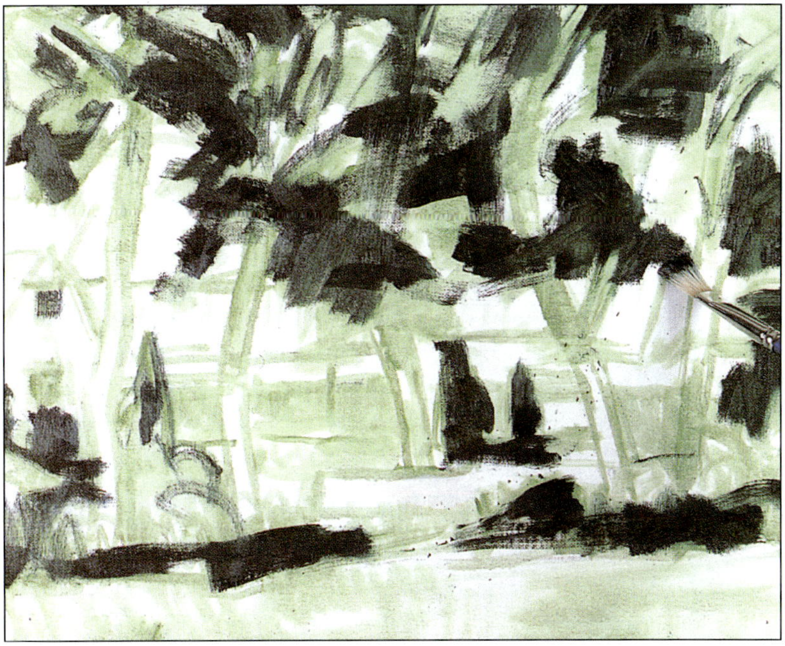

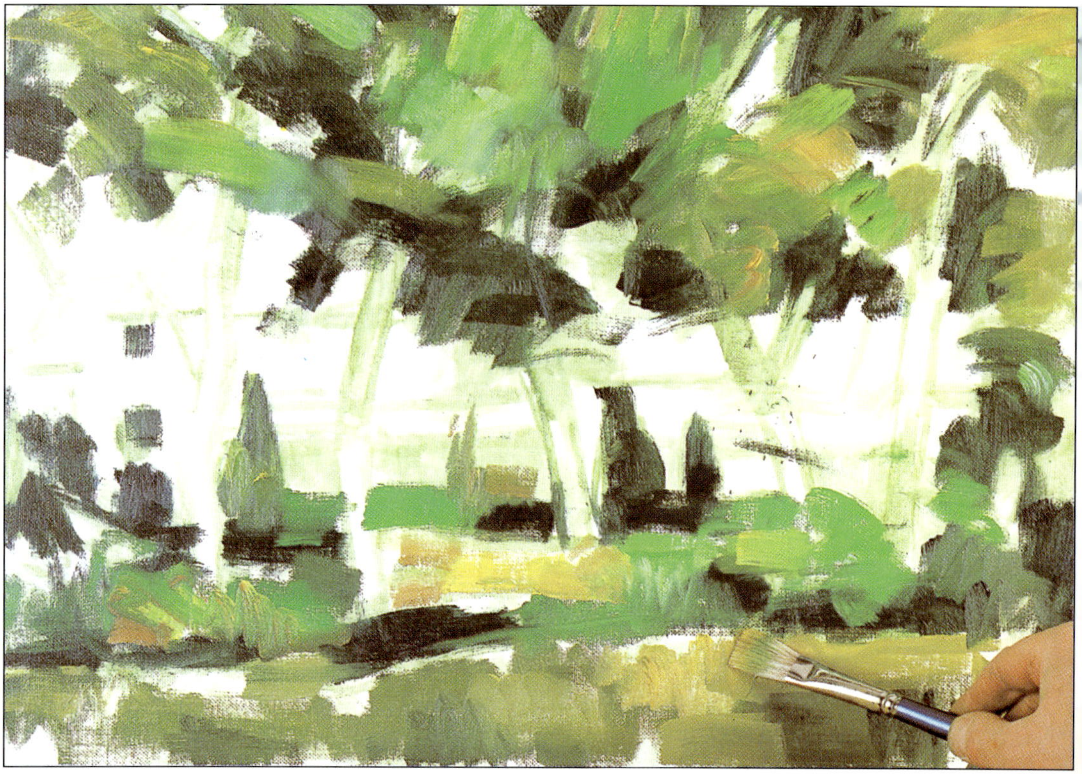

3 Now bring in some yellow ochre, lemon yellow and spectrum yellow, mixing them with the greens and blues in varying proportions to make a range of warmer, lighter greens for the sunlit foliage and grass. Partially blend the colours on the canvas and vary the proportions of the colours in your mixes, adding more yellows to warm up the sunny greens and more blue to cool down the shadowy greens. Add a little titanium white to the palette to introduce light to the picture, but not too much as it tends to make the colours go dull and chalky.

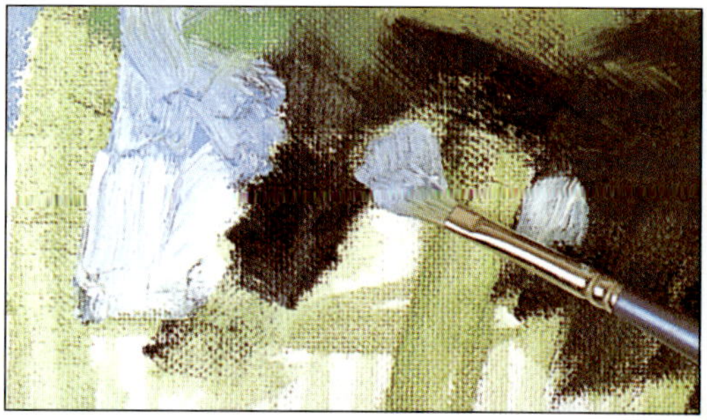

4 Mix a pale blue from cerulean and titanium white and paint the sky, cutting in around the foliage. Paint the clouds with white and a hint of cerulean. Use a no. 5 flat brush for the broad areas and a no. 2 for the smaller patches.

5 With a no. 4 filbert brush, block in the pinks and browns of the buildings in the background with broad strokes. Use a base mixture of Venetian red and titanium white, adding some yellow ochre and spectrum yellow for the warm-coloured roofs and some cobalt violet and cerulean for the slate roof in the middle.

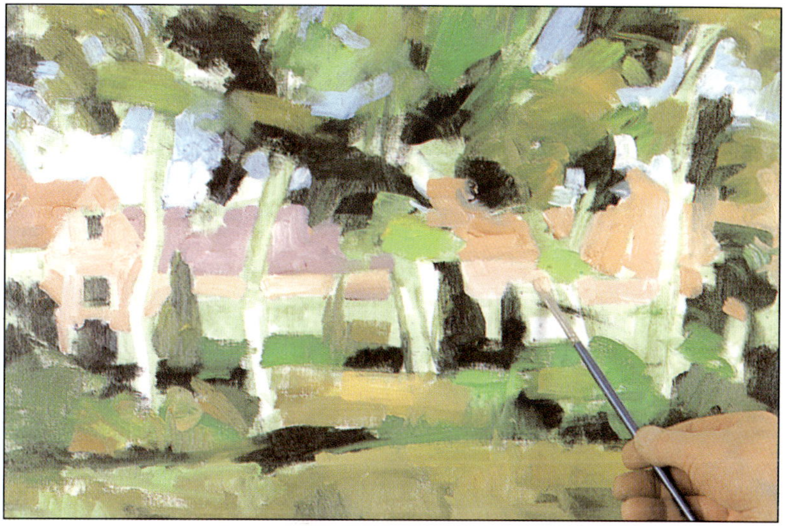

Helpful Hint

TRY TO INTRODUCE TOUCHES OF SIMILAR COLOUR IN DIFFERENT PARTS OF THE PICTURE. THIS WILL CREATE A SATISFYING, HARMONIOUS EFFECT.

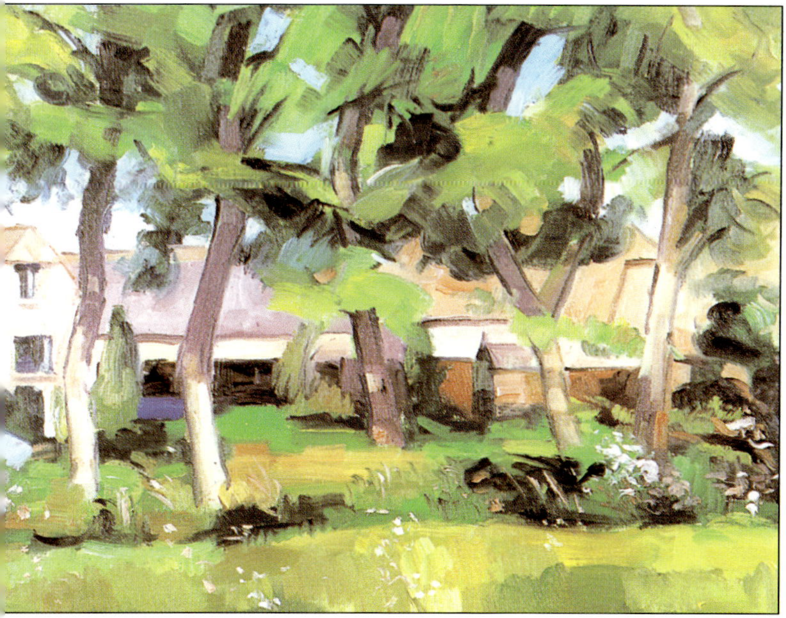

6 The canopy of foliage casts violet-tinged shadows onto the upper parts of the tree trunks; paint these using mixtures of cobalt violet, ultramarine and a little Venetian red, varying the proportions of the colours to create light and dark tones. Now that you have blocked in most of the base colours, you can begin to work over them to develop contrasts of tone and texture.

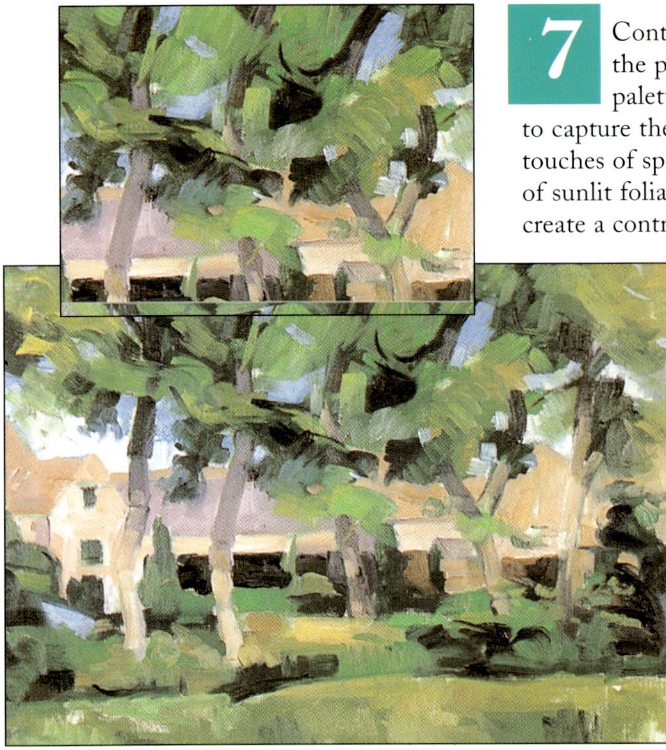

7 Continue working on the green areas of the picture using all the colours on your palette, including a little violet and blue to capture the really deep tones in the trees. Add touches of spectrum yellow to brighten the patches of sunlit foliage at the outer edges of the trees and create a contrast with the dark tones in the shadows. In the detail (left) you can see how the artist has partially blended his colours on the canvas, wet-into-wet, and varied the angle of his brush to create lively marks that give a sense of movement to the foliage.

Helpful Hint

GREENS CAN BE LIGHTENED WITH WHITE OR YELLOW AND DARKENED WITH BLACK, BLUE OR RED. WHITE MAKES SOME COLOURS APPEAR CHALKY, AND BLACK CAN HAVE A DEADENING EFFECT.

8 Go over the buildings with a no. 2 flat brush, putting in outlines and the shadows under the eaves with a mixture of cobalt violet and ultramarine. Darken the shadows on the tree trunks with the same colour; this contrast of dark tone against the lighter tones of the buildings helps to create a sense of space and depth in the picture.

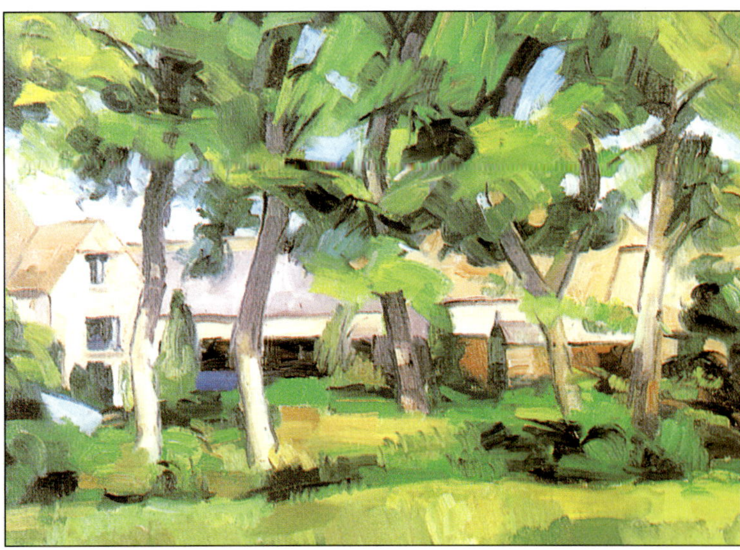

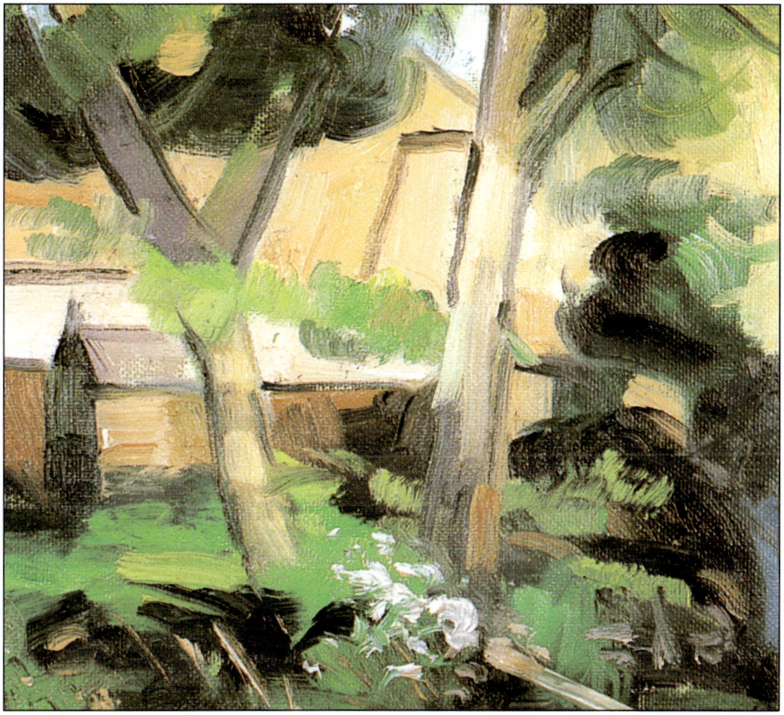

9 Now start adding the details, suggesting the rose bushes in the foreground with dabs of Venetian red and titanium white. Roll the well-loaded brush over the surface to deposit the paint – this technique is known as scumbling.

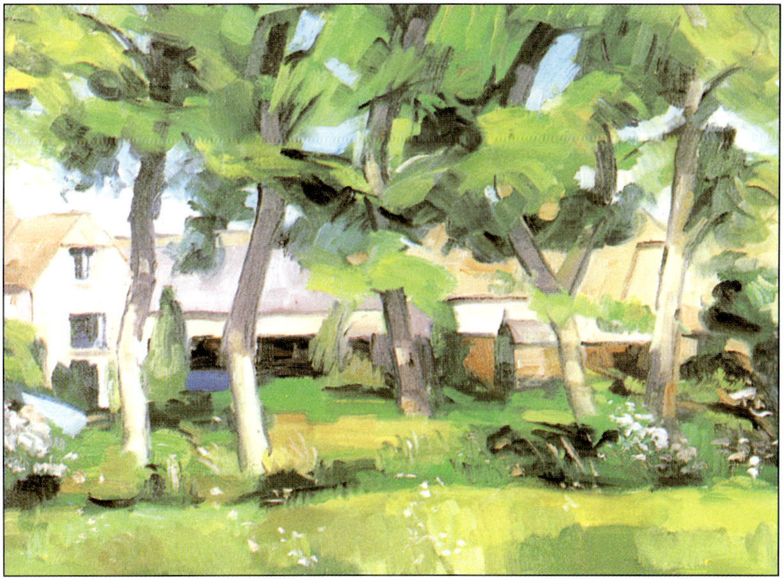

10 The final picture gives a lively impression of sunlight breaking through the shady pine trees. Notice the variety of greens the artist has used, from cool blue-greens through to vibrant yellow-greens. A refreshing note of contrast is provided by the warm, reddish tones of the buildings in the background.

Blending

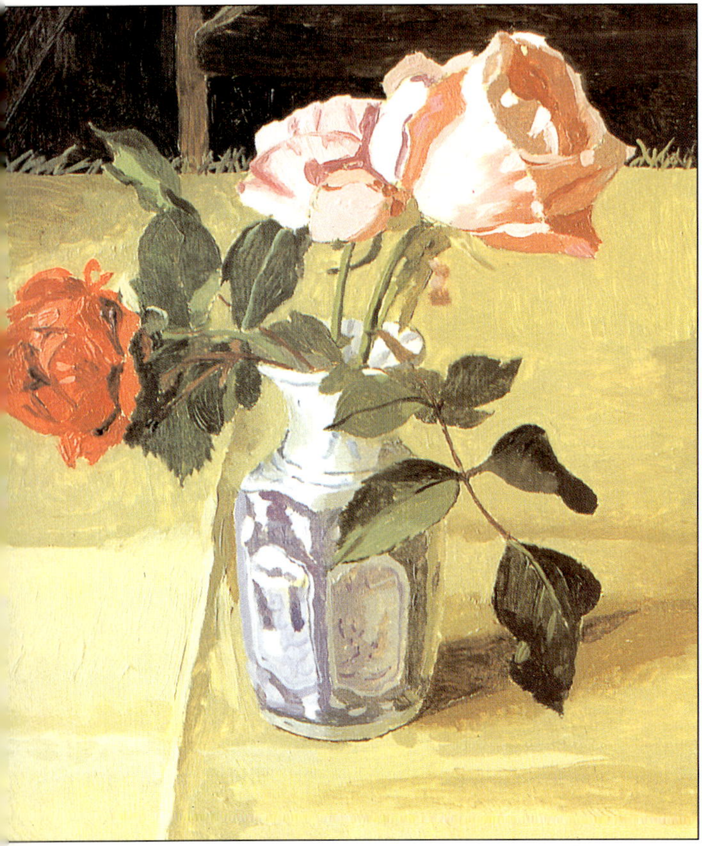

Blending is a means of achieving soft gradations between adjacent tones or colours by brushing them together where they meet, wet-into-wet. Oil paint lends itself readily to the blending technique because its soft, buttery consistency and slow drying time mean the paint can be freely manipulated on the painting surface.

Subjects

Smooth gradations of colour are used in painting to render specific materials and surface qualities such as soft fabrics, skin tones, flowers, fruits and the reflective surfaces of metal and glass. They are also used to describe certain atmospheric impressions found in the landscape, such as skies and clouds, fog and mist, and reflections in water. In landscapes and seascapes, an impression of space, light and atmosphere can be created by softening the line where sky and horizon meet.

Jeremy Galton
ROSES IN BLUE VASE
Too many sharply focused edges can make delicate subjects look hard and brittle. This floral still life shows how the sensitive handling of tones and edges can suggest form without overstatement. Notice how most of the tones and colours are blended wet-into-wet, with just a few crisp touches here and there to bring the picture into focus.

Techniques

The techniques of fusing colour fall between two extremes. On the one hand you can blend the colour with your brush so smoothly and silkily that the brushstrokes are imperceptible even when viewed close-up. At the other extreme it is possible to roughly knit the colours together so that the brushmarks remain visible at close quarters; when viewed at a distance the colours appear to merge together, yet they retain a lively quality because they are only partially blended.

Brushes

Any type of brush can be used for blending, depending on your style of painting. Some artists use stiff-bristled brushes so as to retain the liveliness of the brushstrokes. Others prefer to use softhair brushes to achieve very smooth, perfect gradations. Special brushes called 'fan blenders' – they have long hairs arranged in a fan shape – are specially adapted for smooth blending; work over the edge between two tones or colours using a gentle sweeping motion until a smooth, imperceptible blend is achieved.

David Curtis
HOT AUGUST EVENING, RIVER IDLE
Colour, composition and brushwork all contribute to the peaceful atmosphere of this pastoral scene. A harmonious palette of warm colours sets the mood; and the smoothly blended brushstrokes capture the hazy light of a summer evening.

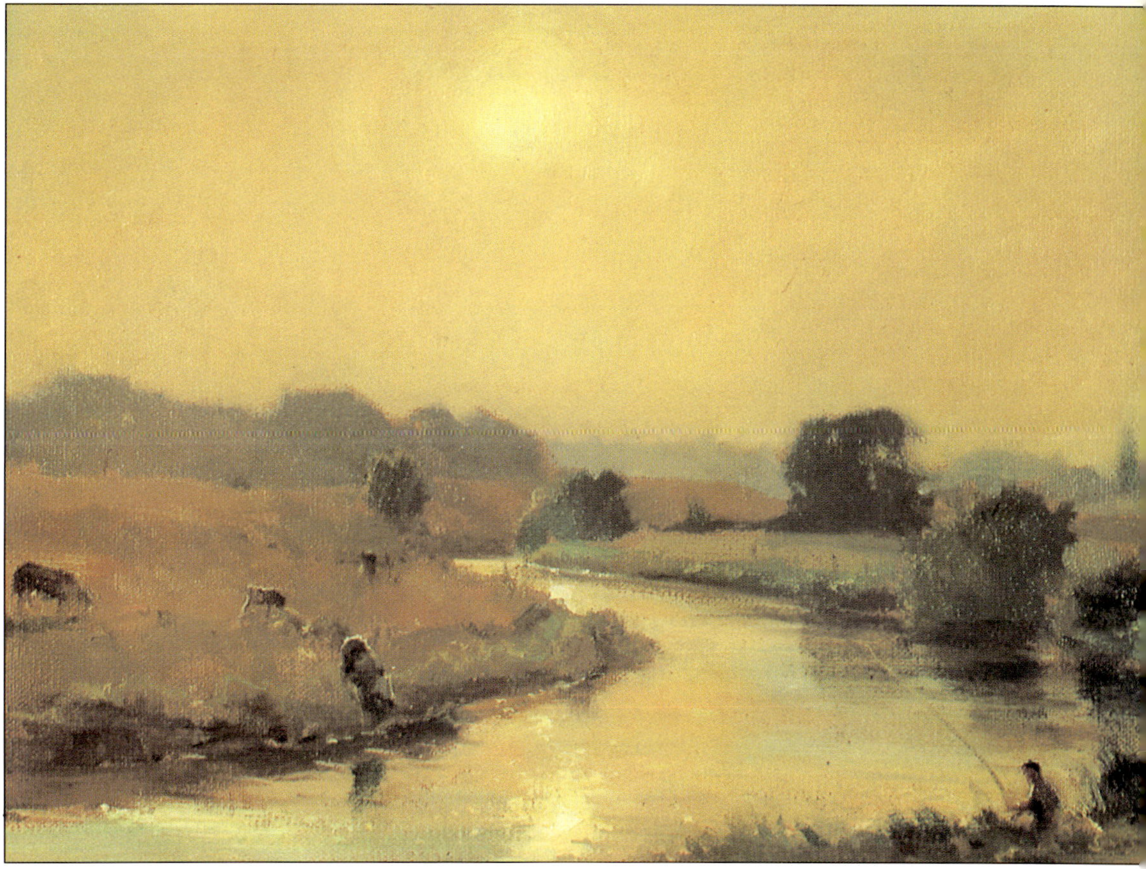

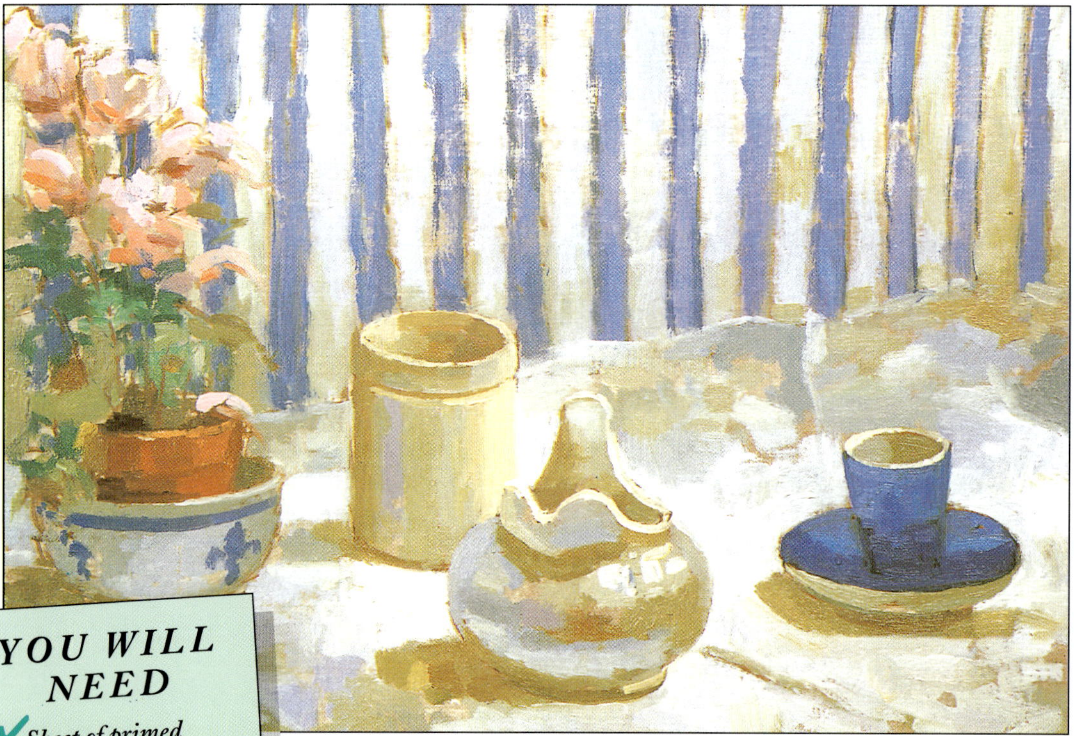

YOU WILL NEED

- *Sheet of primed canvas or board, 12 x 9in (30.5 x 22.8cm)*
- *1½in (38mm) decorating brush*
- *No. 5 round bristle brush*
- *No. 2 round sable brush*
- *No. 4 round sable brush*
- *No. 4 filbert bristle brush*
- *Refined linseed oil*
- *Distilled turpentine*
- *Dammar varnish*

Still Life in Blue and White

In this painting the artist has blended his colours softly into one another, wet-into-wet, producing gentle gradations of tone and hue that describe the rounded forms of the jugs and bowls and give them solidity and weight.

OIL PAINTS IN THE FOLLOWING COLOURS

- *French ultramarine*
- *Cerulean*
- *Yellow ochre*
- *Naples yellow*
- *Veridian*
- *Raw umber*
- *Burnt sienna*
- *Cadmium red*
- *Alizarin crimson*
- *Titanium white*
- *Ivory Black*

1 Start by staining your canvas or board with a thin wash of cadmium red mixed with a little French ultramarine. Use a 11/2in (38mm) decorating brush to spread the colour over the surface in wide sweeps. Leave to dry overnight. Then sketch in the main outlines of the composition with a no. 2 round sable brush and burnt sienna, thinned to a watery consistency with turpentine.

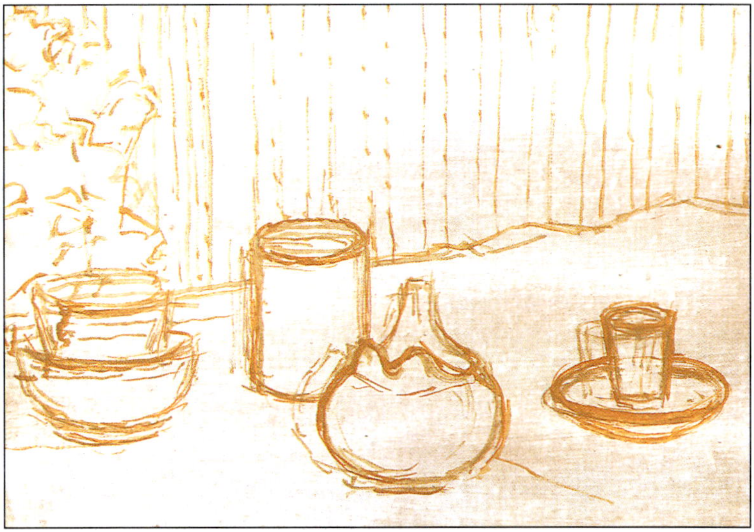

Helpful Hint

THE ARTIST MIXED HIS PAINTS WITH EQUAL PROPORTIONS OF LINSEED OIL AND DAMMAR VARNISH, PLUS TWICE THE VOLUME OF TURPENTINE. THE ADDITION OF DAMMAR VARNISH TO THE BASIC TURPS AND OIL MEDIUM GIVES A RICH, ENAMEL-LIKE QUALITY TO THE PAINT.

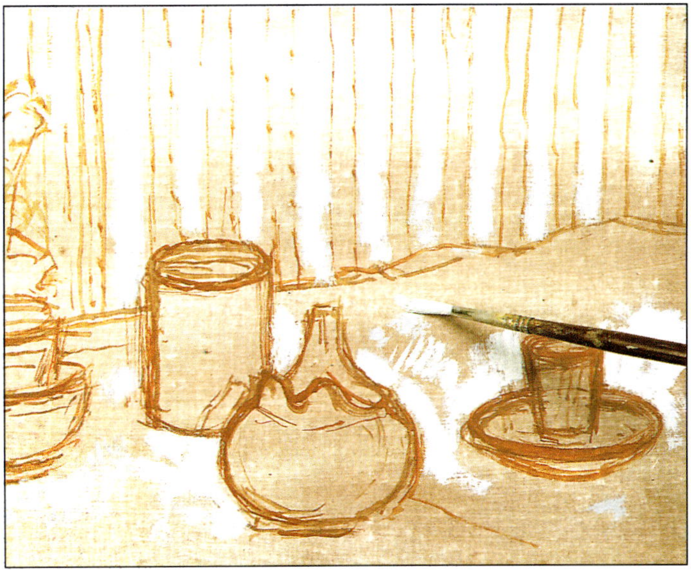

2 From this point, mix your colours with an oil medium (see Helpful Hint above) to make the paint more workable. Squeeze some titanium white onto your palette and blend tiny touches of yellow ochre and raw umber into it, just to take the edge off the white. With a no. 5 round bristle brush, roughly block in the white stripes on the wallpaper and start to paint the white cloth, twisting and turning the brush to create lively strokes.

3 Mix two blues for the blue stripes on the wallpaper: French ultramarine and white for the darker, warmer stripes, and cerulean and white for the cooler, lighter stripes behind the plant. Use fairly dry paint and keep them quite 'sketchy' in feel so that they stay in the background – if they are too clearly defined they will leap forward in the picture plane.

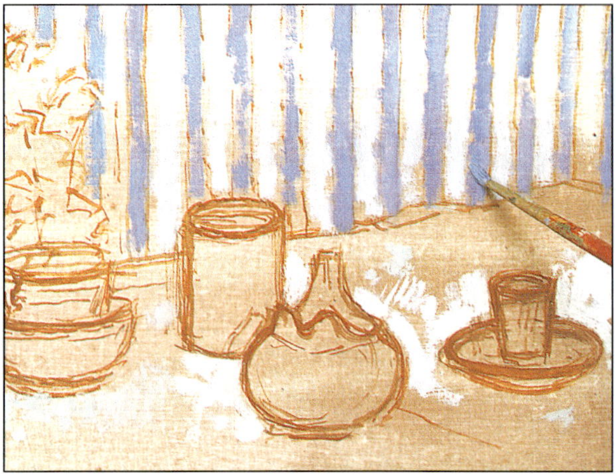

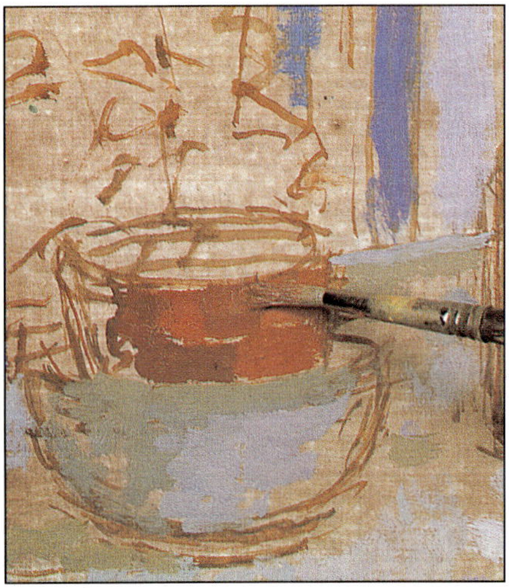

4 Establish the broad areas of light and shade on the china bowl and block them in, using a mix of French ultramarine, ivory black, alizarin crimson and white for the lighter tone, and a darker mix with yellow ochre added for the dark tone. Do the same for the terracotta plant pot, using various proportions of cadmium red, burnt sienna and white to create the light, dark and mid tones. Block these in quite broadly, making no attempt to blend the colours at this stage.

5 Rather than committing to one area in detail, move around the picture putting in touches of colour so that you can assess how the various tones and colours are balancing each other. Paint the deep shadows on the jug and jar with yellow ochre and raw umber, then block in the mid tones using the greys mixed in step 4. Add touches of pale mauve, mixed from ultramarine, alizarin, white and a hint of black, where colour is reflected onto the jug and jar from the pink cyclamen flowers. Mix Naples yellow and white for the highlight on the right side of the jar. Use the same colours to establish the soft shadows on the white cloth.

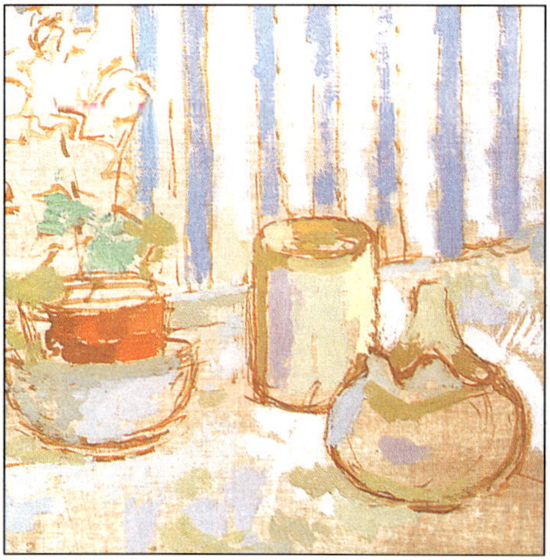

6 Now paint the blue egg cup and saucer with a mixture of ultramarine and cerulean, darkened with alizarin crimson for the shadow areas.

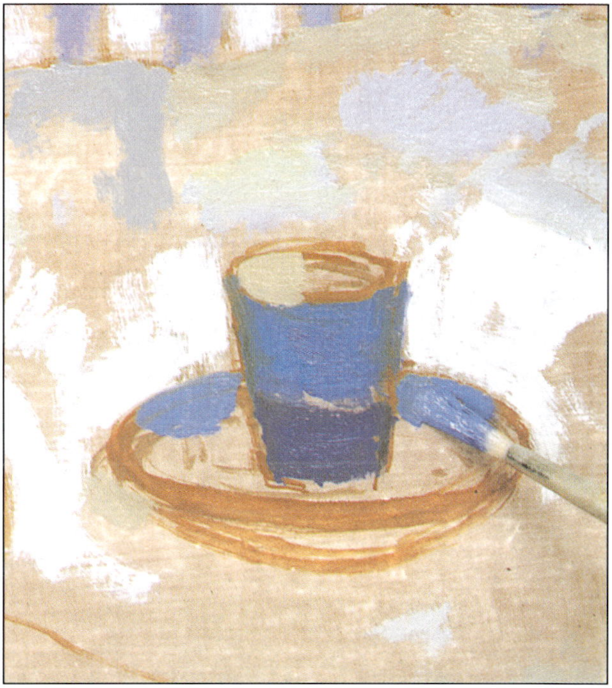

Helpful Hint

IF YOU FIND IT DIFFICULT TO ASSESS THE RELATIVE TONES IN YOUR SUBJECT, TRY LOOKING AT IT THROUGH HALF-CLOSED EYES. THIS CUTS OUT MUCH OF THE DETAIL, ALLOWING YOU TO SEE THE LIGHTS, DARKS AND MID TONES MORE CLEARLY.

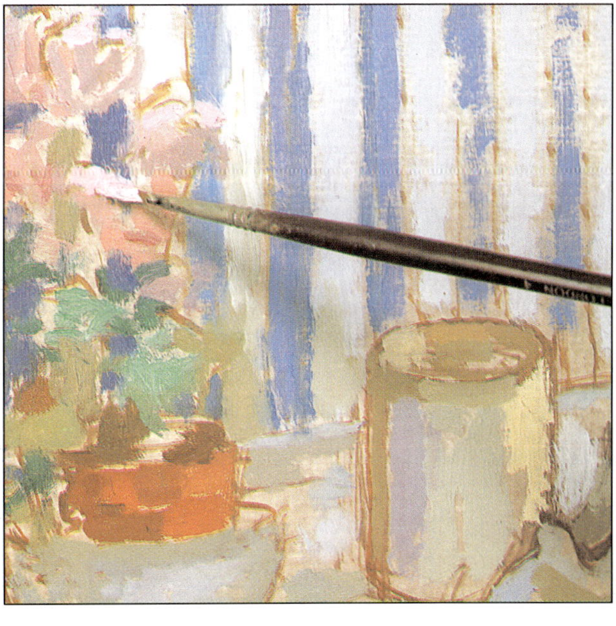

7 Switch to a no. 4 round sable brush and establish the main forms of the cyclamen plant. For the leaves, make up a series of warm and cool greens mixed from varying amounts of viridian, ultramarine, white, and grey from the palette. Do the same for the flowers, mixing warm and cool pinks from cadmium red (a warm red), alizarin crimson (a cool red) and white.

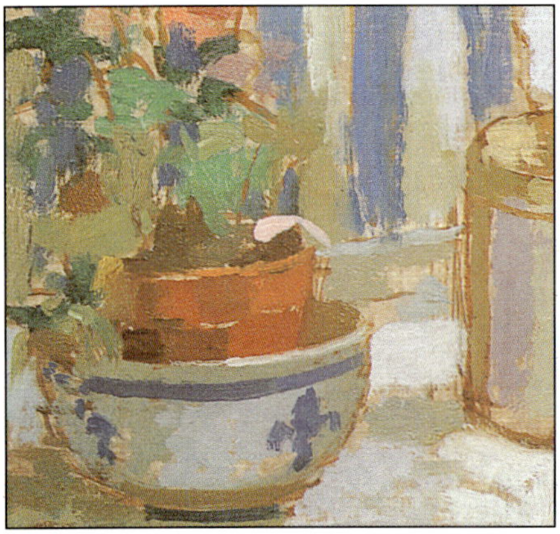

8 Use the same brush to paint the blue pattern on the china bowl with a mixture of ultramarine and white, darkened with a little alizarin crimson where the pattern turns into shadow.

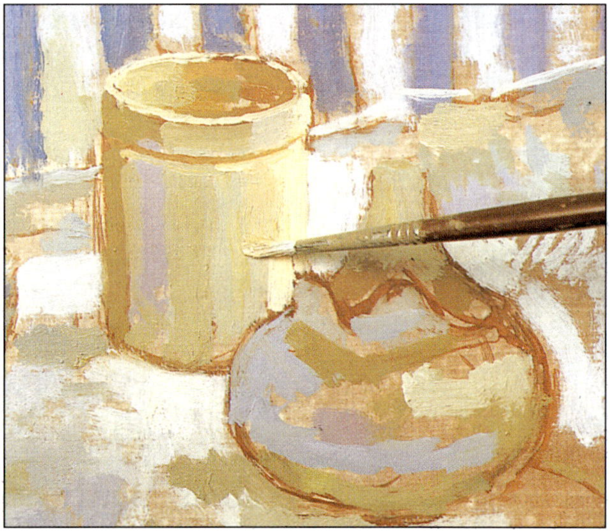

9 With everything in place and the broad tones and colours established, you can start to define the form and volume of the objects by blending the tones together to create smooth gradations. Working on the jar with the no. 4 round sable brush and the same colours used for the initial block-in, create a more even progression of tones from light to dark. Apply the colours wet-in-wet, slightly – but not too smoothly – blending the edge between one tone and the next. Mix white and a little Naples yellow for the highlight on the rim of the jar.

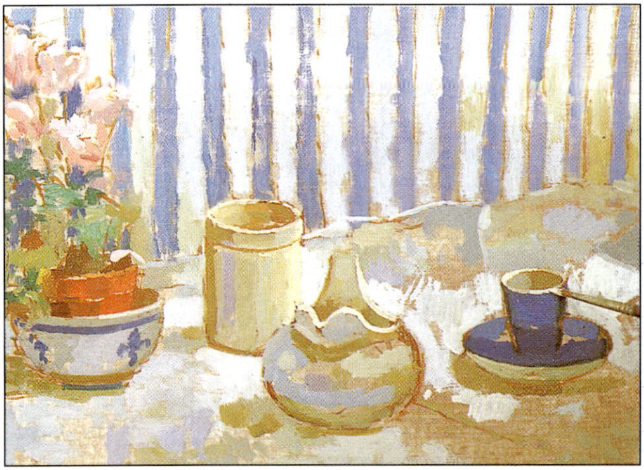

10 Continue to work around the painting, blocking in broad areas of tone and colour and then blending them together. Paint the greenish shadows inside the egg cup, and beneath the saucer, with a combination of yellow ochre plus a little black and white. Then use your Naples yellow and white mix to paint the highlit rims of the jug and the egg cup.

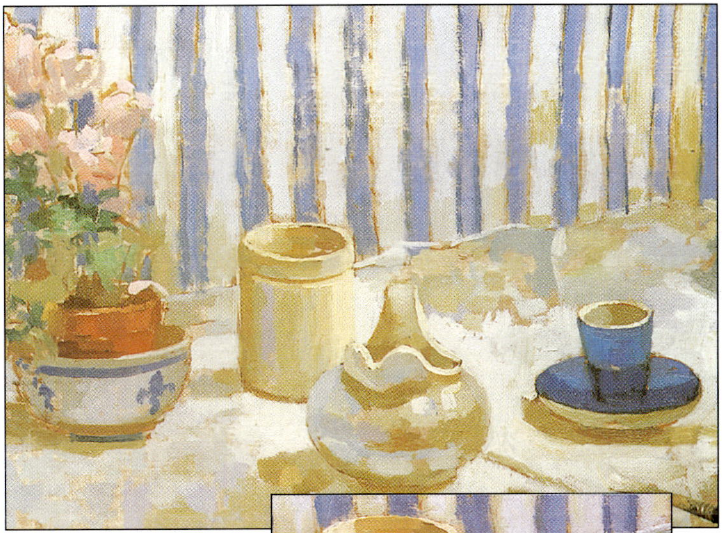

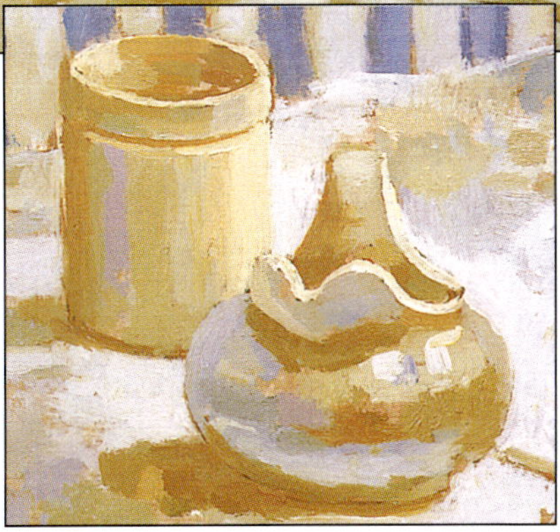

11 Squint up your eyes and look for the subtle changes in hue and tone in the glazed surface of the jug, which picks up and reflects colour from its surroundings. Use the no. 4 sable brush to touch in patches of colour – pale mauves, blues and pinks, greenish greys and bluish greys – using all the colours previously mixed on your palette. Then finish off the white cloth, using pure white for the lightest areas, modifying it with blues and greys from the palette for the shadows. In this detail you can see how the artist has broken down the jug into separate 'patches' of colour. Each one is accurately observed in terms of shape, colour and tone, then its colour is mixed on the palette and applied decisively with brush strokes that follow the form of the jug. The separate tones are blended slightly, but not too much, thus retaining a lively paint quality. Note how the brightest highlights are modified with hints of Naples yellow and ultramarine so that they don't appear too stark.

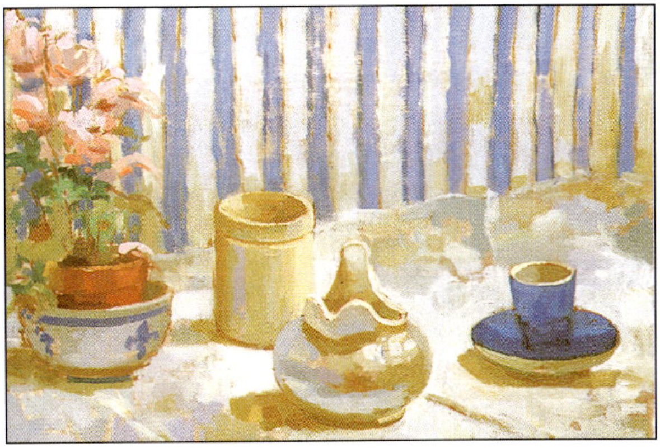

12 Continue making adjustments to the painting until you are satisfied with it, adding tiny touches of colour to modify the tones. Here, for example, the artist felt that the cyclamen flowers needed a little more definition, so he put in some dark pinks and strengthened the shapes of the petals. It is interesting to note the variety of colours that have been put into the whites in the painting – yet they still read as 'white'.

Painting Trees

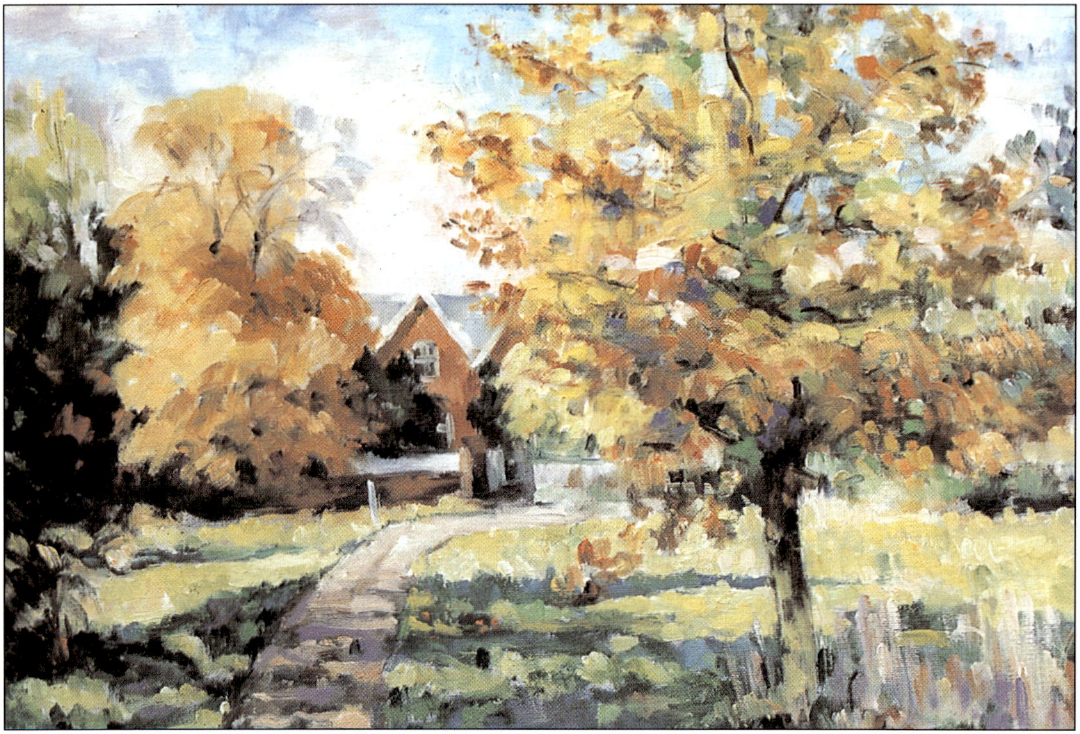

Ted Gould
AUTUMN TREES
Trees in their glorious autumn colours are captured expressively here with thick dabs and strokes of broken colour. Touches of blues and violets make the warm golds really 'sing'.

In a landscape, trees are usually seen from a distance; thus it is more important to capture their overall shape than to try to render every leaf and twig. Try to define the silhouette and 'gesture' of the particular tree species you are painting; an oak tree, for example, has a squat, rounded shape, while a poplar has a tall, distinctive, conical shape.

It is always necessary to simplify to some extent, whether you are painting bare winter trees or foliage-clad summer ones. Look for the large shapes and masses which characterize the tree and block these in broadly with thin paint, noting how each mass is modelled by light and shade. Then use thicker paint to develop the smaller branches and clumps of foliage. Finally, use descriptive brushwork to suggest some of the nearer foliage masses with more definition, and indicate one or two limbs and branches. The most important thing is to express the idea of the tree as a living, animate thing, so keep the edges of the foliage soft and feathery by merging them into the background wet-in-wet.

Proportions

A common mistake is misjudging the size of the leaf canopy in relation to the height of the trunk. Often it is painted too small, making the trees look like lollipops. Establish the correct proportions by comparing the width of the canopy with its height from base to crown, then comparing the height of the visible trunk to the overall height of the tree.

Form and volume

Use light and shade to define the volume of trunks, branches and individual clumps of foliage; without attention to this aspect, your trees will appear flat and one-dimensional. Careful observation will show you that the light side of the tree will pick up warm colours, whereas the shadow side will contain hints of blue and violet reflected from the sky. Note also that not all the branches grow sideways; some will extend towards and away from you.

Sky holes

A tree is seldom, if ever, a solid mass of green. Even when a tree is in full foliage, there are always little light patches where the sky shows through, particularly around the outer edges of the branches. These 'sky holes' can be painted in last, which gives you a chance to redefine the shapes of the clumps of foliage.

Foliage colours

Try to see how many different colours you can find in the trees around you. Green is often the dominant colour, but the particular hue of green depends on the specific tree as well as on the season, the weather and the time of day. The foliage and branches of trees in spring often contain light greens, greys and even pinks. The full trees of summer contain rich, saturated greens, browns and rusts.

David Curtis
SLEET AND SNOW, HATHERSAGE
Trees devoid of their summer foliage make dramatic shapes against a wintry sky. Here the thin, delicate twigs and branches are suggested with feathery drybrush strokes, working the outlines into the sky area to soften them.

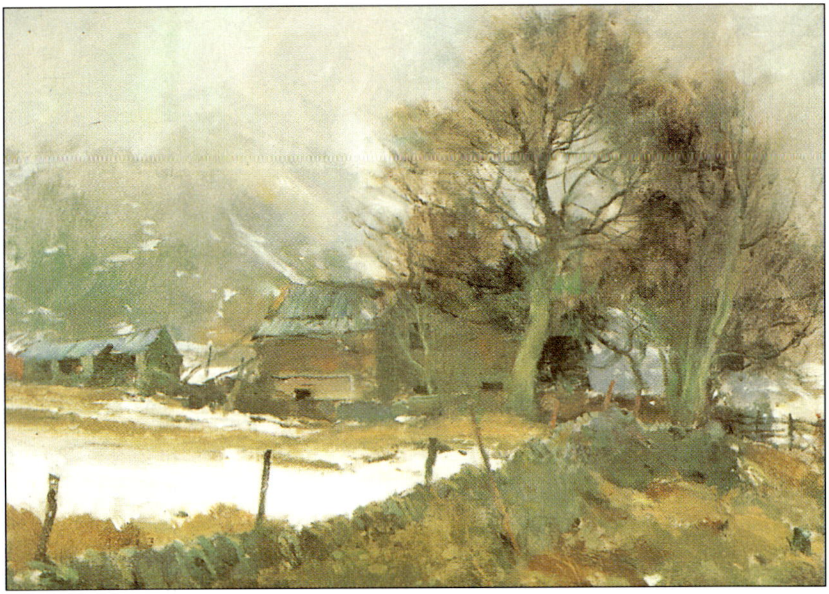

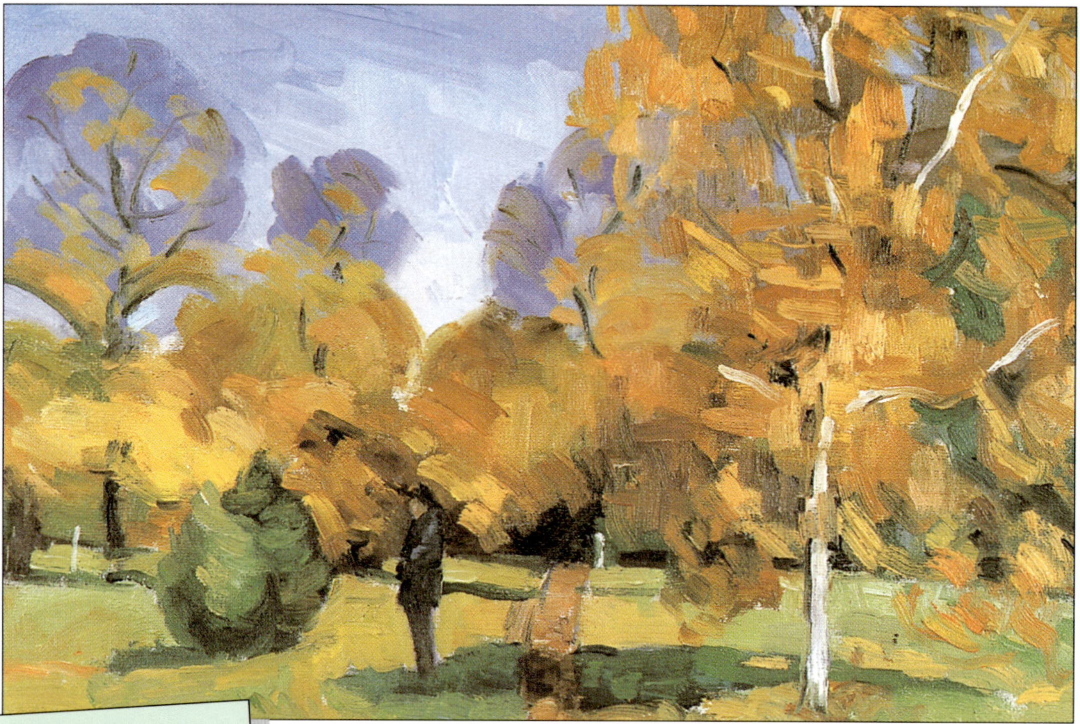

YOU WILL NEED

- *Canvas board, 16 x 12in (40.6 x 30.5cm)*
- *No. 2 round bristle brush*
- *No. 5 flat bristle brush*
- *No. 4 long flat bristle brush*
- *Charcoal*
- *Rag*
- *Distilled turpentine*
- *Purified linseed oil*

Autumn Trees

Landscapes and trees are favourite subjects for all oil painters, especially beginners. In this project we show you how to capture the essential characteristics of trees, their forms and textures, by using a variety of brush techniques to lend vitality and movement to your painting. Use bold, broad strokes to develop the trunk and branches, and descriptive brushwork for the foliage.

OIL PAINTS IN THE FOLLOWING COLOURS

- *Spectrum yellow*
- *Yellow ochre*
- *Indian yellow*
- *Chrome orange*
- *Cobalt violet*
- *French ultramarine*
- *Manganese blue*
- *Chrome green*
- *Titanium white*
- *Mauve*

1 Lightly sketch in the main outlines of the trees with a thin stick of charcoal. Use a clean cloth to gently flick off any excess charcoal dust so that it doesn't mix with the oil colours and dirty them.

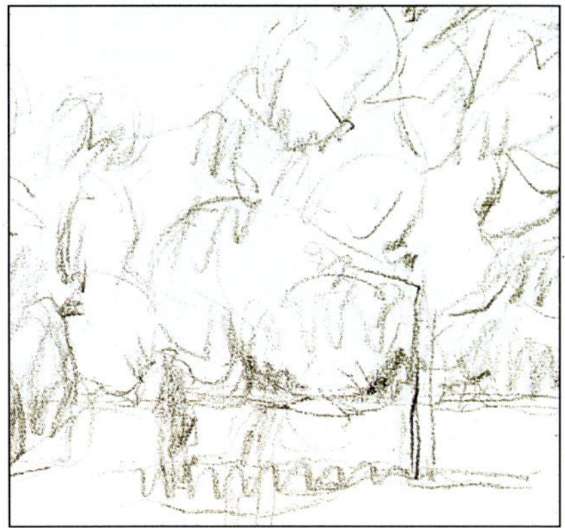

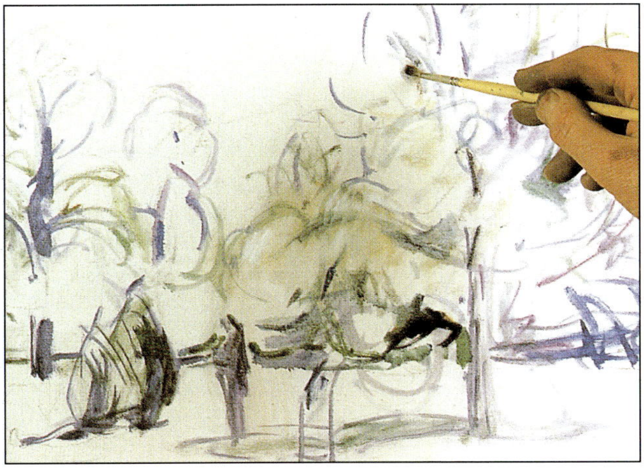

2 Using a no. 2 round bristle brush, mark in the main areas of the painting with mixtures of cobalt violet, French ultramarine, chrome green and yellow ochre. Dilute the paint with turpentine to a thin consistency and scrub it into the weave of the canvas. Add the outline of the figure in the foreground.

3 Block in the sky using a no. 5 flat bristle brush and a varied mix of white, manganese blue and French ultramarine diluted with turpentine. As you paint, use your colours only partially blended to add texture to the sky. Darken the mix with more ultramarine and a little yellow ochre and indicate the trees in the distance. Note how the artist has used vigorous, diagonal brush strokes which suggest the movement of the trees in the breeze (see detail above).

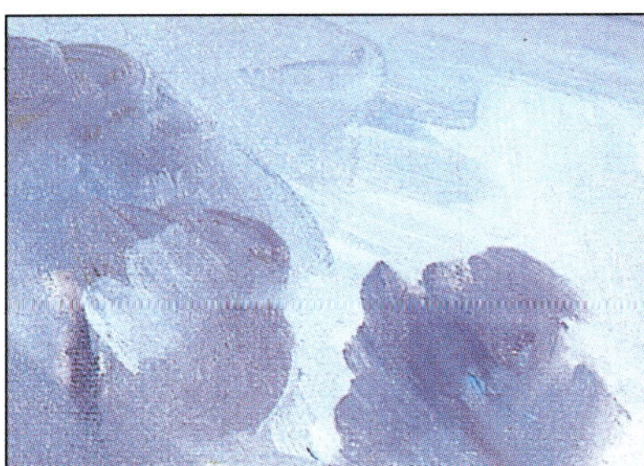

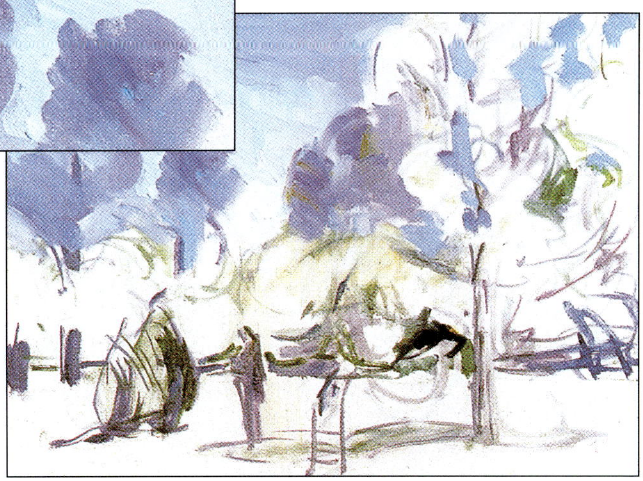

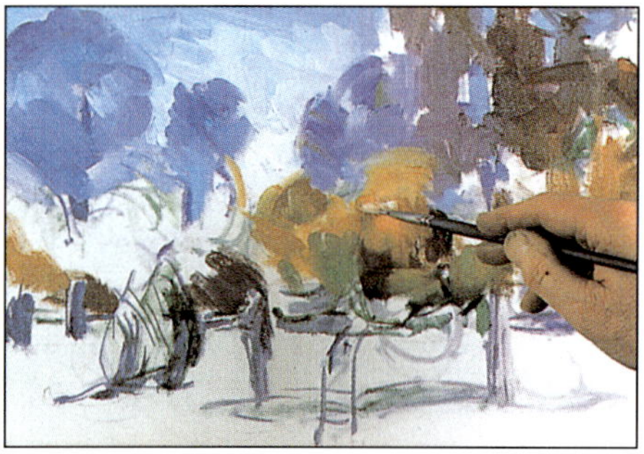

4 Mix a warm brown from cobalt violet and Indian yellow and block in the main clumps of foliage on the righthand tree. Twist and turn your brush to make both vertical and horizontal strokes. Dilute the paint with about 40% linseed oil and 60% turpentine. This makes the paint richer and easier to work with.

Helpful Hint

DON'T HOLD THE BRUSH TOO CLOSE TO THE METAL FERRULE AS THIS RESTRICTS MOVEMENT. HOLD IT WHERE IT FEELS NATURALLY BALANCED SO THAT YOUR BRUSH-MARKS WILL BE CONTROLLED YET CONFIDENT.

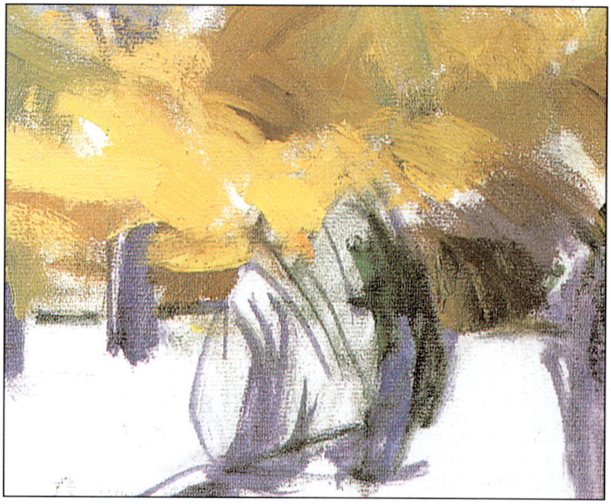

5 Mix yellow ochre and Indian yellow for the autumn foliage on the trees. Add in a little chrome orange, chrome green and spectrum yellow. Work across the painting using varied combinations of green, yellow and orange, gradually filling in all the areas of foliage.

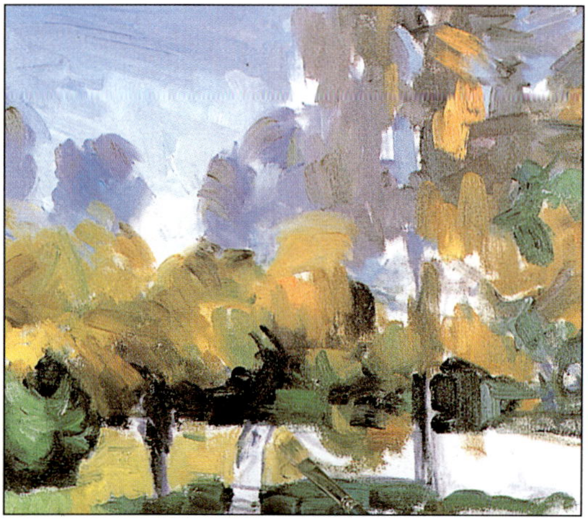

6 Now start painting the foreground using a no. 4 long flat bristle brush. Mix cobalt violet, ultramarine and chrome green to paint the darker, shadowy areas around the base of the trees and on the tree trunks. Mix a lighter green from ultramarine and chrome green for the light-struck foliage near the tops of the trees. Paint the fir trees in the foreground with the darker mix, adding some white to give the effect of light on the trees. Mix spectrum yellow with chrome green and yellow ochre for the grass, varying the proportions of each colour to add variety of tone and texture.

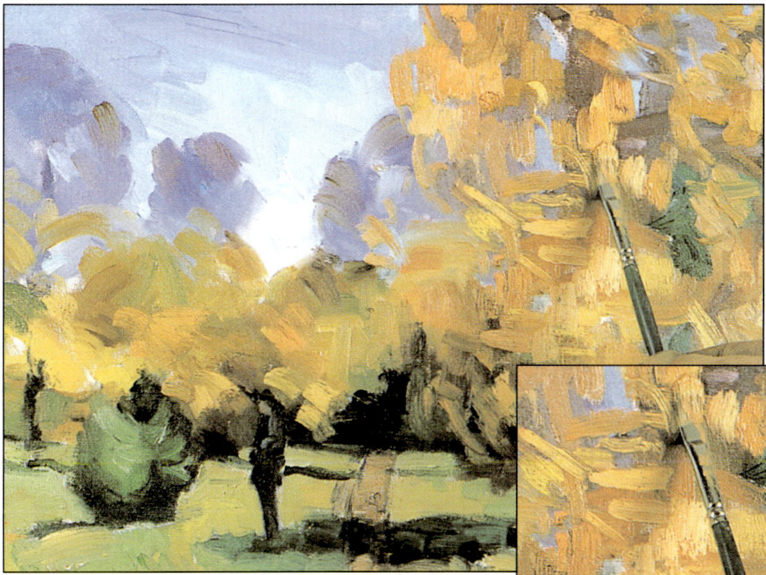

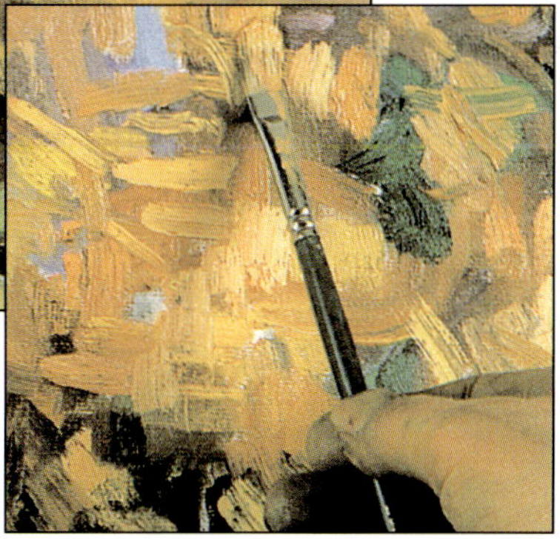

7 For the track in the centre of the picture mix a warm brown from Indian yellow, chrome orange and cobalt violet. Mix yellows, orange and a little violet for the autumn leaves. Once again vary the tones and move the brush vertically and horizontally across the canvas to build up an energetic paint surface (see detail left).

8 Paint the right-hand tree trunk and branches with titanium white, letting the colour underneath break into it. Using the no. 2 round bristle brush, now add the dark trunk and branches using a mixture of ultramarine and mauve. Define the figure in the foreground with the same mixture. Finally, move around the picture adding touches of colour to introduce more detail and texture.

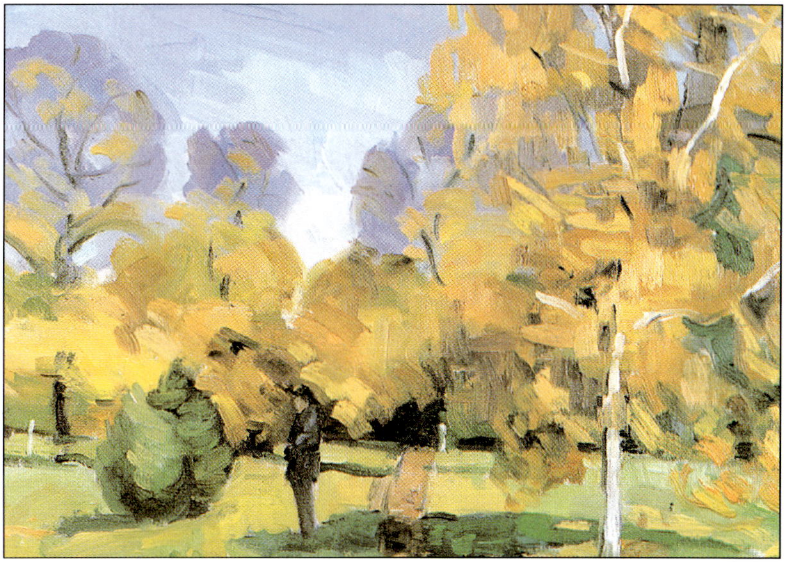

Underpainting

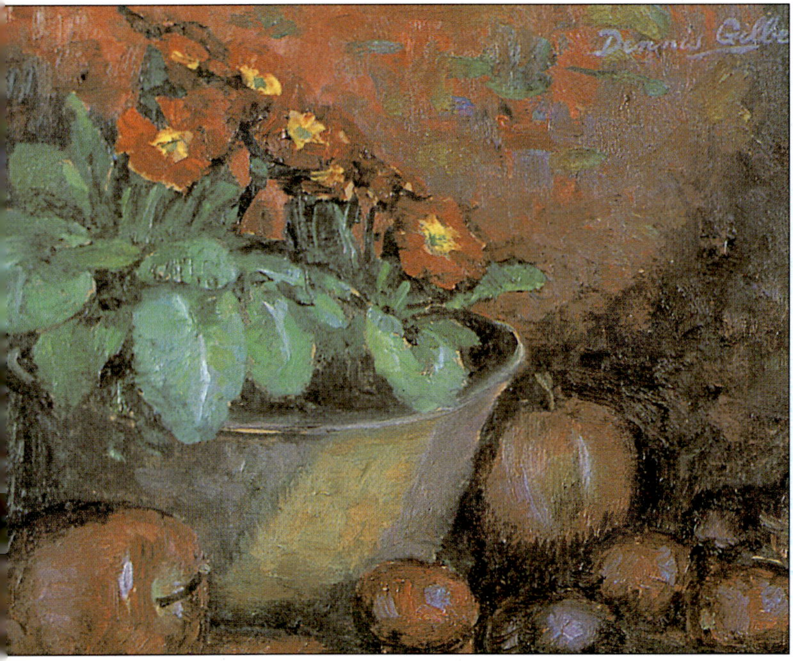

Dennis Gilbert
RED STILL LIFE
When tackling an intricate subject like this one, starting with an underpainting can help by providing a tonal 'blueprint' of the final image. Knowing that the composition and tonal values are sound, you can proceed with confidence and thus retain the freshness of your first impression.

The traditional way of starting an oil painting is to block in the main shapes, masses and tones of the composition with thin paint in a neutral colour, before adding the main details and surface colours and textures. The basic principle is to give you an idea of what the final image will look like before you begin the painting proper.

Composition, drawing, proportion, the distribution of light and shade – all of these elements can be checked, and any alterations made quite easily at this stage. Because the paint used for underpainting is so thin, any alterations needed can be easily effected by wiping the paint with a rag soaked in turpentine; this will not be possible in the subsequent stages, as you run the risk of overworking the painting and spoiling the colour mix.

The result is a practical division of labour; once the underpainting is complete you can begin working in colour, confident that the composition and tonal values are sound. This is the time-honoured method of painting in oils, which was used by Rembrandt, Rubens and many other great masters.

When underpainting in oils, always keep in mind the principle of working 'fat over lean': the paint should be thinly diluted with turpentine and allowed to dry thoroughly before adding further layers. To save time, fast-drying colours such as raw umber, cobalt blue and terre verte are the most convenient to use.

Alternatively, use acrylic paint for the underpainting. This dries within minutes, allowing you to begin the overpainting in oils in the same session.

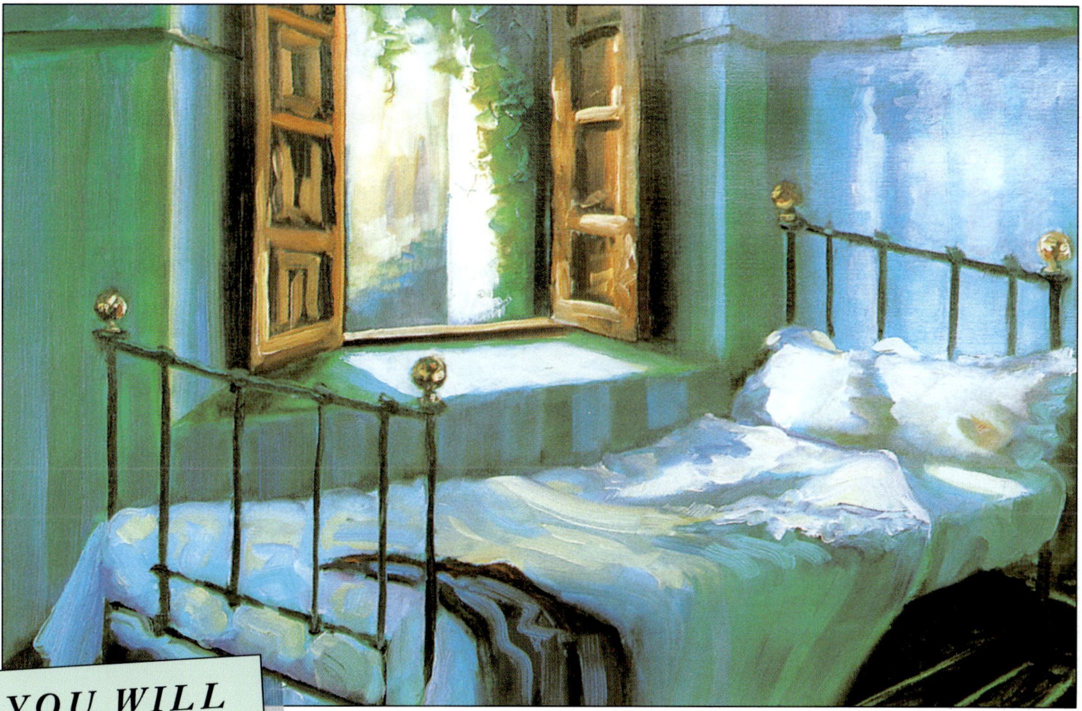

YOU WILL NEED

- Sheet of primed canvas board, 16½ x 12in (41.9 x 30.5cm)
- ¾in (19mm) flat synthetic fibre brush
- No. 4 flat synthetic fibre brush
- No. 6 flat synthetic fibre brush
- HB pencil
- Distilled turpentine
- Small piece of muslin
- Kitchen paper

The Boudoir

It was important to assess the light and dark tones accurately in order to recreate the effect of vibrant light in this sunny interior. By starting with an underpainting, the artist was able to control the tonal balance of the image from the beginning, without being distracted by colour. Tones of blue-grey were used for the underpainting, to harmonize with the cool, shadowy tones of the bedroom.

OIL PAINTS IN THE FOLLOWING COLOURS

- *Monestial turquoise*
- *Monestial blue*
- *French ultramarine*
- *Indigo*
- *Winsor violet*
- *Burnt sienna*
- *Brown ochre*
- *Yellow ochre*
- *Lemon yellow*
- *Rowney red*

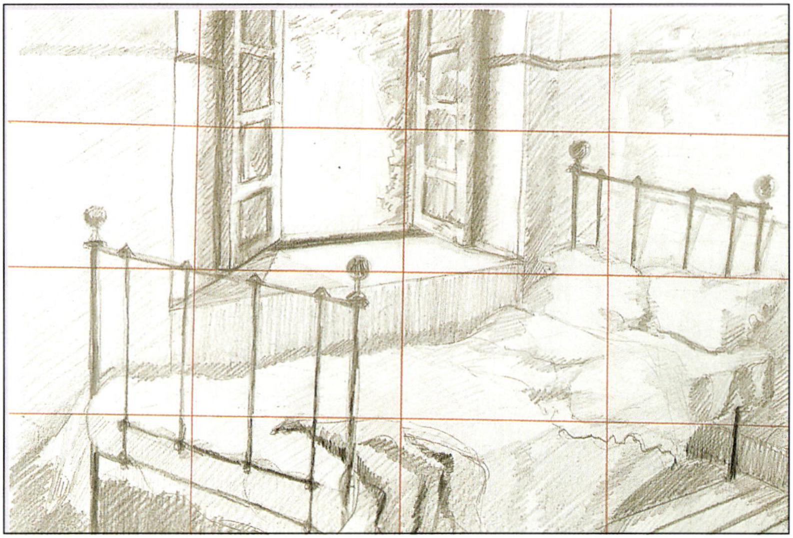

1 When painting a complex subject, it's a good idea to make a pencil sketch of it first. Refer to the sketch as you paint, using it to check the perspective lines and the arrangement of light and dark tones. Drawing a grid over the sketch (use tracing paper if you prefer) makes it easier to transfer the composition to your canvas; draw a grid in the same proportions on the canvas, then transfer the image that appears in each square on the sketch to its equivalent square on the canvas.

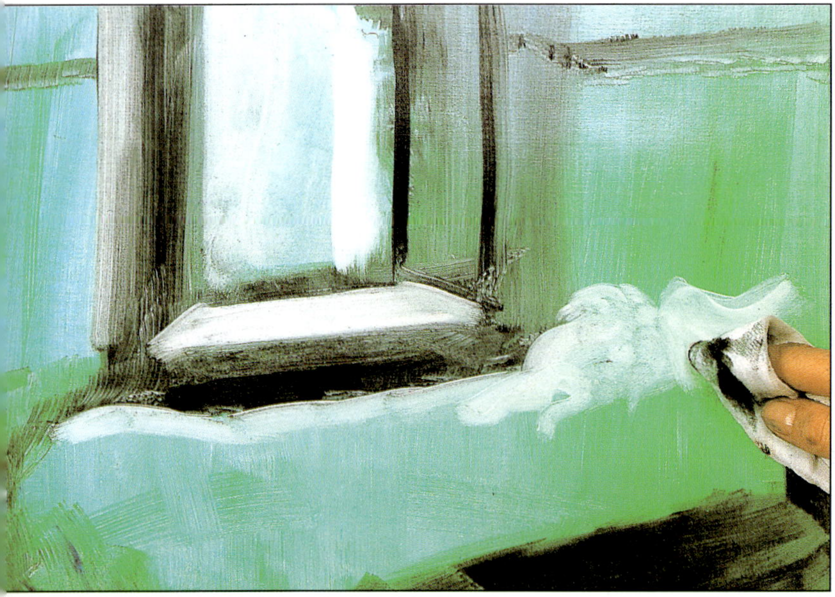

2 Mix a wash of monestial turquoise, thinly diluted with turpentine, and apply this over the entire board with the 3/4in (19mm) flat brush. This eliminates the stark whiteness of the primed canvas board. Add a touch of indigo to the mixture and block in the dark tones – the window frame, the picture rail and the shadows around the bed. Now wrap a piece of muslin round your finger, dip it in turpentine and rub into the wet colour, back to the white priming, to introduce the light tones on the window and the bed.

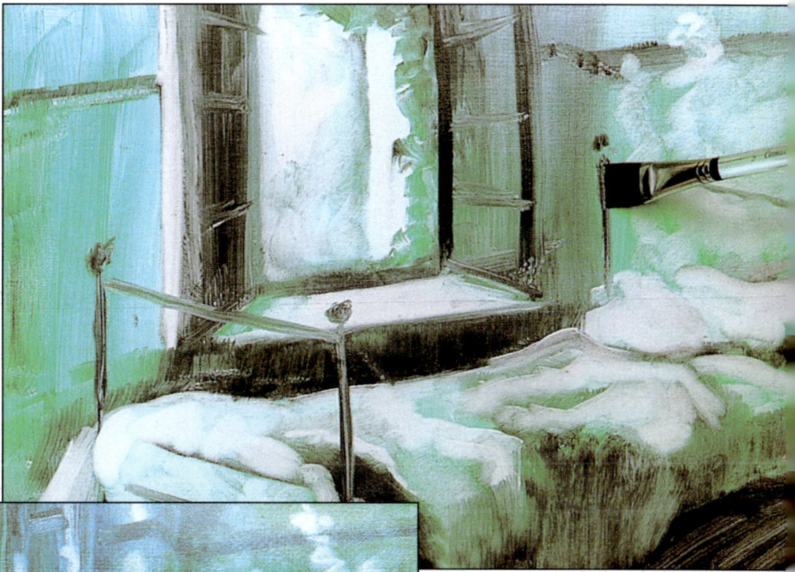

3 Here we see how the artist has described the rumpled sheets and pillows by 'drawing' into the wet paint with the muslin. The tone of the wall on the right has also been lightened. Now, using the chisel edge of the no. 4 flat brush and the monestial turquoise and indigo mixture, put in the lines on the window shutters and paint the metal bedstead.

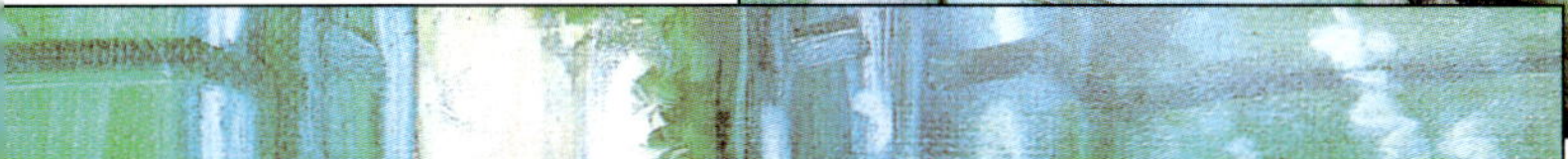

4 Build up an informative under-painting, adding the details on the shutters and bedstead with broad brushstrokes. Start to refine the broad shapes of light and dark on the bed linen and the dressing gown draped over the foot of the bed. Add a little more indigo to the mix and loosely describe the foliage glimpsed through the window. Suggest the frilled edges of the sheets and pillows by working into the wet paint once more with the damp muslin, pushing your fingernail through to the cloth to describe the intricate curves.

Helpful Hint

AS YOU WORK, KEEP CHECKING ONE DARK AREA AGAINST ANOTHER TO SEE WHETHER OR NOT THE TONES ARE SIMILAR, THEN CHECK THEM AGAINST THE LIGHTER AREAS. OVER-ESTIMATING THE DIFFERENCES BETWEEN TONES CREATES A CONFUSED, 'JUMPY' IMAGE. ALWAYS KEEP AN EYE ON THE WHOLE IMAGE AS WELL AS INDIVIDUAL PARTS.

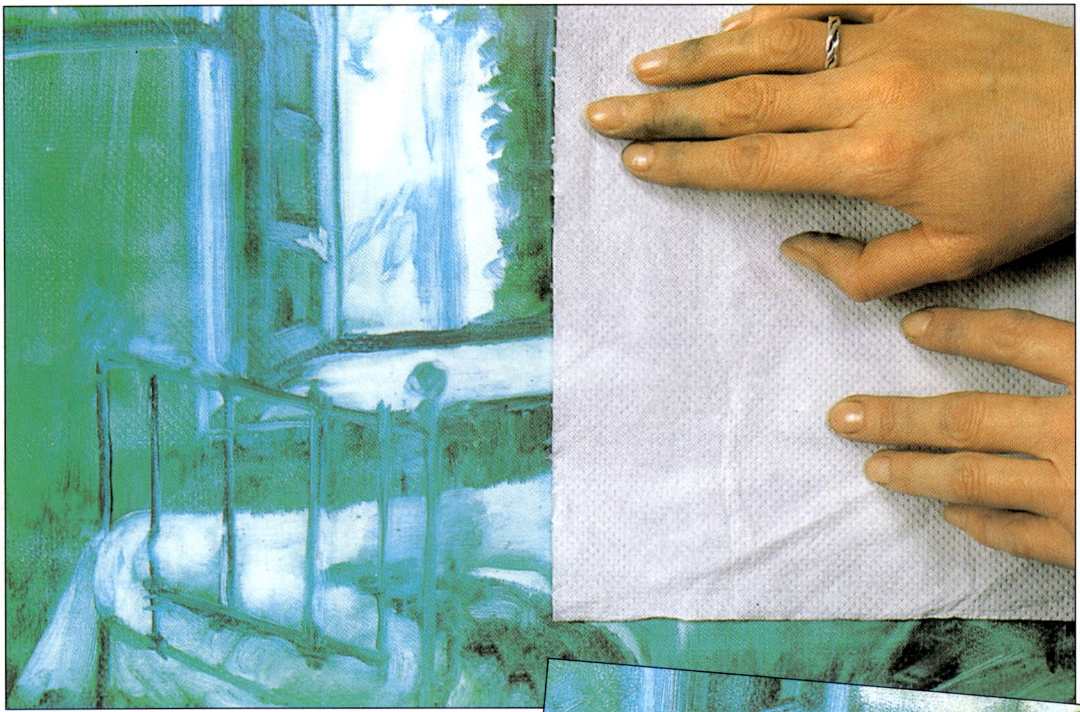

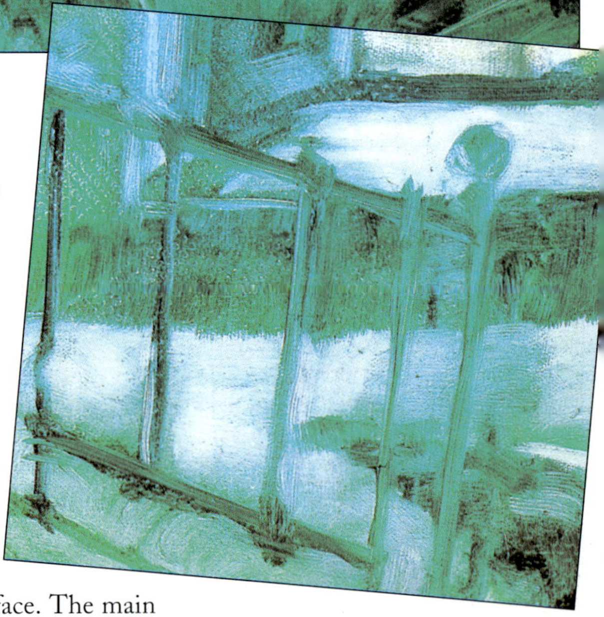

5 Now that the underpainting is completed you can start to build up the details. To create a surface with more 'grip' for the further application of paint, try the following technique: lay a sheet of absorbent paper such as kitchen paper over the painting and gently smooth it down using a circular movement. Then peel away the paper to remove any excess oily paint, creating a more sympathetic surface to work on. Leave the painting to dry for approximately 24 hours. This method is known as 'tonking' (after a former professor of painting named Henry Tonks). In the detail (right) you can see how the tonking method creates a pleasing, softly textured surface. The main structure of the painting is firmly established, but the colours are softened and lightened, making it easier to continue adding more detail on top.

6 Now start to introduce the warm tones in the room. Partially mix titanium white, Winsor purple and brown ochre. Using a no. 4 flat brush, sketch in the view through the window with loose, fluid brushstrokes, working the colours wet into wet. Use pure white on the sunlit wall. Add warm highlights on the sunlit leaves with white and a little yellow ochre. For the shadowy leaves use monestial turquoise and monestial blue. Paint the wooden shutters with a thin wash of burnt sienna. Touch in the knobs on the bedstead with brown ochre.

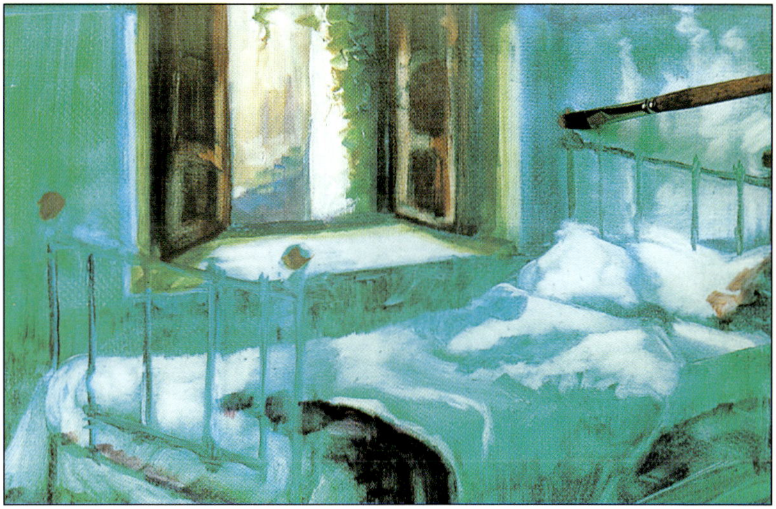

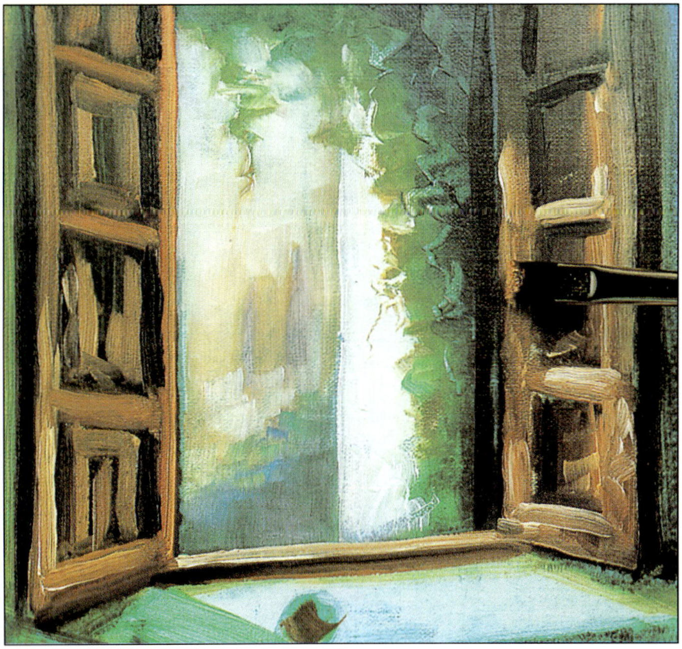

7 To make the view through the window appear to recede, concentrate stronger detail and colour on the window itself to bring it forward. Block in the shutters with a mix of raw umber and indigo. Then mix yellow ochre, burnt sienna and white and define the carved detailing on the shutters. Where warm light strikes the edges of the shutters, use a warm orange mixed from Rowney red, yellow ochre and lemon yellow. For the cooler glints of light, add touches of white and lemon yellow. Paint the shadows cast by the shutters on the windowsill with monestial turquoise and indigo.

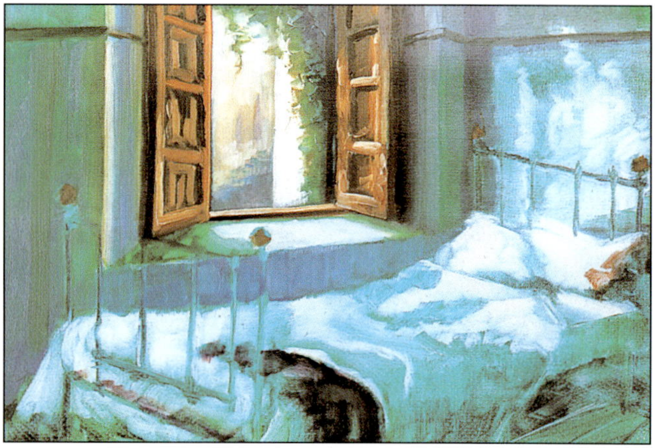

8 Sunlight streaming in through the open window gives the shadows on the walls a luminous blue-violet tint. Use a no. 6 flat brush to paint the walls with monestial turquoise and white, working in some Winsor violet and white for the shadow areas. For the shadow on the wall beneath the window, mix indigo and Winsor violet. Paint the window alcove with a mix of monestial blue, white and a touch of ultramarine. Sketch in the picture rail with a mix of indigo and burnt umber and define the edge of the window alcove with white and lemon yellow.

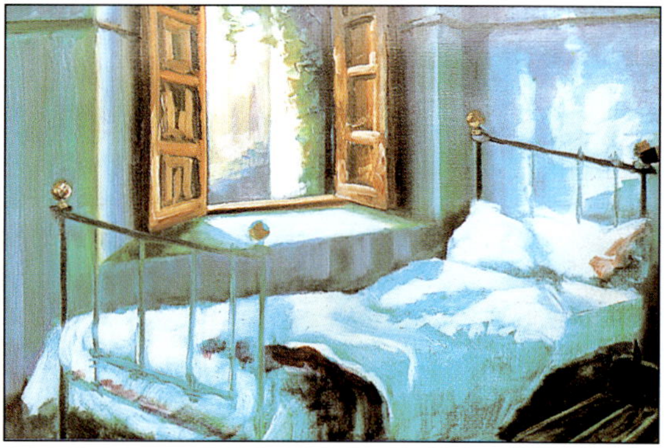

9 Soften the colour of the wall on the right with a mix of ultramarine and white. Work into the shadows under the bed with indigo and a little raw umber, then scratch lines into the wet paint with the end of the brush handle to suggest the floorboards. With the no. 4 brush, define the metal bedstead with indigo. Mix lemon yellow with just a touch of Rowney red and dot in the bright highlights on the shiny brass bed knobs.

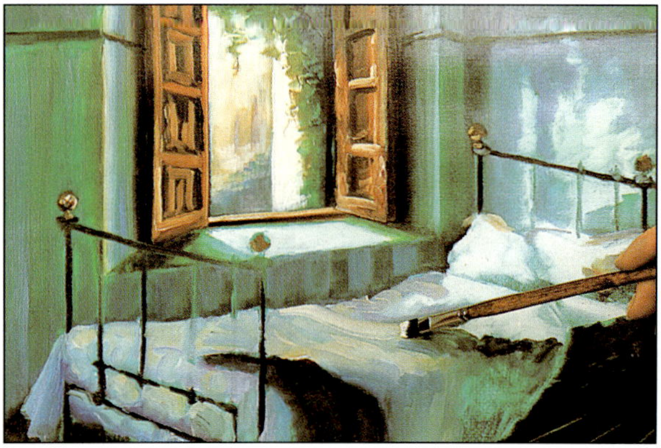

10 Now start to define the cool shadows and warm lights on the white bed linen. Go over the shadows established in the underpainting with shades of ultramarine and monestial blue. Where the sheet folds over the end of the bed the shadows have a more violet cast – paint these with a mix of Winsor violet and white. Then mix white and yellow ochre to pick up the highlights on the pillows and sheets.

11 Suggest the striped pattern of the dressing gown with Rowney red and a mix of monestial blue and white. Finish defining the bedstead with indigo and complete the brass knobs with raw umber for the shadows, a little Rowney red for the reflections and lemon yellow for the bright highlights. Deepen the shadow on the sheet falling over the edge of the bed with a mixture of ultramarine, Winsor violet and white. Mix white with just a hint of ultramarine and begin painting the brighter whites where light from the window is shining directly on to the bed.

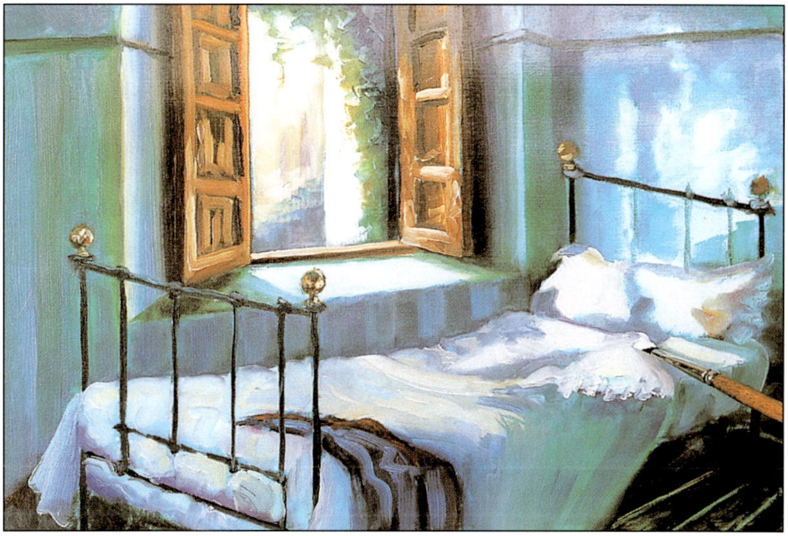

Helpful Hint

WHITE OBJECTS REFLECT COLOUR FROM THEIR SURROUNDINGS, SO THEY RARELY APPEAR PURE WHITE BUT A COMPOSITE OF MANY COLOURS. IN THIS SUNNY ROOM THE WHITE BED LINEN CONTAINS COOL BLUES AND VIOLETS IN THE SHADOWS AND WARM CREAMS AND YELLOWS IN THE HIGHLIGHTS.

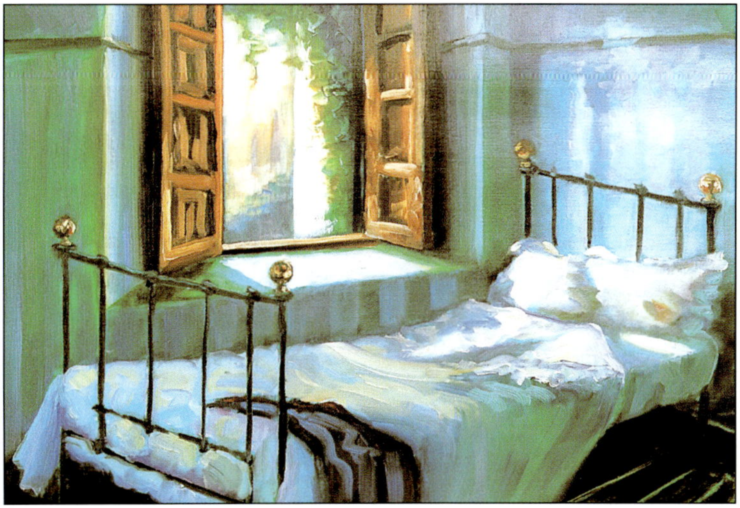

12 Use the same mixture to paint the pillows and suggest their frilled edges, and to soften and blend the shadows and highlights on the righthand wall. Finally, use touches of pure white to accentuate the dappled light that falls across the windowsill and over the bed.

Developing the Painting

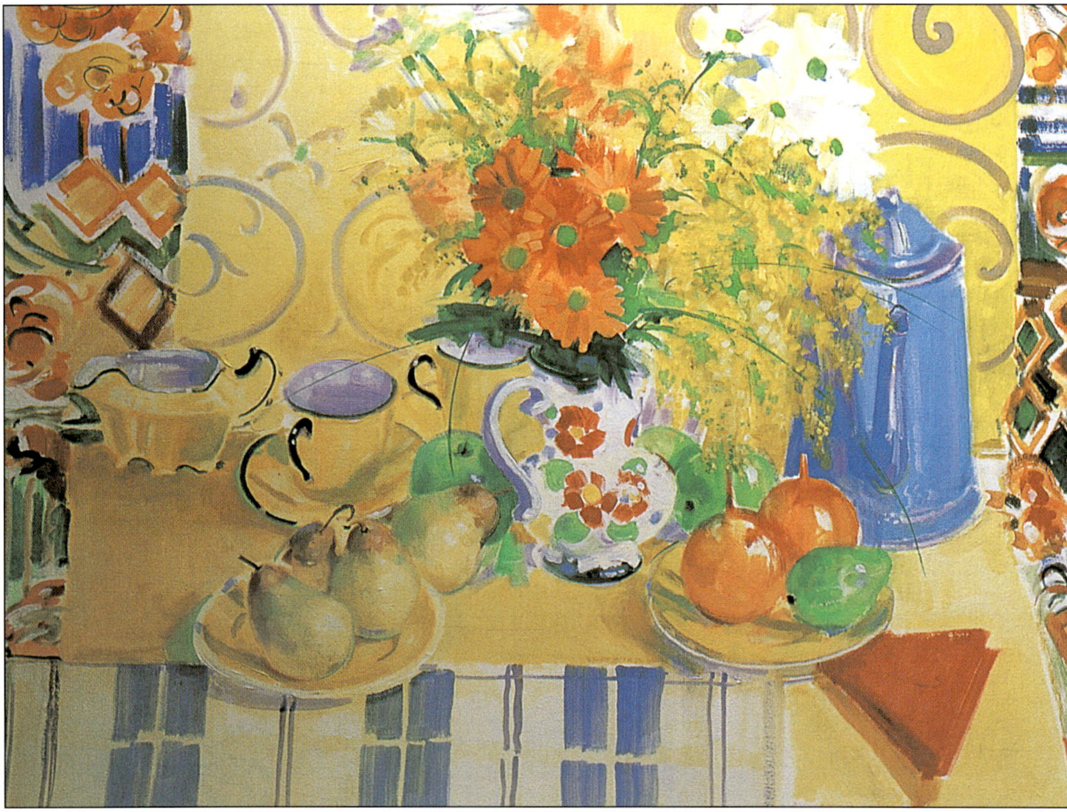

Peter Graham
LE PETIT DÉJEUNER
This artist always starts his paintings with washes of thin colour, well diluted with turpentine, to indicate the broad forms of the composition. By building up the colours gradually, he keeps the final painting fresh and lively.

A mistake sometimes made by inexperienced painters is to work on one small area of a painting until it is 'finished', and then move on to the next area. However, this can result in a confused and disjointed image because each area of tone and colour is separate and unrelated to its neighbours.

Instead of working in this piecemeal fashion, try to work over all areas of the canvas at the same time, moving from foreground to background and letting the composition weave itself into a whole. The image should emerge gradually, similar to the way a photographic image comes into focus in the developing tray.

Balancing colours

Keep your eyes moving around the subject, looking for the way tones, colours and shapes relate to each other and making adjustments as you go. You need to do this because the tones and colours you apply to your canvas do not work in isolation – they are influenced by the tones and colours surrounding them. For example, a tone which appears dark on its own will suddenly appear much lighter when surrounded by darker tones. Similarly, a warm colour may appear quite cool when surrounded by even warmer colours. Painting is a continuous process of balancing, judging, altering and refining – which is what makes it so absorbing.

Building up

If you apply too many heavy layers of paint in the early stages, you may find that the surface quickly becomes clogged and the paint eventually builds up to a slippery, churned-up mess. To avoid this you need to pace yourself in the early stages – it is a mistake to try to get to the finished picture too soon.

When you start a painting, bear in mind the advice of Cézanne: "start with the broom and end with the needle!" In other words, work from the general to the particular. Start by rapidly laying in the broad shapes and colour masses of the composition with thin colour before starting to develop the detail.

Dennis Gilbert
WASHING LINE, MURANO
The harmony and unity of this picture was achieved by working over the whole painting at once, so that colour was picked up on the brush and transferred to other areas, thus allowing the image to emerge gradually from the canvas.

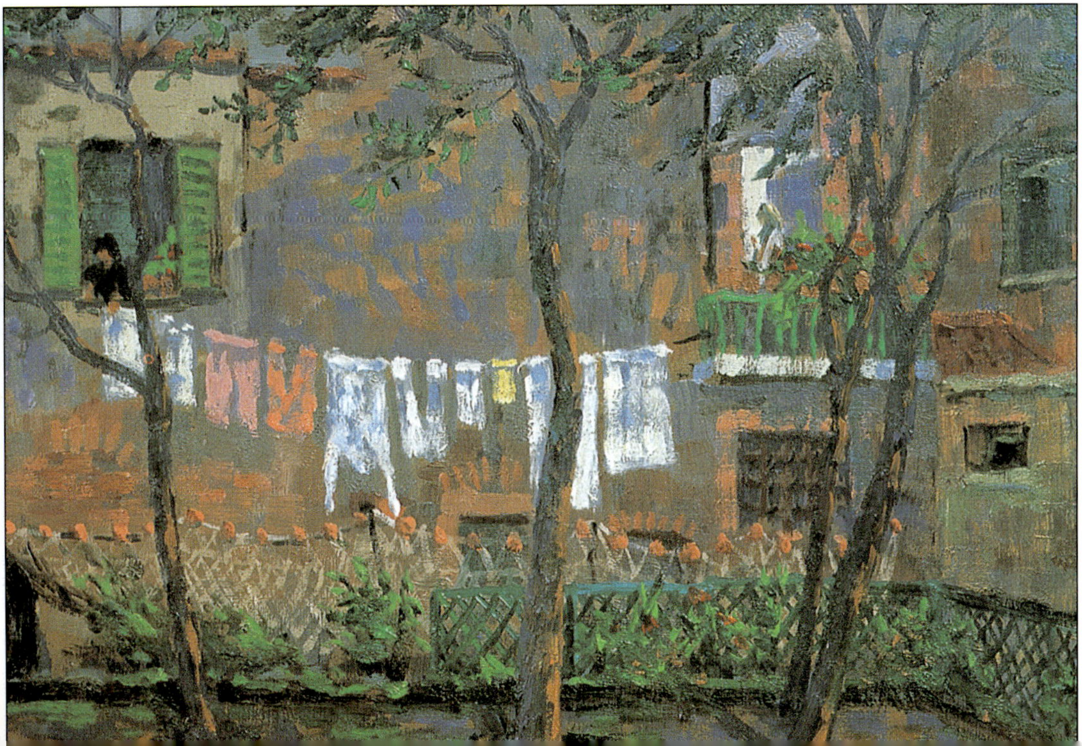

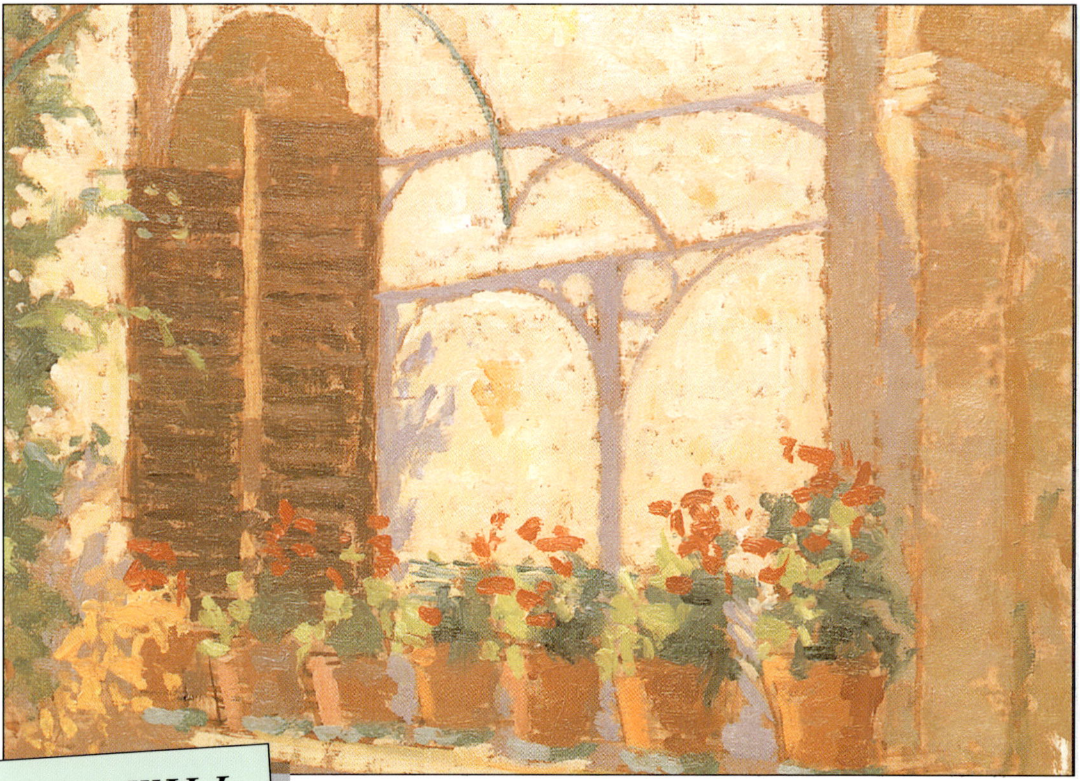

YOU WILL NEED

- Sheet of primed board, 20 x 16in (50.8 x 40.6cm)
- No. 3 round sable bristle brush
- No. 4 round bristle brush
- No. 6 round bristle brush
- Distilled turpentine
- Purified linseed oil
- Dammar varnish

Terrace in Tuscany

A successful composition weaves itself into a whole. To capture the unifying effect of bright sunlight on this scene, the artist worked over the whole painting at once, so that paint was picked up on the brush and transferred to other areas of the canvas.

OIL PAINTS IN THE FOLLOWING COLOURS

- *Raw umber*
- *Raw sienna*
- *Burnt sienna*
- *Cadmium orange*
- *Yellow ochre*
- *Chrome green*
- *Cadmium red*
- *Alizarin crimson*
- *Titanium white*
- *French ultramarine*
- *Ivory Black*
- *Veridian*
- *Lemon yellow*
- *Cobalt blue*
- *Vermilion*

1 Prepare your board in advance by tinting it with a warm brown mixed from raw umber and raw sienna. Dilute the paint with plenty of turpentine and apply it loosely with a 1in (25mm) decorating brush. Leave to dry for 24 hours. Using a no. 3 round sable brush, draw the main outlines of the composition with thinly diluted burnt sienna.

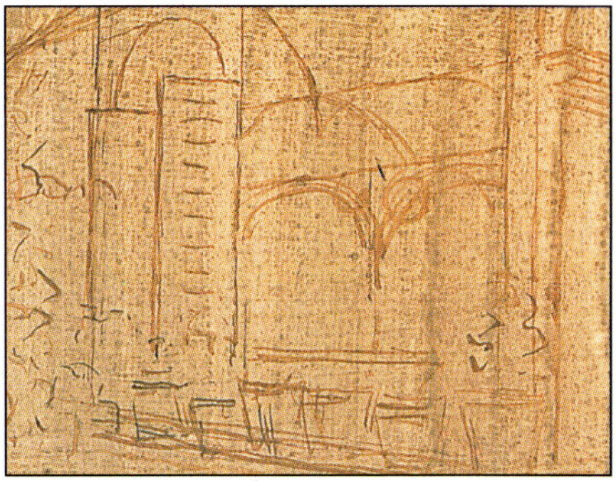

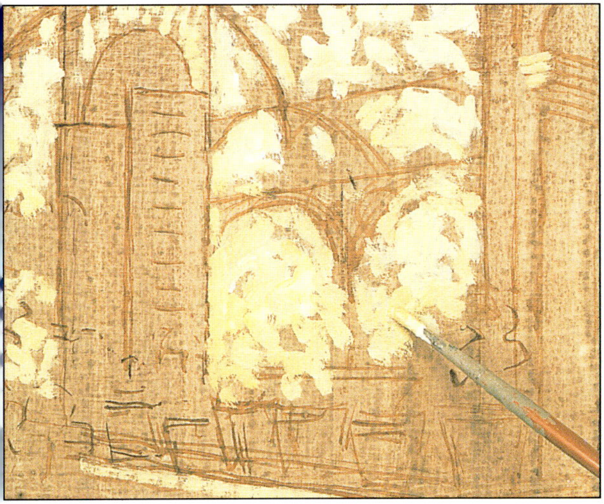

2 Start to block in the stone wall of the house with a light golden yellow mixed from varied combinations of cadmium orange, yellow ochre and titanium white. Mix the paint with a medium consisting of equal parts of linseed oil and dammar varnish plus twice the volume of turpentine. Apply the paint with a no. 6 round bristle brush using short brushstrokes worked in different directions. Allow some of the background wash to show through.

3 Paint the climbing plant on the left with a mixture of French ultramarine, chrome green and ivory black, varying the tones from light to dark. Suggest the slatted wooden shutters with a mixture of burnt sienna, alizarin crimson and a little cadmium red. To paint the part of the wall that falls in shadow on the right you will need chrome green, burnt sienna, alizarin crimson, cadmium red and French ultramarine. Mix the colours in varying combinations to create a variety of tones ranging from grey to a greenish brown.

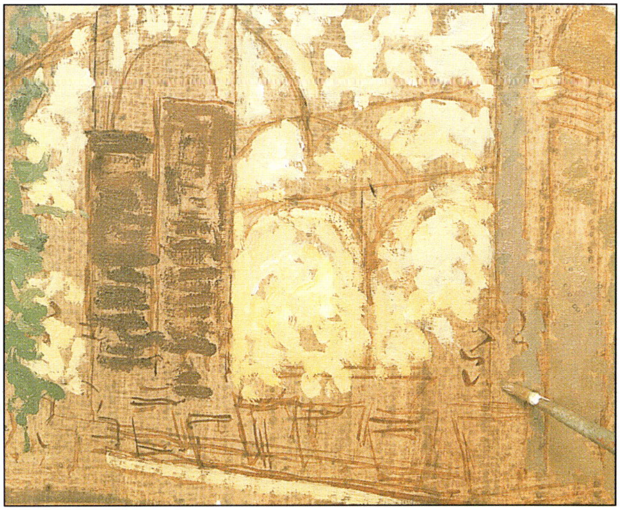

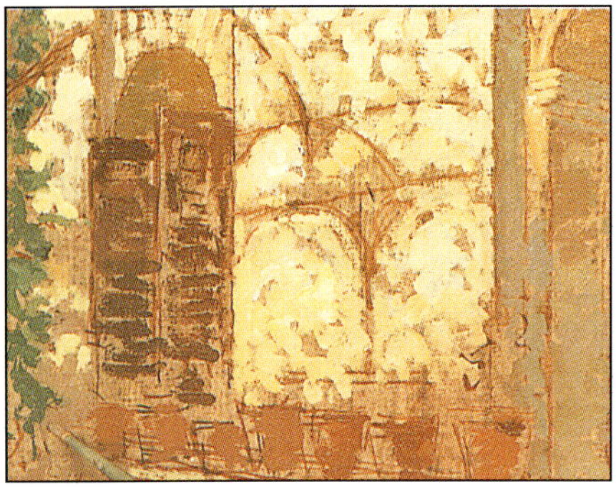

4 Mix burnt sienna, cadmium red, alizarin crimson and white to make a rich terracotta and use this to rough in the shadow sides of the plant pots. Paint the arch above the shutters with the same combination of colours used for the shadowy wall in step 3. Use the same mix to suggest the dappled shadows cast by the foliage on the bottom left of the picture.

5 Continue building up the picture loosely, keeping an eye on the overall effect. Resume work on the background wall and the shutters, using the same colours mixed earlier. Switch to a no. 4 round bristle brush and define the shadow cast by the pergola onto the wall with a purple-grey mixed from ultramarine and cadmium red. Work on the climber and the geranium leaves, adding a little yellow ochre to the original foliage colour used in step 3 for the warmer tones.

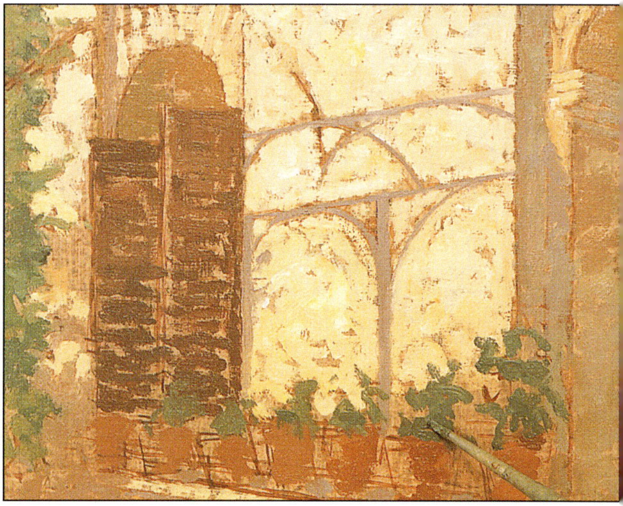

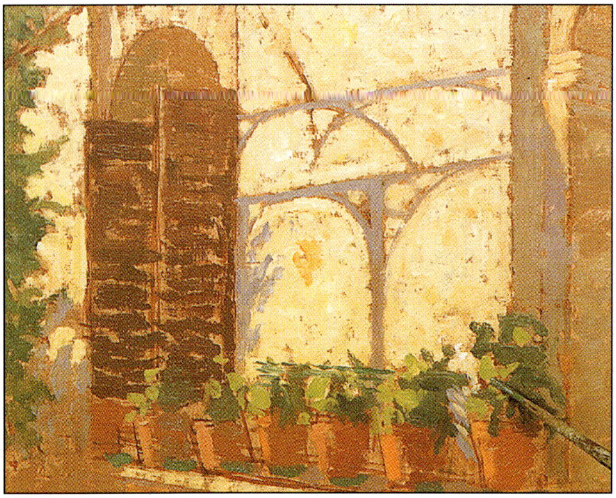

6 Continue building up the colour on the background wall. Add subtle hints of lighter tone to the shadow of the pergola by adding cobalt blue and a little white to the original mix. Use the same colour for the dappled shadows either side of the shutters. Mix viridian and ultramarine for the small trays under the plant pots. Put in the warm lights on the plant pots with touches of cadmium orange and a dusky pink mixed from alizarin, white and a touch of burnt sienna. Paint the sunlit geranium leaves using white, chrome green and lemon yellow.

7 Give more definition to the shutters, adding more alizarin to the original mix for the darker slats and a little white for the highlights. Define the sunlit edge of the shutter with a mix of cadmium orange, lemon yellow and white. Use the same colour to suggest the trailing plant in the lefthand corner. Mix lemon yellow, chrome green and white for the light-struck leaves on the climber. Use a no. 3 round sable brush to paint the green metal arch of the pergola with a mixture of viridian and ultramarine, lightened with white.

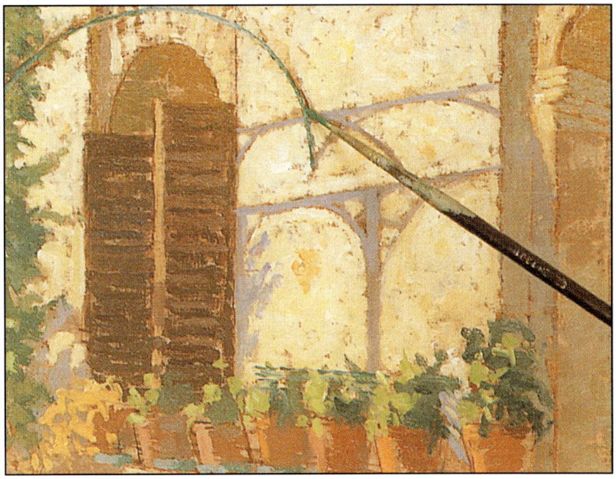

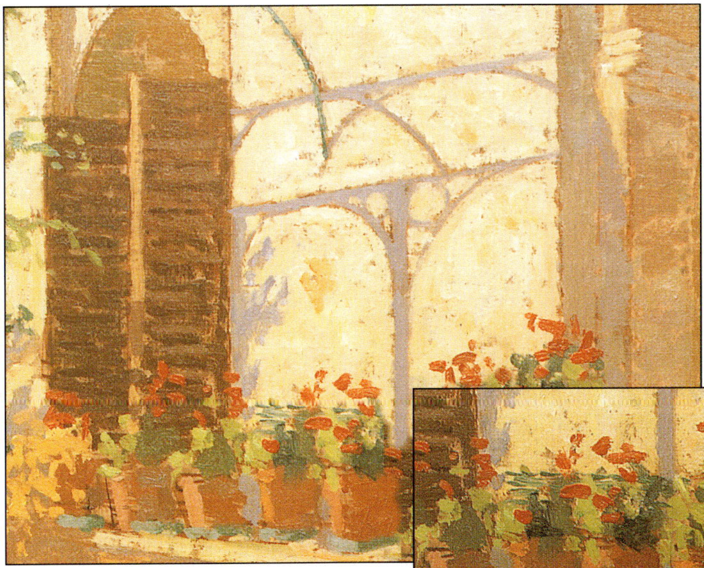

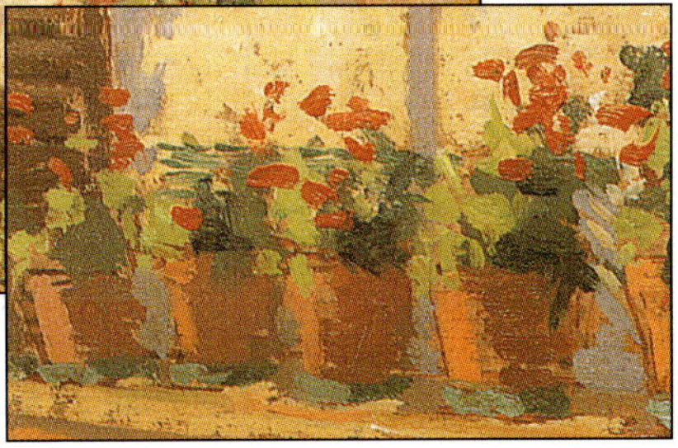

8 Bring some sprigs of foliage out across the shutter on the left to create a sense of three-dimensional space. Add touches of richer colour to the terracotta plant pots with mixes of burnt sienna, cadmium red and cadmium orange. Finally, paint the brilliant red geranium flowers with short strokes of vermilion, letting the brushstrokes themselves form the shapes of the petals. This detail (left) of the geraniums illustrates the way paint can be used to create texture. The flowers and leaves are suggested by short, curving brushstrokes, using thick paint over a still-wet layer beneath it so that each colour is modified by the one beneath.

Helpful Hint

AS YOUR PAINTING NEARS COMPLETION, TAKE A BREAK FROM IT SO THAT WHEN YOU COME BACK TO IT YOU CAN LOOK AT IT AFRESH.

Colour Harmony

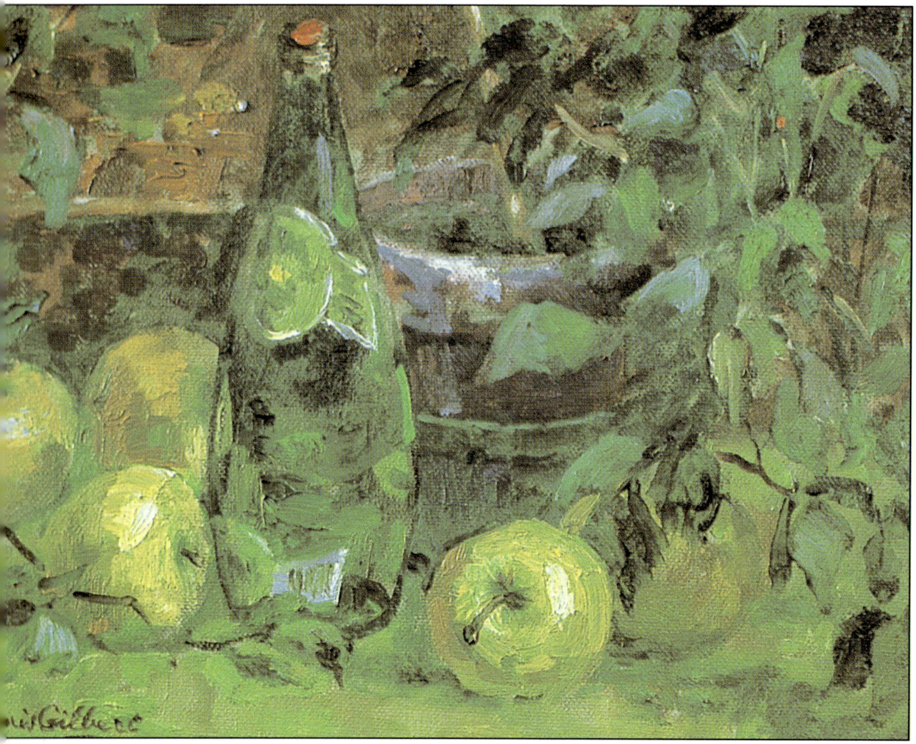

Dennis Gilbert
GREEN STILL LIFE
The cool greens and yellows in this painting are offset by smaller touches of warm earth colours; thus the image is harmonious but not monotonous.

Think of the tones and colours in a painting as musical notes. If you include too many colour 'notes' in your picture it becomes confused and 'out of tune'. But if you use them in a controlled range, you will produce an image that is not only balanced and harmonious but also more powerful and intense.

Analogous colours

An effective way of creating harmony in a painting is to focus on a small selection of colours which lie next to each other on the colour wheel; these are called analogous colours. They work together well since they share a common base colour. Examples of harmonious colour schemes might be blue, blue-green and blue-violet; or orange, red-orange and yellow-orange.

Nature provides ample inspiration for harmonious colour schemes. Think of the golds, arussets and reds of an autumn landscape, the subtle shades of blue and green in a river or sea, or the pinks, violets and indigos of the sky at twilight.

There is a risk, of course, that too much harmony can make a rather bland, insipid painting. One way to avoid this is to include a small area of contrasting colour in the composition; for example, a painting with a predominant theme of blue might benefit from a touch of a brighter colour such as orange or yellow.

Selective palette

Another way to ensure that there are no jarring notes in your picture is by sticking to a selective range of colours and interweaving them throughout the picture. Using a limited number of colours is an excellent way to learn about colour mixing – you'll be surprised at the wide range of subtle and vibrant hues that can be mixed from just half a dozen colours.
Try to work over the whole painting at once, so that paint is picked up on the brush and transferred from one area of the composition to another; when a few colours are continually repeated and intermixed in this way, a certain harmony will naturally arise.

Toned grounds

Toning the canvas with a wash of colour is another way of achieving harmony. It is easier to work out a cool colour scheme of blues and greens on a similarly cool blue-grey ground, for example, than on a white ground. The toning strikes through the patches of overlaid paint and becomes an integral part of the picture, pulling together all the various elements.

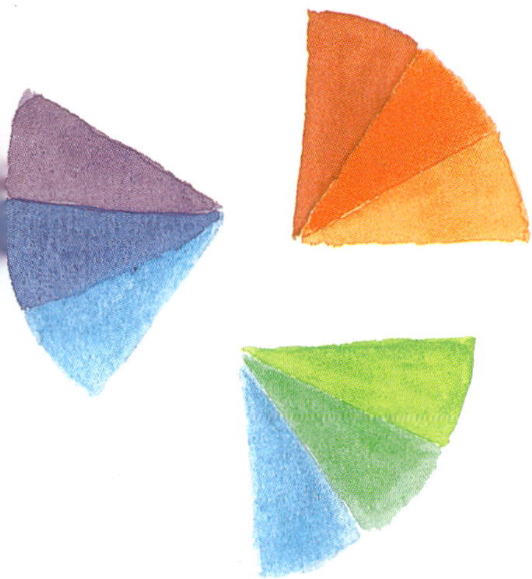

Colours adjacent to one another on the colour wheel form a related, harmonious sequence.

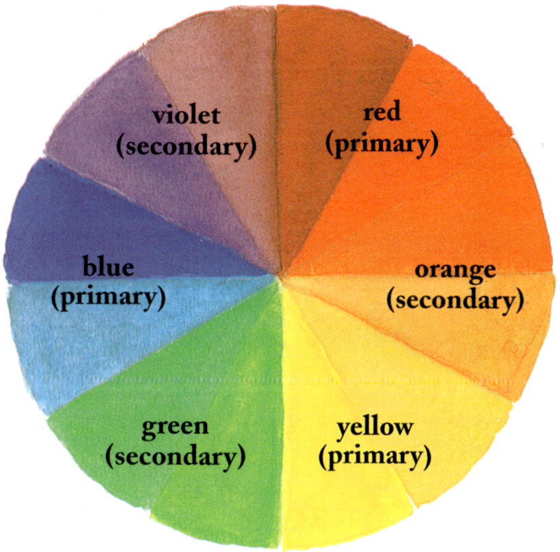

The colour wheel is a handy 'tool' which the artist can refer to when experimenting with colours and the way they react together. It is a simplified version of the spectrum, formed into a circle, showing the arrangement of the primary colours (red, yellow and blue) and the secondary colours (orange, green and violet), from which all other colours are mixed.

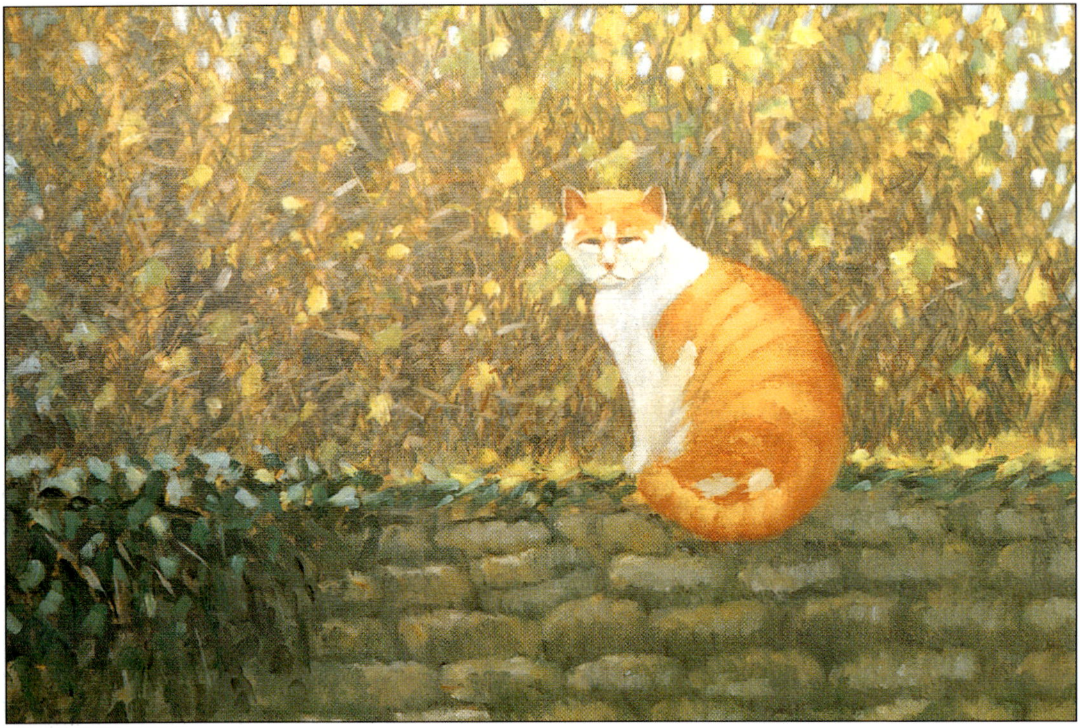

YOU WILL NEED

- Sheet canvas or board, 18 x 14in (45.7 x 35.6cm)
- No. 6 round sable or synthetic brush
- No. 8 round bristle brush
- Refined linseed oil
- Distilled turpentine
- Lint-free cloth
- 1½ (38mm) decorating brush

Marmalade Cat

Although this painting contains a lot of complex detail the artist has kept it under control by sticking to a limited palette of related colours. Yellows and oranges predominate, with touches of green providing a foil for the warmer colours. The yellow toned ground strikes through the overlaid brush-strokes, providing a harmonizing element of its own.

OIL PAINTS IN THE FOLLOWING COLOURS

- *Yellow ochre*
- *Burnt sienna*
- *Cadmium red*
- *Titanium white*
- *Prussian blue*
- *Cobalt blue*
- *Lemon yellow*
- *Cadmium yellow*
- *Cerulean*

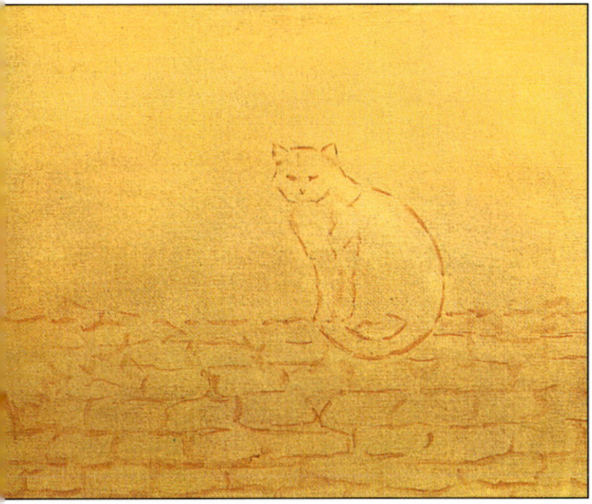

1 Prepare your canvas in advance by toning it with a wash of yellow ochre, well diluted with turpentine and applied with a 11/2in (38mm) decorating brush. Before this dries, rub over the canvas with a clean, lint-free cloth to lighten the colour and soften the brush marks. Leave to dry overnight. This creates a warm, golden undertone that will show through the overlaid colours and harmonize the picture. Sketch the main outlines of the cat and the stone wall. Use burnt sienna thinly diluted with turpentine, applied with a no. 6 round sable or synthetic brush.

Helpful Hint

TO SAVE TIME, WHY NOT TONE THE CANVAS WITH ACRYLIC PAINT? UNLIKE OILS, THIS DRIES IN MINUTES, ALLOWING YOU TO START PAINTING STRAIGHT AWAY. OIL PAINTS CAN BE APPLIED OVER ACRYLICS, BUT ACRYLICS SHOULD NEVER BE APPLIED OVER OILS AS THIS CAUSES THE OIL PAINT TO CRACK.

2 Use the burnt sienna mix to indicate the striped markings on the cat's coat, then block in the shadows on the face and chest with a pale mix of cadmium red and titanium white, thinly diluted with turpentine and linseed oil. Start work on the foliage in the background with a weak mix of Prussian blue and cadmium red, adding white for the lighter tones. Apply the paint with loose, sketchy strokes, leaving plenty of the ground colour visible.

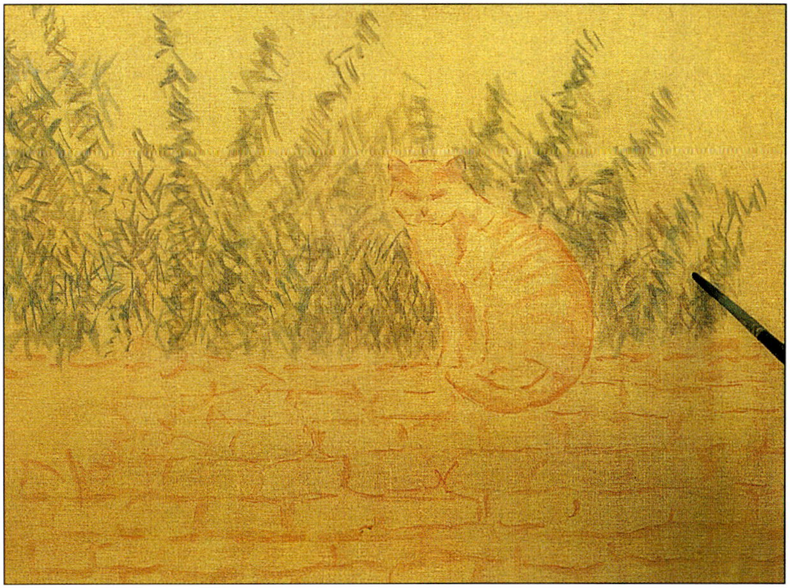

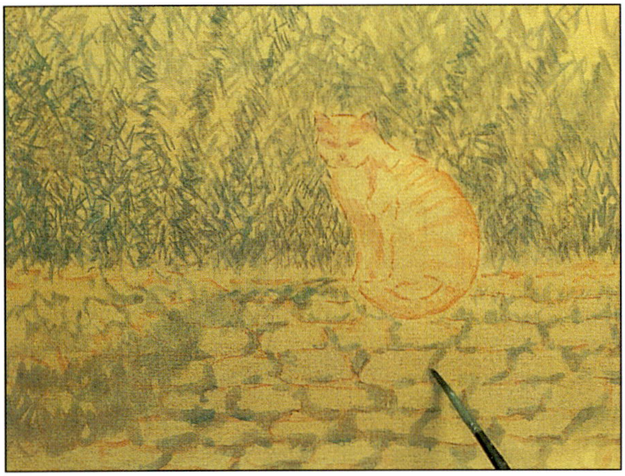

3 Continue working on the foliage, building up the leaves and branches with short, random brushstrokes. Now use the Prussian blue/cadmium red mixture to define the shadows on the individual stones in the wall, and the shadow cast by the ivy climbing over the wall on the left of the picture.

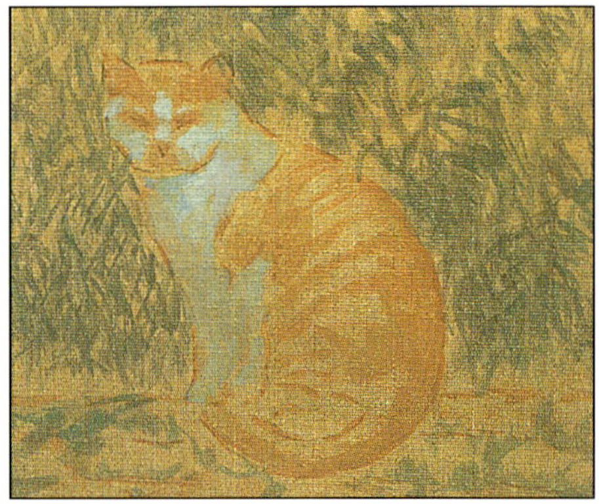

4 Still using the no. 8 brush, mix white with a hint of cobalt blue and carefully paint the pale greyish-white fur on the cat's face and chest with short brushstrokes. Let the pinkish shadows underneath show through the white. Develop the marmalade stripes with a combination of yellow ochre and cadmium red.

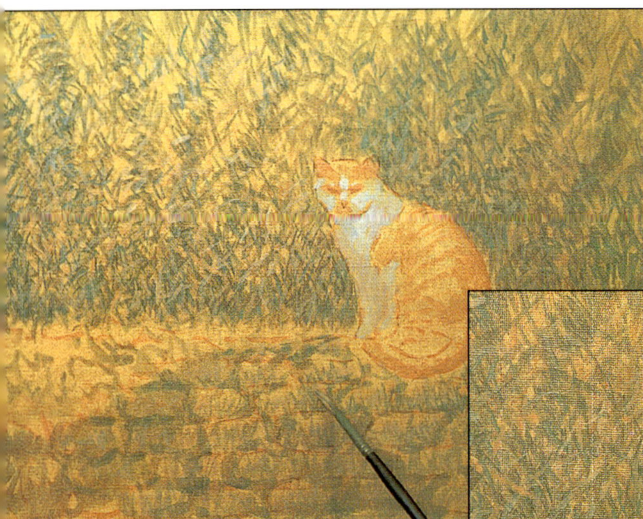

5 Continue working up the background using the same colours as before. Vary the direction of your brushstrokes to suggest the scattered effect of the foliage. Build up the shadows on the wall with loose strokes. The paint should still be quite thin at this stage, allowing the toned ground to show through (see detail). Now make a slightly thicker mix of yellow ochre, cadmium red and white to make a pale peachy colour. Work this loosely into the foliage and on the wall to create soft highlights, flicking the brush gently across the canvas.

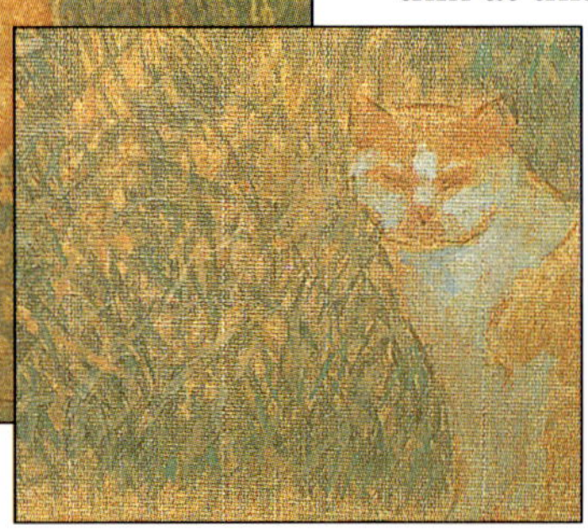

6 Mix lemon yellow, cobalt blue and a touch of yellow ochre to make a dull green and start to paint the ivy creeping over the wall. For the light-struck leaves mix together cobalt blue, lemon yellow and white to make a cool blue-green. For the shadows underneath the foliage use a mixture of Prussian blue, cadmium red, yellow ochre and white. Scumble the colour onto the stone wall, still allowing the toned ground to show through.

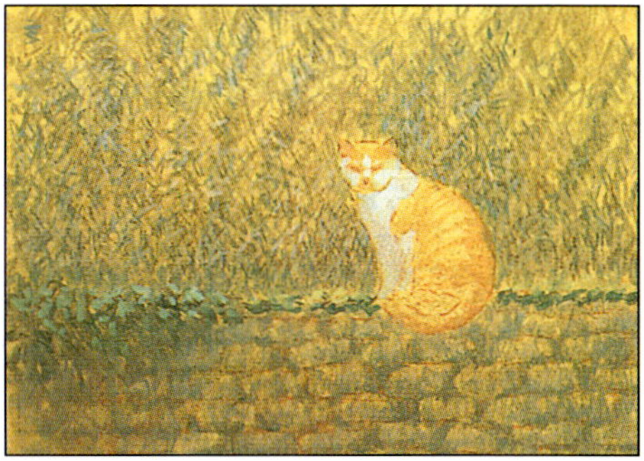

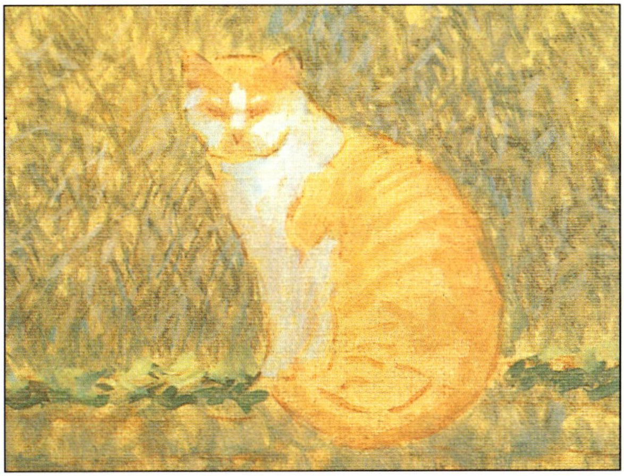

7 Resume work on the cat, adding more of the cobalt blue/white mix for the fur on the face, neck and chest. For the fur between the ears use lemon yellow and white with a touch of cadmium red. Put in the eyes and nose with a dark pink made up of white and cadmium red with a hint of Prussian blue. For the marmalade stripes use white, cadmium yellow, cadmium red and a touch of burnt sienna. Apply the paint with short feathery strokes to give the effect of soft fur.

8 Keep moving from area to area, rather than concentrating on one particular part of the painting. Mix lemon yellow and white and work back into the foliage to introduce some warm highlights with loose dots and dashes. Use the same colour on the ivy along the top of the wall.

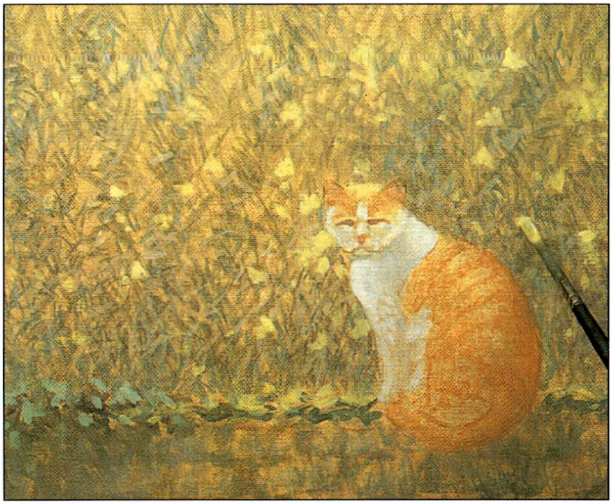

9 Make a thicker mixture of cobalt blue and lemon yellow to make a rich green and use this to build up the foliage, creating a dense patchwork of colour and tone. Then use the white/cobalt blue mix to break a little sky into the foliage at the top of the painting. Switch to a no. 8 round bristle brush and use the same mix to build up the lighter tones on the stone wall.

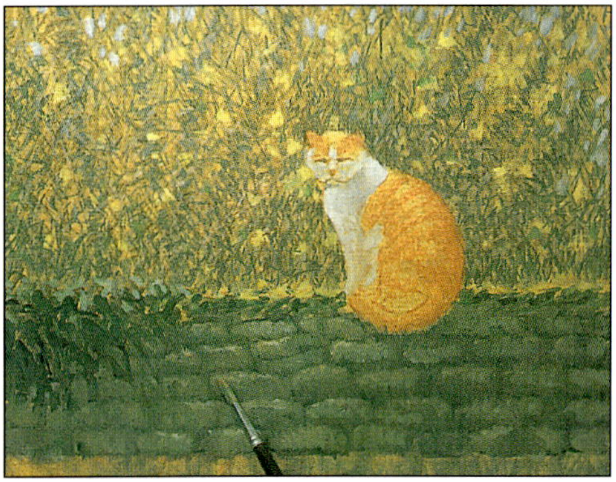

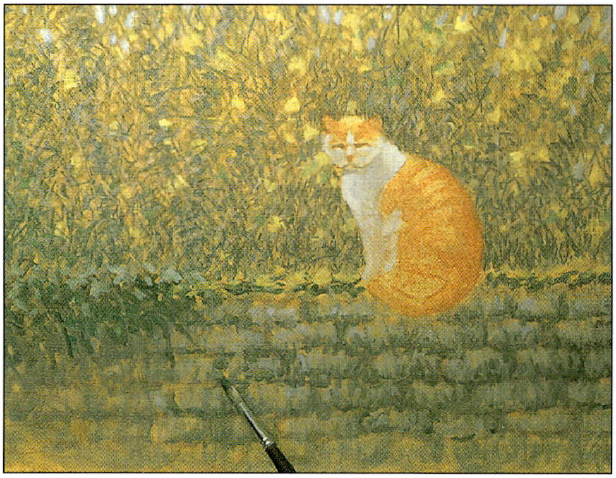

10 Develop the rough texture of the wall with short vertical strokes of thicker paint. Mix cadmium red and Prussian blue to make a dark grey for the shadows between the individual stone slabs, then add a little yellow ochre and white to the mixture to soften the tones. It's important not to let the wall dominate the painting too much – the focus should be on the cat and not on the background.

11 Work over the fur on the cat's face with cadmium yellow to introduce highlights. Paint the ears with a mix of cadmium red, burnt sienna and white, then outline them with a fine line of pure white to separate the cat from the background. Emphasize the striped markings with short strokes of cadmium yellow mixed with white. Add a little cadmium red and yellow ochre to the mixture and darken the orange fur on the back and tail with loose, scumbled strokes.

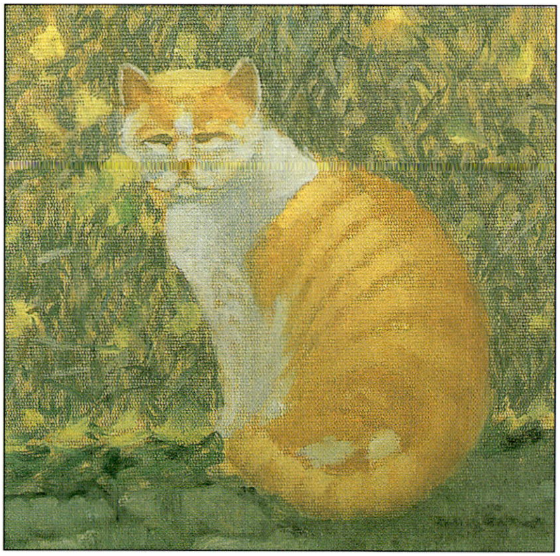

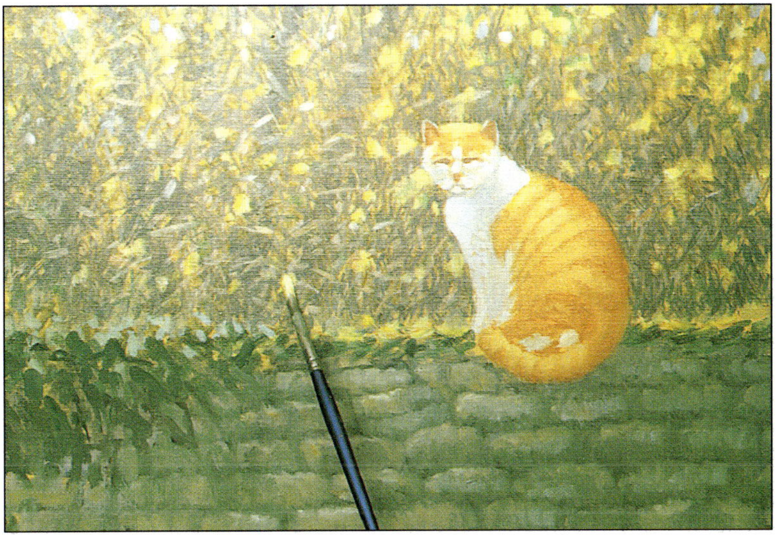

12 Use mixes of cadmium red and Prussian blue to add the deeper tones in the background foliage, then redefine the patches of sky with cobalt blue and white. Moving back to the cat, scumble some strokes of pure white over the fur on the neck and chest to give it a softer appearance. Put in the eyes with a mixture of cadmium red and Prussian blue. Build up the mottled pattern on the stone wall with broken strokes, using varied mixes of yellow ochre, white and touches of cobalt blue.

Helpful Hint

AT AROUND THIS POINT IT'S A GOOD IDEA TO ALLOW THE PAINT TO DRY FOR 24 HOURS OR SO BEFORE CONTINUING. IT IS DIFFICULT TO APPLY THE FINISHING DETAILS ON TOP OF A WET PAINT SURFACE.

13 To finish the picture, add warmer highlights on the wall with mixes of cerulean, cadmium red and white. Accentuate the highlights on the ivy, too, using cerulean, lemon yellow and white. Repeat some of this colour in the background foliage to provide colour balance. Finally, mix cadmium red and white and suggest some pinkish twigs in the background with random strokes.

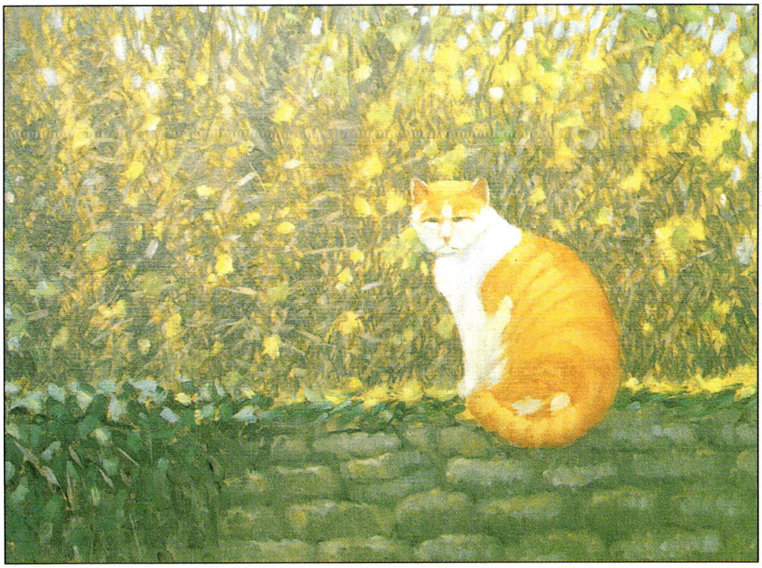

Painting Skies

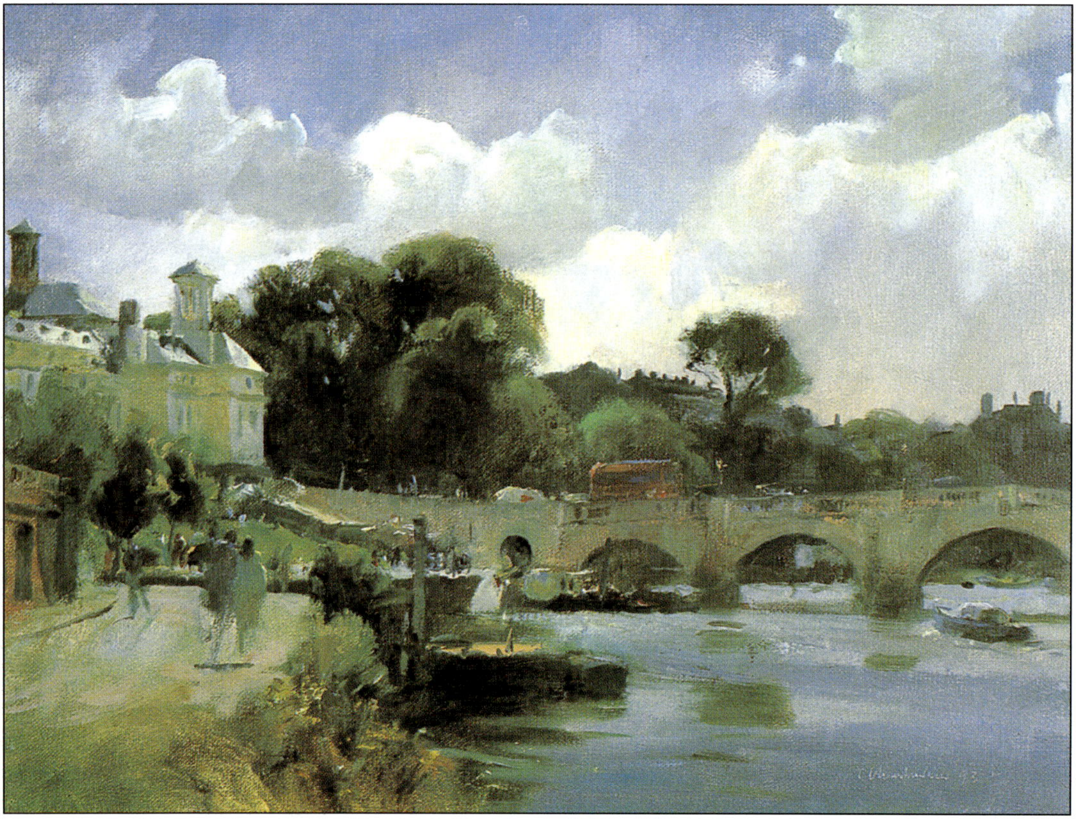

Trevor Chamberlain
SUMMER AT RICHMOND
Clouds directly in front of the sun are particularly exciting to paint because the backlighting makes them appear luminous and gives them a 'silver lining'.

The sky tends to set the mood of a landscape because it is the source of light. It is important, therefore to treat the sky as an integral part of the landscape and not merely as a backdrop. As you paint, try to bring the sky and the land along simultaneously, working from one to the other and bringing some of the sky colour into the land and vice versa.

Techniques

In order to suggest the airiness of the sky and clouds, it is best to work quickly and simplify what you see. Look for the main shapes and block them in with thin paint, then start to introduce detail and modelling. By varying your brushwork and the consistency of the paint, you can create a range of subtle effects that suggest the amorphous nature of clouds and sky. Creamy, opaque colour will suggest groups of dense, advancing clouds; thinly applied, transparent colour gives the impression of atmosphere and receding space, and is ideal for portraying distant clouds and areas of dark, remote sky.

To achieve the effect of distant haze, blend wet colour into wet, taking some of the sky colour into the land and vice versa. This slight softening of the horizon gives a marvellous sense of air and light.

Modelling clouds

Look carefully at cloud structure. Clouds are not flat shapes but have three-dimensional form, with distinct planes of light and shadow. Warm colours – reds, oranges and yellows – appear to come forward, as our eyes are more receptive to them. Cool colours – blues, greens and violets – appear to recede. Therefore the contrast of warm and cool colours can be used to model the advancing and receding planes of clouds. The lit areas of cumulus cloud, for example, may contain subtle hints of warm yellow and pink, depending on the weather and the time of day. Those parts of the cloud which are in shadow may appear grey or even brown in colour, and contain blues and violets.

Too many hard outlines make clouds appear 'pasted on' to the sky and destroy the illusion of form. Partially blend the shadow edges of clouds into the surrounding sky so they blend naturally into the surrounding atmosphere.

John Denahy
SUFFOLK COAST
Instead of painting the sky as a flat area of blue, the artist has used broken strokes of vibrant blues, violets, greens and yellows, laid over a warm-toned ground. This gives a more vivid impression of the sparkle of a summer sky.

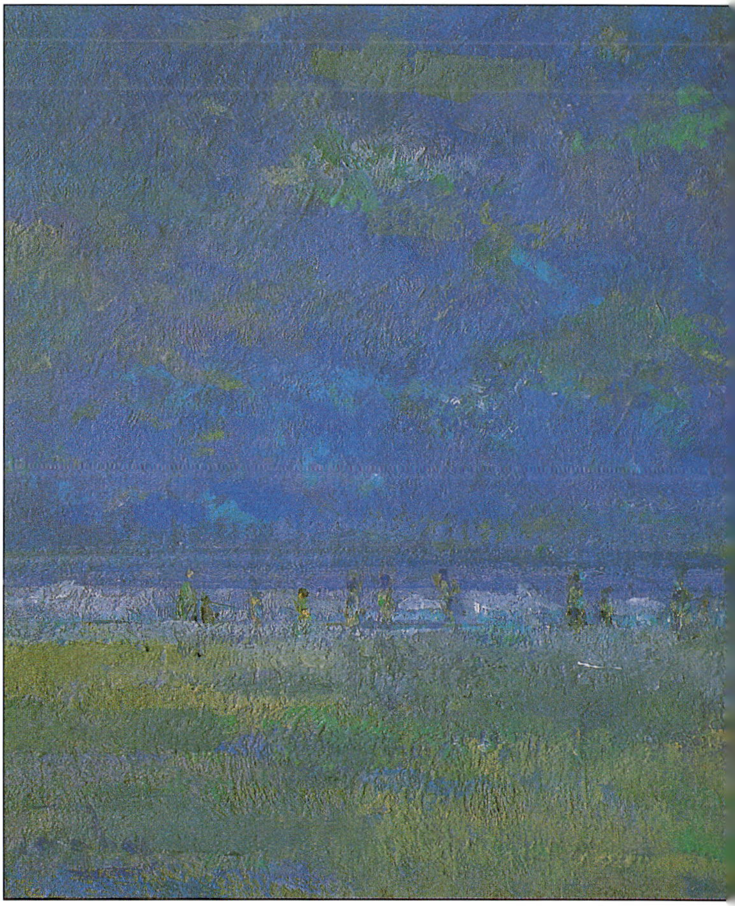

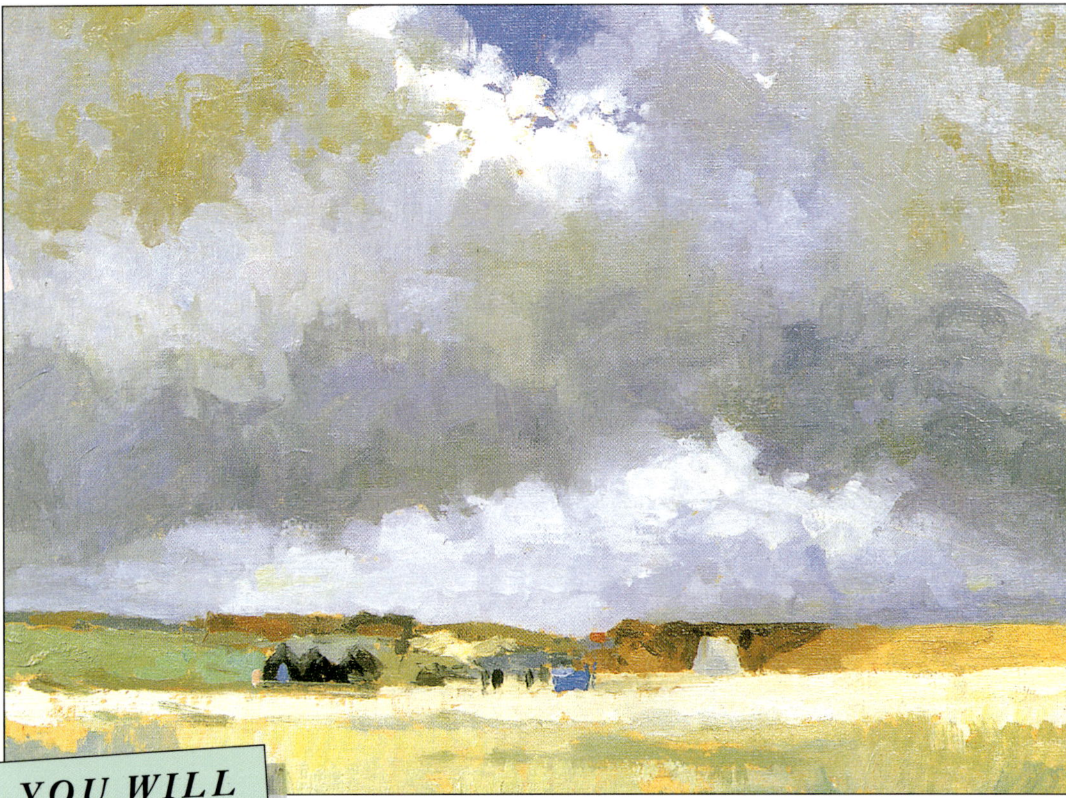

YOU WILL NEED

- ✔ Sheet of primed board, 12 x 10in (30.5 x 25.4cm)
- ✔ No. 3 round sable brush
- ✔ No. 4 flat bristle brush
- ✔ No. 5 round bristle brush
- ✔ Painting knife
- ✔ Refined linseed oil
- ✔ Distilled turpentine

Sky Over Suffolk

The sky need not be a mere backdrop to your landscape paintings – it can sometimes be a subject in its own right. In this painting the dramatic clouds form virtually the whole composition, with the narrow strip of hills and fields serving as an anchor to the movement above.

OIL PAINTS IN THE FOLLOWING COLOURS

- *Burnt sienna*
- *French ultramarine*
- *Lemon yellow*
- *Ivory black*
- *Titanium white*
- *Alizarin crimson*
- *Cadmium yellow*
- *Cadmium orange*
- *Raw umber*
- *Cerulean*

1 Working on a board tinted with a thin wash of burnt sienna, use a no. 3 round sable brush and diluted burnt sienna to sketch in the details on the horizon. Start by establishing the broad tones in the sky and land using a no. 4 flat bristle brush. For the green fields, mix varying amounts of lemon yellow, French ultramarine, ivory black and titanium white. Rough in the sky using ultramarine, white and a touch of alizarin crimson, plus greys mixed from varied proportions of ultramarine, lemon yellow, black and white.

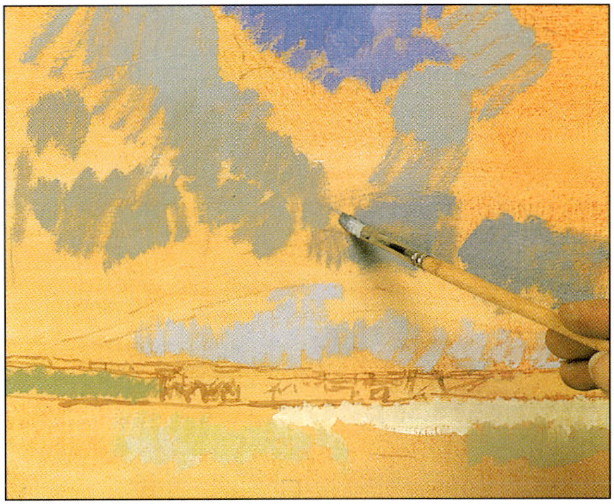

Helpful Hint

LEAVE PATCHES OF THE GROUND BARE IN THE EARLY STAGES SO THAT LATER ADDITIONS OF COLOUR CAN BE SLIPPED INTO THE GAPS. THIS AVOIDS THE DANGER OF OVERWORKING THE AREA WITH PAINT.

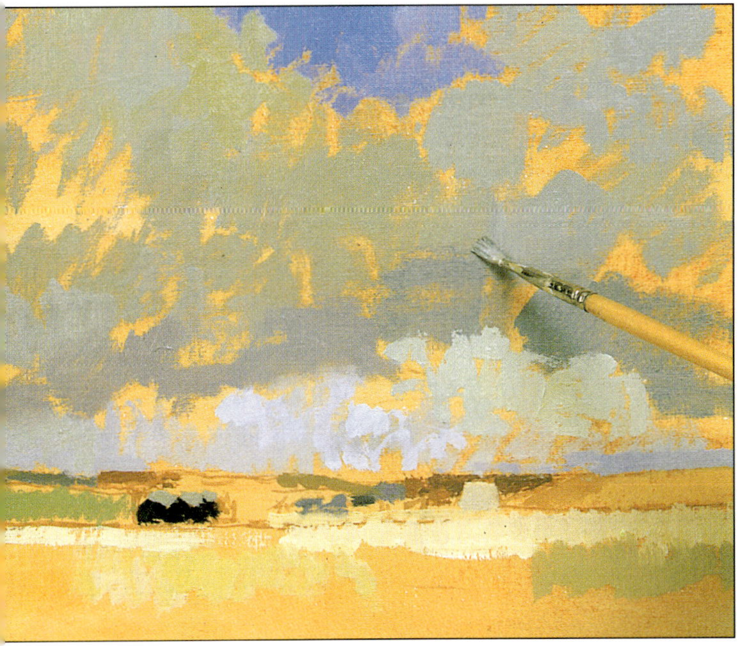

2 Suggest the landscape features in the distance using some of the colours already on your palette. Continue building up the tones in the sky using the same colours mixed in step 1. By varying the proportions of colour used, it is possible to create a wide range of colourful greys ranging from greenish grey through to grey-violet.

3

Work over all the areas of the painting at the same time, moving from the sky to the land and back again and constantly making adjustments to the relative tones and colours. Use a no. 5 round bristle brush to lay in the smaller clouds with rapid brushstrokes, letting some of the colours blend wet-into-wet at the edges.

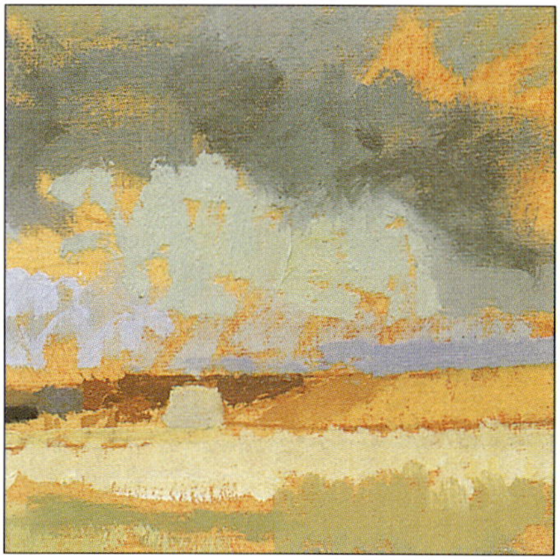

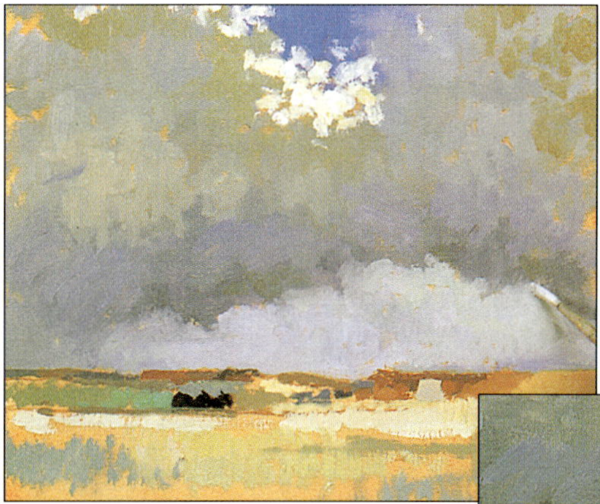

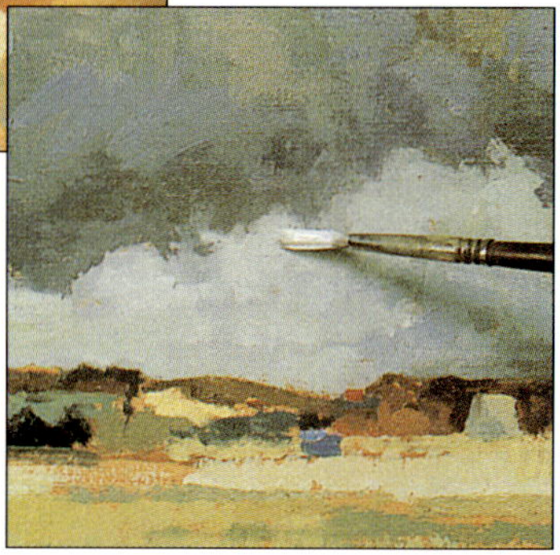

4

Begin to use slightly thicker, creamier paint now, and build up the cloud masses with broad strokes, slurring the colours wet-into-wet. Paint the sunlit white clouds with loose strokes of white, warmed with touches of cadmium orange and cadmium yellow. Now work on the large, light cloud on the horizon with a combination of ultramarine, alizarin, raw umber and plenty of white.

Helpful Hint

TAKE THE TIME TO OBSERVE THE VARIOUS CLOUD TYPES AND THEIR CHARACTERISTICS AND MAKE SKETCHES OF THEM. THESE SKETCHES WILL HELP YOU PAINT SKIES MORE CONVINCINGLY.

5

Mix a pale, cool grey from ultramarine, alizarin crimson and white and scumble this lightly over the brownish clouds near the top of the sky to give the effect of smaller clouds passing across the large mass of cumulus. Now begin to soften some of the edges of the clouds by blending very gently with a painting knife.

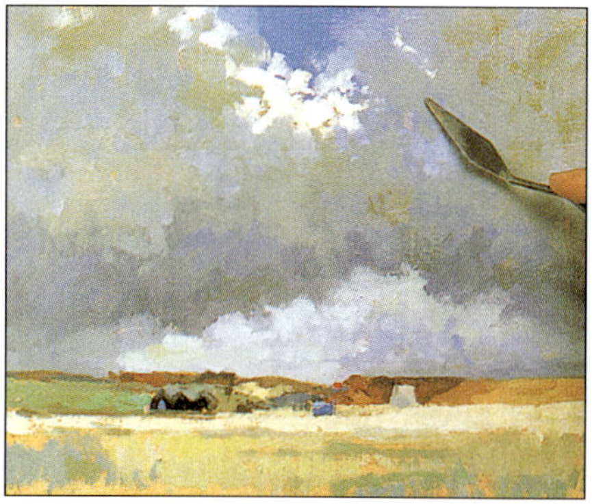

6 At this point it is often a good idea to take a short break from your painting so that you can return to it with a fresh eye and make any necessary corrections or modifications. Here, for example, the cloud mass on the left is a little too heavy, so mix cerulean and white and scumble over the dark grey area to lighten it. Then lighten the brownish area just above it with white, burnt sienna and lemon yellow.

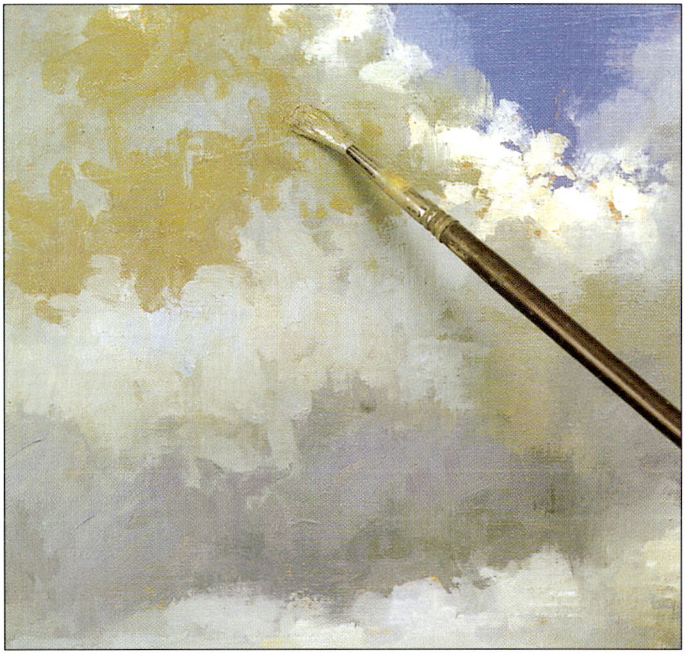

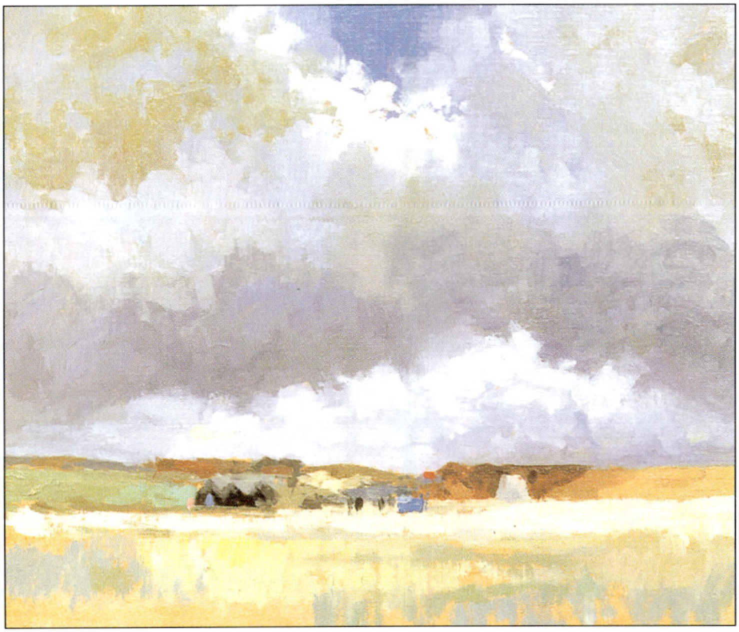

7 Work over the whole picture, modifying colours and softening edges where required; for example, soften the patch of white cloud at the top of the picture to integrate it into the patch of blue sky.

Index